Financial Planning Applications
Volume 2

Huebner School Series
Gary K. Stone, Editor

Fundamentals of Financial Planning
Robert M. Crowe and Charles E. Hughes (eds.)

Readings in Income Taxation
James F. Ivers III (ed.)

McGill's Life Insurance
Edward E. Graves (ed.)

Group Benefits: Basic Concepts and Alternatives
Burton T. Beam, Jr.

Planning for Retirement Needs
Kenn Beam Tacchino and David A. Littell

Readings in Wealth Accumulation Planning
James F. Ivers III and Eric T. Johnson (eds.)

Readings in Estate Planning I
Constance J. Fontaine (ed.)

Readings in Estate Planning II
Ted Kurlowicz (ed.)

Planning for Business Owners and Professionals
Ted Kurlowicz, James F. Ivers III, and John J. McFadden

Financial Planning Applications
William J. Ruckstuhl, Jeffrey B. Kelvin, David M. Cordell, and David A. Littell

Financial Decision Making at Retirement
David A. Littell, Kenn Beam Tacchino, and David M. Cordell

The primary purpose of this series is to provide timely reading materials tailored to the educational needs of those professionals pursuing the Chartered Life Underwriter and Chartered Financial Consultant designation programs offered by the Solomon S. Huebner School of The American College. These publications should also be of interest to other persons seeking further knowledge in the broad area of financial services.

Huebner School Series

Volume 2
Financial Planning Applications
Twelfth Edition

William J. Ruckstuhl
Jeffrey B. Kelvin
David M. Cordell
David A. Littell

The American College/Bryn Mawr, Pennsylvania

This publication is designed to provide accurate and authoritative information about the subject covered. The American College is not engaged in rendering legal, accounting, or other professional advice. If legal or other expert advice is required, the services of an appropriate professional should be sought.

© 1994 The American College
All rights reserved

Library of Congress catalog card number 93-74841
ISBN 0-943590-58-2

Printed in the United States of America

Contents

Acknowledgments	*viii*
Planning for the Self-Employed Professional	*5.1*
Planning for the Small Family-Owned Business and Its Owners	*6.1*
Planning for the Officer of a Large Organization	*7.1*
Planning for a Surviving Spouse	*8.1*
Planning for the Successful Closely Held Corporation and Its Owners	*9.1*
Bibliography and Recommended In-depth Reading	
Index	

Acknowledgments

Gwenda L. Cannon, JD, formerly of The American College, for her creation of the original cases whose elements have survived multiple revisions and continuous changes in the tax and financial environment

Gary K. Stone, PhD, CLU, vice president of academics at The American College, and editor of the Huebner School Series, for his support and encouragement

C. Bruce Worsham, JD, LLM, CLU, director of the Huebner School at The American College, for his assistance in developing the examination for this course

The American College faculty for their gracious and patient assistance with various technical questions and practical recommendations that have added to the quality of the course

Sally Kennedy, manuscript editor at The American College, for her editing of the manuscript

Evelyn M. Rice, executive secretary at The American College, for her able assistance and for unfailing patience in typing numerous revisions of the manuscript

Lillian G. Pedrick, instructional designer at The American College, for her indispensable assistance in operating ExecPlan

Howard E. Hoctor, supervisor of media services at The American College, for his design of the cover and excellent graphics

                                                         William J. Ruckstuhl
                                                         Jeffrey B. Kelvin
                                                         David M. Cordell
                                                         David A. Littell

The computer illustrations contained in this book were generated by a financial planning software system called ExecPlan. We wish to thank Sawhney Software, Princeton, New Jersey, for providing us with continuous cooperation and assistance in the use of version 3.3 of their system to enhance and illustrate various elements of the cases.

Financial Planning Applications
Volume 2

5

PLANNING FOR THE SELF-EMPLOYED PROFESSIONAL

Some professionals, such as physicians, dentists, and attorneys, earn relatively high incomes. However, because of the demands of their practices they often lack the time to inform themselves fully of the merits and problems of various financial planning techniques and are consequently somewhat unsophisticated in financial matters. As a result this type of client is often accumulating disposable income for investment or the achievement of personal objectives at a slower rate than he or she believes is desirable.

In addition, as high income earners, professionals are likely to be on every sort of solicitation, mailing, and prospect list. Consequently professionals have been barraged with solicitations to purchase a large number of services and products, each of which has been touted as the answer to many problems. Frequently professionals have made such purchases, usually with mixed results. Because of the demands on their time that limit the opportunity to compare the advantages and disadvantages of various products or to consult with several service or product providers, the services and products professionals have purchased are likely to be poorly coordinated.

Consequently professionals may be wary about becoming involved in the financial planning process. However, once they are convinced that comprehensive financial planning can save them substantial amounts in taxes and in the cost of other services and products and can materially decrease the amount of time spent evaluating and coordinating services and products, and once they are convinced that the comprehensive financial planner is credible as a client-oriented deliverer of services and product recommendations, professionals usually engage in the planning process enthusiastically. Because professionals are already accustomed to making major decisions, they can be very satisfying clients to work with when they are presented with appropriate information about alternative solutions and asked to adopt a planner's particular recommendations. However, since the professional's time is limited, he or she should be kept adequately involved and informed throughout the planning process without being taken away from professional and personal obligations any more than is absolutely necessary.

For all these reasons planning for the professional is a highly specialized field. Many financial planning firms choose to do planning exclusively for professionals.

CASE NARRATIVE

Personal Information

Dave Anderson, aged 41, is an orthopedic surgeon. His wife, Diana, is 39. They have been married for 16 years. Diana is a registered nurse and was working as an emergency room nurse when they met. Diana enjoyed her career and continued to work until shortly before their first child, Keith, was born 10 years ago. She has not worked outside her home since that time and has no immediate plans to return to her career. She does not know whether she would like to resume nursing if she did return to work. Dave and Diana have two other children, Deidre, 9, and Melissa, 6, and have just discovered that they will have another child in about 7 months. Although they are somewhat concerned about Diana's health and the health of the child, they consider this development a happy surprise.

Dave and Diana own their home, which had an approximate fair market value of $215,000 at the end of 1993. When they purchased the house in March 1980, it cost $79,000. Of that sum they paid $16,000 in cash and financed the balance of $63,000 at 12 percent for 30 years. Property taxes on the house are $1,900 per year. Dave holds title to the house in his name alone.

They plan to take one major trip at least every third year and estimate that such travel will cost $8,000 in today's dollars. In off years family vacations are estimated to cost approximately $4,000 in today's dollars. The Andersons give about $3,000 annually to various charities, and Dave also gives $1,500 to his medical school every year for its endowment fund.

The older Anderson children have done very well in school. Although Melissa is just midway through first grade, it looks as if she will also do well. None appears to have any handicaps or problems that would necessitate expensive special schooling. In fact, they are quite bright. Since the children appear gifted, the Andersons ask that you project the cost of education through the undergraduate level at a higher-quality educational institution. It is too early to tell about postgraduate or professional schools for the Anderson children, but Dave and Diana would like them to be able to pursue their education as far as they wish. Presently the children attend public schools, but there is some interest in transferring them to a private school with more rigorous academic requirements as they enter high school. At present tuition and other expenses for an appropriate private school are approximately $2,500 per year per child.

Dave and Diana do not have a luxurious life-style. They enjoy travel and have tastefully furnished parts of their home with antiques, most of which Diana has discovered on what she calls her "treasure hunts." They do not collect museum-quality antiques because of their attitude that it is more important for them to have a comfortable home than to have a lot of material things that have to be protected from the children and their two Shetland sheepdogs. However, they have acquired a number of very fine old pieces at nominal prices due in large part to Diana's willingness to learn about antique furniture, paintings, and other accessories. Dave and Diana do not view their household furnishings as investment vehicles, whatever their value. They enjoy living with them and are not concerned about whether a particular piece is appreciating in value. They believe their furnishings are worth approximately $50,000.

In truth, Diana is much more interested in furnishing the house than is Dave, who requires only that it be comfortable and in fact is quite content with the furnishings they acquired when they were first married. Dave is more interested in accumulating funds for investment. He is also interested in reducing income taxes to the extent that is still possible under the current federal income tax laws.

In the course of furnishing their house, Diana has acquired an appreciable amount of knowledge about antique Oriental porcelain and thinks that once the children are older, she would enjoy collecting some finer pieces more seriously and perhaps trading in them in a small way. She would also like to increase her knowledge of Oriental rugs and possibly purchase some for personal use and perhaps as an investment. She has even thought that after the children are older and need less of her time at home, she might consider opening a small shop that would specialize in Oriental rugs and antique Oriental porcelain. She had hoped that she could explore this possibility seriously within the next year or two but thinks now that she would like to stay at home full-time with the new baby for at least a year or perhaps two. However, she has not decided whether she wants to remain at home full-time as long as she did with the other children. Dave has mixed feelings about her returning to work and at this time would prefer that she remain at home with the baby at least until the child has started school. He does recognize that this will require Diana to delay any possibility of starting her own business for another 6 to 8 years.

Dave's parents are still living, and as far as he knows, they are in good health and are all right financially, although they have not accumulated a large amount of material wealth. Fred Anderson, his father, is a high school principal and is 63 years old. Amy, his mother, 61, is a violinist who has given music lessons for many years. They were able to help Dave through undergraduate school as a result of careful saving, supplemented by Dave's obtaining a sizable scholarship.

Diana's father died when she was a teenager, and although she believes that he did not leave her mother too well provided for, she does not know for certain. While Diana was growing up, her mother implied that finances were quite limited. However, she was able to provide the funds required for Diana to go to nursing school. Diana's mother, Sarah, now 59, remarried in 1976. Her stepfather, Alex Smythe, now 63, is retired from the U.S. Postal Service after 30 years of service (retiring at 55 years of age) and is currently employed as the clerk of the superior court for Metropolis County. Diana's mother appears to be in good health, but her stepfather had a slight heart attack last year and later had a double heart bypass. While he seems to be recovering well, Diana is concerned about her mother's financial condition and what would become of her if something should happen to Alex. Her mother worked as a secretary after Diana's father died, but she has been a housewife since she married Alex. Diana and Dave have discussed their concerns about Alex's health with Sarah but have not really discussed the matter of her financial future in any depth.

Diana inherited nothing from her father except a coin collection that he and she had accumulated during her childhood. She thought of it primarily in terms of sentimental value and was surprised to learn some years later that its estimated worth was approximately $5,000 when she inherited it in 1968. Dave became interested in the collection and has essentially taken over its management, adding to it from time to time, and he estimates that it is probably worth $20,000 today. They keep the collection in their safety deposit box at the bank.

Dave tells you that he has made some real estate investments over the last few years, some in the form of limited partnerships. In fact, he has purchased the following three such investments: Gate House Properties, one partnership unit—$35,000 in 1983; Northbrook Gardens, one unit—$102,000 in 1984; and Smoky River, Ltd., one unit—$55,500 in 1985.

Gate House Properties has begun to show a positive cash flow of about $6,000 per year. In 1993 Gate House generated neither a loss nor any taxable income. Beginning in 1994, it will produce passive income of $600 that will increase by $600 per year thereafter. Cash flow is projected to remain constant at $6,000 during this period.

The purchase of Northbrook Gardens required a $31,000 payment in 1984, a $46,000 payment in 1985, and an additional payment of $25,000 in 1986. It produced a passive loss of $6,012 in 1993 and will produce passive losses of $3,674, and $1,135 for the following 2 years. In 1996 it will produce income of $2,020. In 1997 and 1998 the income will be $3,000 and $3,800 respectively. Northbrook Gardens is projected to have a level cash flow of $5,600 from 1994 to 1998.

Smoky River, Ltd., was fully paid for in 1986. It had a $2,208 passive loss for 1993 and is projected to produce passive losses from 1994–1996 as follows: $2,208, $1,913, and $850. Smoky River is expected to produce income of $700 in 1997 and $1,800 in 1998. Cash flow for the same period is projected at $1,563, $1,798, $2,054, $2,321, and $2,615.

As an investment Dave purchased a single-family house in November 1982 for $57,000, financing $47,500 at 9 1/2 percent for 25 years. The house is rented for $550 per month and is presently worth about $75,000. Dave has been depreciating the house by the straight-line method for tax purposes over a 20-year useful life with a $10,000 salvage value. For depreciation purposes $5,000 of the purchase price was allocated to the land and the remaining $52,000 to the building.

Dave also purchased an undeveloped commercial lot in March 1983 for $100,000. He paid $20,000 down and financed the $80,000 balance at 10 percent for 20 years. He estimates that the land is worth approximately $160,000, and he has recently been approached by a buyer who is willing to pay him $165,000 if the transaction can be closed early in 1995. Dave is interested because the land does require cash flow to carry the note and taxes, and it produces no income. However, he is uncertain about whether he should sell the lot now.

After the enactment of the Tax Reform Act of 1986, which significantly reduced the tax advantages of investing in passive activities, Dave ceased acquiring any additional ownership interests in real estate or in real estate limited partnerships. In 1986 and 1987 he attempted to sell these investments but was unable to find any buyers who would make a reasonable offer for any or all. Now that it appears that some will start providing a positive cash flow in the near future, he feels that they should be retained.

Now he allocates any investable funds into securities and has benefited from the bull markets in both stocks and bonds that marked the period 1986 to 1993. Table 5-1 summarizes his purchases, sales, income, and current market values of the securities portfolio. Dave's selections followed the rcommendations of an account representative from a local brokerage firm. Initially Dave acquired individual securities, but an article in *Medical Economics* describing the mutual fund features of diversification and professional management convinced him that funds would be a better approach for his personal investment plan. Dave expressed a desire to continue the investment program at the same or greater dollar level, until such time as he plans to retire.

The Andersons own two cars, both in Dave's name. Diana's car was purchased in June 1992 for $12,400; $10,000 of the purchase price was financed at 10 percent for 48 months. The value of the car is approximately $10,000. Dave's car was purchased in December 1993 for $22,000. Dave paid for the car with cash.

The Andersons have no other significant personal assets or liabilities except a $5,000 joint checking account and $10,000 in a joint savings account.

Dave and Diana had some estate planning done about 6 years ago. Their basic estate plan is described below.

Dave's will provides that an amount equal to one-half his adjusted gross estate, including the house, goes to Diana in a marital trust with a testamentary power of appointment if she survives him. The remainder of his estate after the payment of estate taxes is left in a residuary trust for the benefit of Diana, Keith, Deidre, and Melissa for Diana's life. The trustee of the trust is empowered to pay income or corpus to or for the benefit of Diana, Keith, Deidre, or Melissa as necessary for their health, support, maintenance, or education. Diana has a limited power of appointment over the principal of the trust, which can be exercised both during her life and at her death. She can appoint the principal only to Keith, Deidre, or Melissa. At Diana's death the remainder of the trust principal is to be paid equally to Keith, Deidre, or Melissa, if living. If any of them is deceased, the deceased child's portion is to go to his or her living children, per stirpes.

Diana's will leaves all her property to Dave if he survives her, otherwise, equally to her living children or children of a deceased child, per stirpes. Neither will contains a provision dealing with afterborn children.

TABLE 5-1
Dave Anderson's Portfolio Transactions, 1986 through 1994

Security Name	Quantity Bought	Date Bought	Total Cost	Date Sold	Sales Price	Market Value 12/31/94	Current Annual Income	Past Growth Rate	Current Yield
Clean Soap Inc.	250 sh[1] 250 sh[1] 500 sh[1]	12/86 1990/ 7/1991	12,000 2-for-1 split 2-for-1 split	— — —	— — —	35,000	$1/sh	14.0%	2.80%
Job River Textile	20 bonds	9/87	19,800	6/92	24,000	—	—	—	—
High Fly Airlines	10 bonds	11/87	10,500	—	—	In Chapter 11 bankruptcy	zero	—	—
Nationwide Oil Co.	200 sh[1]	6/88	9,000	—	—	12,000	$2.50	5.0%	4.20%
Houseboat Finance Co.	10 bonds due 2010	1/89	10,100	—	—	12,500	9.0%	4.5%	7.20%
Deep Snow Maker Inc.	300 sh[1]	9/89	6,000	—	—	14,000	$0.10/sh	18.0%	0.20%
Burp Soda Inc.	400 sh[1] 400 sh[1]	9/89 1992	20,000 2-for-1 split	—	—	32,000	$0.80/sh	9.0%	2.00%
Economic Fund	300 sh	11/89	3,000	—	—	1,500	$0.08/sh	-13.0%	1.60%
Wellington Mfg Corp (c)	400 sh[1] 200 sh[1]	10/90 1994	16,000 3-for-2 split	—	—	24,000	$0.50/sh	10.0%	1.25%
Fund Mgrs Growth Fund	500 sh[1] 600 sh[1]	8/91 7/92	19,500 24,000	—	—	21,000 25,200	$1.22/sh $1.22/sh	2.5%	2.90%
Atlantic Rim Fund	800 sh[1]	10/92	8,000	—	—	9,500	$0.57	9.0%	4.80%
Southern Fund	500 sh[1]	10/92	8,200	—	—	10,200	$0.79/sh	11.5%	3.90%
5-7 Year Bond Fund	500 sh[1]	10/92	6,000	—	—	6,200	$0.79/sh	1.6%	6.40%
Town Hall Munibonds	10 bonds due 2013	9/93	10,500	—	—	10,600	5.40%	1.0%	5.10%
State School System	15 bonds due 2013	9/93	14,900	—	—	15,150	5.25%	1.3%	5.20%

[1] Common stock

Assumptions
Expected growth rate for divs: 2%
Expected growth rate for price of stock: same as past
No growth in either bond current yields or growth rates

The First Trust Company is named executor and trustee under Dave's will. Dave is named executor of Diana's will, with the First Trust Company named as successor if he is unable to serve. Diana is not happy with the fact that all her property would be tied up in a trust. She says she hates the idea of having to deal with a bank officer "for every little thing I need." Dave says he is only interested in having Diana and the children taken care of and in Diana's having someone to help her manage and direct the investment of the funds. He is also anxious to avoid unnecessary estate taxes. These are subjects they have discussed at various times since their last wills were drawn, and neither has changed his or her original position. Diana is also concerned that virtually all their assets are held in Dave's name.

Dave purchased a $100,000 term life insurance policy in 1986. In 1988, as part of their estate planning, the insurance policy was gifted to an irrevocable insurance trust. Diana is the trustee of the trust until Dave's death, when the First Trust Company becomes the successor trustee. The dispositive provisions of the insurance trust are identical to those of the residuary trust under Dave's will. The trust document does not give the beneficiaries the right to withdraw funds gifted to the trust. The annual premiums for the years 1994–1998 are $279, $327, $377, $443, and $521.

Dave also carries a personal disability income policy that would provide disability income coverage after a 30-day waiting period in the event of a disabling accident or illness. If an accident causes the disability, the monthly benefits are as follows:

Date of disability through 30th day	$ 0
31st through 90th day	2,900
91st day through end of first year	5,400
First day of second year through age 60	4,900
After age 60 throughout life	4,700

If illness causes the disability, the monthly benefits are as follows:

Date of disability through 30th day	$ 0
31st through 90th day	2,900
91st day through end of first year	5,400
First day of second year through fifth year	4,900
Sixth and seventh years	2,900
Eighth year throughout life	1,400

Disability is defined under these policies as being disabled from one's own occupation for 5 years, and after that being unable to perform any occupation for which one is otherwise suited by reason of education, experience, or training. The cost of the disability income coverage is $1,539 annually.

Dave has $180,000 in homeowners coverage that provides replacement-cost coverage on the family house. There is a residential rental property policy covering the rental house for 90 percent of its replacement value.

Both these policies have inflation-adjustment provisions. The automobiles are new enough to warrant the collision and comprehensive coverage that is included in Dave's auto policies. The liability limits carried in these auto policies are the maximum available in the standard premium classification, and they dovetail with the Andersons' personal umbrella policy, which provides up to $1 million in protection over the homeowners and automobile policy limits.

Business Information

Dave went to medical school at Johns Hopkins University and did his internship at Johns Hopkins Hospital. He then served 2 years in the Air Force as a physician and returned to Johns Hopkins to complete his residency in orthopedic surgery. After finishing his residency, he set up his own practice in a large metropolitan area in Georgia, where he has been in practice a little over 10 years. The practice is well established and has become more profitable in recent years. Dave presently operates his practice as a sole proprietorship. He does, however, share office space with Larry Brown and Janet Cole, two other orthopedic surgeons who are also sole practitioners. They all share office overhead (rent, telephone, and the like) equally, except for direct staff costs, malpractice insurance, and some equipment, for which each physician is responsible individually. The physicians have occasionally covered each other's calls at night and on weekends, but they do not share profits in any way. They sometimes refer patients to one another but have no formal professional relationship.

Dave estimates that his office equipment is worth about $45,000 and that the office furniture is worth about $20,000. Both the equipment and the furniture have been fully depreciated for tax purposes.

The total rent for the office space is $5,000 a month, and Dave's share for his office space is $2,000 a month. It is quite likely that the building in which he is located will be sold within the next 2 years. A realtor acquaintance gave Dave a casual estimate that the property (land and building) currently has a market value of $550,000 and probably would have a market value of $600,000 in 2 years. Operating expenses and property taxes, according to the realtor, would total about $10,000 annually. Dave would not like to relocate his practice because it is located conveniently near the three hospitals at which he has staff privileges. For the past 6 years his practice has provided him with net income of over $100,000 per year, and it has increased approximately 6 to 8 percent each year. Last year after his Keogh contribution his net earnings were approximately $150,000, and he anticipates that he will earn $170,000-$175,000 after the Keogh contribution this year. He feels that he devotes the maximum possible time to his practice and that the number of patients cannot expand appreciably. Dave expects that his yearly income will continue to increase but estimates that it will level off at no more than $250,000 in today's dollars. He could increase his income to a greater degree if he were willing to devote more of his time to the practice, but he feels that he is already committing so much of his time to it that his family obligations are barely being met, and he is unwilling to curtail further the time he can spend with Diana and his children. Diana would like him to spend more time with her and the children, particularly while they are growing up, and they indicate that this issue causes some friction between them. He is strongly committed to his career and must even spend some of his at-home hours trying to keep up with advances in his field.

Dave employs three full-time employees: Martha Ann Hammond, 23, his secretary-receptionist; Jeanne Smith, 22, a radiology technician; and Sally Evans, 31, a nurse. Martha Ann Hammond was hired in August 1993 and is paid $15,000 annually. Jeanne Smith was hired in November 1993 and is paid $18,500 annually. Sally Evans has been with Dave since shortly after he opened his practice and usually works with him in surgery as well as at the office. She is paid $24,000 annually.

When asked how he feels about his employees, Dave says that they are all hardworking and that they earn their salaries. He volunteers that he would not be interested in planning for employee benefits that unduly discriminate against them. When asked to clarify what he means by unduly discriminatory benefits, he says that he has no objection, for example, to providing retirement benefits to his employees at or near the current levels. In fact, he feels obligated to do so. However, he is interested in maximizing benefits for himself while minimizing costs.

In the second year of his practice Dave established a profit-sharing Keogh plan, under which participants become 100 percent vested in their plan benefits after the completion of 3 years of service. The plan now provides for immediate 100 percent vesting upon an employee's entry into the plan. However, employees are not eligible for entry into the plan until they have completed 2 years of service. Of the present members of Dave's staff only Sally Evans and Dave have vested benefits under the plan.

Dave has contributed the maximum legally available amount to the Keogh plan for the past 7 years. The Keogh account is presently invested in 30-month CDs, which pay 8 percent and were purchased in June 1990. The trustee of the account is the First Bank and Trust of Georgia. Diana is the named beneficiary of the Keogh plan.

Dave includes his three employees in his Keogh plan when they become eligible. He also provides them with medical insurance coverage that provides a $1 million lifetime benefit with a $100 annual deductible. Eighty percent of the first $3,000 of covered expenses is paid by the insurer and 20 percent by the employee. After $3,000 of covered expenses, the plan pays 100 percent. The costs are $200 per month for employee coverage and $275 per month for employee and dependent coverage. Dave provides medical coverage but not dependent coverage for his employees. However, he participates in the plan and carries dependent coverage despite the fact that the cost is not fully tax deductible.

In the normal course of his practice, Dave usually has $25,000 in excess funds from his practice, which he deposits in a separate money market deposit account until they are needed for quarterly tax liabilities or other expenses. In addition, he says that his accounts receivable usually average $45,000–$55,000 and that most are covered wholly or partially by insurance, so there are rarely significant uncollected receivables.

Drs. Brown and Cole have discussed with Dave the possibility that the three of them could combine their practices and perhaps take on a younger doctor to help expand the practice. They have discussed a professional partnership or incorporating all their practices together. Dave is not too interested in this concept because he is not convinced that he would be willing to be part of a larger organization, but he is considering incorporating his own practice. He has considered incorporation in the past but has always decided it was too much trouble and expense. He is wondering whether incorporation is still as beneficial under the current tax laws. Dave does not wish to change his form of ownership unless a change would bring him significant tax or economic benefits.

When asked to rank the following standardized list of general financial objectives in order of their priority, the Andersons' response was the following:

Provide college educations for all their children	1
Take care of the family in the event of Dave's death	2
Maintain their standard of living	3
Reduce tax burden	4
Take care of self and family during a period of long-term disability	5
Invest and accumulate wealth	6
Enjoy a comfortable retirement	7
Develop an estate plan	8

Next the Andersons were individually asked to rate their responses to a standardized list of various investment vehicles from 0 to 5, with 0 representing an aversion and 5 representing a substantial preference.

Dave's responses were the following:

Savings account	2
Money market fund	2
U.S. government bond	1
Corporate bond	2
Corporate stock (growth)	4
Mutual fund (growth)	4
Mutual fund (income)	1
Municipal bond	3
Real estate (direct ownership)	4
Insurance and annuities	1
Limited partnership units (real estate, oil and gas, cattle, equipment leasing)	3
Commodities, gold, collectibles	2

Diana's responses were the following:

Savings account	3
Money market fund	4
U.S. government bond	2
Corporate bond	3
Corporate stock (growth)	2
Mutual fund (growth)	2
Mutual fund (income)	3
Municipal bond	1
Real estate (direct ownership)	3
Insurance and annuities	2
Limited partnership units (real estate, oil and gas, cattle, equipment leasing)	1
Commodities, gold, collectibles*	4

The Andersons then each responded to a list of general personal financial concerns by rating the concerns from 0 to 5, with 5 indicating a strong concern and 0 indicating no concern.

Dave's ratings are below:

Liquidity	2
Safety of principal	3
Capital appreciation	5
Current income	2
Inflation protection	4
Future income	3
Tax reduction/deferral	4

Diana's ratings are as follows:

Liquidity	3
Safety of principal	3
Capital appreciation	3
Current income	3
Inflation protection	4
Future income	4
Tax reduction/deferral	3

---

*Diana says she would not be interested in commodities or gold, but she thinks collectibles can be very good investments.

INSTRUCTIONS TO STUDENTS

Based on this information, prepare a working outline for the Andersons' financial plan. When this has been completed, it can be compared with the suggested solution that follows. After comparing your working outline to the suggested solution, turn to page 5.19 for further instructions.

WORKING OUTLINE

I. Clients' objectives
   A. For lifetime planning
      1. Fund special schools and college education for children
      2. Accumulate enough wealth to maintain their life-style and to be secure at retirement
      3. Reduce tax burden
      4. Investigate the possibility of the sale of the commercial lot
      5. Investigate the benefits of incorporating Dave's practice
      6. Explore the advisability of Diana's wish to start her own business

   B. For dispositions at death
      1. Ensure that the family will have sufficient assets to maintain their life-style if Dave should die prematurely
      2. Avoid unnecessary taxes at the death of either Dave or Diana

II. Business planning
   A. Tax planning
      1. Present position
      2. Choosing the appropriate business form
         a. Continuing as a sole proprietorship
         b. Forming a professional partnership
         c. S corporations
         d. C corporations
         e. Recommendations
      3. Qualified plans of deferred compensation
         a. Forfeitures in account balances
         b. Present situation
         c. Integration with social security
         d. Recommendation for qualified plans for Dave
            - Self-directed accounts and self-trusteed plans
      4. Buy-sell agreements to ensure that Dave's practice is marketable at death or disability

   B. Insurance planning
      1. Funding the buy-sell agreement(s)
      2. Medical, disability, and life insurance plans
         a. Medical expense insurance
         b. Disability income insurance
      3. Property and liability insurance for the business
      4. Professional liability insurance
      5. Business overhead expense disability insurance

III. Personal planning
   A. Tax planning
      1. Present situation
      2. Fund private school and/or college education for children
         a. Gifting
            - Outright gifts
            - UGMA and UTMA gifts

     b. Income shifting
        - Sec. 2503(b) trusts
        - Sec. 2503(c) trusts
        - Family partnership
        - Caveat: parental obligations
  3. Reduce tax burden
     a. Achieve personal objectives through income-shifting devices to reduce cost
     b. Defer tax liability on a portion of Dave's income from the practice through the use of qualified plans
     c. Individual retirement accounts
  4. Ensure adequate protection in the event of Dave's disability
     a. Design buy-sell to become operative in the event of Dave's disability
     b. Personal disability income coverage
  5. Ensure a comfortable retirement
  6. Consider various problems Diana might encounter in setting up her own business
     a. Preliminary general planning
     b. Taking advantage of start-up losses
  7. Dispositions at death
     a. Analysis of present plans
     b. Recommendations
     c. Failure of present estate planning documents to contemplate the birth of Dave and Diana's fourth child
     d. Considerations regarding Diana
     e. Diana's dissatisfaction with leaving all assets in trust
     f. Problems with present life insurance trust

B. Insurance planning
  1. Life insurance
     a. Ordinary whole life insurance
     b. Single-premium whole life insurance
     c. Variable life policy
     d. Universal life policy
     e. Term policy
     f. Recommendations
  2. Disability insurance
  3. Personal property and liability insurance

C. Investment planning
  1. Financial status of the clients
  2. Funding the children's education
     a. Secondary school expenses
     b. College expenses
     c. Investment alternatives for education funding
        - Moderately high-risk income bond funds
        - Growth-oriented no-load mutual fund
     d. Investment media selection
        - Use of corporate bonds
        - Use of higher-risk investments
  3. Repositioning of existing assets
     a. Earned income
     b. Investment income

  c. Passive income
- Concept of passive income
- Special real estate rules
- Special transition rules

  d. Recommendations
- The commercial lot
- Real estate investments

4. Increasing net worth
    a. Collectibles (coins, porcelain)
    b. Growth-oriented no-load mutual fund
    c. Selected issues of common stock
    d. Preferred stock
    e. Corporate bonds
    f. Municipal bond fund
    g. Leveraged, closed-end bond funds
    h. Junk bonds
    i. Real estate
5. Recommendations

INSTRUCTIONS TO STUDENTS

Now prepare a financial plan for the Andersons. When you have prepared your solution, it should be compared with the suggested solution that follows.

Suggested Solutions

PERSONAL FINANCIAL PLAN

for

DAVE AND DIANA ANDERSON

CLIENTS' OBJECTIVES

A. For lifetime planning
   1. Fund special schools and college education for children
   2. Accumulate enough wealth to maintain their life-style and to be secure at retirement
   3. Reduce tax burden
   4. Investigate the possibility of the sale of the commercial lot
   5. Investigate the benefits of incorporating Dave's practice
   6. Explore the advisability of Diana's wish to start her own business
   7. Investigate possibility of purchasing office building

B. For dispositions at death
   1. Ensure that the family will have sufficient assets to maintain their life-style if Dave should die prematurely
   2. Avoid unnecessary taxes at the death of either Dave or Diana

BUSINESS PLANNING

TAX PLANNING

Present Situation

Dave has a well-established and profitable private practice as an orthopedic surgeon. The practice is conducted as a sole proprietorship, even though there is a space-sharing arrangement with two other orthopedic surgeons. The practice has produced over $100,000 in income for Dave for each of the past 6 years. Last year he earned $150,000 after his Keogh contribution, and he expects to earn at least $170,000–$175,000 in the current year.

Dave employs three full-time employees in his practice: Martha Ann Hammond, 23, his secretary-receptionist; Jeanne Smith, 22, a radiology technician; and Sally Evans, 31, a nurse. Martha Ann Hammond was hired in August 1993 and is paid $15,000 annually. Jeanne Smith was hired in November 1993 and is paid $18,500 annually. Sally Evans is a long-time employee and is paid $24,000 annually. Dave has indicated that his employees work very hard and are well worth the salaries he pays them and that he does not want to implement employee benefits that would unduly discriminate against them, although he is interested in maximizing his own benefits.

Dave has been approached by Drs. Brown and Cole about consolidating their practices either through a professional partnership or by incorporating the three practices as one corporation.

Dave believes that bigger is not necessarily better and thinks that it would probably be a mistake to consolidate the practices. He also thinks that such a plan would greatly increase administrative problems. He has not totally refused to consider the idea despite his reservations, but he is more interested in incorporating his own practice if he decides to incorporate at all. Prior to changing the form of his business he would like information on his options so that he can assess the changes that would be necessary in his practice under the available forms of doing business.

Dave presently provides a good medical insurance plan for each of his employees. He is also a participant in this plan, although the payments in his behalf are not tax deductible for federal income tax purposes. He has set up a defined-contribution Keogh plan for himself and his employees, and he makes the maximum annual contribution to the plan. On the following pages are 5-year projections of the Andersons' tax, net worth, and cash-flow positions if they continue their present life-style without making any significant changes.

[text continues on page 5.39]

BASE CASE

CASE ASSUMPTIONS — BASE CASE

1. The checking account balance is maintained at $5,000; the account is non-interest-bearing.

2. The joint savings account balance of $10,000 earns 3 percent interest annually. Interest accumulates in the account.

3. The money market deposit account has an average balance of $25,000 and earns 3 percent interest annually. Interest does not accumulate in the account but is added to surplus cash.

4. Surplus cash is invested and earns 4 percent annually.

5. Dave's gross receipts and business expenses are expected to increase at 8 percent annually.

6. Diana inherited a coin collection from her father in 1968. Fair market value of the collection is presently $20,000 and is expected to increase annually at 6 percent.

7. The 1994 value of the personal residence ($215,000) will increase at 8 percent annually. The residence was purchased in March 1980. The original amount of the mortgage was $63,000 at an interest rate of 12 percent for a term of 30 years.

8. The 1994 value of the commercial lot ($160,000) will increase at 4 percent annually. The lot was purchased in March 1983. The original amount of the mortgage was $80,000 at an interest rate of 10 percent for a term of 20 years.

9. The 1994 value of the rental property ($75,000) will increase at 6 percent annually. The rental property was purchased in November 1982. Currently the property rents for $550 per month and has operating expenses of approximately $900 annually. All these amounts will increase at 6 percent annually.

10. Limited partnership interests are shown at cost.

11. Dave has office furniture valued at approximately $20,000 and office equipment valued at $45,000. No increase or decrease in value has been assumed.

12. Dave's accounts receivable average $50,000.

13. Property taxes on the personal residence are expected to increase at 6 percent annually.

14. Nondeductible living expenses are expected to increase at 6 percent annually.

15. Charitable contributions are expected to increase at 6 percent annually.

16. Dave's Keogh plan is presently invested in 30-month CDs earning 8 percent. This earning assumption has been projected through 1998. He makes a maximum contribution to this plan in each year.

17. Automobiles decrease in value at a rate of 15 percent annually.

18. The expected growth rate of all dividends is 2 percent.

19. The expected growth rate for prices of all stocks is the same as the past growth rate for each stock.

20. No growth is expected in either bond current yields or total returns.

1994   INCOME STATEMENT

DAVE & DIANA ANDERSON

BASE CASE	1994	1995	1996	1997	1998
Earned Income					
Business Inc-Cl	200,000	216,000	233,280	251,942	272,098
Keogh Plans	-22,500	-22,500	-22,500	-22,500	-22,500
	177,500	193,500	210,780	229,442	249,598
Interest/Dividends					
Saving/NOW Acts	300	300	300	300	300
Money Market Fund	750	750	750	750	750
Houseboat Finance	900	900	900	900	900
Clean Soap Inc	1,000	1,020	1,040	1,061	1,082
Nationwide Oil Co	500	510	520	531	541
Deep Snow Maker Inc	30	31	31	32	32
Burp Soda Inc	640	653	666	679	693
Economic Fund	24	24	25	25	26
Wellington Mfg Corp	300	306	312	318	325
FundMgrsGrowthFund	1,342	1,369	1,396	1,424	1,453
Atlantic Rim Fund	456	465	474	484	494
Southern Fund	395	403	411	419	428
5-7 Year Bond Fund	395	403	411	419	428
Investable Cash	1,455	4,525	7,962	11,827	16,120
	8,487	11,659	15,199	19,170	23,571
Investments					
Invest--House Loan	-3,575	-3,435	-3,282	-3,114	-2,928
Invest--House Expen	-900	-954	-1,011	-1,072	-1,136
Invest--House Rent	6,600	6,996	7,416	7,861	8,332
Invest--House Depre	-2,100	-2,100	-2,100	-2,100	-2,100
Invest--Lot Loan	-5,371	-4,962	-4,512	-4,015	-3,465
	-5,346	-4,455	-3,489	-2,440	-1,297
Other					
State Tax Refund	0	2	2	2	3
	0	2	2	2	3
Adjustments					
S.E. Tax Dedctn	6,398	6,761	7,142	7,559	7,996
	6,398	6,761	7,142	7,559	7,996
Adj Gross Income	174,243	193,953	215,358	238,623	263,891
Deductions					
Charitable 50%	4,500	4,770	5,056	5,360	5,681
State Tax Paid	8,535	9,637	10,835	12,139	13,556
Prop Taxes--Home	1,900	2,014	2,135	2,263	2,399
Home Mortgage	6,584	6,432	6,262	6,070	5,853
Reductn For High Inc	-1,966	-2,444	-2,967	-3,542	-4,174
Gross Deductions	19,553	20,409	21,321	22,290	23,315
Standard Deduction	6,200	6,400	6,600	6,850	7,100
Allowed Deductions	19,553	20,409	21,321	22,290	23,315
Pers Exemptions	10,575	9,555	8,415	6,760	5,130
Taxable Income	144,115	163,988	185,622	209,573	235,446
Fed Income Tax	50,206	57,568	65,593	74,504	84,134
Fed Tax Bracket	36.0	36.0	36.0	36.0	36.0

1994   **BALANCE SHEET**

DAVE & DIANA ANDERSON

BASE CASE	1994	1995	1996	1997	1998
LIQUID ASSETS					
Cash Balance	4,851	4,867	4,945	4,973	5,099
Cash Deposits					
Saving/NOW Acts	10,000	10,000	10,000	10,000	10,000
Investable Cash	74,209	156,575	249,477	353,678	468,442
Money Market Fund	25,000	25,000	25,000	25,000	25,000
	109,209	191,575	284,477	388,678	503,442
Stocks & Bonds					
Houseboat Finance	12,508	12,426	12,338	12,243	12,142
Town Hall Munibonds	10,600	10,585	10,572	10,556	10,540
State School System	15,150	15,152	15,157	15,161	15,165
Clean Soap Inc	35,000	39,900	45,486	51,854	59,114
Nationwide Oil Co	12,000	12,600	13,230	13,892	14,586
Deep Snow Maker Inc	14,000	16,520	19,494	23,002	27,143
Burp Soda Inc	32,000	34,880	38,019	41,441	45,171
Economic Fund	1,500	1,305	1,135	987	859
Wellington Mfg Corp	24,000	26,400	29,040	31,944	35,138
FundMgrsGrowthFund	46,200	47,355	48,539	49,752	50,996
Atlantic Rim Fund	9,500	10,355	11,287	12,303	13,410
Southern Fund	10,200	11,373	12,681	14,139	15,765
5-7 Year Bond Fund	6,200	6,299	6,400	6,502	6,606
	228,858	245,150	263,377	283,777	306,636
Overpaid Taxes					
Overpaid State Tx	2	2	2	3	3
	2	2	2	3	3
Liquid Assets	342,920	441,594	552,801	677,432	815,180
NONLIQUID ASSETS					
Retirement Plans					
Keogh Plans	91,168	122,761	156,882	193,733	233,532
	91,168	122,761	156,882	193,733	233,532
Investments					
Investment--House	75,000	79,500	84,270	89,326	94,686
Investment--Lot	160,000	166,400	173,056	179,978	187,177
Gate House Property	35,000	35,000	35,000	35,000	35,000
Northbrook Gardens	102,000	102,000	102,000	102,000	102,000
Smoky River Ltd	55,500	55,500	55,500	55,500	55,500
	427,500	438,400	449,826	461,804	474,363

5.32

1994 **BALANCE SHEET** (cont.)

DAVE & DIANA ANDERSON

BASE CASE	1994	1995	1996	1997	1998
Personal Property					
Home	232,200	250,776	270,838	292,505	315,906
Dave's Car	18,700	15,895	13,511	11,484	9,762
Diana's Car	8,500	7,225	6,141	5,220	4,437
Furnishings--Home	30,000	30,000	30,000	30,000	30,000
Furnishings--Office	65,000	65,000	65,000	65,000	65,000
Coin Collection	21,200	22,472	23,820	25,250	26,765
Business Accts Rec	50,000	50,000	50,000	50,000	50,000
	425,600	441,368	459,310	479,459	501,869
Nonliquid Assets	944,268	1,002,529	1,066,018	1,134,996	1,209,765
Total Assets	1,287,188	1,444,123	1,618,819	1,812,428	2,024,945

LIABILITIES

Mortgage Loans					
Home Mortgage	54,208	52,864	51,350	49,644	47,721
	54,208	52,864	51,350	49,644	47,721
Notes Payable					
Diana's Car--Loan	4,223	1,478	0	0	0
	4,223	1,478	0	0	0
Investments					
Invest--House Loan	36,858	35,313	33,615	31,749	29,697
Invest--Lot Loan	51,565	47,263	42,511	37,262	31,463
	88,423	82,576	76,126	69,011	61,160
Total Liabilities	146,854	136,918	127,476	118,655	108,881
Net Worth	1,140,334	1,307,205	1,491,343	1,693,773	1,916,064

1994   CASHFLOW STATEMENT

DAVE & DIANA ANDERSON

BASE CASE	1994	1995	1996	1997	1998
BEGINNING OF YEAR					
Idle Cash On Hand	5,000	4,851	4,867	4,945	4,973

SOURCES OF CASH

Cash Income					
Business Inc-Cl	200,000	216,000	233,280	251,942	272,098
Interest+Dividends	8,360	8,461	8,565	8,671	8,778
	208,360	224,461	241,845	260,613	280,876
Investments					
Gate House - Cash	6,000	6,000	6,000	6,000	6,000
Northbrook - Cash	5,600	5,600	5,600	5,600	5,600
Smoky River - Cash	1,563	1,798	2,054	2,321	2,615
InvestHouse - Depre	2,100	2,100	2,100	2,100	2,100
	15,263	15,498	15,754	16,021	16,315
Tax Refund					
State Tax Refund	0	2	2	2	3
	0	2	2	2	3
Total Cash Inflow	223,623	239,961	257,601	276,636	297,194
Tot Cash Available	228,623	244,812	262,468	281,581	302,167

USES OF CASH

Fully Tax Deductible					
Keogh Plans	22,500	22,500	22,500	22,500	22,500
Home Mortgage	6,584	6,432	6,262	6,070	5,853
	29,084	28,932	28,762	28,570	28,353
Partly Deductible					
Charity Contrb-50%	4,500	4,770	5,056	5,360	5,681
	4,500	4,770	5,056	5,360	5,681
Not Tax Deductible					
Diana's Car--Loan	559	299	44	0	0
Vacations	4,000	4,240	4,494	4,764	5,050
Life Ins Prem--Dave	279	327	377	443	521
Home Ins Prem--Home	600	636	674	715	757
Ins Prem--Cars	995	1,055	1,118	1,185	1,256
Dis Ins Prem--Dave	1,539	1,539	1,539	1,539	1,539
Living Expenses	30,000	31,800	33,708	35,730	37,874
	37,972	39,896	41,955	44,376	46,998

5.34

1994   **C A S H F L O W S T A T E M E N T** (cont.)

DAVE & DIANA ANDERSON

BASE CASE	1994	1995	1996	1997	1998
Taxes Paid					
Fed Tax Paid	50,206	57,568	65,593	74,504	84,134
State Tax Paid	8,535	9,637	10,835	12,139	13,556
Prop Taxes--Home	1,900	2,014	2,135	2,263	2,399
	60,641	69,219	78,563	88,906	100,089
Purchase/Deposits					
Investable Cash	72,754	77,841	84,940	92,374	98,644
	72,754	77,841	84,940	92,374	98,644
Investments					
Invest--House Loan	4,980	4,980	4,980	4,980	4,980
Invest--House Expen	900	954	1,011	1,072	1,136
Invest--Lot Loan	9,264	9,264	9,264	9,264	9,264
	15,144	15,198	15,255	15,316	15,380
Liability Liquidation					
Home Mortgage	1,192	1,344	1,514	1,706	1,923
Diana's Car--Loan	2,485	2,745	1,478	0	0
	3,677	4,089	2,992	1,706	1,923
Tot Cash Outflow	223,772	239,944	257,523	276,608	297,068
END OF YEAR					
Cash Balance	4,851	4,867	4,945	4,973	5,099

5.35

1994   SUPPORTING SCHEDULE

DAVE & DIANA ANDERSON

	JOINT 1994	JOINT 1995	JOINT 1996	JOINT 1997	JOINT 1998
BASE CASE	----	----	----	----	----
Income					
Earned Income	177,500	193,500	210,780	229,442	249,598
Adj Gross Income	174,243	193,953	215,358	238,623	263,891
Allowed Deductions	19,553	20,409	21,321	22,290	23,315
Pers Exemptions	10,575	9,555	8,415	6,760	5,130
Taxable Income	144,115	163,988	185,622	209,573	235,446
Investments					
Ordinary Income	6,600	6,996	7,416	7,861	8,332
Depreciation	2,100	2,100	2,100	2,100	2,100
Invstmt Interest	8,946	8,397	7,794	7,129	6,393
Other Expenses	900	954	1,011	1,072	1,136
Investment Income	-5,346	-4,455	-3,489	-2,440	-1,297
Investment Interest					
Inv Int Sch E	8,946	8,397	7,794	7,129	6,393
Federal Tax Liab					
Regular Tax	37,410	44,046	51,310	59,387	68,142
Gross Fed Inc Tax	37,410	44,046	51,310	59,387	68,142
Self Employmt Tax	12,796	13,522	14,283	15,117	15,992
Fed Income Tax	50,206	57,568	65,593	74,504	84,134
Fed Tax Analysis					
Indexing Factor	46	51	56	62	68
Fed Tax Bracket	36.0	36.0	36.0	36.0	36.0
$ To Next Bracket	105,885	94,762	82,228	67,627	51,454
Next Bracket	39.6	39.6	39.6	39.6	39.6
Previous Bracket	31.0	31.0	31.0	31.0	31.0
$ To Prev Bracket	4,115	19,038	35,622	54,323	74,746
Alt Minimum Tax					
Adj Gross Income	174,243	193,953	215,358	238,623	263,891
State Tax Refund	0	-2	-2	-2	-3
Contributions	-4,500	-4,770	-5,056	-5,360	-5,681
Home Mortgage	-6,584	-6,432	-6,262	-6,070	-5,853
Adjusted AMTI	163,159	182,749	204,038	227,191	252,354
AMT Exemptions	-41,710	-36,813	-31,491	-25,702	-19,412
AMT Taxable Inc	121,449	145,936	172,547	201,489	232,942
Gross Alt Min Tx	31,577	37,943	44,862	52,917	61,724
Fed Tax Less FTC	-37,410	-44,046	-51,310	-59,387	-68,142

1994 **SUPPORTING SCHEDULE** (cont.)

DAVE & DIANA ANDERSON

BASE CASE

	JOINT 1994	JOINT 1995	JOINT 1996	JOINT 1997	JOINT 1998
Other Tax Liabs					
Adj Gross Inc	174,243	193,951	215,356	238,621	263,888
GA AGI Adjstmnts	1,328	1,326	1,326	1,326	1,325
GA Adj Grss Inc	175,571	195,276	216,681	239,947	265,212
GA Standard Ded	4,400	4,400	4,400	4,400	4,400
GA Itemized Ded	21,519	22,853	24,288	25,832	27,489
GA Exemptions	7,500	7,500	7,500	7,500	7,500
GA Taxable Inc	146,552	164,923	184,893	206,615	230,224
GA Regular Tax	8,533	9,635	10,833	12,136	13,553
GA Income Tax	8,533	9,635	10,833	12,136	13,553
Georgia Tax	8,533	9,635	10,833	12,136	13,553
Tot State/Local Tx	8,533	9,635	10,833	12,136	13,553
Total Inc Tax	58,739	67,203	76,426	86,640	97,687

1994   **FINANCIAL SUMMARY**

DAVE & DIANA ANDERSON

BASE CASE	1994	1995	1996	1997	1998
Gross Real Income					
Personal Earnings	200,000	216,000	233,280	251,942	272,098
Interest Income	4,733	7,803	11,240	15,105	19,398
Dividends Rcvd	5,082	5,184	5,287	5,393	5,501
Gate House - Cash	6,000	6,000	6,000	6,000	6,000
Northbrook - Cash	5,600	5,600	5,600	5,600	5,600
Smoky River - Cash	1,563	1,798	2,054	2,321	2,615
InvestHouse - Depre	2,100	2,100	2,100	2,100	2,100
	225,078	244,484	265,561	288,461	313,311
Income & Inflation					
Gross Real Inc	225,078	244,484	265,561	288,461	313,311
Total Inc Tax	-58,739	-67,203	-76,426	-86,640	-97,687
Net Real Income	166,339	177,281	189,135	201,821	215,624
Cur Real Inc =	166,339	172,160	178,186	184,422	190,877
At Infltn Rate Of	4	4	4	4	4
Cash Flow					
Idle Cash On Hand	5,000	4,851	4,867	4,945	4,973
Norml Cash Inflow	223,623	239,961	257,601	276,636	297,194
Norml Cash Outflw	151,018	162,103	172,583	184,234	198,424
Cash Invested	72,754	77,841	84,940	92,374	98,644
Cash Balance	4,851	4,867	4,945	4,973	5,099
Net Worth					
Personal Assets	430,451	446,235	464,256	484,432	506,968
Investment Assets	856,735	997,886	1,154,562	1,327,993	1,517,973
Personal Liabilities	-58,431	-54,342	-51,350	-49,644	-47,721
Investmt Liabilities	-88,423	-82,576	-76,126	-69,011	-61,160
Personal Net Worth	372,020	391,893	412,906	434,788	459,247
Investment Net Worth	768,312	915,310	1,078,436	1,258,982	1,456,813
Net Worth	1,140,334	1,307,205	1,491,343	1,693,773	1,916,064

Choosing the Appropriate Business Form

Continuing as a Sole Proprietorship

The sole proprietorship is the most informal type of business ownership because there is such a close identity between the business and the business owner. Sole proprietorships are not separate entities for tax-reporting purposes (as are partnerships) or for taxpaying purposes (as are corporations). The taxpayer for a sole proprietorship for both tax-reporting and taxpaying purposes is the proprietor. There is no separate income tax form to file since all business income and losses from a proprietorship are computed on the proprietor's Form 1040 and added to (or subtracted from) his or her gross income from other sources, if any. All ordinary and necessary business expenses are deducted from the gross income from the business, and any gains are taxed at the tax rate for individuals up to the maximum rate of 39.6 percent. Bona fide business losses can be used to offset other income of the proprietor, if any, without the constraints of such limitations as the basis rules for partnerships. Taxable years for sole proprietorships must be the same as those of the owner.

In a sole proprietorship the proprietor owns all assets and therefore has total control over the business. A proprietor can retain total control or delegate some authority to employees on his or her own terms. There is no board of directors, and there are no partners or shareholders to answer to or to question the proprietor's decisions. Some business owners enjoy the informality, flexibility, control, and freedom that the sole proprietorship affords.

Sole proprietorships are not, however, without their drawbacks. The close identity between the proprietor and the business can leave the proprietor personally vulnerable to liability for acts of employees or agents. Such a situation does not normally exist when business is carried on in a corporate form. There is also no opportunity for the sole proprietor to take advantage of splitting income (and thereby the income tax liability) between himself or herself and another taxpayer, as is the case in regular (C) corporations. In addition, there are still some restrictions with regard to qualified retirement plans that apply to self-employed persons and owner-employees that are not applicable to other employees. One such important restriction is that a loan to an owner-employee (defined in IRC Sec. 401(c)(3) to include self-employed persons and certain partners) will constitute a prohibited transaction that will subject the borrower to excise taxes and may even jeopardize the plan's qualified status.

Certain employee benefits that are available to shareholder-employees of C corporations free of tax cost, such as group life and medical insurance, are paid with after-tax dollars by self-employed persons.

As a physician, Dave is personally liable for his own acts in the event of an action against him for negligence or malpractice, regardless of whether he operates as a sole proprietor, a partner, or a corporation. His relationship with Drs. Brown and Cole is not of a type that could result in Dave's being held liable for their acts. Therefore with respect to personal liability exposure, incorporation would not provide him with a significant advantage over his present situation.

Forming a Professional Partnership

Like the sole proprietorship, the partnership is a nontaxpaying entity. While it is a tax-reporting entity that has taxable income or losses and must file a tax return, the partnership itself is a mere conduit, and the partnership income and losses are passed through to the partners individually. This does not mean, however, that the partnership itself does not have significant importance in determining the amount and type of taxes that the partners will pay. For example, the characterization of income or losses as capital or ordinary is made at the partnership level and merely passed on to the individual partners for reporting on their individual income tax returns. The partnership can be used to pass through tax losses (limited to the partner's basis in his or her partnership interest) to the individual partners in order to offset income from other sources.

The Internal Revenue Code defines a partnership as any business, financial operation, or venture carried on through a syndicate, group, pool, joint venture, or other unincorporated organization other than trusts, estates, or corporations (IRC Sec. 7701(a)(2)). The definition is a broad and flexible one, and the partnership can in fact be a very flexible form of business ownership that allows for a substantial amount of informality in business operations. It is not without its potential problems, however, regarding both legal and tax issues.

One of the most troubling problems in operating a business, particularly a professional practice, in the form of a partnership is that as a legal matter all the general partners are responsible for all the debts of the partnership as well as the debts of other partners arising out of the partnership business. For a group of professionals such as physicians this means that a malpractice suit resulting in a proven claim of professional liability is the responsibility of each of the partners to the full extent of the liability. In other words, if the person who made the professional error is unable to pay all the liability, each of the other partners is fully liable for the payment of the required amount. In strict legal terms each partner is "jointly and severally liable" for the total liabilities of the partnership and of the individual partners arising out of the partnership business. This can necessitate one partner's making huge payments on behalf of another partner. It should be noted that the amount of a partner's liability in this regard is not limited to the assets the partner has in the partnership but extends to personal assets as well. Therefore each partner can lose everything he or she owns through the liabilities of the partnership or the acts of the partners. It should also be noted that joint and several liability extends to all obligations of the partnership and of general partners arising from the partnership business and is not restricted to the area of professional liability.

As a tax matter, partnerships, like sole proprietorships, do not offer the opportunity to split income between a business entity and an individual. Because the partnership is not a taxpaying entity, all income is taxed to the partners. If the partnership has taxable income, each partner must pay tax on his or her portion of that amount in the year in which it is recognized by the partnership regardless of whether it is actually distributed to that partner.

In addition, there are benefits available to shareholder-employees of regular (C) corporations on a tax-advantaged basis that are unavailable to partners. These benefits include

- group medical, disability income, and life insurance plans
- certain loans to shareholder-employees from the corporation's qualified plans under IRC Sec. 72(p)

Primarily because of the increased personal liability exposure, forming a professional partnership is not recommended in this case.

S Corporations

S corporations have long been treated as corporations for tax purposes (for example, the computation of taxable income according to regular corporate rules) except that the income from such corporations was essentially treated as if the individual shareholders had earned or received it as a dividend, regardless of whether it was actually distributed to the shareholders. It was primarily this tax attribute of having S corporation taxable income taxed to the individual shareholders that made the gift of S corporation stock an effective income-shifting device. For example, income could be shifted to a child by a gift of S corporation shares without raising difficult tax issues such as reasonable compensation. Since taxable income was generally taxed to the shareholders, S corporations have always been loosely compared to partnerships despite the many differences in taxation between these two forms of business entities. In fact, until recent years S corporations were actually taxed in some ways as combinations of partnerships and regular corporations. Under current federal income tax law, however, the rules governing S corporation income are much closer to the rules governing partnership income than to the rules governing regular corporations. There are, however, significant differences between the formation and the eligibility requirements of an S corporation and those of a partnership.

IRC Sec. 1361 requires that in order to elect S corporation status, a corporation must be a domestic corporation that is not an ineligible corporation. Ineligible corporations include

- affiliated corporations as defined in IRC Sec. 1504(a) regardless of whether they are eligible to file a consolidated return
- banks and financial institutions that are allowed deductions for bad debts under IRC Sec. 593 and that would be defined as a financial institution under IRC Sec. 585
- an insurance company subject to tax under Subchapter L
- a corporation electing the Puerto Rico and possessions tax credit under IRC Sec. 936, as amended
- a domestic international sales corporation (DISC) or former DISC

In addition, the corporation must satisfy the following four requirements:

1. The electing S corporation may have no more than a total of 35 shareholders; however, a husband and wife or their estates, each owning stock individually, are treated as one shareholder.
2. Each individual shareholder must be a citizen or resident of the United States; that is, no shareholder can be a nonresident alien.
3. Each shareholder must be an individual, an estate, or a specified type of trust. The definition of individual shareholders does not include corporations or partnerships. However, there are basically four types of trusts that are permitted to be shareholders:

    a. a grantor trust or a trust that distributes all its income to a sole beneficiary who is treated as the owner of the trust under IRC Sec. 678, provided that the grantor or owner of the trust would be an eligible shareholder
    b. a trust created primarily as a voting trust, although each beneficiary of the voting trust is treated as a separate shareholder for purposes of the maximum-35-shareholder limitation
    c. any trust, but only as to stock transferred to it under the terms of a will and only for 60 days beginning with the date of transfer
    d. a qualified Subchapter S trust, which is a trust that owns stock in one or more S corporations and distributes or is required to distribute all its current income to its sole income beneficiary, who must be an individual United States citizen or resident. If there is a distribution of corpus during the term of the trust, it can be made only to the income beneficiary.

4. The corporation must have no more than one class of stock outstanding, and these shares must be absolutely identical as to the shareholders' rights in the profits and assets of the corporation. Recently released Treasury regulations set forth many situations in which a second class of stock will be deemed to have been issued by the S corporation.

Any qualifying corporation (one meeting all the criteria listed above) can elect S corporation status. The election may be made at any time during the taxable year preceding the year the election is to go into effect. For example, for a corporation with a calendar-year taxable year, the election could be made on November 1, 1994, and would become effective on January 1, 1995. The election can also be made on or before the 15th day of the third month of the year in which the election is to be effective; that is, an election made on or before March 15, 1995, would be effective as of January 1, 1995. If the corporation fails to make the election until after the 15th day of the third month of the year in which the election is intended to be effective, it will be treated as an election made for the succeeding tax year. The consent of all shareholders on the day the election is made is required. In the case of an election made on or before the 15th day of the third month of the election year, the consent of anyone who was a shareholder during the preelection portion of the year is also necessary to effect the election.

A new shareholder who wants to revoke the S election may do so if he or she owns more than 50 percent of the corporation's stock and refuses to affirmatively consent to the election within 60 days after acquiring the stock. If a new shareholder owning less than 50 percent of the corporation's stock becomes a shareholder while an S election is in effect, the new shareholder will be bound by the election.

Once a valid election for Subchapter S status is made, the election is in effect for the tax year for which it was made and continues in effect for all subsequent years unless it is terminated or voluntarily revoked. The election may be terminated or revoked in any of the following ways:

- Shareholders owning more than 50 percent of the stock consent to a voluntary revocation.
- The corporation fails to continue to satisfy any one of the qualification requirements (for instance, it exceeds the allowable number of shareholders or issues a second class of stock).
- More than 25 percent of the S corporation's gross receipts for 3 successive tax years is from certain types of passive income, and the corporation has accumulated earnings and profits from a period prior to the S status election when it had operated as a C corporation.

An S corporation can elect to revoke the election provided the shareholders of more than 50 percent of the stock consent.

An involuntary termination of S status (such as the issuance of stock to a prohibited shareholder) is effective as of the day the disqualifying event occurs and not retroactively to the beginning of the taxable year. The IRS may waive the effect of an inadvertent termination for any period, provided the corporation corrects the event that created the termination, and the corporation and its shareholders agree to be treated as if the election had been in effect for the entire period.

A revocation of Subchapter S status can be elected on or before the 15th day of the third month of the present taxable year and will be effective for that entire taxable year unless the revocation specifically requests a date in the future. In the event that a future date is specified (for example, an election to revoke on January 1, 1995, was made on November 30, 1994), the revocation will be effective on that date (January 1, 1995). If no future date of revocation is specified but the election is filed after the permissible period, the revocation is effective at the beginning of the following taxable year. Voluntary revocations result in an inability to reelect Subchapter S status for 5 years without obtaining IRS consent to the reelection. In appropriate circumstances the IRS can waive the 5-year waiting period and permit the corporation to make a new election effective for the following taxable year.

The law requires that the S corporation's choices of a taxable year be generally the same as those of a partnership or a personal service corporation. A new S corporation is required to have a taxable year ending December 31 unless it can establish to the satisfaction of the IRS that it has a business purpose for choosing another taxable year. For most businesses this will be difficult to establish.

Shareholder-employees of new S corporations who own (either individually or by attribution under IRC Sec. 318) more than 2 percent of the outstanding stock of the S corporation or stock having more than 2 percent of the voting power of all the S corporation's stock are ineligible for tax-free benefits that are available to regular (C) corporation shareholder-employees. These benefits primarily include certain group medical, disability, and life insurance benefits (IRC Sec. 1372 applying IRC Sec. 7701(a)(2)). There are also constraints on borrowing from qualified plans for shareholder-employees who own more than 5 percent of the outstanding stock of the corporation (IRC Sec. 4975(d)). The overall effect of these rules is to treat S corporation shareholders as if they were partners when determining the tax status of fringe benefits and borrowing from qualified plans.

Income from an S corporation is not taxed at the corporate level. Instead it is passed through to the individual shareholders in proportion to their percentage of stock ownership and taxed at their tax rates as in a partnership. This eliminates any possibility of reducing the individual shareholder's tax liability by splitting income between the shareholder and the corporation. While the S corporation can work effectively, especially in passing through the start-up losses of a new business to offset other income of shareholders and in limiting the personal liability of shareholders, care should be taken in making a Subchapter S election or in revoking such an election once it has been made. Professionals can incorporate and elect Subchapter S status. The limited personal liability is an advantage in some situations.

C Corporations

As a general rule property can be transferred from a proprietorship or a partnership into a regular corporation (or to an S corporation) without the recognition of gain or loss on the transfer (IRC Sec. 351). The regular or C corporation is both a tax-reporting and a taxpaying entity. There are separate rates of corporate taxation, and the benefits of splitting the taxation of corporate profits between the corporation and the individual shareholders can be material, especially when the shareholders are in high tax brackets. The corporate tax rate for the first $50,000 of taxable income is 15 percent for C corporations (except for qualified personal service corporations). However, leaving excessive funds in the corporation to avoid taxation at the individual level can lead to additional tax problems such as the accumulated-earnings penalty tax, which is a punitive tax, with additional tax rates of 39.6 percent imposed on all accumulated taxable income (IRC Secs. 531–537). The accumulated-earnings tax is an attempt to prevent individuals from retaining funds in the corporation for other than the reasonable needs of the business. However, operating businesses can maintain up to $250,000 in the corporation without subjecting themselves to the accumulated-earnings tax. Professional corporations such as a medical practice are personal service corporations and are allowed to accumulate up to $150,000 without subjecting themselves to the accumulated-earnings tax. If accumulated taxable income exceeds these amounts, the retention of earnings and profits must be to meet reasonable business needs or the corporation will be subject to the accumulated-earnings tax. This tax is imposed in addition to regular corporate tax rates. Except in unusual circumstances the accumulated-earnings tax is not a major problem in a professional corporation, since most income can be paid out in the form of salaries and tax-advantaged benefits for the shareholder-employees.

There are few intricate rules for setting up a regular corporation for tax purposes. There is no limitation on the number or type of persons or entities that can be shareholders. Any enterprise doing business in a corporate form, as defined under state law, and indeed some associations that are not technically legal corporations but that have centralized management, continuity of life, limited liability, and free transferability of interests are treated as corporations for tax purposes. Owners of regular corporations may also be employees of the corporations and as such are entitled to withdraw monies in the form of reasonable salaries and to receive certain tax-free fringe benefits.

An important nontax advantage of the corporate form, whether it is an S corporation or a regular C corporation, is the limited personal liability of the shareholders. The general rule is that in a suit or claim against the corporation the shareholder's potential liability is limited to the amount of money that he or she has invested in the corporation.

However, the liability situation is different in the case of a professional corporation. Each professional is personally responsible for any professional negligence of his or her own, regardless of whether the practice is conducted in corporate form. This risk cannot be shifted to the entity and must be insured against. Also in Georgia one shareholder in a professional corporation may be subject to liability for the actions of another shareholder. Therefore incorporation of a medical practice does not produce a significant liability advantage in Georgia.

There is additional expense in changing the form of any business from a sole proprietorship to a corporation. These expenses will result primarily from the necessity of filing separate tax returns. There are also significant organizational expenses involved in establishing a corporation.

Recommendations

Because of the nature of Dave's professional relationship with Drs. Brown and Cole, he should not seriously consider forming a professional partnership with them at this time. In fact, Dave has indicated clearly that he has no wish to be part of a larger organization.

Therefore the remaining issue is whether Dave should continue to operate as a sole proprietor or incorporate his practice either as a C or as an S corporation.

As previously stated, incorporation in this case does not present significant protection from personal liability, since Dave is personally liable for his own professional acts regardless of whether he incorporates, and he has no partners for whose acts he would be liable. As long as Dave maintains adequate professional liability insurance, his personal assets should be protected. There is no compelling reason for Dave to incorporate at this time. Although the costs of incorporation are not dramatic, it is not appropriate to incur them without obtaining any significant advantage. Moreover, a C corporation could present tax problems if Dave decided to liquidate the corporation, since *both* the shareholder and the C corporation are taxed on the distribution of appreciated assets in a liquidation, pursuant to the current federal income tax laws. Dave could obtain tax-free group insurance and borrow from his qualified plan under the corporate form, but these advantages do not appear to outweigh the costs in this case.

An S corporation would not provide Dave with any significant advantages. Therefore the recommendation in this case is to continue operating as a sole proprietorship in the absence of any compelling reason to incorporate.

Qualified Plans of Deferred Compensation

NOTE TO STUDENTS

To avoid repetition, the technical information on defined-benefit and defined-contribution plans such as that contained on pages 3.39–3.45 has been omitted from this discussion. In an actual plan this type of information should be presented to the client for completeness. In addition, if the student is not completely familiar with this material, it should be reviewed before proceeding through this suggested solution.

Dave's Keogh plan is of the profit-sharing type. In a profit-sharing plan, the employer may make an annual deductible contribution of up to 15 percent of covered compensation. A separate rule (Sec. 415 limits) requires that no single employee may have more than the lesser of 25 percent of pay or $30,000 allocated to his or her account annually.

Since Dave's plan is a Keogh plan, the maximum 15 percent deduction limit is complicated by the fact that compensation for a self-employed person is defined as his or her "earned income." Earned income is calculated after taking into account all appropriate business deductions, which includes the contribution to the plan. This rule has the impact of reducing the maximum contribution for the self-employed to 13.043 percent of earned income (disregarding the plan contribution).

Also note that a deduction is currently allowed for one-half of an individual's self-employment social security taxes. Dave is required to pay a total of $13,314 in social security taxes. This is calculated as follows:

the OASDI tax: 12.40 percent x $60,600 = $7,514
plus
The HI tax: 2.9 percent x $200,000 = $5,800.

(Note when making this calculation that the Omnibus Reconciliation Act of 1993 removed the cap on wages subject to tax under the HI tax. This has the effect of increasing the total social security taxes for those who earn more than the old cap of $135,000.)

Since Dave's total social security taxes are $13,314, he can take a deduction of $6,657. This deduction also has the result of reducing his maximum contribution, by lowering his compensation to $193,343. Under these rules, the maximum contribution on his behalf is $25,217 ($193,343 x 13.043 percent).

However, a third rule also has to be considered, which may reduce the maximum contribution further. Under the Omnibus Reconciliation Act of 1993, the maximum amount of compensation that can be considered in determining contributions or benefits cannot exceed $150,000. This compensation cap is used for calculating benefits and for determining the maximum allowable deduction. For example, in Dave's nonintegrated plan he is contributing 15 percent of compensation to the plan for each employee. This means that the contribution for himself is 15 percent of $150,000, or $22,500. In addition, when determining the maximum deductible contribution the $150,000 limit also applies. For example, since all participants in Dave's plan are receiving 15 percent of compensation, the contribution is at the maximum deductible 15 percent limit. Note that it would be possible for Dave to get somewhat more than $22,500 under this rule if other participants were receiving contributions less than 15 percent of compensation. One way to do this would be to integrate the plan with social security (see below).

Integration with Social Security

Dave has indicated that he is not interested in unduly discriminating against his employees with regard to benefits in the plan, although he is interested in minimizing costs. With these two considerations in mind, Dave might consider integrating his plan with social security. In this way, Dave can continue to make a contribution for himself in the amount of 15 percent of compensation while somewhat reducing the contribution for his employees. In the existing nonintegrated plan, contributions are allocated to participants on a pro rata basis, based on each individual's compensation. Therefore if Dave makes a contribution of 15 percent for himself, he is also making a contribution of 15 percent of compensation for each employee. With an integrated plan, Dave can make a 15 percent contribution on his behalf, while contributing only 11.60 percent of compensation for his employees. The integrated contribution results in a significant savings, while still providing his employees with an excellent retirement plan.

Mechanics of Social Security Integration. The nondiscrimination rules provide that in a profit-sharing plan, employer contributions can be allocated to participants as a level percentage of compensation. In addition, a larger portion of the employer's contribution (as a percentage of compensation) may be allocated to those employees who earn more than the taxable wage base ($60,600 for 1994). This "disparity" is allowed in the private pension system due to the fact that employers are required to make higher contributions (as a percentage of salary) to the social security system for those individuals who earn less than the taxable wage base. In other words, since the social security system discriminates in favor of nonhighly compensated employees, the employer is allowed to make up for this in a private pension plan by discriminating in favor of the highly compensated (to the extent allowed under the rules).

In any defined-contribution plan (which includes a profit-sharing plan), the sponsor can provide a higher rate of contributions to the participant for compensation above the integration level (referred to as the excess contribution percentage) than for compensation below the integration level (the base contribution percentage). The integration level is usually the taxable wage base.

When the integration level is the taxable wage base, the difference between the two percentages (the permitted disparity) cannot exceed the lesser of the base contribution percentage or 5.7 percent. For example, a plan providing a contribution percentage of 4 percent for contributions based on compensation below the integration level could provide no more than a contribution percentage of 8 percent for contributions based on compensation above the integration level. If a plan provides 7 percent below the integration level, it could provide up to 12.7 percent above the integration level (the disparity equals 5.7 percent).

If the integration level is reduced below the taxable wage base, the 5.7 percent maximum disparity is adjusted as follows:

Integration Level	Maximum Disparity
Taxable wage base (TWB)	5.7 percent
80 percent or more of TWB	5.4
20 to 80 percent of TWB	4.3
Less than 20 percent of TWB	.7

In Dave's case, if he wants to contribute 15 percent of the $150,000 compensation cap for himself ($22,500), while reducing the contributions made on behalf of his staff, he will look to maximize the disparity allowed under the integration rules. In this case, if Dave chooses the taxable wage base as the integration level, a contribution of $22,500 is the same as an allocation of 5.7 percent of compensation in excess of $60,600 ($5,095) and 11.60 percent of total compensation ($17,405). Since each of his employees earns less than the taxable wage base, 11.60 percent will have to be contributed on behalf of each employee.

To maximize the disparity, the planner should test whether integrating at various integration levels will result in smaller contributions for the nonhighly compensated employees. In this case integrating at $48,480 (80 percent of the integration level) and at $12,120 (20 percent of the integration level) will not significantly lower the required contribution for nonhighly compensated employees.

Money-Purchase Pension Plan

Another option that Dave has is to add a second plan to supplement his profit-sharing plan. Due to the various Keogh profit-sharing limits described above, Dave is making a contribution of only $22,500 on his own behalf to the profit-sharing plan. However, under law, he can have a maximum of $30,000 allocated to his accounts under all defined-contribution plans. To make up for this difference Dave might consider adopting a money-purchase pension plan. With a money-purchase profit-sharing combination, the maximum deductible contribution is 25 percent of compensation. This higher combined deduction limit would allow Dave the opportunity to contribute the full $30,000.

Unlike a profit-sharing plan, a money-purchase plan must have a predetermined contribution formula. At the present time Dave is making maximum contributions to the profit-sharing plan. However, if at any time he wants to make a smaller contribution, he is allowed to do so. If he establishes a money-purchase pension plan, he will have less flexibility. Due to the required contributions, Dave should establish the money-purchase plan as a supplemental plan that requires the minimum contribution necessary to make up the difference between the $22,500 and the maximum of $30,000. In other words, he may want to establish a money-purchase pension plan with a 5 percent contribution formula ($150,000 x 5 percent equals $7,500).

Recommendation for Qualified Plans for Dave

Adding this supplemental plan is an interesting solution for Dave since the second plan provides him with additional benefits (and a larger tax deduction). If he combines this new plan with an integrated profit-sharing plan, Dave's employees will end up with only slightly higher contributions than they have currently under the nonintegrated profit-sharing plan. Therefore we have offered Dave two choices—either integrate the profit-sharing plan to reduce his costs, or increase the contribution on his behalf while keeping the contribution level stable for his employees with the money-purchase integrated profit-sharing plan example.

Dave should seek the assistance of a pension attorney or consultant if he decides to integrate the profit-sharing plan or adopt a money-purchase pension plan. Such assistance will help Dave to determine exactly how to best meet his objectives. Also, if Dave decides to change his profit-sharing plan or add a money-purchase plan, he will incur additional expenses. Dave needs to fully understand these costs so that he can compare the cost savings of the plan redesign against the additional costs that he will incur.

Other Methods of Creating Disparity. In the last several years, a new plan design called *age-weighting* has emerged that could, in Dave's case, be used to create a larger disparity between the contribution made on Dave's behalf and the contributions made for other employees.

Age-weighting is a method of allocating employer contributions to a profit-sharing plan. An age-weighted allocation formula takes into consideration an individual's age and his or her compensation. Age-weighting results in larger contributions (as a percentage of compensation) for older employees. When the highly compensated employees are older than the nonhighly compensated employees, age-weighting can be even more advantageous for the highly compensated employees than integrating the plan with social security.

The reason that age-weighting is allowed is that the nondiscrimination rules allow a plan to demonstrate that either contributions or benefits are provided in a nondiscriminatory manner. In an age-weighted profit-sharing plan, contributions will discriminate in favor of highly compensated employees. However, benefits will not be discriminatory. Larger contributions can be justified as necessary to support the same level of benefits for older employees as for younger employees. An analogous situation is the purchase of a single-premium annuity. The price for an annuity with a specific monthly retirement benefit will increase as the age of the purchaser increases. In the same way, in an age-weighted profit-sharing plan, larger contributions can be made for older employees if the contributions result in a similar level of monthly retirement benefits for each employee.

The theory of age-weighting is simple, although the mechanics can be somewhat complex. In Dave's case, age-weighting could work since he is 8 years older than the next oldest employee. However, Dave is not a good candidate for an age-weighted profit-sharing plan since he is not interested in substantially reducing contributions for his employees.

Buy-Sell Agreements to Ensure That Dave's Practice Is Marketable at Death or Disability

One of the Andersons' most important assets is Dave's practice; in fact, it is presently their most important asset in terms of income production. However, there is no guarantee that the practice could be translated into cash within a reasonable time after his death or disability because Dave has never implemented a legally enforceable agreement for the sale of his practice to take effect at his death or disability. The failure to implement a legally enforceable buy-sell agreement that is appropriately funded often causes significant losses on the disposition of a closely held business. Dave's death could make it necessary for his executor to find a buyer for his practice unless Dave had entered into a postdeath purchase arrangement with another physician.

In the event that Dave continues to live but becomes disabled, his business interest should be convertible to cash to provide him with additional monies throughout the period of his disability. The design and implementation of an appropriate buy-sell agreement is the most effective way to ensure the accomplishment of these objectives.

Because buy-sell agreements are usually funded wholly or partially with life insurance, they are particularly troublesome when the parties are of widely disparate ages or if one of the parties' health is impaired. The difference in ages or health conditions can result in the younger or healthier parties' being forced to personally pay nondeductible high premiums for insurance on the life of an older or impaired party.

We have no information that would indicate whether such a problem might arise in this case. In the absence of these problems the recommendation would be that Dave discuss the possibility of a buy-sell agreement with either Dr. Cole or Dr. Brown or both, as they have expressed an interest in expanding their practices. Since Dave is not particularly interested in expanding his practice, it may be possible to interest one or both of the other physicians in agreeing to purchase his practice should he die or become disabled. On the other hand, it may be necessary for Dave to agree to a reciprocal purchase agreement if he wants the assurance that his practice can be quickly converted to cash. Based on the results of these negotiations, Dave must make a decision on whether to proceed.

If Dave decides to proceed with buy-out arrangements, the provisions and funding of the agreement should be carefully considered. At a minimum the agreement(s) should provide for the other party or parties to become obligated to purchase Dave's shares if he is deceased or becomes disabled. Death is an absolutely ascertainable event, and there are no arguable facts to impede the buy-sell agreement's becoming operative.

In the event of disability, however, the definition of disability that will make the buy-sell operative must be contained within the document in order to make the document effective for this purpose.

A buy-sell agreement should not be designed to provide for the immediate buyout of a disabled party. An appropriate waiting period should be adopted to balance the client's need for disability income and the time at which the client can psychologically deal with the fact that he or she will be unable to resume professional duties.

Without question the most difficult aspect of any buy-sell agreement is deciding on a valuation for the business interest. Of course the surest way to ascertain the value of a going business is to have the business appraised by an appropriate professional. In many cases, however, closely held business owners are reluctant to engage an appraiser because of the expense. In addition, even if an appraisal is made currently and a firm dollar value is entered into the buy-sell agreement, it is likely that the agreement may not become operative for many years. In that event the appraisal figure is meaningless because it is badly outdated. This does not mean, however, that the parties to the buy-sell agreement can ignore the stated dollar figure. In fact, the value of the business could have risen tenfold or fallen to half its stated value, yet if the dollar figure stated in the buy-sell agreement has not been revised, the purchasing party is obligated to pay only the original price as stated in the agreement. This can result in significant hardships to the estate or beneficiaries of the closely held business owner if the value of the business has increased or to the purchaser if the value of the business has decreased.

It is human nature that even with a buy-sell in effect, most parties to such agreements will not meet to revalue the valuation figure on a regular basis because they are usually too preoccupied with their lives. Therefore absolute dollar figures are problematic and should be avoided.

In the case of a personal service business such as Dave's professional practice, if he can be persuaded to obtain an appraisal on the current value of the business, that value can be used as the starting point for the valuation of the buy-sell agreement. Furthermore, the appraisal will almost certainly provide the criteria upon which an appropriate ongoing valuation formula for the practice can be based. Such a formula should be included in the buy-sell agreement in lieu of a stated dollar figure if possible. The formula approach is preferable to any other since it allows the value of the business to be determined at any point in time.

Buy-sell agreements may also be made effective for establishing estate tax value if appropriately structured. In order to be binding for estate tax purposes the buy-sell agreement must (1) have a valid business purpose, (2) be binding on transfers both during the life and at the death of the present owner, (3) have a value that is predetermined or ascertainable according to a formula, and (4) obligate the business owner's estate to sell at the contract price at the death of the business owner. This approach is sometimes referred to as "pegging" for value and is discussed at length in Rev. Rul. 59-60.

As long as no attempt is made to reach an outrageously low valuation, the IRS is usually bound by such an agreement. However, if any one of the four conditions is not met, the IRS is not bound by the agreement and the results can be very distressing. It is possible for the purchaser to pay the beneficiaries of the deceased business owner at the lower value stated in the buy-sell agreement while the IRS attacks the valuation formula and seeks to tax the value of the business in the estate at a much higher value. In this event there is a case, *Estate of Dickinson v. Comm'r,* 63 T.C. 771 (1975), that holds that a buy-sell agreement can validly contain a provision stating that if the Internal Revenue Service is successful in an attack on the stated valuation, the estate is no longer bound by the lower value in the buy-sell agreement.

IRC Sec. 2703, enacted as part of chapter 14 of the Internal Revenue Code dealing with estate freezes, prohibits the use of any agreement for the purpose of affixing the value of a business interest unless (1) the arrangement is a bona fide business arrangement, (2) the arrangement is not a device to transfer the business interest to members of a decedent's family for less than full and adequate consideration, and (3) the arrangement is comparable to similar arrangements entered into by persons in an arm's-length transaction.

In this case a unilateral purchase agreement between one or both of Dave's professional colleagues and Dave should be explored. If a unilateral purchase agreement can be negotiated, it should be entered into although such an agreement is clearly difficult to negotiate successfully. It should be expected that Dave's colleagues would want a reciprocal buy-sell arrangement, in which case Dave will have to decide whether he is willing to rethink his decision about increasing the size of his practice. The agreement should be funded partially or wholly by insurance to the extent that it is available. A realistic value for Dave's practice should be established, preferably by an appraisal, and maintained by a formula throughout the life of the buy-sell agreement.

INSURANCE PLANNING

Funding the Buy-Sell Agreement(s)

As already indicated, the recommendation for funding the buy-sell agreements is full or partial funding with life insurance. At this point, without further information about whether the buy-sell agreements will be unilateral or cross-purchase agreements, specific funding recommendations for a death buyout would be inappropriate. However, such buy-sell arrangements can be fully funded by life insurance.

The other element that must be considered in funding the buy-sell agreement is the appropriate amount and availability of coverage if Dave's disability triggers the buy-sell.

Insurers are generally unwilling to provide coverage with lump-sum benefits for professionals who are sole practitioners. Therefore it will be necessary for Dave to discuss with Dr. Cole or Dr. Brown or both whether one or both would be willing to enter into a buy-sell agreement that would protect him in the event of his becoming disabled without such an agreement's being insured. If one or both of the other physicians are interested in these terms, the recommendation would be that the business valuation price according to the formula in the buy-sell agreement be paid in installments over the shortest possible period that he and his attorneys can negotiate.

The crucial issues in this type of uninsured disability buyout are really not materially different from the issues in the case of those that are insured. They include primarily the definition of disability and the waiting period before the agreement becomes operative. The parties must agree to the definition of disability, and the length of the waiting period must be set forth in unambiguous terms in the buy-sell agreement.

There is a real danger in selecting too short a waiting period for a buyout agreement as it could result in a mandatory sale of Dave's business interest because of a relatively short-term disability that lasts longer than the waiting period specified by the agreement. It would be advisable to have a waiting period of at least 24 months before triggering the buyout agreement.

Medical, Disability, and Life Insurance Plans

If Dave decides not to incorporate his practice, there does not appear to be any significant advantage to having the existing proprietorship provide additional group insurance benefits, as proprietors are not considered employees of proprietorships, and therefore contributions in their behalf are not tax deductible. Therefore no tax savings could be achieved, except for his medical coverage as discussed below.

Medical Expense Insurance

The medical insurance plan that Dave presently provides for his employees and in which he and his family participate appears to provide excellent benefits at a competitive price. The premiums paid on behalf of the employees are deductible as a business expense. However, since Dave operates as a sole proprietorship, the tax treatment of health benefits provided for himself and his family is different. Sole proprietors are allowed to deduct against gross income only 25 percent of the cost of purchasing health insurance coverage for themselves and their own families. The deduction is not available if the self-employed individual is eligible for a medical plan sponsored and subsidized by an employer or if the cost of the insurance exceeds earned income. (The remainder of the insurance cost is part of the itemized medical expense deductions that are subject to the 7.5 percent threshold for deductibility.) Neither of these exceptions applies in Dave's case. The Revenue Reconciliation Act of 1993 retroactively extended the 25 percent deduction. Although this provision of the tax code had expired on June 30, 1992, the 1993 tax law extended the availability of the provision from June 30, 1993, to December 31, 1993. A further extension is to be considered as part of health care reform.

Disability Income Insurance

Although Dave presently has an individual disability plan, a review of its coverage limits makes it apparent that it is insufficient to allow him to maintain his present life-style. In all likelihood it will be impossible to achieve this objective solely with disability income protection, as insurers will not provide such a high ratio of coverage to total income. Generally a higher upper limit of coverage is available if an employer purchases the disability income coverage than if the employee individually purchases the coverage. In this case, however, the overall limit would be approximately $6,000 per month of benefits either through an employer plan or (as in this case) if Dave purchases the coverage individually. This results from the fact that at this high level of income, maximum benefit limits tend to merge.

Upper-limit coverage that would pay benefits if Dave is unable to perform his own occupation for a period of 5 years and thereafter unable to perform any occupation for which he is otherwise suited by reason of education can be obtained for an annual premium of $2,617 for either a corporate plan or for an individually owned policy, each with a 90-day elimination period. A 180-day elimination period would reduce the premium to $2,486, a savings of $131 annually.

Our recommendation would be that disability income coverage with a 90-day waiting period be purchased by Dave individually. Since Dave is not incorporated, coverage through a group plan would be more costly and provide no tax advantage. The 90-day elimination period is worth the approximate additional cost of $131 per year.

Property and Liability Insurance for the Business

With little information given in the case about the business assets to be covered by property and liability insurance, it is difficult to make any recommendations other than noting the necessity of having these coverages thoroughly reviewed by a professional in the field of property and liability insurance.

Professional Liability Insurance

Professional liability coverage for physicians and surgeons is often referred to as medical malpractice insurance. As a result of the significant premium increases in this type of insurance and the objections to those increases by physicians, a newer type of lower-cost policy has become popular.

The original type of coverage, known as occurrence-based coverage, protected the insured from any claims stemming from medical procedures performed while the policy was in force. This coverage would pay benefits for liability even if the incident giving rise to the liability was first discovered many years after the policy expiration date and when no further premiums were being paid. Thus the premium charged while the policy was in force had to be high enough to cover inflation applicable to future claims amounts.

The newer type of policy, known as claims-made coverage, pays only for claims made during the time the policy is in force. Claims will be payable by the insurer only if the medical treatment giving rise to the claim was performed after the retroactive date specified in the policy and before the policy termination date. This type of policy necessitates continuation of coverage after the medical professional retires or otherwise discontinues practice. The extended reporting-period endorsements keep this protection in place after the base policy terminates. Premiums must generally be paid for the first 3 years of the extended reporting-period endorsements. If the professional does not engage in any aspect of practice for the entire 3-year period, a single additional premium of less than the regular premium will extend the claims-made protection to perpetuity.

In cases where the physician changes back to an occurrence-based coverage after having a period of claims-made coverage, it will also be necessary to extend the reporting period by endorsements. Without such extension there would be a gap in coverage. The occurrence-based coverage would not cover procedures performed during the period the claims-made coverage was effective.

In terms of cost the claims-made coverage can be as low as one-quarter of the premium for occurrence-based coverage in the first year. The claims-made premiums will increase to about 85 percent of occurrence-based premiums after 5 or more years.

The potential liability for an orthopedic surgeon is quite high. In fact, there have already been single-case liability judgments in medical cases that exceeded $5 million. It is therefore suggested that professional liability coverage with policy limits of $10 million be carried. If the policy acquired is claims-made coverage, it is important to seek a retroactive date that coincides with the termination date of the most recent occurrence-based professional liability coverage. Although coverage for $1 million of liability protection is available at a cost of approximately $12,000 annually, Dave's sole proprietorship can obtain the recommended $10 million of protection on Dave and his nursing staff for about $27,000 a year. This provides 10 times the liability protection for 2.25 times the cost.

Business Overhead Expense Disability Insurance

Because of the limitations that insurers impose on the upper limits of disability income benefits, it is virtually impossible to get adequate coverage to ensure that all the usual and normal expenses of one's life are covered by insurance benefits, especially when the disabled person has continuing business overhead expenses. Business overhead expense disability coverage is an additional source of benefits aimed at closing this gap. In a case such as Dave's this coverage will normally pay for continuing business expenses, such as office rent, utilities, nurses' salaries, postage, office equipment and supplies, and business taxes. This type of policy disability is usually defined as the inability to perform the duties of the insured's own occupation. While various benefit durations are available, benefits should not exceed the effective date of the disability buyout provisions of the buy-sell agreement if such an agreement is entered into between Dave and Drs. Brown and/or Cole.

Based on the facts of this case approximately $5,000 in monthly benefits would be the maximum available coverage, and such benefits would be available for a period of 24 months.

Representative annual premiums for $5,000 in monthly benefits with various elimination periods are listed below.

Elimination Period	Annual Premium
30 days	$1,025
60 days	630
90 days	385

The elimination period should be based on Dave's available cash flow. The recommendation is that an elimination period of no less than 60 days be elected.

PERSONAL PLANNING

TAX PLANNING

Present Situation

Dave and Diana have been married for 16 years. They have three children: Keith, 10, Deidre, 9, and Melissa, 6, and have just discovered that they will have another child in about 7 months. The older children are very intelligent, and the Andersons are considering sending them to a private high school with rigorous academic standards, where tuition is $3,500 per school year. Dave and Diana would also like to plan now to finance college educations for their children.

In 1980 they purchased a home for $79,000 that has appreciated to its present value of $215,000. The house is furnished with some lovely antiques that Diana has acquired over the years. They own two relatively new cars.

Dave has invested in three real estate limited partnerships. In addition, he owns a single-family residential rental property and an undeveloped commercial lot. A potential buyer has made an offer for the commercial lot, and Dave is interested in a recommendation as to whether the lot should be sold. During recent years Dave has been beginning a portfolio of stocks, bonds, and mutual fund shares.

Dave earns a substantial income from his practice as an orthopedic surgeon, and the Andersons enjoy a good life. They want to maximize their wealth accumulation, provide themselves with retirement funds sufficient to continue their life-style, and provide for the family if Dave should die prematurely.

Fund Private School and/or College Education for Children

Dave and Diana have asked that an estimate of projected costs for educating their children at a top-quality institution be prepared.

As discussed in the investment planning section, the cost of funding the college educations for Keith, Deidre, and Melissa would be in excess of $256,000 if the funding was accomplished with a lump sum in today's dollars, given reasonable assumptions regarding inflation and rates of return. If college education funding is done on an annual basis from the present until each child completes college, the annual funding amount would be approximately $26,000. Since the Andersons are in a 36 percent federal tax bracket and also pay state income tax, they must earn at least $1.61 for every $1 they can accumulate for accomplishing this goal.

Obviously the best way to accumulate this sum is on a tax-advantaged basis. One of the ways this is accomplished in harmonious family situations is through the mechanism of gift giving.

Gifting

Outright Gifts. Under the current federal gift tax provisions a person (donor) can give any other person (donee) up to $10,000 per year per donee, gift tax free (IRC Sec. 2503(b)). That amount can be doubled if the spouse agrees to join in the gift regardless of whether the spouse actually contributes any portion of the gift (IRC Sec. 2513). This annual gift tax exclusion is often touted as an effective way for clients to shift assets to their children and take advantage of the children's lower tax brackets. However, outright gifting presents some significant problems. The person giving the gift (the donor) must part forever with the property that is gifted, including any earning capacity that it has. All but the wealthiest clients are reluctant to part with assets that they may need for their later years.

The Andersons could utilize outright gifting to supplement other accumulation techniques if actual college costs exceed those that are anticipated and funded for. If these "gifts" were made in the form of actual tuition payments to a qualified educational institution, the amounts would be totally exempt from federal gift taxes (IRC Sec. 2503(e)). They would, however, have to be made with after-tax dollars; therefore there are better techniques for funding the bulk of their children's educations.

UGMA and UTMA Gifts. In addition to the problems already described with outright gifting, there are problems with giving gifts to minors. The Uniform Gifts to Minors Act (UGMA) and the Uniform Transfers to Minors Act (UTMA) provide mechanisms by which a donor can give a gift to a minor without necessitating the appointment of a guardian of the minor's property. (About half of the states have adopted the newer Uniform Transfers to Minors Act.) Instead, a custodian of the gift, who has full powers over the gifted property and its income in behalf of the minor child, is designated. In many cases the donor is the minor child's parent, who also functions as the custodian of the UGMA or UTMA account. Gifts under the Uniform Acts qualify under the federal gift tax provisions as present-interest gifts without the necessity of withdrawal rights or annual payments of income and as such are subject to the $10,000-per-year-per-donee gift tax exclusion (IRC Secs. 2503(b), 2503(c)).

There are, however, some problems with UGMA and UTMA gifts:

- If the donor is the parent of the minor and also the custodian of the UGMA or UTMA account and dies while still the custodian, the total amount of the account will be included in his or her estate for federal estate tax purposes because of the control he or she can exercise over the account (IRC Sec. 2036(a)).
- The type of property that can be transferred effectively under the Uniform Acts is severely restricted in some states. In other words, the Uniform Acts are *not* uniform from state to state. When the original UGMA was being lobbied for, the most effective lobbying group consisted primarily of securities dealers attempting to facilitate gifts of stock and securities to minors. The result of this lobbying effort is that many of the UGMA statutes enacted by the various states, including Georgia, restrict UGMA gifts to money, securities,

life insurance, or annuity contracts. In other words, other types of property such as real estate cannot be effectively transferred by UGMA gifts in many states. (If this is the result in the state in which a particular client is located, as it is in Georgia, and the client needs to transfer property other than money, securities, life insurance, or annuity contracts, the UGMA transfer can be made under the UGMA statute in one of the several states that allows for transfers of almost any type of property, including real estate, by having the instrument state that the transfer is being made pursuant to the Uniform Gifts to Minors Act of the more favorable state.) In states that have adopted the Uniform Transfers to Minors Act, there is more flexibility regarding the types of assets that may be transferred.
- The custodianship generally terminates when the minor reaches either age 21 or the local legal age of majority. At that time all funds in the custodial account must be distributed to the beneficiary. This gives the 18-, 19-, or 21-year-old (depending on local law) unfettered discretion over the disposition of the assets, which may result in the assets' being squandered rather than being used for the purpose for which the custodianship was established, such as education.
- Income from assets in such accounts will be subject to the kiddie tax for minors under 14 years of age, regardless of whether the income is distributed to the minor. This is so because such an account, unlike a trust, is not a separate taxpayer from the minor beneficiary.

While gifts to minors under UGMA or UTMA can be utilized effectively for relatively small sums, they are generally not the technique of choice for larger sums because of the mandatory distribution at the legal age of majority, the potential kiddie tax problems, and potential federal estate tax inclusion for the donor-parent who acts as custodian.

Income Shifting

One of the most effective ways to accumulate assets for such objectives as the funding of education for children is to use a technique that splits income from family assets between highly taxed adults in the family and the children, who are taxed in lower brackets, if at all. It has long been settled under federal tax law that one cannot assign a portion of the income that one earns to another and avoid taxation (*Lucas v. Earl,* 281 U.S. 111 (1930)). One can, however, assign property one owns to another, either irrevocably or for a statutorily required period of time, and have the income taxed to the donee or assignee. The techniques for accomplishing this are called income-shifting techniques and can result in substantial net family tax savings. However, recent federal tax legislation has reduced these savings by limiting available vehicles and compressing the tax rate structure.

Sec. 2503(b) Trusts. A trust device that can be utilized to provide gifts to minors is the IRC Sec. 2503(b) trust, which provides certain advantages as well as certain disadvantages that are not present under the Sec. 2503(c) trust, discussed later in this section. The principal advantage of the Sec. 2503(b) trust is that it need not terminate at the beneficiary's attaining the age of 21. A principal disadvantage is that the trust must pay the net income to the beneficiary annually or in more frequent installments. That is, it cannot accumulate income even during the minority of the beneficiary. This means that income from the trust that is paid to beneficiaries under the age of 14 will be taxed at the marginal rate of the beneficiary's parents, generally to the extent that such income exceeds $1,000 per year (under the so-called kiddie tax). This substantially reduces the income-shifting benefits of the 2503(b) trust.

Another disadvantage of the Sec. 2503(b) trust is that the value of the income interest and the value of the remainder interest (the property that composes the principal of the trust) are computed separately for gift tax purposes. Only the value of the income interest is eligible for the $10,000-per-year-per-donee annual gift tax exclusion.

The Sec. 2503(b) trust may not contain discretionary payments to more than one beneficiary. In addition, there can be no postponement or delay in the commencement of the payment of the net income of the trust. Indeed, if there are any restrictions on distribution of trust income—for example, if the income is conditional or discretionary in any way—the annual exclusion will be unavailable.

Obviously the mandatory payment of the trust income can be a major tax and nontax disadvantage when the beneficiary is a minor. This is especially true if significant sums are involved, since it could necessitate the appointment of a guardian of the minor's property. This procedure is both expensive and tedious, as guardians are subject to court supervision in handling the funds of the minor and are statutorily prohibited from entering into certain investment transactions.

Because of the mandatory payment requirement and the fact that the trust beneficiaries—the Anderson children—are minors under age 14, it would not be advisable to utilize the 2503(b) trust to fund college education for the children.

Sec. 2503(c) Trusts. If a trust is structured according to the terms of IRC Sec. 2503(c), gifts to the trust qualify for the $10,000-per-year-per-donee gift tax exclusion without giving the beneficiary a right to withdraw funds or without the necessity for paying the beneficiary the income at least annually. The Sec. 2503(c) trust can be more advantageous than transfers to an UGMA custodianship because no statutory restriction on the type of property transferred is applicable in the case of 2503(c) trusts. In addition, the property can be maintained in the trust at least until the beneficiary reaches age 21, regardless of whether the age of legal majority in the state of the trust situs is less than 21. There is no return of the Sec. 2503(c) trust principal to the donor.

The Internal Revenue Code requires that both the property and the income from the property be available to be expended by or for the benefit of the beneficiary during the time before he or she attains the age of 21. In addition, to the extent that it has not already been expended by or for the beneficiary before his or her attainment of the age of 21, the property and the income therefrom must pass to the beneficiary at the time he or she attains the age of 21. If the beneficiary fails to live to the age of 21, the accumulated income and the principal must be payable to the estate of the beneficiary unless he or she can appoint it to another under a general power of appointment.

Let us examine separately each of the statutory requirements for qualification as a 2503(c) trust. As already noted, the Internal Revenue Code requires that the principal and income must be available for distribution in the time period before the donee reaches age 21. The regulations, however, go further. Treas. Reg. Sec. 25.2503-4(b)(1) prohibits "substantial restrictions" on the trustee's power to make distributions of trust income and principal. This might prohibit any specific restrictions in the trust instrument on the distributions of income and principal to certain specified purposes, such as illness or education. However, as a practical matter the trustee can make distributions or accumulate income for the purposes intended by the donor in his or her discretion as trustee.

In addition, the Sec. 2503(c) trust cannot be used for the benefit of a class of beneficiaries. Trust instruments routinely describe payments to a class of beneficiaries in substantially the following language: "All the net income from the trust is to be distributed annually or at more frequent intervals to or for the benefit of the grantor's three children, as necessary, in such amounts as the trustee in his sole discretion shall deem necessary." Although under this type of provision the terms of the trust provide that all the net income of the trust is to be distributed at least annually, the amount of the income receivable by any one of the beneficiaries remains within the discretion of the trustee and is not presently ascertainable. Accordingly the annual exclusion is disallowed with respect to the transfers to such a trust. It is possible to utilize Sec. 2503(c) trusts for more than one beneficiary, however, by using either a separate trust for each beneficiary or what is known as a separate-share trust. A separate-share trust divides the trust principal into definite portions, each having a specified beneficiary.

Another statutory requirement of the Sec. 2503(c) trust appears to be that the trust cannot exist past the time of the beneficiary's 21st birthday. The Treasury regulations, however, provide that the trust will not be disqualified provided that the donee (beneficiary) has the right to extend the term of the trust upon reaching the age of 21 (Treas. Reg. Sec. 25.2503-4(b)(2)). The right to continue the trust can apparently require that the beneficiary must affirmatively compel distribution at age 21 (Rev. Rul. 74-43, 1974-1 C.B. 285). The right to compel distribution at age 21 may exist for only a limited period of time, as long as the period of time is reasonable. Thirty to sixty days have been deemed reasonable in a number of private letter rulings (PLR 7824035; PLR 7805037). If the beneficiary fails to compel the distribution from the trust during the permissible period or otherwise affirmatively allows the trust to continue, the trust will continue until it terminates under the terms of the trust instrument.

The next statutory section deals with the death of the beneficiary before attaining the age of 21. It is often undesirable to allow the trust principal and accumulated income, if any, to pass through the estate of a minor, as the minor may be legally incompetent to make a will, and the funds must pass by intestacy. However, the Treasury regulations provide that if the beneficiary is given a general power of appointment over the trust principal and accumulated income and fails to exercise this power of appointment, regardless of whether he or she is competent as a minor to do so under local law, the trust continues to qualify for the annual exclusion. In fact, the trust instrument may provide that in the absence of the exercise of the power of appointment there is a gift in default of the exercise of the power. This gift-over may be made to whomever the grantor of the trust desires, including his other children. This is an especially advantageous provision, the inclusion of which should be considered in any Sec. 2503(c) trust.

The practical use of the 2503(c) trust involves several important factors. If the income is accumulated until the child reaches age 14, there is no kiddie tax problem with this arrangement. The income of the trust will be taxed at the trust's marginal rate and not the marginal rate of the parents (unless the trustee distributes income to the child). The first $1,500 of trust income is taxed at a rate of 15 percent. Therefore the parents can save up to 21 percent in taxes on the income if they are in a 36 percent bracket. Also even though the child must be given access to both income and principal no later than age 21, smart parents can minimize the amount of money they must transfer. If the trust invests in fixed-rate-of-return investments such as bonds, a precise calculation can be made to determine how much should be contributed annually to the trust to fund a specific dollar-amount funding objective. In this way the trust fund can be fully exhausted to pay education expenses so that there is no money left in the trust when the child finishes college. The only actual risk the parents take in transferring funds is that the child does not use the money for college education but instead drops out of school and uses the money for a frivolous purpose when he or she turns 21.

The Revenue Reconciliation Act of 1993 raised the effective income tax rate imposed upon trust (and estate) income in excess of $1,500 beginning with 1993. The following table displays the income level and income tax rates that apply to trust (and estate) income.

TABLE 5-2	
If Taxable Income Is:	The Tax Is:
Not over $1,500	15% of taxable income
Over $1,500 but not over $3,500	$225 plus 28% of the excess over $1,500
Over $3,500 but not over $5,500	$785 plus 31% of the excess over $3,500
Over $5,500 but not over $7,500	$1,405 plus 36% of the excess over $5,500
Over $7,500	$2,125 plus 39.6% of the excess over $7,500

This new rate schedule reduces the effectiveness of 2503(c) trusts as a device for sheltering income being accumulated for any purpose, including education funding.

Having the first $1,500 of trust income taxed at 15 percent may not seem like a substantial tax savings. However, if the trust is funded when the beneficiary is young, savings can be substantial.

The numbers in table 5-3 below are based on these assumptions: The trust accumulates income until the beneficiary reaches age 18, the contributions are made annually beginning at the stated age, the trust funds earn 7.5 percent annually, and the parents' marginal tax rate is 36 percent. These savings are calculated on the assumption that without the trust the same income would be taxed at the parents' rate. The calculations do not include allowances for the cost of establishing and managing the trust.

However, if Dave and Diana's attorney can set up a separate trust for each child, act as a trustee, and work with their CPA to file estimated and annual tax returns for the trusts (a relatively simple procedure), the tax benefits should still substantially outweigh the total costs. Typically an attorney will not charge a full fee for each separate trust if the provisions are nearly identical. Dave and Diana should be able to set up these trusts for each of their children at a total cost of $1,000 to $2,000. Annual administration and tax return preparation expenses must be paid, but these costs should be modest and substantially less than the tax savings that can be realized.

TABLE 5-3
Tax Savings from the 2503(c) Trust When Beneficiary Reaches Age 18—Assuming 7.5 Percent Return and Parents in 36 Percent Tax Bracket

Annual Gift to Trust	Age of Beneficiary When Trust Is Established		
	5	10	15
$ 1,000	$1,872	$ 660	$ 99
5,000	5,313	2,525	493
10,000	5,786	3,544	863
20,000	3,949	3,609	1,297

In the case of the Andersons care should be exercised as to the amount of annual funding they will contribute in behalf of Melissa, aged 6. Based on the data in table 5-3, the tax saving is reduced if they contribute $20,000 annually instead of $10,000 due to the trust's large amount of income taxed at the 39.6 percent rate starting in the fifth year.

Despite its complexities the Sec. 2503(c) trust is the best vehicle for the Andersons to utilize as an income-shifting device. The use of this vehicle will be further discussed in the investment planning section.

Family Partnership. Family partnerships are another income-splitting device that can be valuable in allowing higher-bracket taxpayers to shift income to lower-bracket family members. In order to be effective for this purpose, however, the partnership must be a bona fide partnership and not merely an attempt to assign the income of a high-bracket taxpayer to taxpayers in a lower tax bracket. In order to test whether a family partnership could withstand an assignment-of-income attack by the IRS, the following guidelines provided by the Regulations should be considered. The production of income by a partnership is attributable to the capital or services, or both, contributed by the partners. The provisions (of the determination of tax liability portions of the partnership tax rules of the Internal Revenue Code) are to be read in the light of their relationship to Sec. 61 of the Code (dealing with gross income) that requires, among other things, that income be taxed to the person who earns it through his or her own labor and skill and the utilization of his or her own capital (Treas. Reg. Sec. 1.704(e)(1)). In other words, an impermissible assignment of income has not occurred if (1) the income tax liability for income derived from personal services remains with the person who performed the services and (2) the income tax liability for income produced by utilizing capital remains with the owner of the capital. (Note that a shift in the ownership of the capital under this principle would result in the shifting of the income tax liability.)

For family partnerships in which "capital is a material income-producing factor," the tax status of a partner is recognized if he or she owns a capital interest in the partnership, whether such an interest was acquired by purchase or by gift (IRC Sec. 704(e)(1)). The tax status of partners in a family partnership in which capital is not a material income-producing factor is much more troublesome. Therefore in deciding to consider a recommendation to create a family partnership one should generally concentrate only on those partnerships in which capital will be a material income-producing factor.

The statutory protection of the status of partner for tax purposes does not apply if the ownership of the capital interest in the partnership is not bona fide. In most family partnerships the partnership interest will be a direct or indirect gift to a family member; that is, a capital interest in the partnership will either be a direct gift, or the funds necessary to purchase a capital interest will be gifted. The fact that the interest is the result of a gift does not necessarily make it suspect. There are, however, some other tests that are applied to ascertain the genuineness of the transfer. Among those tests are the following:

- a donor partner's retention of the right to control the distribution of the income of the partnership, which tends to indicate that the transfer is less than genuine unless the income is retained with the other partners' consent for the reasonable needs of the business
    The donor partner can, however, retain the right to control and distribute partnership income without any negative implications provided that right is retained and exercised in a fiduciary capacity (Treas. Reg. Sec. 1.704-1(e)(2)).

- retention of control over the donee's disposition or liquidation of the donated interest beyond reasonable business restrictions
- retention of control over assets essential to the partnership's business (such as ownership of a crucial asset leased to the partnership) that would give the donor partner unusual power to affect the partnership's viability or business

Minors can be recognized as general partners for tax purposes without the minor's interest being held in trust (Treas. Reg. Sec. 1.704-1(e)(2)). The fact that a minor is very young, however, may result in the minor's losing his or her tax status as a partner, as it must be demonstrated that the minor is competent to manage his or her own property and participate in the partnership activities in accordance with his or her interest in the property (Treas. Reg. Sec. 1.704-1(e)(2)). The test is not based on the legal age of majority under the local law of the state but is a test of the minor's maturity and experience (Treas. Reg. Sec. 1.704-1(e)(2)). Because of these limitations, minors in their individual capacity should generally not be made general partners. If a general partnership interest is desirable for a minor, the partnership interest should be conveyed to a trust for the minor's benefit.

Another option is to make minors limited partners in family partnerships. Gifts can be made of either the limited partnership interests or of money to purchase the partnership units. Limited partners by definition do not participate in the management of the partnership business. The Treasury Regulations state that in order for a limited partnership to be recognized for federal tax purposes it must be organized and conducted in accordance with the applicable state limited partnership law. The Treasury regulations further provide that the absence of services and participation in management by a donee partner in a limited partnership is immaterial (Treas. Reg. Sec. 1.704-1(e)(2)). This allows for a great deal of control to be retained by the donor general partner. That control cannot extend, however, to placing restrictions on the disposition of the partnership interest that would not be acceptable to unrelated limited partners.

The Andersons could form a family limited partnership and contribute the residential rental property to it; however, the cash flow and appreciation from this property are not sufficient to make it an effective mechanism for funding the children's educations. In addition, an interest in a limited partnership does not qualify for the special $25,000 real estate allowance under the passive-loss rules discussed in the investment planning section. For these reasons the family partnership is not the recommendation of choice.

Caveat: Parental Obligations

If an income-shifting device such as the 2503(c) trust is utilized, care must be taken that the resulting income is not used to satisfy legal parental obligations for support. If the parental obligations of a father (both parents in some states) are satisfied with these funds, the funds are taxed to the father despite the fact that the income-shifting device is otherwise fully effective. The extent of parental obligations is a matter that is decided under local state law. In all states the parental obligation of support extends to "necessaries"—food, clothing, shelter, and the like. In some states the legislatures or the courts have extended the scope of these parental obligations to include such things as college educations and private schools when those are consistent with the family's life-style and are within their financial means.

In Georgia parental obligations have generally not been extended to include sending children to private schools or to college. There is a case, however, that holds that a father who enters into an agreement—incorporated into a divorce decree while a child is a minor—to send a child to college is legally obligated to provide that college education even after the child's majority.

State laws vary widely in this area. Some states make parental obligations the legal responsibility of the father only, while some states extend the duty to the mother as well. This is an area that should be thoroughly investigated prior to implementing any income-shifting device.

Reduce Tax Burden

Achieve Personal Objectives through Income-Shifting Devices to Reduce Cost

As has already been discussed, it is often advantageous to divide income among harmonious family members through the use of income-shifting devices. This allows income from certain assets to be taxed to lower-bracket family members. The use of an outright gift of a fairly nominal sum (when compared to the required accumulation amount) combined with a Sec. 2503(c) trust to fund the college education objectives of the Anderson children is such an income-shifting device. The appropriate investment techniques for educational funding will be discussed in the investment planning section.

Defer Tax Liability on a Portion of Dave's Income from the Practice through Use of Qualified Plans

Dave and Diana will be paying federal taxes in the 36 percent bracket in 1994 and thereafter. Dave is contributing $22,500 a year to his Keogh plan on a tax-deductible basis. This contribution will not be taxable to Dave until it is distributed to him. Although this will mean that the Andersons forgo this amount in immediate cash flow, the net effect to the family is a cash-flow shrinkage of approximately 62 percent annually on an after-tax basis. At the time a distribution of the plan benefits takes place, there is favorable income tax treatment available for lump-sum distributions from qualified plans. This method, called 5-year forward averaging, basically takes the lump-sum distribution from the qualified plan as separate income in the year of the distribution, assumes that the participant is being taxed as a single individual with no dependents, and computes the income tax liability as if the income had been received by this individual in fifths, 1/5 in each of 5 years. This method can result in significantly lower tax liability on the lump-sum distribution as compared to the regular tax computation. However, a lump-sum distribution is only one of several options available to Dave at retirement with respect to his profit-sharing plan account. The alternatives regarding distribution should be closely examined as Dave approaches retirement age.

Individual Retirement Accounts

Under the current federal income tax laws, deductible IRA contributions are restricted to

- individuals who are not active participants in an employer-maintained retirement plan for any part of the retirement plan year ending with or within the individual's taxable year
- any other individual, as long as the individual (or married couple if a joint return is filed) has adjusted gross income below a specified limit. If the adjusted gross income exceeds this limit, the $2,000 IRA limit is reduced under a formula that eventually permits no deduction.

The *active participant* restriction applies if the individual (or if a joint return is filed, either the individual or spouse) is an active participant in a regular qualified plan, a Sec. 403(b) tax-deferred annuity plan, a simplified employee pension (SEP), or a federal, state, or local government plan, not including a Sec. 457 nonqualified deferred-compensation plan.

Active plan participants can make deductible IRA contributions only if their income falls within certain income limits, as shown by table 5-4:

TABLE 5-4
IRA Deduction/Compensation Limits (Taxpayer or Spouse Active Plan Participant)

Filing Status	Full IRA Deduction	Reduced IRA Deduction	No IRA Deduction
Individual	Up to $25,000	$25,000–$35,000	$35,000 or over
Married couple, joint return	Up to $40,000	$40,000–$50,000	$50,000 or over
Married, filing separately	Not available	$ 0–$10,000	$10,000 or over

The reduction in the IRA deduction for those affected is computed by multiplying the IRA limit ($2,000 or 100 percent of compensation) by a fraction equal to

$$\frac{\text{taxpayer's adjusted gross income in excess of full deduction limit}}{\$10,000}$$

For example, a married couple, one of whom is an active participant in a regular qualified plan, files a joint return and has an adjusted gross income of $43,000. The computation is as follows:

$$\frac{\$43,000 - \$40,000}{\$10,000} \times 2,000 = \$600$$

$2,000 - \$600 = \$1,400$. This is the IRA deduction limit.

If a married couple has a "spousal IRA," the same formula is applied except that $2,250 is substituted for the $2,000 figure. Another major IRA change may soften the blow administered by the new limits just described. Individuals not permitted to make deductible IRA contributions may nevertheless make such contributions on a nondeductible basis, up to the usual $2,000/100 percent/$2,250 limit. Nondeductible contributions (but not income on those contributions) are tax free when ultimately distributed to the individual. If nondeductible contributions to an IRA are made, any amounts withdrawn are treated as partly tax free and partly taxable under rules similar to the exclusion-ratio calculation for annuities under IRC Sec. 72.

The benefits, however, of making nondeductible contributions can be marginal. In Dave and Diana's case Dave's income is far in excess of the range in which deductible contributions can be made. Since Dave's profit-sharing plan will provide him with substantial retirement funds from deductible contributions, the establishment of an IRA is not recommended in this case.

Ensure Adequate Protection in the Event of Dave's Disability

Design Buy-Sell Agreement to Become Operative in the Event of Disability

In discussing the buy-sell agreement in the business plan, it has already been noted that while such agreements can be designed to become operative in the event of the disability of a shareholder, insurers generally will not provide coverage for professional sole proprietors. The agreement that has been recommended for Dave's practice could be designed to become operative in the event of disability if he can get his professional colleagues to agree to an installment payout in lieu of the availability of insurance funding.

Personal Disability Income Coverage

The primary advantage of personally acquired disability income coverage is that the proceeds are received tax free. The primary disadvantage of personal disability income coverage is that the premiums for such coverage are not tax deductible. In addition, there are different limitations on coverage amounts available under personal and corporate coverage plans. Generally the amounts available under personal disability coverage are lower than those available under employer disability coverage. In Dave's case the total amount available under either personal disability income coverage or employer coverage is approximately $6,000 a month, because his high income has effectively caused the coverage limits to merge. As discussed in the business planning section, Dave should obtain the maximum amount of coverage through a personally owned policy.

Ensure a Comfortable Retirement

Dave's Keogh plan is the Andersons' primary vehicle for accumulating funds for retirement. The plan balance at year end is projected at $95,041. Contributions are projected to remain constant unless tax laws affecting Keogh plans change.

Although the plan balance is presently earning 8 percent, a more conservative rate of return should be assumed beyond the 5-year plan horizon. Dave will reach age 65 in the year 2018. If an inflation-adjusted rate of return of 4 percent is assumed for the Keogh plan (to express his retirement date plan balance in today's dollars), the plan balance in 24 years will be approximately $1,180,000.

Dave and Diana will have a number of options at that point. They could take the plan proceeds in a lump-sum distribution and systematically liquidate the principal over life expectancy. They could also choose to live on the income only. Alternatively they could use the plan balance to purchase a joint and survivor annuity with an installment refund feature. This decision, of course, will be based on their total situation at that time.

However, it does appear that the Andersons will enjoy a comfortable retirement under the given assumptions. For example, a joint and survivor annuity with an installment refund would pay Dave and Diana approximately $12,000 per month using current rates if the funds were fully applied to the annuity. This would provide them with a before-tax income of over $144,000 per year.

Sec. 4980A could be a factor in the case as well since this 15 percent excise tax on excess pension accumulations and distributions could apply to Dave's Keogh plan in the future. Specifically the 15 percent excise tax on excess retirement accumulations will apply to all excess retirement accumulations in existence at the date of death of the decedent/plan participant. We are told by the Internal Revenue Code that an excess retirement accumulation is the value for federal estate tax purposes of the decedent-participant's interest in all plans, less the present value of a hypothetical life annuity in the amount of the "applicable annual exemption" for the decedent's attained age using the interest rate and mortality assumptions that the IRS accepts for valuing life annuities. The Internal Revenue Code further clarifies the situation by defining the *applicable annual exemption* as the greater of (a) $150,000 or (b) $112,500 as indexed for inflation with October 1, 1986, as the base period. It should be noted that the 15 percent excise tax is to be assessed as an additional federal estate tax, which is computed independently of the regular federal estate tax computations. Therefore neither the unified credit, other credits, the federal estate tax marital deduction, the federal estate tax charitable deduction, nor other federal estate tax deductions can be used to reduce the imposition of this 15 percent excise tax. However, it is impossible to predict what the tax laws will be when this issue comes up. Since it will not be a problem over the current 5-year planning horizon, it is not a significant planning consideration at this time.

The Andersons' current committed and discretionary expenses (excluding taxes and investment outlays) are approximately $66,000 per year. The retirement plan assumptions include an inflation-adjusted rate of return to express the future plan balance in today's dollars. Therefore either the annuity or an alternative payout method should provide the Andersons with sufficient funds for a comfortable retirement under the assumptions.

Assuming further that the social security system remains intact, the Andersons would probably receive a total monthly benefit of at least $1,900 (combined benefit) in inflation-adjusted dollars, based on the retirement benefit formulas currently in place.

As discussed in the business plan, Dave can consider the implementation of a defined-benefit plan in combination with his profit-sharing plan if he wants to provide additional security for his retirement.

Consider Various Problems Diana Might Encounter in Setting Up Her Own Business

Preliminary General Planning

Since the new baby will delay the actual start of Diana's proposed business specializing in antique Oriental porcelain and Oriental rugs, the detailed planning for that venture should be postponed until closer to the time she will be free to devote her time to such an effort. This may not be for several years, depending on a family decision about how long she should stay home with the baby. However, it is appropriate to begin doing some preliminary long-range planning in this regard.

During the interim Diana can continue developing her expertise through classes and independent study of the subject matter. After the baby is old enough to be left with babysitters or in nursery school, she might consider taking a part-time job for a few hours each week at a shop specializing in some of the items she wishes to feature in her business. This would allow her to continue developing her expertise and also to deal with some of the actual day-to-day problems that exist in such businesses.

If she finds that she is still interested in her own shop, she might consider opening it only during school hours for a few years and then expanding the shop's hours if business warrants as her need to be home decreases. Many specialty shops have restricted hours, and their owners will see customers at other times by appointment only. The most important point is that Diana should not feel that she must delay opening her own business until she can devote 10 hours a day 6 days a week to it, as it is doubtful that she will realistically be able to do that until all her children have left home.

Taking Advantage of Start-Up Losses

When Diana does start her own business, it may not be profitable at the very beginning. It would be helpful to the Andersons' tax situation if any start-up losses could be used to offset some of Dave's income. This result can generally be accomplished by operating the business as a sole proprietorship or as an S corporation. While the operation of the business in any of these forms can pass through start-up losses, both sole proprietorships and S corporations are subject to the limitations regarding deductions for hobby-type businesses under IRC Sec. 183, which should be explored prior to making a decision about the form in which to operate the business.

Dispositions at Death

Analysis of Present Plans

Dave's present will provides that an amount equal to one-half of his adjusted gross estate goes to Diana in a marital trust, with the remainder going to a residuary trust for the benefit of Diana and the children.

The problem with this arrangement is that it does not take full advantage of the unified credit if Dave were to die in the very near future. This unnecessarily increases Diana's taxable estate should Dave predecease her.

Moreover, as Dave's estate increases, the current arrangement will result in a federal estate tax payable in Dave's estate if Dave should die first and if one-half of Dave's adjusted gross estate was more than $600,000, the unified credit exemption equivalent amount.

Recommendations

Dave's estate plan should be revised to provide that $600,000 of his adjusted gross estate should pass to a residuary credit shelter trust with provisions similar to his present residuary trust. The remaining assets should pass to Diana under the marital trust arrangement. This will avoid payment of federal estate taxes in Dave's estate if he predeceases Diana. Diana can subsequently take steps to reduce her estate and thereby reduce the total federal estate taxes ultimately payable.

The following schedules illustrate the difference in results between Dave's current estate plan and the suggested revision under the current asset situation. The illustrations assume that Dave predeceases Diana in 1994 and Diana dies in 1994. An appreciation rate of 5 percent annually is applied to most assets.

(text continues on page 5.84)

COMPREHENSIVE ESTATE TAX REPORT

DAVE & DIANA ANDERSON
CURRENT ESTATE

	DAVE Predeceasing DIANA		DIANA Predeceasing DAVE	
Date: Dec 31, 1994 Under Present Will	DAVE's Estate	DIANA's Estate	DIANA's Estate	DAVE's Estate
Individually Held Assets	1,277,186	0	0	1,277,186
Share from Joint Assets	5,000	10,000	5,000	10,000
Life Insurance Proceeds	100,000	0	0	100,000
Gross Estate	1,382,186	10,000	5,000	1,387,186
Own Liabilities	146,854	0	0	146,854
Adjusted Gross Estate	1,235,332	10,000	5,000	1,240,332
Marital Deduction	5,000	0	5,000	0
Taxable Estate	1,230,332	10,000	0	1,240,332
Total Taxable Amount	1,230,332	10,000	0	1,240,332
Fed Tax Before Credit	440,236	1,800	0	444,336
Unified Tax Credit	192,800	1,800	0	192,800
Net Federal Estate Tax	247,436	0	0	251,536
Net Federal + State Tax	247,436	0	0	251,536
Combined Tax	$247,436		$251,536	

ESTATE ANALYSIS
ASSET DISTRIBUTION

DAVE & DIANA ANDERSON
CURRENT ESTATE

	DAVE Predeceasing DIANA		DIANA Predeceasing DAVE	
Date: Dec 31, 1994 Under Present Will	DAVE's Estate	DIANA's Estate	DIANA's Estate	DAVE's Estate
Liquid Assets	$529,086	$10,000	$5,000	$531,586
Non-liquid Assets	853,100	0	0	855,600
Total Assets	1,382,186	10,000	5,000	1,387,186
Passing to Spouse	5,000	0	5,000	0
Passing to Trust/Heirs	982,896	10,000	0	988,796
Estate Shrinkage	394,290	0	0	398,390

5.73

ESTATE ANALYSIS

LIQUIDITY SITUATION

DAVE & DIANA ANDERSON
CURRENT ESTATE

	DAVE Predeceasing DIANA		DIANA Predeceasing DAVE	
Date: Dec 31, 1994 Under Present Will	DAVE's Estate	DIANA's Estate	DIANA's Estate	DAVE's Estate
Debt	146,854	0	0	146,854
Administration Expenses	0	0	0	0
Estate Taxes	247,436	0	0	251,536
Charitable Contributions	0	0	0	0
Need for Liquid Capital	394,290	0	0	398,390
Liquid Capital Available	529,086	10,000	5,000	531,586
Addt'l Liquidity Needed	0	0	0	0

ESTATE ANALYSIS
MARITAL DEDUCTION

DAVE & DIANA ANDERSON
CURRENT ESTATE

	DAVE Predeceasing DIANA		DIANA Predeceasing DAVE	
Date: Dec 31, 1994 Under Present Will	DAVE's Estate	DIANA's Estate	DIANA's Estate	DAVE's Estate
Marital Deduction is--	Ok		Overqualified	
Best Deduction Amount	$615,166		-Same-	
Your Amount Exceeds by	$0		$0	
Resulting Additional Cost	$232,514		$0	
Total Family Assets	$1,387,186		$1,387,186	
Joint Estate Taxes	$247,436 18.00%		$251,536 18.00%	
Total Shrinkage	$394,290 28.42%		$398,390 28.72%	
Remaining for Heirs	$992,896 71.58%		$988,796 71.28%	

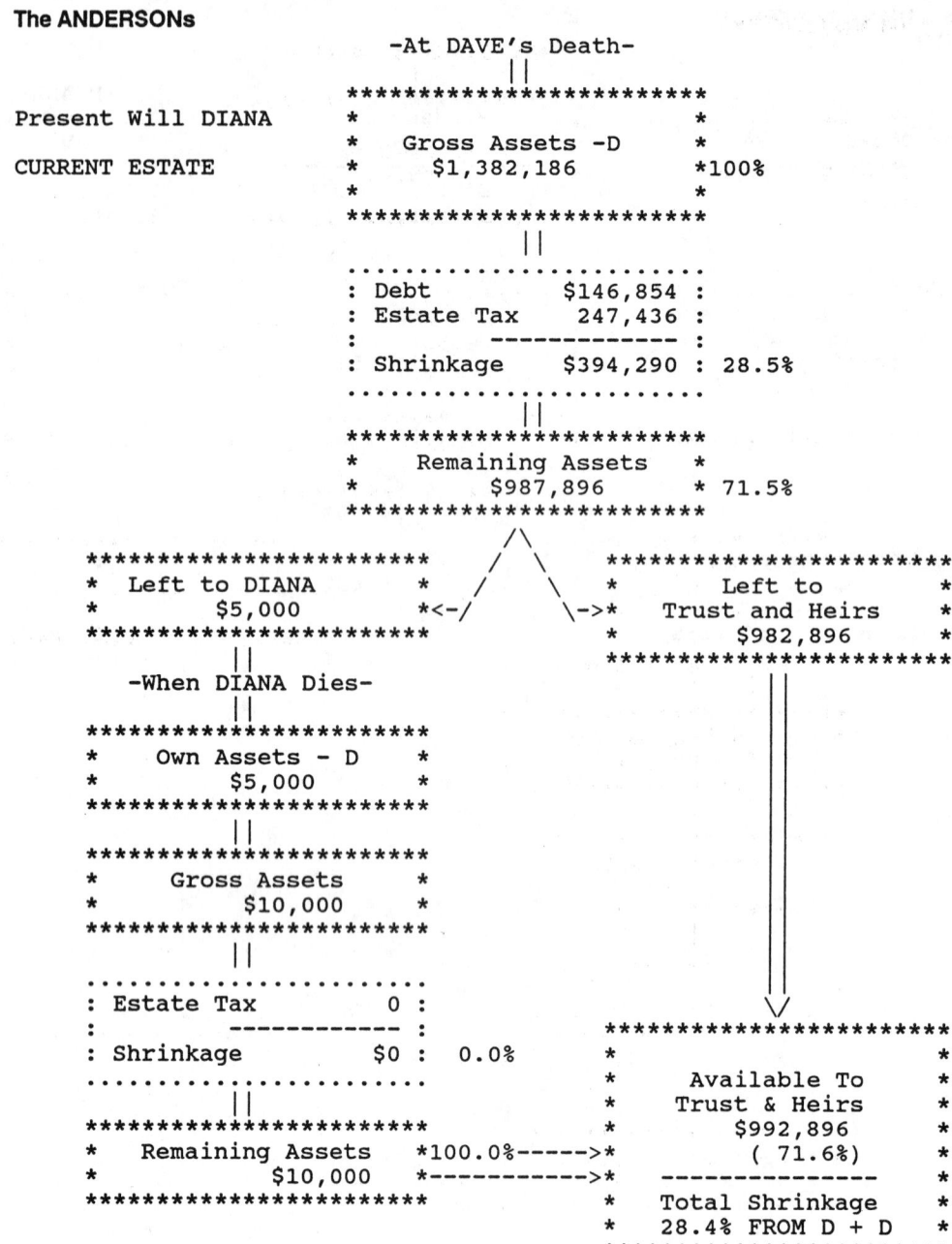

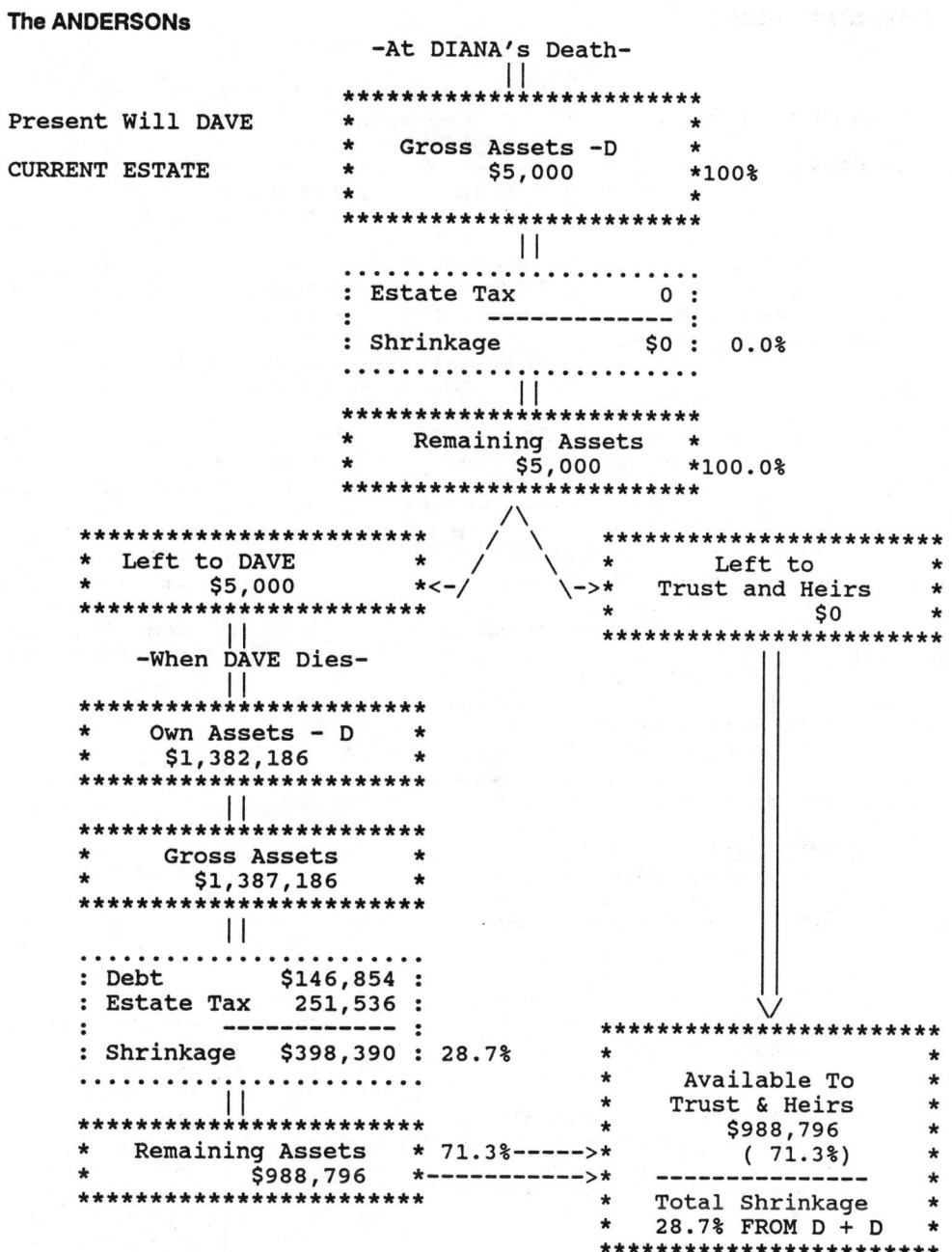

COMPREHENSIVE ESTATE TAX REPORT

DAVE & DIANA ANDERSON
REVISED ESTATE

	DAVE Predeceasing DIANA		DIANA Predeceasing DAVE	
Date: Dec 31, 1994 Maximized Unified Credit Will	DAVE's Estate	DIANA's Estate	DIANA's Estate	DAVE's Estate
Individually Held Assets	1,277,186	0	0	1,277,186
Share from Joint Assets	5,000	10,000	5,000	10,000
Life Insurance Proceeds	100,000	0	0	100,000
Assets Received from Spouse	0	630,332	0	0
Gross Estate	1,382,186	640,332	5,000	1,387,186
Own Liabilities	146,854	0	0	146,854
Adjusted Gross Estate	1,235,332	640,332	5,000	1,240,332
Marital Deduction	635,332	0	5,000	0
Taxable Estate	600,000	640,332	0	1,240,332
Total Taxable Amount	600,000	640,332	0	1,240,332
Fed Tax Before Credit	192,800	207,723	0	444,336
Unified Tax Credit	192,800	192,800	0	192,800
Net Federal Estate Tax	0	14,923	0	251,536
Net Federal + State Tax	0	14,923	0	251,536
Combined Tax	$14,923		$251,536	

ESTATE ANALYSIS
ASSET DISTRIBUTION

DAVE & DIANA ANDERSON
REVISED ESTATE

Date: Dec 31, 1994
Maximized Unified Credit Will

	DAVE Predeceasing DIANA		DIANA Predeceasing DAVE	
	DAVE's Estate	DIANA's Estate	DIANA's Estate	DAVE's Estate
Liquid Assets	$529,086	$387,232	$5,000	$531,586
Non-liquid Assets	853,100	253,100	0	855,600
Total Assets	1,382,186	640,332	5,000	1,387,186
Passing to Spouse	635,332	0	5,000	0
Passing to Trust/Heirs	600,000	625,409	0	988,796
Estate Shrinkage	146,854	14,923	0	398,390

ESTATE ANALYSIS
LIQUIDITY SITUATION

DAVE & DIANA ANDERSON
REVISED ESTATE

	DAVE Predeceasing DIANA		DIANA Predeceasing DAVE	
Date: Dec 31, 1994 Maximized Unified Credit Will	DAVE's Estate	DIANA's Estate	DIANA's Estate	DAVE's Estate
Debt	146,854	0	0	146,854
Administration Expenses	0	0	0	0
Estate Taxes	0	14,923	0	251,536
Charitable Contributions	0	0	0	0
Need for Liquid Capital	146,854	14,923	0	398,390
Liquid Capital Available	529,086	387,232	5,000	531,586
Addt'l Liquidity Needed	0	0	0	0

ESTATE ANALYSIS
MARITAL DEDUCTION

DAVE & DIANA ANDERSON
REVISED ESTATE

	DAVE Predeceasing DIANA		DIANA Predeceasing DAVE	
Date: Dec 31, 1994 Maximized Unified Credit Will	DAVE's Estate	DIANA's Estate	DIANA's Estate	DAVE's Estate
Marital Deduction is--	Overqualified		Overqualified	
Best Deduction Amount	$615,166		-Same-	
Your Amount Exceeds by	$20,166		$0	
Resulting Additional Cost	$1		$0	
Total Family Assets	$1,387,186		$1,387,186	
Joint Estate Taxes	$14,923		$251,536	
	1.00%		18.00%	
Total Shrinkage	$161,777		$398,390	
	11.66%		28.72%	
Remaining for Heirs	$1,225,409		$988,796	
	88.34%		71.28%	

ESTATE DISTRIBUTION FLOWCHART

(DAVE Predeceasing DIANA on Dec 31, 1994)

The ANDERSONs

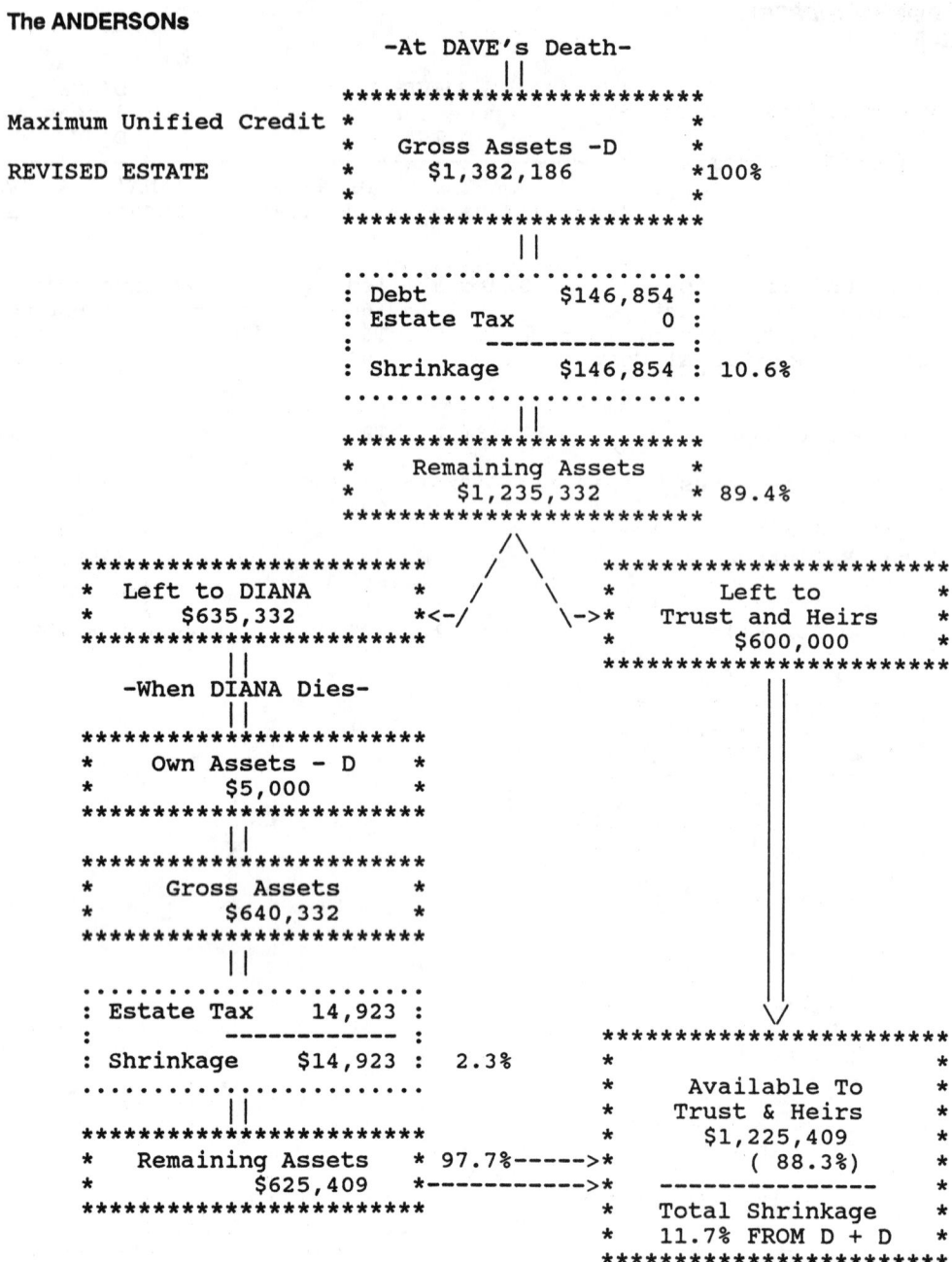

5.82

ESTATE DISTRIBUTION FLOWCHART

(DIANA Predeceasing DAVE on Dec 31, 1994)

The ANDERSONs

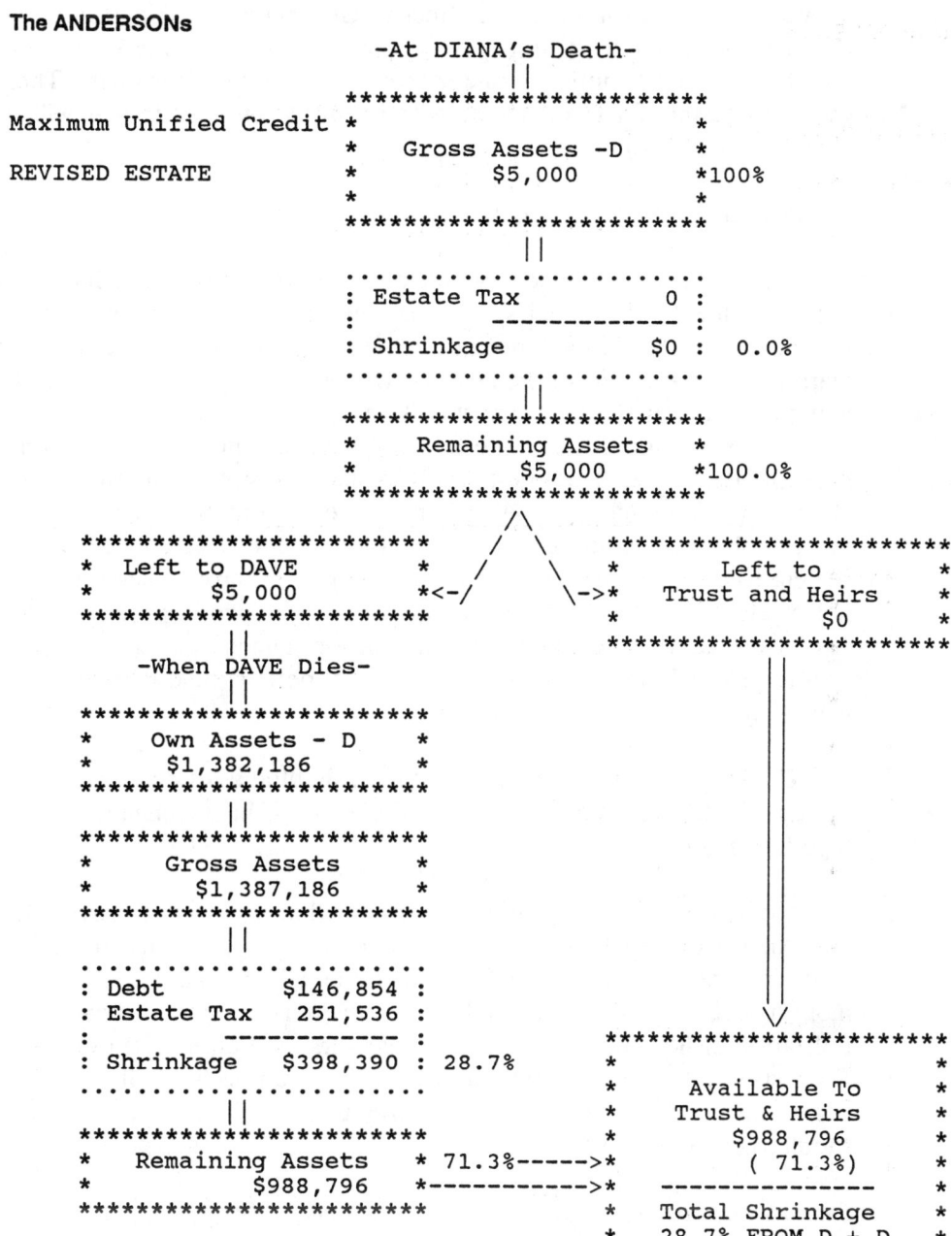

5.83

Failure of Present Estate Planning Documents to Contemplate the Birth of Dave and Diana's Fourth Child

The failure of the Andersons' wills to contain a provision contemplating an afterborn child will have the effect in Georgia of revoking their wills at the birth of the child. The insurance trust would not be revoked; however, the child is not a beneficiary under that trust based on our facts. Therefore it will be necessary for the Andersons to include provisions in new wills to eliminate these problems.

Considerations Regarding Diana

The primary tax problem with the marital trust that Dave has in his present will is that it includes the personal residence (a non-income-producing asset). This will not disqualify the trust for the federal estate tax marital deduction. However, because Diana has only a testamentary power of appointment over the property, it will deprive her of the nonrecognition-of-gain provision should she desire to sell the house and purchase another for a principal residence. The one-time $125,000 exclusion from federal income tax (IRC. Sec. 121) could also be lost under the present arrangement. To avoid these problems one-half of the house could currently be conveyed to Diana subject to the indebtedness as a joint owner with Dave. Such a transfer does not produce any federal gift tax consequences and could probably have significant psychological benefits. In addition, Diana's car could be transferred to Diana outright now. Such property should not be placed in a marital trust.

Dave's new will should also contain a simultaneous death provision to protect the federal estate tax marital deduction if he and Diana were to die together in a common disaster.

Diana's present will is adequate except that it does not provide for the new child and should be redrafted to contain a provision that the new will is made in contemplation of the birth of the new baby. Also as she acquires more assets, it would be advisable to review her estate plan regarding utilization of her unified credit if she dies first and a provision requiring that Dave survive her by 6 months in order to take under her will. Such provisions will avoid adding unnecessarily to Dave's taxable estate if Diana should die first.

Diana's Dissatisfaction with Leaving All Assets in Trust

Under existing facts and recommendations previously made, Diana would no longer have all her assets tied up in trust. There are joint checking and savings accounts, and she has been named the beneficiary of Dave's Keogh plan; consequently the funds in the account balance will go directly to her and will not pass under his will to the marital trust. The house will be held in joint ownership and she will hold title to her car. She will also have a special power of appointment over the irrevocable insurance trust, as discussed in the insurance planning section. If Diana is still concerned about the inaccessibility of the funds in the residuary and marital trusts, she can be given some additional powers in the trust instrument that will give her absolute access to some of these funds without triggering adverse estate tax consequences. One example of such a power is an annual noncumulative right to withdraw the greater of 5 percent of the trust corpus or $5,000. Neither the exercise nor lapse of such a power will cause gift or estate tax problems. In fact, Diana could be the trustee or a cotrustee of the residuary trust with the bank while remaining a beneficiary without risking inclusion of the trust in her estate as long as her ability to distribute trust funds (income and corpus) to herself is limited by an ascertainable standard. The statutory language describing an appropriate ascertainable standard is that funds may be distributed for "health, education, support, or maintenance" without risking estate tax inclusion as a general power of appointment (IRC Sec. 2041(b)(1)(A)).

Problems with Present Life Insurance Trust

The present irrevocable life insurance trust does not contain a Crummey provision (that is, a provision allowing the beneficiaries of the trust to currently withdraw amounts gifted to the trust). For this reason the gifts to the trust fail to qualify as present-interest gifts and do not qualify for the $10,000-per-year-per-donee annual exclusion (IRC Sec. 2503(b)). The result is that each time Dave makes a gift to the trust for the payment of the insurance premium, a taxable gift results. Although the amounts of the gifts are small, gift tax returns reflecting the total amount gifted annually should be filed. (It should be noted, of course, that there will not actually be any federal gift tax liability created since the unified credit will be available to prevent the actual imposition of any federal gift tax. However, it is not desirable to reduce the amount of unified credit available at death.)

A properly structured irrevocable insurance trust is being recommended for the newly acquired insurance. The question of what to do with the present trust remains. The trust can be effectively discontinued by an immediate cessation of gifts to pay premiums; however, serious consideration should be given to maintaining this trust, even though it generates some small annual gift tax liability, at least until the new insurance is in place. It would also probably be prudent to maintain the present coverage until contestability periods under the new coverage have passed.

The dispositive provisions of the new irrevocable insurance trust can (but are not required to) be the same as the terms of the residuary trust under Dave's will. Certainly the trust should empower (but not require) the trustee to loan money to or purchase assets from either Dave's or Diana's estate.

INSURANCE PLANNING

Life Insurance

Should Dave die prematurely, the Anderson family would experience a loss of cash inflow of more than $177,000 annually. While there would also be a reduction in expenses and income taxes, the family's needs after Dave's death would still run between $70,000 and $80,000 annually to maintain their present life-style. This amount could be partially covered by the cash flow from existing investments, which would be approximately $20,000 to $25,000 annually. Assume that Dave wants to provide an $80,000 annual income to Diana and the children and that his investment assets will generate $20,000 of annual income. Dave needs to provide about $60,000 of additional annual income to maintain his family's life-style. The funds available from the existing Keogh plan are not adequate to make up the shortfall for a period of more than 2 years. There is an immediate need for additional insurance protection that could be reduced over a period of years in concert with the buildup of retirement fund balances and other investment assets.

Dave has a $100,000 term life insurance policy in an irrevocable life insurance trust. As discussed previously, a new irrevocable insurance trust with a Crummey provision has been recommended. If the additional life insurance is applied for, owned, and paid for by the trust and the trust is the named beneficiary, the proceeds will not be included in Dave's estate for federal estate tax purposes. The trust will invest the life insurance proceeds and use the income for the benefit of Diana and the children. If the trust could earn 10 percent on this money over a long period of time, the family would have an additional income flow of $60,000. The total life insurance needed, based on a 10 percent rate of return, would be $600,000. Alternatively should the trust earn only 8 percent on the proceeds, a total of $750,000 would be needed to generate $60,000 per year and still preserve principal. Thus Dave needs between $500,000 and $650,000 of additional insurance on his life.

This additional protection should cover the family income needs if prices remain relatively stable in the future. If there is significant inflation, however, there will be a need to increase the insurance coverage. However, as the children reach college age, the funds set aside for their education will provide much of their needed support. Also the longer Dave lives, the greater will be the accumulation of investment assets and contributions to the benefit plan that can provide income to Diana. When Diana reaches the age of eligibility for social security benefits, her income will also increase, so the need for insurance protection should always be periodically reviewed.

The selection of life insurance products involves choices among many available designs. Dave should consider using one of the following types of policies to provide the additional survivor protection needed.

Ordinary Whole Life Insurance

This form of insurance is based on the assumption that premiums will be paid on a level annual basis throughout the insured's lifetime. In the early years of the policy the premium exceeds the cost of protection, thereby providing the basis for cash values within the policy. The cash values of a policy depend on the size of the policy, the insured's age at the time of issue, and whether the policy is rated. Cash values are guaranteed by the contract and can be borrowed at a rate either stated therein or established by an index. In addition, the increase in cash value each year is not taxable to the policyowner. Even though the assumption is that the premium will be paid over the life of the insured, many owners often convert their policies to either a reduced paid-up policy when the need for this protection decreases, such as when any children become self-supporting, or to an annuity upon retirement.

Single-Premium Whole Life Insurance

This form of insurance differs from the ordinary whole life policy in that only one premium, paid at policy inception, is made. These policies enjoy the customary life insurance advantage of tax-free internal cash value increases and income-tax-free death benefits. Of course if owned by the insured, the proceeds would be includible in the insured's estate for estate tax purposes.

In single-premium whole life policies there is typically an initial cash value equal to the premium paid to acquire the policy. These policies also have a guaranteed minimum interest rate stated in the policy, but frequently the actual return is higher than the minimum guaranteed return. The interest rate applicable to policy loans is either equal to or a given percentage above the current rate credited to the cash value. These policies also impose a surrender charge if they are terminated within a specified period of time. They enjoy tax-deferred accumulation of especially substantial up-front cash values.

However, the current Internal Revenue Code imposes a series of rules that have altered the traditional attractiveness of single-premium whole life insurance contracts unless the policyowner plans to leave the cash values with the insurer and looks to the death benefit as the primary purpose for purchasing the contract. IRC Sec. 7702A specifies that if a contract is a modified endowment contract, any cash withdrawals including policy loans will be deemed to be interest earnings first and then a withdrawal of premium. Any withdrawal treated as income is obviously subject to taxation at the policyowner's marginal tax rate. In addition, a 10 percent penalty tax applies.

A modified endowment contract exists if at any time the accumulated amount of the first 7 years' premiums paid on the contract exceeds the accumulated amount of "net level premiums" that would be payable if the contract provided for paid-up future benefits after the payment of seven level annual premiums. The first year's death benefit will be deemed to apply for the purpose of computing the "net level premium" if there is no reduction in the death benefit during the first 7 years even though such a reduction might occur in a subsequent year, such as the tenth year. If a death benefit smaller than the first year's death benefit becomes the face amount during the first 7 years of the policy, then the reduced benefit is used for calculating the amount of the net level premium. Sec. 7702A defines net level premium in such a way that the 7-pay test premium varies from one insurance product to another.

A material change automatically makes a policy subject to the 7-pay premium test. If the test is failed, the policy will be characterized as a modified endowment contract. Any increase in future benefits provided under the policy is a material change, with three exceptions: (1) an increase in benefits attributable to cost-of-living adjustments (CPI or similar index related), (2) the payment of premiums to fund the lowest death benefit payable during the first 7 years, and (3) the crediting of interest and policyholder dividends to the premium paid to meet the requirements of the second exception. Special rules apply to life insurance contracts having an initial death benefit of no more than $10,000. We know from the latest clarifications added to the federal income tax laws that a material change includes (1) any increase in the death benefit under the contract or (2) any increase in, or addition of, a qualified additional benefit under the contract.

These tax limitations on the use of single-premium policies have limited the benefits and flexibility previously available with such policies.

Variable Life Policy

A variable life insurance policy is also a fixed, level-premium policy for the lifetime of the insured. With variable life the insured selects the investment medium used within the policy, usually with a choice restricted to specific funds managed by the insurer. This policy differs from the ordinary whole life policy in that the face amount of the policy changes with the investment performance of the investment instrument(s) chosen by the insured. Often a minimum guaranteed floor below which the policy's face will not fall is an integral part of the policy. However, all investment risk shifts to the policyowner. Since the investment risk is transferred to the owner, no guarantees are included as to the amount of the policy's cash values. If cash values do exist within the policy, borrowing of these values is permissible. However, borrowing from the policy can result in taxation if the policy is defined as a modified endowment contract under IRC Sec. 7702A. Some policies specify a variable interest rate on the borrowing that fluctuates with changes in some previously established standard interest rate. Other policies do have fixed borrowing rates. Since these policies have a substantial surrender charge during their early years, the client should realize that a long-term commitment is being made if this policy is chosen.

In addition, the insured needs to monitor carefully the performance of the investment instrument(s) selected. If the initial choice was incorrect, or if the insured has failed to shift funds as economic conditions change, the amount of protection could fall sizably. This form of fluctuating death benefit might not be suitable to the client when the primary reason for acquiring additional insurance at this time is protection for survivors.

Universal Life Policy

A universal life insurance policy differs from the previous policies in that it has a flexible premium. Universal life is available in two forms—either a level or an increasing death benefit. In addition, a changing face amount of any life insurance death benefit payable under universal life contracts as a consequence of changes in the amount of the annual premium being paid will result in the policy being subject to the 7-pay test at the time of the change. The insured has the option to either increase or decrease or to omit the premium. However, all premiums when paid are added to the policy's cash value account, and all mortality charges are deducted from the same account. Interest is credited to this account with a minimum guarantee. Another unique characteristic of this policy, compared to the three previous policies, is that some mortality risk is shifted to the insured by the potential for increases in the mortality rate. Also a minimum interest rate on the cash value is guaranteed, and interest in excess of the guarantee depends on investment performance and insurer discretion. Any interest buildup in the policy is currently tax free. Although the cash values can be borrowed, the insured can also make withdrawals from the cash values that are not considered a loan, so interest does not have to be paid to the insurer for the withdrawals. Furthermore these withdrawn funds do not have to be repaid to the insurer. However, there may be income tax consequences of such withdrawals. As with the variable life policy, there are significant surrender charges during the early years.

Term Policy

Over the lifetime of the insured this policy has an increasing premium used solely to provide life insurance protection. Important features of this policy are its guaranteed renewability, convertibility of the policy to permanent insurance up to age 65, and no cash value buildup over the life of the insured.

Recommendations

If this protection is purchased as whole life insurance other than the single-premium form, the premium will be in the range of $15 to $23 per $1,000 of protection. The premium for a universal life policy is somewhat lower since the premium can change over the life of the policy. The single-premium policy entails an insurance premium of 30 to 35 percent of the policy's face amount. Term costs will start at about $2.25 per $1,000 of protection and reach the $20-per-$1,000 rate at or beyond age 56.

Dave's personal insurance should be applied for and owned by a properly structured irrevocable life insurance trust that should also be the beneficiary of the insurance policies. This avoids the necessity of transferring policies to the trust, which would cause the insurance proceeds to be included in Dave's estate should he die within 3 years of the transfer (IRC Sec. 2035). The insurance trust should contain provisions similar to or identical with the terms of the residuary trust under Dave's will. It must also contain a valid Crummey provision. If the terms of the insurance trust and the residuary trust are substantially identical, a provision in either or both trusts allowing the trustee to combine them can achieve savings in administrative costs. Diana can continue to function as trustee of this trust until it is funded at Dave's death, and the trust instrument should provide that the corporate trustee should then automatically take over as the successor trustee to avoid having the trust taxed in Diana's estate at her death.

The trust might contain a special power of appointment allowing Diana to make gifts of the trust principal to individuals other than herself, her creditors, her estate, and her estate's creditors. In this way the trust can purchase cash value life insurance on Dave's life, and the Andersons can have access to the inside buildup and/or side funds through Diana's special power. This power should not result in the inclusion of the insurance proceeds in either Dave's or Diana's estate. In addition, Diana has expressed concern that virtually all the Andersons' assets are in Dave's name. Such a special power would provide Diana with some control over the property in the irrevocable insurance trust. However, this technique, involving the use of a special power of appointment in this context, is aggressive and its tax effects are uncertain. Therefore the advice of a tax attorney must be obtained before its use is seriously considered.

Dave and Diana should keep in mind that even though the investment features and tax advantages of some of the permanent forms of insurance are attractive, the primary function of insurance is to protect survivors. However, that does not prevent them from considering or even using additional permanent life insurance as part of their planning for both investment and the protection of their survivors.

Dave and Diana do have some need for temporary insurance to provide for their survivors, at least until the children are finished with college. For this purpose term insurance would provide the protection at the lowest cost. The use of term insurance will be discussed in the education funding section. However, there is a need for permanent survivorship protection extending beyond the time the children have finished their education and are self-supporting. For this purpose Dave and Diana should discuss with their life agent the possibility of using one of the forms of permanent life insurance.

A reasonable estimate of the cost of the life insurance needed at this time is about $9,000 annually. This includes the premiums for additional term insurance as recommended in the next section to assure the funds will be available for the children's college education expenses.

Disability Insurance

The maximum available levels of both disability income and disability business overhead coverage have been recommended. As additional investments are made that could be relied on to produce income, these amounts should be reviewed to ensure that these coverage levels are still needed.

Personal Property and Liability Insurance

On the facts of our case the property and liability coverage carried by the Andersons is good, and additional protection is available through a personal liability umbrella policy. No changes appear necessary in this area.

INVESTMENT PLANNING

Refinancing Clients' Home

Before embarking on any plans to achieve their financial objectives, consideration should be given to the terms and conditions of the mortgage on their home. The mortgage for the Andersons' residence was taken out when interest rates were quite high. Dave was unaware that mortgages can be paid off early and a replacement mortgage obtained that will provide substantial cash-flow savings as a result of lower market interest rates.

Because of the accumulation of home mortgages as the backing for collateralized mortgage obligation bonds, today's mortgage market conditions require that the duration of individual mortgages be standardized. With few exceptions—such as a close relationship with a lending institution that will hold, rather than sell, an individual's mortgage—the choices available to consumers are either 15- or 30-year mortgages. Due to their financial position the Andersons would not be looking at refinancing as a means of having only an additional $100 or so dollars of disposable income to meet their expenses. In addition, they are not desirous of extending the duration of the mortgage that has about 16 years remaining, but they are interested in refinancing their home with a 15-year mortgage at the current interest rate of 7.75 percent with zero points. Dave is not interested in paying points as a means of lowering the nominal interest rate on the loan since—unlike initial financing points, which are immediately deductible—points associated with a refinancing have to be amortized over the life of the loan.

The monthly mortgage payment for the original 30-year, 12 percent mortgage is $648.03, and for the new 15-year, 7.75 percent mortgage it is $510.25, or a reduction in the monthly payment of $137.78. The new mortgage payment, with a lower interest component, will reduce the mortgage interest that the Andersons can deduct against their federal income tax. Given that their income results in their being subject to the reductions for high income, the effect of the reduced interest deductibility is not as severe as it would be for those with lower adjusted gross income.

The current mortgage, still retained by the issuing local bank, can be prepaid without penalty. The bank also is willing to refinance this mortgage and estimates that the total costs to the Andersons for refinancing will be approximately $1,000.

In light of the more than $1,600 reduction in the annual expenses for their home, it is recommended that they refinance. The full arrangements for the refinancing will be completed by March 1995.

The Andersons have four general financial objectives that may be met by proper investment planning, selection, and monitoring. They have stated these objectives in the following order of priority:

- to fund their children's education
- to reduce their tax burden
- to increase their net worth
- to enjoy retirement

The Andersons have also stated their desire to "maintain their life-style." This can be interpreted as a constraint on meeting the other objectives, three of which may be classified as wealth-accumulation objectives. The objective of reducing their tax burden can be met while achieving the other wealth-accumulation objectives.

There is a variety of investment vehicles suitable in various degrees to the achievement of the Andersons' objectives. The planner must consider this entire array and advise the Andersons on the suitability of these vehicles and the proportion of investable funds the Andersons should place in each vehicle, keeping in mind the clients' stated preferences for particular investments. The planner must also be prepared to reposition assets within the portfolio as the clients' financial environment and preferences change.

Once the family and the business are established, the first financial objective is to provide protection to the family in case of Dave's premature death or disability. Insurance is also needed to protect the clients' assets, as previously discussed. After insurance needs have been met, any investable funds remaining must be used to best meet the clients' other needs. Therefore once properly insured, the Andersons should establish an emergency reserve fund to finance their everyday affairs, to handle unexpected contingencies, and to take advantage of favorable prices. This emergency fund could be kept in a money market fund where it earns interest and is highly liquid. Since Dave is self-employed, owns few income-producing liquid assets, and is the breadwinner for a family of five (soon to be six), an increase in their liquid financial assets to the upper 6-month limit would be appropriate. Although Dave does have $50,000 of accounts receivable from his medical practice, he will also have continuing expenses for his medical practice. Therefore it would be inappropriate to consider these accounts receivable as his emergency reserve.

Most of their surplus cash flow for 1995 *should* be appropriated for this purpose.

Financial Status of the Clients

The Andersons are in a strong financial position. They can maintain their current standard of living and have no need to borrow or to lower their standard of living while achieving their desired objectives. Their projected cash flows, if managed prudently, are sufficient to permit the Andersons to fund their children's education, increase their net worth, and enjoy their retirement without borrowing or cutting down.

The planner in this situation should be concerned with how best to achieve the objectives by recommending various investment vehicles that will be effective for the Andersons in accumulating wealth and reducing the tax burden.

Funding the Children's Education

The Andersons have yet to do any funding of the education expenses for their three children. At this time any accumulating for the expected child would be premature. That need can be addressed after the birth of the child next year.

They have two distinct education expenses for each of their three children: those associated with tuition for secondary (high school) education and those for a 4-year college education.

Secondary School Expenses

The expenses for a 4-year private school, estimated at $3,500 per child per school year, are not considered a legal support obligation in Georgia. Therefore a Sec. 2503(c) trust, possibly in conjunction with college education funding, could be used to shift the taxation of income earned on assets set aside for this purpose. However, the Andersons expect their income to keep growing. Since the secondary school expenses are not very burdensome relative to their income, the Andersons could consider paying for these expenses from current income even if the expenses are adjusted for an 8 percent inflation rate as shown in table 5-5.

TABLE 5-5
Projected Private Secondary School Costs
(Inflated at 8 Percent per Year)

Year	Cost
1994	$3,500
1995	3,780
1996	4,082
1997	4,409
1998	4,762 *Keith*
1999	5,142 *Deidre*
2000	5,554
2001	5,998
2002	6,478 *Melissa*
2003	6,996
2004	7,556
2005	8,160
2006	8,813
2007	9,518
2008	10,279 *Expected Baby*
2009	11,101
2010	11,989
2011	12,948
2012	13,894

College Expenses

The Andersons plan to have their children attend high-quality, private colleges. They estimate expenses to be $15,000 ($12,000 for tuition, $2,500 for room and board, and $500 for other expenses) in current dollars each college year for each child. An appropriate inflation adjustment needs to be applied to this current value to estimate the future annual college expenses, ascertain the lump-sum funding needed in today's dollars, and determine the amount of annual funding needed to meet this objective.

Since an 8 percent inflation rate for college expenses seems appropriate in the current environment, this rate will be used in making projections.

Because education expenses begin at a specified time and are nondeferrable, a conservative investment strategy is the most effective way to ensure adequate funding for meeting this objective. An appropriate conservative investment vehicle should yield a 7.5 percent before-tax return on average, for their three children. The available return might be somewhat less for Keith and Deidre since their expenses start within a shorter period of time than Melissa's. However, any difference could be slight. Investment performance, however, should be monitored to verify that expected returns are being realized, and adjustments should be made if needed.

If the Andersons retain ownership of the assets used in funding this objective, their marginal tax rate of 36 percent would apply. The 7.5 percent before-tax yield converts to an after-tax yield of 4.8 percent. This after-tax yield of 5.9 percent and an 8 percent inflation rate for college expenses are used in the education funding schedules on the following pages. Summarizing the data contained in the three schedules, the Andersons' education funding needs appear as follows:

TABLE 5-6
Education Funding—4.8 After-tax Return

	Lump-Sum Funding	Annual Funding
Keith	$ 80,796	$ 9,157 (through 2005, $4,579 in 2006)
Deidre	83,461	8,888 (through 2006, $4,444 in 2007)
Melissa	91,846	8,406 (through 2009, $4,203 in 2010)
	$256,103	$26,451

(text continues on page 5.98)

KEITH

Keith's Education Fund 1995-2006
School Starting Date Sep 1, 2002
$72,362 Present Value of Education Need
4.80 Expected Rate of Return
Monthly Payments of $732 Made Until School End

1994 **EDUCATION FUNDING SCHEDULE**

DAVE & DIANA ANDERSON

Annual Cash Flow Statement
Monthly Payments Until School Ends

Invest $763 each month from Jan 1995 through Jun 2006

Year	Investment Needed	Education Expenses	Investment Earnings	Balance in Fund
1995	9,157	0	242	9,399
1996	9,157	0	703	19,259
1997	9,157	0	1,187	29,604
1998	9,157	0	1,694	40,455
1999	9,157	0	2,227	51,840
2000	9,157	0	2,785	63,783
2001	9,157	0	3,371	76,312
2002	9,157	13,868	3,792	75,393
2003	9,157	29,451	3,174	58,273
2004	9,157	31,896	2,270	37,805
2005	9,157	34,543	1,196	13,616
2006	4,579	18,332	138	0
	105,311	128,090	22,779	

DEIDRE

Deidre's Education Fund 1995-2007
School Starting Date Sep 1, 2003
$74,794 Present Value of Education Need
4.80 Expected Rate of Return
Monthly Payments of $706 Made Until School End

1994   **EDUCATION FUNDING SCHEDULE**

DAVE & DIANA ANDERSON

Annual Cash Flow Statement
Monthly Payments Until School Ends

Invest $741 each month from Jan 1995 through Jun 2007

Year	Investment Needed	Education Expenses	Investment Earnings	Balance in Fund
1995	8,888	0	235	9,122
1996	8,888	0	682	18,692
1997	8,888	0	1,152	28,732
1998	8,888	0	1,644	39,264
1999	8,888	0	2,161	50,313
2000	8,888	0	2,703	61,905
2001	8,888	0	3,272	74,065
2002	8,888	0	3,869	86,822
2003	8,888	15,019	4,284	84,975
2004	8,888	31,896	3,573	65,540
2005	8,888	34,543	2,550	42,435
2006	8,888	37,410	1,342	15,255
2007	4,444	19,854	154	0
	111,099	138,721	27,622	

MELISSA

Melissa's Education Fund 1995-2010
School Starting Date Sep 1, 2006
$79,629 Present Value of Education Need
4.80 Expected Rate of Return
Monthly Payments of $654 Made Until School End

1994   **EDUCATION FUNDING SCHEDULE**

DAVE & DIANA ANDERSON

Annual Cash Flow Statement
Monthly Payments Until School Ends

Invest $701 each month from Jan 1995 through Jun 2010

Year	Investment Needed	Education Expenses	Investment Earnings	Balance in Fund
1995	8,406	0	222	8,628
1996	8,406	0	645	17,679
1997	8,406	0	1,089	27,174
1998	8,406	0	1,555	37,136
1999	8,406	0	2,044	47,586
2000	8,406	0	2,557	58,549
2001	8,406	0	3,095	70,050
2002	8,406	0	3,659	82,115
2003	8,406	0	4,251	94,772
2004	8,406	0	4,872	108,051
2005	8,406	0	5,524	121,981
2006	8,406	19,078	5,940	117,249
2007	8,406	40,515	4,919	90,059
2008	8,406	43,878	3,498	58,085
2009	8,406	47,520	1,834	20,805
2010	4,203	25,219	210	-1
	130,294	176,209	45,914	

At today's schedule of market interest rates, retaining the accumulated funds in the Andersons' name when the funding instrument generates taxable income would require that they contribute slightly more each year to this objective than if the funding instrument was a tax-free, public-purpose municipal bond, since currently these municipal bonds are yielding 5.6 percent. If carefully selected, the income could be exempt from state and local income taxation.

If the Andersons use the Sec. 2503(c) accumulation trust provisions as discussed in the tax planning section and establish separate trusts for each child, each trust will be taxed as a separate entity. If the trust accumulates the income, the first $1,500 of interest income the trust earns each year is subject to a 15 percent marginal tax rate regardless of the beneficiary's age. However, if the trust distributes income to a child under age 14, the kiddie tax can become a problem. After the child reaches age 14, the trust income can be distributed and will be taxed at the child's applicable tax rate at that time. At a 7.9 percent before-tax rate of return on trust assets during the accumulation period, the trust assets must exceed $95,000 before sufficient income is earned to place the trust in a higher (39.6 percent) income tax bracket than Dave is in. Assuming that each trust is in a 31 percent bracket, each earns an after-tax rate of 5.4 percent. This earnings rate and the 8 percent college expense inflation rate are used to develop the education funding schedules on the following pages. Summarizing the data contained in those three schedules, the Andersons' education funding needs appear as follows:

TABLE 5-7 Education Funding—5.4 After-tax Return		
	Lump-Sum Funding	Annual Funding
Keith	$ 76,358	$8,923 (through 2005, $4,461 in 2006)
Deidre	78,303	8,629 (through 2006, $4,315 in 2007)
Melissa	73,293	8,072 (through 2009, $4,036 in 2010)
	$227,954	$25,624

The interest earned by the education trusts as shown on pages 5.100–5.102 reports after-tax trust income (7.5 percent x .72 = 5.4 percent) during some of the years that would be taxed to the trust at the 31 percent tax bracket rather than the assumed 28 percent bracket. Because of this tax difference the annual funding as indicated in table 5-7 would be inadequate to fully fund these future education costs. The deficiency is about $200 in annual funding for each trust. The Andersons must recognize this potential accumulation shortage, and they should choose one of the following courses of action to handle this occurrence.

First, they could simply do nothing and expect to pay the shortfall during the college years.

Second, since these are projections, the anticipated results must be carefully monitored during the accumulation period. Earning rates on fund assets or annual contributions could change, the taxation of trust income could be altered by future income tax laws, and the projected rate of increase in college costs could change. Increases or decreases in the annual funding can be made as future events unfold. Or if Dave has a particularly stellar year financially, larger contributions can be made at that time.

Third, they could add $200 to the annual funding each year, which would largely offset the effect of the 31 percent tax bracket in future years.

Fourth, during the years when the trusts would have taxable income in excess of $5,500, trust income could be distributed to each child whose age is at least 14. Thus there would be no kiddie tax consequence, and the child would be taxed on the income at a lower rate than the trust. Of course, the Andersons must make sure that the funds so distributed are set aside for accumulation for college costs and not frittered away on frivolous items. No decision need be made at this time to have trust income distributed in this manner, but the Andersons can keep this alternative in mind as a potential solution. Only when the children reach age 14 would Dave and Diana have to continue implementing this alternative, providing the children have the necessary maturity and commitment to attend college.

Last, Dave and Diana could use investments that have a higher after-tax return. However, these investments would have a higher risk and might have too much price fluctuation to justify their use to accomplish a financial objective that is not postponable.

Considering how much money will be needed to fund the children's educations, the recommendation is for the Andersons to become accustomed to these funding amounts for several years, after which they should address the shortfall. The following analysis is based on this recommendation.

(text continues on page 5.103)

KEITH

Keith's Education Fund 1995-2006
School Starting Date Sep 1, 2002
$64,058 Present Value of Education Need
5.40 Expected Rate of Return
Monthly Payments of $688 Made Until School End

1994   **EDUCATION FUNDING SCHEDULE**

DAVE & DIANA ANDERSON
Annual Cash Flow Statement
Monthly Payments Until School Ends

Invest $744 each month from Jan 1995 through Jun 2006

Year	Investment Needed	Education Expenses	Investment Earnings	Balance in Fund
1995	8,923	0	265	9,188
1996	8,923	0	774	18,885
1997	8,923	0	1,311	29,118
1998	8,923	0	1,877	39,919
1999	8,923	0	2,475	51,316
2000	8,923	0	3,106	63,345
2001	8,923	0	3,772	76,040
2002	8,923	13,868	4,256	75,351
2003	8,923	29,451	3,571	58,394
2004	8,923	31,896	2,561	37,982
2005	8,923	34,543	1,353	13,715
2006	4,461	18,332	156	0
	102,612	128,090	25,478	

DEIDRE

Deidre's Education Fund 1995-2007
School Starting Date Sep 1, 2003
$64,499 Present Value of Education Need
5.40 Expected Rate of Return
Monthly Payments of $657 Made Until School End

1994   **EDUCATION FUNDING SCHEDULE**

DAVE & DIANA ANDERSON

Annual Cash Flow Statement
Monthly Payments Until School Ends

Invest $719 each month from Jan 1995 through Jun 2007

Year	Investment Needed	Education Expenses	Investment Earnings	Balance in Fund
1995	8,629	0	257	8,886
1996	8,629	0	748	18,263
1997	8,629	0	1,268	28,160
1998	8,629	0	1,815	38,605
1999	8,629	0	2,394	49,627
2000	8,629	0	3,004	61,260
2001	8,629	0	3,648	73,537
2002	8,629	0	4,327	86,494
2003	8,629	15,019	4,808	84,911
2004	8,629	31,896	4,020	65,665
2005	8,629	34,543	2,877	42,628
2006	8,629	37,410	1,518	15,365
2007	4,315	19,854	175	0
	107,864	138,721	30,858	

MELISSA

Melissa's Education Fund 1995-2010
School Starting Date Sep 1, 2006
$65,840 Present Value of Education Need
5.40 Expected Rate of Return
Monthly Payments of $593 Made Until School End

1994 **EDUCATION FUNDING SCHEDULE**

DAVE & DIANA ANDERSON

Annual Cash Flow Statement
Monthly Payments Until School Ends

Invest $673 each month from Jan 1995 through Jun 2010

Year	Investment Needed	Education Expenses	Investment Earnings	Balance in Fund
1995	8,072	0	240	8,312
1996	8,072	0	700	17,083
1997	8,072	0	1,186	26,341
1998	8,072	0	1,698	36,110
1999	8,072	0	2,239	46,421
2000	8,072	0	2,810	57,302
2001	8,072	0	3,412	68,786
2002	8,072	0	4,048	80,905
2003	8,072	0	4,719	93,696
2004	8,072	0	5,427	107,194
2005	8,072	0	6,174	121,440
2006	8,072	19,078	6,661	117,095
2007	8,072	40,515	5,532	90,183
2008	8,072	43,878	3,944	58,321
2009	8,072	47,520	2,073	20,946
2010	4,036	25,219	238	0
	125,110	176,209	51,100	

A comparison of table 5-6 with table 5-7 shows that the Andersons will reduce the annual funding needed by $827 if they use trusts. This reduction, as well as the difference in the amount of lump-sum funding needed ($28,149), results from the difference in the assumed tax rate on trust income during the accumulation period compared with the tax rate if the Andersons retained ownership of the assets.

At the moment the Andersons do not possess sufficient assets to fully fund the education needs unless Dave were to sell the commercial lot or some of his securities. However, the commercial lot, which produces zero taxable income, would be converted into one generating income taxed at their 36 percent bracket, if the funds were kept in Dave's name. If the proceeds from the sale were used to fund the trusts, each trust would soon have income in excess of $3,500 per year and would be taxed at the higher rate of 31 percent if this income was accumulated. The lump-sum funding, accomplished by using the proceeds from the sale of the commercial lot, is not the best solution. Annual funding is the recommended procedure for the Andersons.

The annual funding that is needed for each of the three separate trusts is less than the annual gift tax exclusion whether Dave makes the gift himself ($10,000) or is joined by Diana in making the gifts ($20,000) to each trust.

Consideration must also be given to the nature of Dave's profession. As a practicing physician he has liability for his professional conduct. Even though insurance is carried to protect him and his family from the consequences of malpractice, a catastrophic judgment (however unlikely) against both the business and personal assets should at least be recognized as a possibility in this planning process. Since the 2503(c) trust is an irrevocable trust, the trust assets are ultimately the property of the children and should be beyond the reach of any judgment levied against Dave. Therefore even if the tax savings from using the trusts are not large, the protection afforded by placing the assets beyond the reach of any judgment levied against Dave might be sufficient reason to justify their establishment.

The Andersons specified that the highest priority among their financial objectives is to provide college education for each of their children. Since they will be funding this objective from now until the time the last child completes college, additional assurance that the funding will be achieved should appeal to the Andersons. One effective way to obtain this assurance would be to utilize decreasing term insurance in conjunction with educational funding, with disability riders added to the policies. Thus if Dave died prematurely, the funding would be self-completing. One policy for each child's lump-sum funding need should be obtained now on Dave's life. Dave should apply for, be the owner of, and pay the premium for three decreasing term insurance policies, each equal to the amount needed to provide lump-sum funding of a child's educational fund. Each child's trust should be the beneficiary of that child's policy. The trusts should not own the policies, because such an arrangement could result in a loss of the desired income shifting. The annual premium for the three policies combined will not be over $350.

This recommended insurance in the amount of $195,000 for ensuring total funding for the children's education does not reduce the amount of life insurance that Dave needs as discussed in the insurance planning section. The assumption was made that the money Diana would have from insurance proceeds was for maintaining the current life-style and that the funding for college education would be treated separately.

The use of a Sec. 2503(c) accumulation trust in this situation provides significant benefits. First, since the trusts are irrevocable, the contributions are completed gifts. The trust assets ultimately belong to the children and are not included in the estates of Dave or Diana for estate tax purposes, assuming Dave is not named trustee. Second, the trust assets, are beyond the reach of any professional judgments levied against Dave and beyond the reach of any of Dave's and/or Diana's personal creditors. Third, there are some income tax advantages, as described above, since much of the trust income will be taxed at a lower tax bracket than the Andersons' bracket. This income tax saving is modest for both Keith and Diedre since the accumulation time is relatively short. In Melissa's case, where the time horizon is longer, larger tax savings result.

Once a trust is created for one child, the additional costs for drafting trust instruments and for the management of additional trusts for the other two children are relatively modest. Use of a trust only for Melissa might generate future sibling animosity the Andersons want to avoid. Even though the income tax savings are modest for Keith and Diedre, should anything happen to Dave and Diana simultaneously, Melissa would be in a favored position financially unless provisions of Dave and Diana's wills considered the existence of her trust.

One additional factor to consider is the cost of establishing and maintaining these trusts. First, between $1,000 and $2,000 of expense will be incurred to have the trust instruments drafted by an attorney. If appropriate, the same attorney could also be named as trustee and be responsible for the annual income tax returns for the trust. A portion of the expenses of establishing (but not maintaining) these three trusts qualifies as a tax planning expense and therefore would be deductible by Dave and Diana in the year the trusts are established. Second, the annual expenses incurred for trust asset management and income tax preparation should be significantly less than the tax savings generated. These expenses are tax deductible by the trust, but not by Dave and Diana. Each trust would deduct its portion of the annual expense against trust income for that year. Consequently the Andersons may wish to increase their annual contributions to meet these expenses.

The expense of establishing and maintaining an UGMA custodial account is less. However, as previously discussed, income from an UGMA account would be subject to the kiddie tax until the beneficiary reaches the age of 14.

Although the Sec. 2503(c) trust, given its previously described advantages, is the best method of achieving the desired college education funding for the Andersons, clients are often uncomfortable about making irrevocable transfers. If so, alternatives do exist.

One alternative available to Dave and Diana will be to purchase Series EE bonds for the purposes of funding the children's expenses. Since recognition of the income earned on these bonds can be deferred until redemption occurs, the interest earnings will accumulate in a tax-advantaged manner. Moreover, existing federal law provides an additional incentive for parents to use EE bonds as the educational funding vehicle. The following rules must be met to qualify the interest as tax-exempt upon redemption of the bonds:

- The proceeds of the redemption must be used for qualified educational expenses such as higher education tuition.
- The total proceeds—initial acquisition cost plus accumulated interest—must not exceed the amount of incurred qualified educational expenses in the year of the redemption.
- The expenses must be made on behalf of a dependent of the taxpayer.
- The bonds must initially be acquired by the taxpayer (or spouse).
- The bond purchaser must be at least 24 years of age at the time the bond is issued.
- The bonds must have been purchased after December 31, 1989.

Currently Series EE bonds yield 4 percent. For taxpayers such as the Andersons, who are in the 36 percent tax bracket, this translates into a before-tax yield of 6.25 percent. Unfortunately, as with other tax matters, the taxpayer must have income below a certain amount to obtain the full benefit of this exemption. The exemption benefit is then phased out as income exceeds the specified limit. In the case of married couples filing a joint return, such as the Andersons, the phaseout begins if the modified adjusted gross income exceeds $60,000 and ends at $90,000. These income limitations are adjusted for inflation beginning January 1, 1991. Due to Dave's income level the Andersons cannot benefit from this exclusion. The best they could achieve if they use Series EE bonds as the accumulation device would be the tax deferral until redemption, at which time the deferred interest will be taxable to them.

Another alternative would be for Dave and Diana to purchase municipal bonds, hold the bonds in their names, and use the interest income and sale proceeds to meet the college expenses. These bonds will earn about 5 to 5.5 percent tax free. This yield is similar to the after-tax income that could be earned on corporate bonds held in their name. However, since a higher after-tax yield can be obtained by using the Sec. 2503(c) trusts, the use of the municipal bonds cannot be justified unless Dave and Diana do not wish to make irrevocable gifts at this time or if they feel the cost of establishing and maintaining the trusts is excessive.

Considering all factors and particularly the placing of these funds beyond the reach of any potential lawsuits arising from Dave's medical practice, the 2503(c) trusts are the recommended education funding vehicles. Investment selections for the trusts will be discussed in the next section.

The following projections (case II) illustrate the Andersons' tax, net worth, and cash-flow positions if

- under the general insurance recommendations $9,000 of cash flow is allocated annually toward additional coverage on Dave's life beginning in 1995
- the amount of $25,624 is gifted annually to education funding trusts beginning in 1995
- the Andersons refinance their house

(text continues on page 5.119)

CASE II

CASE ASSUMPTIONS—CASE II

New Assumptions

1. Beginning in 1995 an additional $9,000 of cash flow is allocated each year to additional life insurance on Dave.

2. Beginning in 1995 the amount of $25,624 is gifted each year to education funding trusts.

3. In March 1995 the unpaid balance of the home mortgage will be refinanced at 7.75 percent for 15 years. A one-time, nondeductible cost of $1,000 will be paid.

Continuing Assumptions

1. The checking account balance is maintained at $5,000; the account is non-interest-bearing.

2. The joint savings account balance of $10,000 earns 3 percent interest annually. Interest accumulates in the account.

3. The money market deposit account has an average balance of $25,000 and earns 3 percent interest annually. Interest does not accumulate in the account but is added to surplus cash.

4. Surplus cash is invested and earns 4 percent annually.

5. Dave's gross receipts and business expenses are expected to increase at 8 percent annually.

6. Diana inherited a coin collection from her father in 1968. Fair market value of the collection is presently $20,000 and is expected to increase annually at 6 percent.

7. The 1994 value of the personal residence ($215,000) will increase at 8 percent annually. The residence was purchased in March 1980. The original amount of the mortgage was $63,000 at an interest rate of 12 percent for a term of 30 years.

8. The 1994 value of the commercial lot ($160,000) will increase at 4 percent annually. The lot was purchased in March 1983. The original amount of the mortgage was $80,000 at an interest rate of 10 percent for a term of 20 years.

9. The 1994 value of the rental property ($75,000) will increase at 6 percent annually. The rental property was purchased in November 1982. Currently the property rents for $550 per month and has operating expenses of approximately $900 annually. All these amounts will increase at 6 percent annually.

10. Limited partnership interests are shown at cost.

11. Dave has office furniture valued at approximately $20,000 and office equipment valued at $45,000. No increase or decrease in value has been assumed.

12. Dave's accounts receivable average $50,000.

13. Property taxes on the personal residence are expected to increase at 6 percent annually.

14. Nondeductible living expenses are expected to increase at 6 percent annually.

15. Charitable contributions are expected to increase at 6 percent annually.

16. Dave's Keogh plan is presently invested in 30-month CDs earning 8 percent. This earning assumption has been projected through 1998. He makes a maximum contribution to this plan in each year.

17. Automobiles decrease in value at a rate of 15 percent annually.

18. The expected growth rate of all dividends is 2 percent.

19. The expected growth rate for prices of all stocks is the same as the past growth for each stock.

20. No growth is expected in either bond current yields or total return.

1994　　　　　　　　　　　　　　INCOME STATEMENT

DAVE & DIANA ANDERSON

CASE II	1994	1995	1996	1997	1998
Earned Income					
Business Inc-Cl	200,000	216,000	233,280	251,942	272,098
Keogh Plans	-22,500	-22,500	-22,500	-22,500	-22,500
	177,500	193,500	210,780	229,442	249,598
Interest/Dividends					
Saving/NOW Acts	300	300	300	300	300
Money Market Fund	750	750	750	750	750
Houseboat Finance	900	900	900	900	900
Atlantic Rim Fund	456	465	474	484	494
Burp Soda Inc	640	653	666	679	693
Clean Soap Inc	1,000	1,020	1,040	1,061	1,082
Deep Snow Maker Inc	30	31	31	32	32
Economic Fund	24	24	25	25	26
5-7 Year Bond Fund	395	403	411	419	428
FundMgrsGrowthFund	1,342	1,369	1,396	1,424	1,453
Nationwide Oil Co	500	510	520	531	541
Southern Fund	395	403	411	419	428
Wellington Mfg Corp	300	306	312	318	325
Investable Cash	1,455	2,779	3,764	6,200	9,032
	8,487	9,913	11,001	13,543	16,483
Investments					
Invest--House Loan	-3,575	-3,435	-3,282	-3,114	-2,928
Invest--House Expen	-900	-954	-1,011	-1,072	-1,136
Invest--House Rent	6,600	6,996	7,416	7,861	8,332
Invest--House Depre	-2,100	-2,100	-2,100	-2,100	-2,100
Invest--Lot Loan	-5,371	-4,962	-4,512	-4,015	-3,465
	-5,346	-4,455	-3,489	-2,440	-1,297
Other					
State Tax Refund	0	2	2	2	3
	0	2	2	2	3
Adjustments					
S.E. Tax Dedctn	6,398	6,761	7,142	7,559	7,996
	6,398	6,761	7,142	7,559	7,996
Adj Gross Income	174,243	192,207	211,160	232,996	256,803
Deductions					
Charitable 50%	4,500	4,770	5,056	5,360	5,681
State Tax Paid	8,535	9,635	10,726	11,948	13,280
Prop Taxes--Home	1,900	2,014	2,135	2,263	2,399
Refinanced Mortgage	0	3,095	3,989	3,820	3,639
Original Mortgage	6,584	1,623	0	0	0
Reductn For High Inc	-1,966	-2,391	-2,841	-3,373	-3,961
Gross Deductions	19,553	18,746	19,065	20,018	21,037
Standard Deduction	6,200	6,400	6,600	6,850	7,100
Allowed Deductions	19,553	18,746	19,065	20,018	21,037
Pers Exemptions	10,575	9,800	8,925	7,540	5,940
Taxable Income	144,115	163,661	183,170	205,439	229,826
Fed Income Tax	50,206	57,450	64,710	73,016	82,111
Fed Tax Bracket	36.0	36.0	36.0	36.0	36.0

1994   B A L A N C E   S H E E T

DAVE & DIANA ANDERSON

CASE II	1994	1995	1996	1997	1998
LIQUID ASSETS					
Cash Balance	4,851	5,032	4,975	4,985	5,052
Cash Deposits					
Saving/NOW Acts	10,000	10,000	10,000	10,000	10,000
Investable Cash	74,209	67,540	124,436	191,772	268,872
Money Market Fund	25,000	25,000	25,000	25,000	25,000
	109,209	102,540	159,436	226,772	303,872
Stocks & Bonds					
Houseboat Finance	12,508	12,426	12,338	12,243	12,142
State School System	15,150	15,152	15,157	15,161	15,165
Town Hall Munibonds	10,600	10,585	10,572	10,556	10,540
Atlantic Rim Fund	9,500	10,355	11,287	12,303	13,410
Burp Soda Inc	32,000	34,880	38,019	41,441	45,171
Clean Soap Inc	35,000	39,900	45,486	51,854	59,114
Deep Snow Maker Inc	14,000	16,520	19,494	23,002	27,143
Economic Fund	1,500	1,305	1,135	987	859
5-7 Year Bond Fund	6,200	6,299	6,400	6,502	6,606
FundMgrsGrowthFund	46,200	47,355	48,539	49,752	50,996
Nationwide Oil Co	12,000	12,600	13,230	13,892	14,586
Southern Fund	10,200	11,373	12,681	14,139	15,765
Wellington Mfg Corp	24,000	26,400	29,040	31,944	35,138
	228,858	245,150	263,377	283,777	306,636
Overpaid Taxes					
Overpaid State Tx	2	2	2	3	3
	2	2	2	3	3
Liquid Assets	342,920	352,724	427,790	515,538	615,562
NONLIQUID ASSETS					
Retirement Plans					
Keogh Plans	91,168	122,761	156,882	193,733	233,532
	91,168	122,761	156,882	193,733	233,532
Investments					
Investment--House	75,000	79,500	84,270	89,326	94,686
Investment--Lot	160,000	166,400	173,056	179,978	187,177
Gate House Property	35,000	35,000	35,000	35,000	35,000
Northbrook Gardens	102,000	102,000	102,000	102,000	102,000
Smoky River Ltd	55,500	55,500	55,500	55,500	55,500
	427,500	438,400	449,826	461,804	474,363

1994   B A L A N C E   S H E E T   (cont.)

DAVE & DIANA ANDERSON

CASE II	1994	1995	1996	1997	1998
Personal Property					
Home	232,200	250,776	270,838	292,505	315,906
Dave's Car	18,700	15,895	13,511	11,484	9,762
Diana's Car	8,500	7,225	6,141	5,220	4,437
Furnishings--Home	30,000	30,000	30,000	30,000	30,000
Furnishings--Office	65,000	65,000	65,000	65,000	65,000
Coin Collection	21,200	22,472	23,820	25,250	26,765
Business Accts Rec	50,000	50,000	50,000	50,000	50,000
	425,600	441,368	459,310	479,459	501,869
Nonliquid Assets	944,268	1,002,529	1,066,018	1,134,996	1,209,765
Total Assets	1,287,188	1,355,253	1,493,808	1,650,534	1,825,327
LIABILITIES					
Mortgage Loans					
Refinanced Mortgage	0	52,417	50,319	48,052	45,604
Original Mortgage	54,208	0	0	0	0
	54,208	52,417	50,319	48,052	45,604
Notes Payable					
Diana's Car--Loan	4,223	1,478	0	0	0
	4,223	1,478	0	0	0
Investments					
Invest--House Loan	36,858	35,313	33,615	31,749	29,697
Invest--Lot Loan	51,565	47,263	42,511	37,262	31,463
	88,423	82,576	76,126	69,011	61,160
Total Liabilities	146,854	136,471	126,445	117,063	106,764
Net Worth	1,140,334	1,218,782	1,367,363	1,533,471	1,718,563

1994   CASHFLOW STATEMENT

DAVE & DIANA ANDERSON

CASE II	1994	1995	1996	1997	1998
BEGINNING OF YEAR					
Idle Cash On Hand	5,000	4,851	5,032	4,975	4,985
SOURCES OF CASH					
Cash Income					
Business Inc-Cl	200,000	216,000	233,280	251,942	272,098
Interest+Dividends	8,360	8,461	8,565	8,671	8,778
	208,360	224,461	241,845	260,613	280,876
Investments					
Gate House - Cash	6,000	6,000	6,000	6,000	6,000
Northbrook - Cash	5,600	5,600	5,600	5,600	5,600
Smoky River - Cash	1,563	1,798	2,054	2,321	2,615
InvestHouse - Depre	2,100	2,100	2,100	2,100	2,100
	15,263	15,498	15,754	16,021	16,315
Sale/Withdrawals					
Investable Cash	0	9,448	0	0	0
	0	9,448	0	0	0
Tax Refund					
State Tax Refund	0	2	2	2	3
	0	2	2	2	3
Total Cash Inflow	223,623	249,409	257,601	276,636	297,194
Tot Cash Available	228,623	254,260	262,633	281,611	302,179
USES OF CASH					
Fully Tax Deductible					
Keogh Plans	22,500	22,500	22,500	22,500	22,500
Refinanced Mortgage	0	3,095	3,989	3,820	3,639
Original Mortgage	6,584	1,623	0	0	0
	29,084	27,218	26,489	26,320	26,139
Partly Deductible					
Charity Contrb-50%	4,500	4,770	5,056	5,360	5,681
	4,500	4,770	5,056	5,360	5,681

1994 CASHFLOW STATEMENT (cont.)

DAVE & DIANA ANDERSON

CASE II	1994	1995	1996	1997	1998
Not Tax Deductible					
Diana's Car--Loan	559	299	44	0	0
Educ Funding Trusts	0	25,624	25,624	25,624	25,624
Vacations	4,000	4,240	4,494	4,764	5,050
Life Ins Prem--Dave	279	327	377	443	521
Addtl Life Ins-Dave	0	9,000	9,000	9,000	9,000
Home Ins Prem--Home	600	636	674	715	757
Ins Prem--Cars	995	1,055	1,118	1,185	1,256
Dis Ins Prem--Dave	1,539	1,539	1,539	1,539	1,539
Living Expenses	30,000	31,800	33,708	35,730	37,874
	37,972	74,520	76,579	79,000	81,622
Taxes Paid					
Fed Tax Paid	50,206	57,450	64,710	73,016	82,111
State Tax Paid	8,535	9,635	10,726	11,948	13,280
Prop Taxes--Home	1,900	2,014	2,135	2,263	2,399
	60,641	69,099	77,571	87,227	97,789
Purchase/Deposits					
Investable Cash	72,754	0	53,132	61,136	68,068
	72,754	0	53,132	61,136	68,068
Investments					
Invest--House Loan	4,980	4,980	4,980	4,980	4,980
Invest--House Expen	900	954	1,011	1,072	1,136
Invest--Lot Loan	9,264	9,264	9,264	9,264	9,264
	15,144	15,198	15,255	15,316	15,380
Liability Liquidation					
Refinanced Mortgage	0	1,470	2,098	2,267	2,448
Diana's Car--Loan	2,485	2,745	1,478	0	0
Original Mortgage	1,192	54,208	0	0	0
	3,677	58,423	3,576	2,267	2,448
Tot Cash Outflow	223,772	249,228	257,658	276,626	297,128
END OF YEAR					
Cash Balance	4,851	5,032	4,975	4,985	5,052

1994　　　　　　　　SUPPORTING SCHEDULE

DAVE & DIANA ANDERSON

CASE II	JOINT 1994	JOINT 1995	JOINT 1996	JOINT 1997	JOINT 1998
Income					
Earned Income	177,500	193,500	210,780	229,442	249,598
Adj Gross Income	174,243	192,207	211,160	232,996	256,803
Allowed Deductions	19,553	18,746	19,065	20,018	21,037
Pers Exemptions	10,575	9,800	8,925	7,540	5,940
Taxable Income	144,115	163,661	183,170	205,439	229,826
Investments					
Ordinary Income	6,600	6,996	7,416	7,861	8,332
Depreciation	2,100	2,100	2,100	2,100	2,100
Invstmt Interest	8,946	8,397	7,794	7,129	6,393
Other Expenses	900	954	1,011	1,072	1,136
Investment Income	-5,346	-4,455	-3,489	-2,440	-1,297
Investment Interest					
Inv Int Sch E	8,946	8,397	7,794	7,129	6,393
Federal Tax Liab					
Regular Tax	37,410	43,928	50,427	57,899	66,119
Gross Fed Inc Tax	37,410	43,928	50,427	57,899	66,119
Self Employmt Tax	12,796	13,522	14,283	15,117	15,992
Fed Income Tax	50,206	57,450	64,710	73,016	82,111
Fed Tax Analysis					
Indexing Factor	46	51	56	62	68
Fed Tax Bracket	36.0	36.0	36.0	36.0	36.0
$ To Next Bracket	105,885	95,089	84,680	71,761	57,074
Next Bracket	39.6	39.6	39.6	39.6	39.6
Previous Bracket	31.0	31.0	31.0	31.0	31.0
$ To Prev Bracket	4,115	18,711	33,170	50,189	69,126

1994   **SUPPORTING SCHEDULE** (cont.)

DAVE & DIANA ANDERSON

	JOINT 1994	JOINT 1995	JOINT 1996	JOINT 1997	JOINT 1998
CASE II	----	----	----	----	----
Alt Minimum Tax					
Adj Gross Income	174,243	192,207	211,160	232,996	256,803
State Tax Refund	0	-2	-2	-2	-3
Contributions	-4,500	-4,770	-5,056	-5,360	-5,681
Home Mortg Int	-6,584	-4,718	-3,989	-3,820	-3,639
Adjusted AMTI	163,159	182,717	202,113	223,814	247,480
AMT Exemptions	-41,710	-36,821	-31,972	-26,546	-20,630
AMT Taxable Inc	121,449	145,896	170,141	197,268	226,850
Gross Alt Min Tx	31,577	37,933	44,237	51,735	60,018
Fed Tax Less FTC	-37,410	-43,928	-50,427	-57,899	-66,119
Other Tax Liabs					
Adj Gross Inc	174,243	192,205	211,158	232,994	256,800
GA AGI Adjstmnts	1,328	1,326	1,326	1,326	1,325
GA Adj Grss Inc	175,571	193,530	212,483	234,320	258,124
GA Standard Ded	4,400	4,400	4,400	4,400	4,400
GA Itemized Ded	21,519	21,137	21,906	23,391	24,999
GA Exemptions	7,500	7,500	7,500	7,500	7,500
GA Taxable Inc	146,552	164,893	183,077	203,429	225,626
GA Regular Tax	8,533	9,633	10,724	11,945	13,277
GA Income Tax	8,533	9,633	10,724	11,945	13,277
Georgia Tax	8,533	9,633	10,724	11,945	13,277
Tot State/Local Tx	8,533	9,633	10,724	11,945	13,277
Total Inc Tax	58,739	67,083	75,434	84,961	95,388

1994 **FINANCIAL SUMMARY**

DAVE & DIANA ANDERSON

CASE II	1994	1995	1996	1997	1998
Gross Real Income					
Personal Earnings	200,000	216,000	233,280	251,942	272,098
Interest Income	4,733	6,057	7,042	9,478	12,310
Dividends Rcvd	5,082	5,184	5,287	5,393	5,501
Gate House - Cash	6,000	6,000	6,000	6,000	6,000
Northbrook - Cash	5,600	5,600	5,600	5,600	5,600
Smoky River - Cash	1,563	1,798	2,054	2,321	2,615
InvestHouse - Depre	2,100	2,100	2,100	2,100	2,100
	225,078	242,738	261,363	282,834	306,223
Income & Inflation					
Gross Real Inc	225,078	242,738	261,363	282,834	306,223
Total Inc Tax	-58,739	-67,083	-75,434	-84,961	-95,388
Net Real Income	166,339	175,655	185,929	197,873	210,836
Cur Real Inc =	166,339	172,160	178,186	184,422	190,877
At Infltn Rate Of	4	4	4	4	4
Cash Flow					
Idle Cash On Hand	5,000	4,851	5,032	4,975	4,985
Norml Cash Inflow	223,623	239,961	257,601	276,636	297,194
Assets Sold	0	9,448	0	0	0
Norml Cash Outflw	151,018	249,228	204,526	215,490	229,060
Cash Invested	72,754	0	53,132	61,136	68,068
Cash Balance	4,851	5,032	4,975	4,985	5,052
Net Worth					
Personal Assets	430,451	446,400	464,285	484,444	506,920
Investment Assets	856,735	908,851	1,029,521	1,166,087	1,318,403
Personal Liabilities	-58,431	-53,895	-50,319	-48,052	-45,604
Investmt Liabilities	-88,423	-82,576	-76,126	-69,011	-61,160
Personal Net Worth	372,020	392,505	413,966	436,392	461,316
Investment Net Worth	768,312	826,275	953,395	1,097,076	1,257,243
Net Worth	1,140,334	1,218,782	1,367,363	1,533,471	1,718,563

Investment Alternatives for Education Funding

The next step is to assess the suitability of various investment media for meeting the objective.

INSTRUCTIONS TO STUDENTS

To avoid repetition of background material on the various investment risks, investor profiles, the need to match the risk-return tradeoff associated with the various instruments, suggestions for matching investments in the general risk category with financial objectives, and selected investments appropriate for education funding, that material has been omitted from this chapter. In an actual plan material such as that on pages 3.97–3.118 should be presented to the client. If the student is not familiar with the noted material from the previous chapter, it should be reviewed prior to proceeding through this section of the suggested solution.

In addition to the investment media previously discussed, investments that entail slightly higher degrees of risk could be considered for this client.

Moderately High-Risk Income Bond Funds. These bond mutual funds, sometimes referred to as junk bond funds, possess a greater degree of business and interest-rate risk since they invest in a portfolio of corporate bonds at minimum or slightly below what are deemed investment-grade quality as a means of obtaining a higher yield. Other than the composition of their portfolios, they do not differ from other bond funds. Since the Andersons have a relatively high income and since Dave appears willing to take some degree of risk, these could be a viable investment medium for the education funding purposes.

Growth-Oriented No-Load Mutual Fund. The Andersons could use a no-load diversified mutual fund consisting of growth-oriented blue-chip common stock. The advantages would be capital appreciation and an inflationary hedge as investment media for their children's education funds.

The no-load fund should be chosen because there is no shrinkage of productive assets as a consequence of a sales charge being deducted from the purchase price, as in a load fund. With a 6 percent sales charge found in some load funds, the investor has only 94 cents out of each dollar with which to purchase shares in the fund. With the no-load fund the full dollar of investment purchases shares in the fund. If both funds were to earn a 10 percent return on assets, for example, the return in the first year for a purchase of $10,000 would be $1,000 for the no-load fund and $940 for the load fund. Another way to express this difference is that a load fund earns $940 on a $10,000 investment (cost to the Andersons) and thus has a yield of 9.4 percent ($940/$10,000). Since studies show, on the average, little if any difference in investment performance between these two forms of funds, no-load funds should be the Andersons' choice unless extenuating circumstances favor the use of the load fund.

Recently several no-load mutual funds have instituted so-called 12(b)(1) fees that are assessed on an annual basis against fund assets. These fees range from .25 percent to 1.25 percent. The proceeds raised by this assessment are used to pay for marketing expenses of the fund, which include advertising expenses and disguised forms of sales commissions paid to brokers. Since this is an annual fee, its compound result affects the performance of an investment in the fund. Unless there is a compelling reason to purchase a no-load with a 12(b)(1) fee, the Andersons should avoid buying no-load funds with such a fee in their expense schedule. For an investor having the choice of either a 12(b)(1) fee of 0.75 percent annually or a front end load of 6.5 percent and both funds earning 9 percent, if the planned holding period exceeds 8 years, the best choice is the load fund.

Mutual funds should also be attractive to this client since they provide professional management of the assets by handling the day-to-day needs for selection and timing of securities transactions. As a practicing physician, Dave may not have the time, expertise, or inclination to perform these tasks. In addition, ownership of shares in a mutual fund provides diversification of the portfolio due to the fund's ownership of securities spread over various sectors of the economy, thus reducing most of the business risk.

No-load mutual funds are purchased and redeemed at their net asset value. Immediately after dividends are declared (and paid), the net asset value of the shares falls. Consequently if the Andersons select no-load mutual funds as one of their investment choices, they should purchase shares shortly after the fund declares (and pays) its periodic dividend. If shares are purchased shortly before the dividend date, the Andersons will use after-tax savings to purchase the shares and then have taxable dividend income returned to them. In addition, the net amount of their investment working for them in the fund will be reduced by the amount of the distributed dividend.

One disadvantage of this investment vehicle is the necessity of converting the growth-oriented asset into an income-producing asset when needed for their stated objective, a taxable event. Another disadvantage of investing in a growth fund is that like any mutual fund, it cannot be expected to consistently outperform the market. Unfortunately, however, a badly managed fund can continually underperform the market.

For the education funding, the first priority of the Andersons, the trust established for each child should use relatively conservative funding instruments. However, the potential for taking some risk should not be overlooked.

Investment Media Selection

Use of Corporate Bonds. Since high-quality, investment-grade corporate bonds would, if used as the investment medium for the educational expenses, fulfill the objectives of having a fixed return during the accumulation period and a known value upon maturity, the specific amount of money will be available when needed.

Currently investment-grade bonds are providing about a 7.5 percent return. It is anticipated that this return, as an average, is sustainable during the funding period, although economic conditions could cause this expected return to change.

Each trust should acquire as many corporate bonds as possible each year using the annual contribution and any interest earnings. Idle funds (the excess of the contribution and interest earnings over the value of any bonds that can be purchased) should be placed in a money market fund until such time as sufficient funds are accumulated to make additional bond purchases.

The maturity schedules for the bonds selected for each trust should recognize the annual contribution being made as well as any interest earnings. For example, Keith's trust will have approximately 76 bonds (approximately $76,000 in value) as assets when he enters college. His estimated costs or cash outflow from the fund are about $13,800 for his first semester. The annual funding will approximate $8,900, and about $4,200 interest will be earned by the trust. Thus Keith's trust will have a cash inflow of $13,100 and a deficit of $1,000. Thus one bond should be sold. In year 2003, the cash flow will be a deficit of $17,000 ($29,451−$12,400), and about 17 bonds will need to mature at that time. This approach can be used to establish an appropriate maturity schedule to facilitate each trustee's portfolio management.

The above discussion was based on the assumption that the trustee acquired corporate bonds that paid their annual interest in cash each year. Obviously this cash flow, after payment of taxes along with the annual funding contribution, has to be used to acquire additional bonds. If the trustee acquired zero coupon bonds, the problem of reinvesting each year's accumulated interest would be eliminated. Although the trust would have no cash inflow from interest, the IRS would still deem the accrued interest to be income for tax purposes. However, the trust could use the annual funding contribution as the source of cash to pay the income tax, which in these trusts never exceeds the annual contribution.

Use of Higher-Risk Investments. Since Dave and Diana's cash flows are expected to be substantial over the foreseeable future, they can afford to take somewhat higher risk on the investment vehicles used to fund the education objectives.

For instance, assume that a moderately high-risk income bond fund or a moderate growth mutual fund can be expected to have an after-tax yield during the accumulation period of approximately 8.5 percent rather than the 5.4 used in the above discussion. If these higher-risk investment instruments were used, the present value of the amount required to fund Keith's education would be approximately $55,000 instead of the $76,000, or a saving, in present-value amounts, of $21,000. This would necessitate a $7,524 annual funding payment to the trust established for Keith's benefit. Slightly larger savings in present-value amounts would result for the other two children. The annual reduction in funding for the existing three children's college educations could fund the education for the expected baby starting after the child's arrival.

However, it must be recognized that the total funds required for the annual education expenditure might not be available when needed if more risky investment vehicles are used. For the college years until Deidre graduates, there will be two children in college simultaneously. Despite Dave's relatively high income, shortfalls could impose a financial strain on the family. Because of this potential Dave and Diana might consider investing a portion of each year's contribution into the higher-risk investments. Perhaps 20 to 30 percent of the annual contribution to each trust could be placed in higher-yielding, higher-risk investments. This is a potential way to make up the $200-per-trust shortfall as described earlier. Should this course of action be undertaken, the Andersons will need to carefully monitor the perform- ance of the trusts, and if lower-than-anticipated investment returns occur, then either a change in their annual funding or strong recommendations to the trustee to alter the investment mix would be appropriate.

The Andersons could opt to use the higher-risk, higher-return investments. However, for illustrative purposes this discussion is based on their using corporate bonds as the investment medium.

Repositioning of Existing Assets

The Andersons' existing assets reflect Dave's strong desire to invest initially in real estate and lately in individual securities and mutual funds. The consequences of the real estate investments require some consideration for repositioning of these assets. However, any repositioning must consider the passive-loss rules that affect the deductibility of losses from real estate investments, either directly or through limited partnership arrangements.

Under current federal income tax law individuals must think in terms of three different categories of income for tax purposes: earned income, investment income, and passive income.

Earned Income

Earned income for tax purposes includes wages, salaries, and profits from unincorporated businesses in which the owner actively participates, such as Dave in his medical practice, a partner in a law firm, or the proprietor of a clothing store or beauty salon would have.

Investment Income

Net investment income under the federal tax law means the excess of investment income over investment expenses. Taxpayers will need net investment income to make investment interest payments deductible for tax purposes.

Until December 31, 1992, investment income was income from interest, dividends, rents, royalties, and capital gains arising from the disposition of investment assets. For tax years after 1992, as a general guideline, net capital gain from the disposition of investment property no longer qualifies as investment income that can be used to determine the amount of investment interest (expense) deductible for income tax purposes. However, individuals can elect to have all or a portion of capital gains treated as investment income by paying tax on the elected amount at their ordinary income tax rate rather than the more favorable maximum 28 percent rate applicable to these gains.

Investment expenses are all deductible expenses other than interest that are directly connected with the production of investment income.

As a result of changes in the federal income tax law, individual investors can deduct investment interest expense only up to the amount of their net investment income. Any year's nondeductible investment interest can be carried forward and deducted against net investment income in future years.

Passive Income

Concept of Passive Income. In general, the term *passive activity* means any activity that involves the conduct of any trade or business in which the taxpayer does not materially participate. Rental activity of either real or tangible personal property is defined as a passive activity for tax purposes and is deemed not to be an activity in which the individual materially participates. However, working interests in any oil or gas property that the taxpayer holds directly or through an entity that does not limit the taxpayer's liability with respect to that interest will not be subject to the passive-loss rules.

A taxpayer will be treated as materially participating in an activity only if the taxpayer is involved in the operations of the activity on a regular, continuous, and substantial basis. Generally limited partnership interests are treated as an activity in which the taxpayer does not materially participate.

The passive-loss rules generally deny any individual the right to use losses generated by passive activities to offset other income such as salary, interest, dividends, and active business income. Credits from passive activities are generally limited to the tax attributable to income from passive activities. Passive-activity losses may be deducted against income from other passive activities.

The IRS has released regulations on passive-activity losses and credits. These regulations are quite detailed and introduce many new rules for the application of the limitations on deductibility of losses from passive activities. Included in these regulations are definitions of what constitutes an *activity* under the passive-activity rules and what constitutes material participation in a trade or business.

Generally a rental will be considered a "rental activity" if the average rental period is more than 30 days. If the average rental period is 30 days or less and significant personal services are provided to the customers, the activity will not be considered a rental activity. If the average rental period is 7 days or less, the activity is not treated as a rental activity.

The definition of *material participation* under the temporary regulations provides several alternative tests, including the nature of the activity and the time spent by the taxpayer in participating in the activity. A detailed explanation of these tests is beyond the scope of the discussion. However, it is interesting to note that the regulations provide a new concept called *significant participation*. If a taxpayer's participation in an activity constitutes *significant* but not *material* participation, net losses from the activity will be treated as passive losses, but net income from the activity will not be treated as passive income against which other passive losses can be deducted. Therefore activities in which a taxpayer has significant participation are a "heads I win, tails you lose" situation for the IRS.

Taxpayers who engage in passive activities in closely held C corporations other than personal-service corporations are subject to a somewhat less restrictive rule. Passive-activity losses of such corporations are allowable as a deduction against "net active income," which includes business income but not portfolio income. Consequently taxpayers who both manage rental real estate and own passive interests in rental real estate may wish to consider the closely held C corporation as a choice of business entity. In addition, taxpayers who own tax-shelter investments and cannot deduct the losses from these investments because of the passive-activity loss limitations may consider selling their investments through a brokerage firm to C corporations that are subject to the more liberal rules.

If a taxpayer does not have enough income from passive activities to absorb all the losses from other passive activities, the losses are suspended. These suspended losses, disallowed by the passive-loss rules, are not lost permanently. Rather they are deferred. These suspended losses may be applied against income from passive activities in later years. If not used to offset future passive income, the previously suspended losses from a particular passive activity are allowable losses in the taxable year in which the taxpayer disposes of his or her entire interest in that passive activity in a fully taxable transaction. If all gain or loss realized on such disposition is recognized in one taxable year, the current and suspended losses from that passive activity are generally allowable as a deduction against the taxpayer's income in the following order:

- income or gain from that passive activity for the taxable year (including any gain recognized on the disposition)
- net income or gain for the taxable year from all passive activities
- any other income or gain of the taxpayer from whatever source derived

Consequently taxpayers may still use losses from passive tax-shelter activities to offset income or gains from other sources but only if the taxpayer disposes of his or her entire interest in the tax-shelter activity creating the losses. It should be noted that there is no limitation imposed on the amount of suspended losses that will trigger a deduction in the taxable year of the disposition.

Special Real Estate Rules. To mitigate the effects of the new passive-loss rules on certain individual investors who actively participate in managing real estate property, the current tax law contains one special provision. This special provision permits up to $25,000 of losses from one real estate activity to be used to offset up to $25,000 of gains from other real estate activities in which the individual *actively participates* (a concept distinct from the concept of *material participation*). If there are no other such gains to offset a $25,000 loss, the full $25,000 is deductible against other income, provided the individual actively participates in the real estate activity and had no more than $100,000 of adjusted gross income from other sources. An individual will be deemed *not* to be an active participant if he or she has less than a 10 percent ownership interest in the real estate. Adjusted gross income is determined for this purpose without regard to IRA contributions and taxable social security benefits.

If the adjusted gross income is more than $100,000 but not more than $150,000, then for each dollar that adjusted gross income exceeds $100,000, fifty cents of the special real estate loss is disallowed. For example, if adjusted gross income is $110,000, then $5,000 ($10,000 x .50) of the maximum $25,000 special real estate loss deduction is nondeductible. This $5,000 becomes a suspended loss that must be used under the general rules covering suspended losses described in the preceding section.

If the individual's adjusted gross income exceeds $150,000, then none of any real estate loss is deductible under the special provision. It is an allowable deduction under the general passive-loss rules.

Revenue Reconciliation Act of 1993 changes. Although the 1993 tax act changes do nothing with regard to the material participation requirement, a taxpayer will be able to successfully deduct losses stemming from a rental activity as long as more than 50 percent of his or her personal services have been undertaken in a trade or business involving real property. The taxpayer must, of course, materially participate. A C corporation may take advantage of this new rule as long as more than one-half of the corporation's gross receipts are derived from real property business activities.

Because the Andersons' income level is so high, any losses generated by the four passive investments will become suspended passive losses and will not be available to offset any income tax liability.

Recommendations

The Commercial Lot. This lot, acquired as an investment, is vacant and is not held for the anticipation of earning rental income. Dave's sole objective in acquiring and holding the property is its appreciation in value, subsequent sale, and resulting capital gain. This property should qualify as investment property, rather than as a passive activity, since it is not rental property and Dave materially participates in the investment. Therefore the

Andersons' annual interest payments should be treated as investment interest expenses deductible against their investment income.

Since the lot is investment property, the carrying costs (interest and property tax) qualify as investment expenses, so the after-tax carrying costs are reduced for the Andersons. Since their investment income for 1994 is almost $8,500 and their investment interest expense is $3,575 per year, the full amount of the investment interest expense is deductible.

Whether Dave should accept the offer to sell the lot depends in part on the potential taxation of the capital gain resulting from the sale as well as the tax treatment of his carrying costs. Regarding the potential capital gain, the full amount of all net capital gains is now included as income for tax purposes. Therefore the full amount of the gain will be subjected to the federal capital gains tax rate of 28 percent. Dave does not currently need the funds from selling the lot and might wish to consider retaining it to benefit from its tax-deferred appreciation.

Real Estate Investments. The real estate investments in Gate House Properties, Northbrook Gardens, and Smoky River, Ltd., fall within the passive-loss limitations. Since they are rental real estate partnerships, the issue of whether Dave "materially participates" in the partnership under the new Treasury regulations is irrelevant. The passive-loss limitations will apply. The rental property is subject to the special $25,000 loss allowance for real estate in which the taxpayer "actively participates." However, this property will produce a net positive income beginning in 1993. On the other hand, Dave's income exceeds $150,000, thereby disqualifying him from taking the special allowance. In the aggregate the real estate will produce a positive passive income beginning in 1996. Dave will have a carryover of unused passive losses that may be deducted against future passive income. The Andersons should consider retaining these assets for the time being. Alternatively Dave could sell these investments to a C corporation that is permitted to deduct these losses. Such a possibility could be discussed with a securities account executive that provides a "corporate resale" program for tax-shelter investments.

Security Portfolio. Dave has a sizable portfolio of stocks and bonds, some of which have been performing quite well during his holding period. An examination of the portfolio (as listed on page 5.6) shows that Dave has largely, with but one exception, followed a buy-and-hold policy. A careful review of the portfolio is needed and should be made now.

First, an examination of his investment objectives (p. 5.91) indicates that his preferences do not include the ownership of bond funds. Since the portfolio contains this type of investment, it could be a candidate for disposal and the funds placed into securities better matched to his objectives. Therefore, the first recommendation is to dispose of the 5–7 Year Bond Fund. Subsequent portfolio recommendations will be able to offset this long-term capital gain of $200 with long-term capital losses.

Second, Economic Fund's per share NAV has fallen sharply since the shares were acquired. Since no estimate could be made of its future performance, this investment should likewise be sold. Part of this loss of $1,500 can be used to offset the gain from the sale of 5–7 Year Bond fund.

Third, Fund Managers Growth Fund seems to not live up to its title. For a holding period of 3 years, a growth rate of 2.5 percent is relatively meager for a fund having such an objective. Also, the fund did not, at least in this year, realize large capital gains that it distributed to shareholders. The total cash flow was $1.22 per share for shares that have a NAV of $42. This nearly 3 percent return added to the NAV rise of 2.5 percent should warrant its sale. The sale results in a realized long-term capital gain of $2,700.

Fourth, the Chapter 11 bankruptcy filing of High Fly Airlines requires careful examination. It must be determined whether the existing bondholders will realize anything as a result of the financial reorganization that might prevent High Fly Airlines from emerging as an ongoing venture. If it appears that existing bondholders will realize little, this is an opportune time to either find a buyer, or if conditions are right, to write the investment off as a total long-term capital loss that would more than offset the accumulated capital gains from the first three portfolio recommendations. For any excess long-term capital loss, $3,000 could be used to reduce the Andersons' other income for this year. Unused net capital losses are carried forward and used to offset either future capital gains or offset $3,000 of other income each year until the entire amount of the loss is extinguished. For initial planning purposes, it is assumed that High Fly Airlines will not emerge from bankruptcy and that this investment is now worthless.

Fifth, the most recent purchases of municipal bonds mesh exceptionally well with the Andersons' financial objectives and level of income. The tax-exempt income they generate, along with additional investments in municipals, will further strengthen the benefits arising from their portfolio.

Last, the remainder of their portfolio tends to track well with their objectives. The portfolio does not spin off that much taxable income, so draconian measures requiring the disposal of virtually all holdings at this time are not warranted. For both the Atlantic Rim and the Southern Fund Dave should consider having automatic reinvestment of the dividends into additional fund shares. The tax burden of their income, absent any cash inflow from them, can easily be absorbed by their cash flow. An examination should be made as to whether the corporations in which Dave has equity positions have dividend reinvestment plans. If so, Dave might consider also participating in these plans.

Portfolio Repositioning

	Selling Price	Cost	Gain (Loss)
Sale: 5-7 Bond Fund	$ 6,200	$ 6,000	$ 200
Economic Fund	3,000	1,500	(1,500)
Fund Managers Growth Fund	43,500	46,200	2,700
High Fly Airlines	–0–	10,000	(10,000)
Total Gain			($ 8,600)
Loss used			$ 3,000
Carryover loss			$ 5,600

Based on making the above sales, Dave now has to place the $52,700 of sales proceeds into investments suited to his objectives. One possibility is to purchase additional municipal bonds that are also exempt from Georgia income taxation. Alternatively, he could acquire shares of growth common stocks or growth common stock mutual funds. A third alternative is to distribute these proceeds over the investment recommendations on page 5.127. Since the 1993 tax changes reduced the amount that Dave could shelter in the Keogh plan and also raised income tax brackets, the first alternative of using municipal bonds is the recommended course of action.

In summary, the Andersons should not reposition any other of their assets at the present time. They should, however, continue to further diversify their investment assets.

Increasing Net Worth

This objective is to increase wealth. Now that plans have been established to satisfy the Andersons' other financial objectives of funding their children's education and having an emergency reserve, they wish to invest their disposable income in such a way as to increase their net worth and maintain and improve their life-style. To a large extent this objective overlaps with that of reducing their tax burden. The primary concern is seeking growth while reducing the tax burden.

Collectibles (Coins, Porcelains)

One method of generating an inflation hedge while achieving growth is to invest part of one's disposable income in collectibles. Diana has already had experience in collectibles; she has a coin collection she inherited. She also has a strong interest in porcelain. Given the Andersons' age and the years until retirement, it seems appropriate to invest some portion of their disposable income in enhancing the coin collection and in porcelains. The advantages would be the growth potential of these assets, the inflationary hedge the assets might provide, the pride of ownership, and the lack of current income for tax purposes.

The disadvantages would include the illiquidity of the investment: there is an expense in terms of time and money in converting these assets to cash. A second disadvantage is the negative cash flow during the holding period: the investment has to be insured and appraised and may be warehoused. Finally, there is an opportunity cost involved.

The opportunity cost is the interest forgone on the funds invested in the porcelain or the coin collection. The Andersons are now 24 years from retirement. A commitment of $50,000 to the coin collection and the porcelains, for example, that would normally earn 8 percent in a conservative bond fund incurs an opportunity cost of $4,000 a year. This amount compounded at 8 percent per year for 24 years grows to a future value of $267,000, a significant amount. This is the result of interest forgone on funds invested in the collectibles. It may be offset somewhat by appreciation realized if the collectibles are ultimately sold.

Investing in collectibles requires a high degree of expertise on the part of the investor to avoid unknowingly purchasing counterfeits or being swayed by an improper appraisal. Another possible disadvantage is the *loss* of value that may occur from reduced demand for the collectible. Collectibles go in and out of vogue quickly. The investor must also exercise care to avoid buying at retail and later selling at wholesale, as has occurred with investments in diamonds.

If the Andersons invest in collectibles, they can potentially benefit from the inflationary hedge and capital appreciation that they desire. Despite being somewhat risky as an investment, collectibles are consistent with their risk profile. In addition, they have strong appeal to Diana. Thus the Andersons should place some of their annual investment funds into collectibles.

Growth-Oriented No-Load Mutual Fund

As stated, the Andersons are concerned with capital appreciation and obtaining an inflation hedge, both of which will be accomplished by investing in a growth-oriented mutual fund. The Andersons also seek to reduce their tax burden. That will also be achieved to some extent through a growth mutual fund in that the fund seeks capital appreciation in lieu of income. Growth in value is not taxed until the fund sells securities at a profit.

Selected Issues of Common Stock

The discussion of selected issues of common stock presented for the funding of the education objective is applicable here. However, the need for a precise dollar amount available at a specified date, such as exists with education funding needs, is not critical when considering potential investment assets to meet this objective of increasing net worth.

Since the Andersons are approximately 24 years away from retirement, if they continue to purchase selected issues of common stock for their portfolio, the stock will require some monitoring and repositioning as events and profit situations change. It appears that the Andersons do not have the time or the ability to manage a portfolio of common stocks. They could be much better off investing in a common stock mutual fund; the manager of the fund monitors, reevaluates, and repositions the fund to seek maximum growth as recommended in the previous section.

However, the "efficient markets hypothesis" suggests that a buy-and-hold strategy, applied to common stocks, will perform at least as well as a strategy of active trading. A buy-and-hold strategy of carefully selected growth-oriented blue-chip common stocks should increase a portfolio's value over time and could well provide the Andersons with their growth and inflation-protection objectives. Occasional repositioning, but not active management, might be needed. For both the selection and the periodic revision the Andersons could rely on an investment adviser.

One advantage of common stock investments is that the value of a carefully chosen portfolio has the potential of increasing faster than inflation over a long period of time. If emphasis is placed on growth securities, current income from dividends will be little, since these firms reinvest their earnings within the business rather than pay them out in the form of dividends. This would be a plus for the Andersons since they do not need additional current income at this time. The growth will, of course, be taxed at a later time, but they will have the opportunity to determine when the tax liability will occur by deciding when to sell. If the appreciated assets remain in either Dave's or Diane's portfolio at death, the stock obtains a step-up in basis that avoids any income taxation on the stock's increase in value. A distinct advantage of a buy-and-hold strategy is that transaction costs are minimal and do not erode profits as they do in an actively traded portfolio.

The Andersons should recognize the disadvantages of common stock investments. First is the presence of market risk, which could sharply reduce the value of a portfolio. If the common stock portfolio is not diversified, then a second factor, the business risk, can also produce sizable losses should one or two firms in which they own common stock fall on hard times.

Their risk attitudes appear to favor the undertaking of some risk to achieve their objectives. A portion of their annual investable funds, therefore, should be placed in growth-oriented common stocks. Each year's investment can purchase round lots in two or three different companies so that within 4 or 5 years sufficient diversification in the portfolio will result. The existing portfolio can provide the base around which other stocks can be acquired. However, with the real estate currently owned and some purchasing of collectibles and growth common stock mutual funds, their total portfolio will have some diversification even in the first few years of direct purchases of common stock.

Preferred Stock

Preferred stock is a unique financial instrument in that it has the legal characteristics of a stock and the financial characteristics of a bond.

As a financial instrument the preferred stock pays dividends expressed as a fixed percentage of par value, offers very little opportunity for capital growth, and does not have a maturity date. Because corporate shareholders can exclude at least 70 percent of the dividends earned on stock, preferred stocks generally have a dividend yield slightly less than that obtainable from bonds and of equal risk.

Because preferred stocks are primarily an income-generating device with little possibility of capital gain, preferred stock investments are used to preserve the wealth of the investor, not to accumulate wealth. Therefore preferred stocks are not recommended for inclusion in the growth portfolio of the Andersons.

Corporate Bonds

Like preferred stock, corporate bonds are generally acquired to generate current income and to preserve wealth.

Briefly, the advantages of corporate bonds are safety if the bonds are investment quality, the certainty of receiving a known amount of income at specific dates, and the receipt of par value upon maturity of the bond. The disadvantages are the lack of an inflationary hedge, which is of special concern in inflationary times, and the lack of real growth opportunity. Also all income from the bonds is taxable.

Given their income tax bracket and the recommended use of corporate bonds as the investment medium for funding their children's education requirements, additional corporate bonds are not recommended for the Andersons.

Municipal Bonds

General obligation municipal bonds are the safest of all municipal bonds because the obligation to repay the investor is a legal obligation of the taxing authority. Thus the investor is guaranteed repayment out of the taxing power of the community or the state that issues the bonds. The public-purpose feature is important because if the bonds are so classified, the interest payments the Andersons receive will be exempt from both regular income taxation and the alternative minimum tax. Revenue bonds are riskier because the bondholders will be repaid from the revenue generated from whatever purpose the proceeds of the bond were used to finance. For instance, if a community issues revenue bonds to build mass transit facilities, the bondholders are to be repaid out of the revenues generated by the system. A risk element is that if the revenues are not forthcoming, the bondholders might not be repaid. Moreover, the interest earned on new revenue bonds, although exempt from ordinary income taxation, will be taxable to taxpayers who are subject to the alternative minimum tax.

Dave has acquired some municipal bonds during the past year due to the attractiveness of their tax-exempt interest income. He could consider further purchases of such bonds as a means of sheltering the income from taxation. These bonds have risks and limitations similar to those of corporate bonds.

Municipal Bond Funds

Selecting a no-load municipal bond fund is also a practical and desirable method for the Andersons to reduce their tax burden. The fund should invest in general obligation municipal bonds that are also "public-purpose" bonds within the provisions of the income tax Code.

To minimize risk, the Andersons should invest in a fund in which 80 percent of the portfolio consists of general obligation bonds. The bond portfolio should contain only bonds rated AA or better. The AA rating, although not a guarantee of investment performance, is a strong indicator that default will not occur and that the investor will be repaid on time.

The advantages of a municipal bond fund include professional management, diversification, minimal record keeping, and a high degree of liquidity. Other benefits of the fund may include automatic reinvestment of income distributions, withdrawal plans, exchange privileges, and check-writing privileges.

Perhaps the most significant and best-known advantage of a municipal bond fund is that the interest earned on the fund is free of federal income tax if the fund invests in public-purpose bonds. To the extent that the fund invests in bonds issued by the state in which the Andersons live, interest on those bonds should also be free of state income tax.

The disadvantages of a municipal bond fund are the possibility of erosion of value in inflationary times, the possibility of a risk of default, and the possibility that the fund might produce an after-tax return less than that from a taxable bond fund of similar investment-quality rating.

The equivalent taxable yield of a tax-exempt investment can be computed under the following formula:

$$\text{Taxable yield} = \frac{\text{tax-free yield}}{1 - t}$$

where t = the investor's marginal tax bracket

Currently municipal bond funds investing in long-term obligations are paying approximately 5 percent. The taxable equivalent yield for investors such as the Andersons who are in the 31 percent marginal tax bracket is as follows:

$$\text{Taxable yield} = \frac{5}{1 - .36}$$

$$= 7.81$$

As illustrated, an 5 percent tax-free yield is equivalent to a taxable 7.81 percent yield to an investor who is in the 36 percent tax bracket. In comparing taxable to nontaxable yields, it should be apparent that the higher the investor's tax bracket, the more desirable are tax-free municipals. As noted, the Andersons will be in the 36 percent marginal tax bracket this year and are expected to be in that bracket over the next few years.

Disadvantages of the fund also include the possibility of a sales charge, a redemption fee, a high management fee, and interest-rate risk.

The interest-rate risk has previously been described in the discussion of corporate bonds for the children's education funding. Briefly, interest-rate risk occurs when interest rates rise, causing the present value of bonds to decline. If the bondholders sell the bonds, they can only do so at a lower price. On the other hand, if the bondholders hold the bonds until maturity, interest risk will not have created a capital loss. However, reinvestment of interest income will be at a lower rate than anticipated and cause the fully compounded return actually earned on the investment to be less than what was anticipated.

A municipal bond fund is appropriate for the Andersons' portfolio because the fund achieves one of their major objectives: tax reduction. If they invest in a fund that owns AA or higher-rated general obligation bonds, there is a minimal level of default risk. Given the Andersons' high tax bracket, these funds should provide a satisfactory return on their investment. The Andersons could also benefit from the possibility of capital appreciation, depending on future movements in interest rates.

Leveraged, Closed-End Bond Funds

Instead of raising the full amount of capital from the sale of equity shares in the fund, some bond funds also obtain a portion of their investable funds by issuing either short-term or intermediate-term fixed-cost instruments. One form of these fixed-cost instruments is 7- to 30-day adjustable preferred stock. When the preferred matures, new preferred is issued as a replacement. Other funds raise their fixed return by arranging 30- to 90-day adjustable bank lines of credit or issue either money market notes or fixed 5-year notes. This additional capital, along with the original capital, is used to acquire a portfolio of either taxable or tax-exempt bonds, depending on the fund's stated purpose. The leverage from the borrowed funds (typically between 25 and 45 percent of total capital, although the SEC permits as much as 50 percent), if favorable, will enhance the yield to the fund's shares if a sufficient difference exists between the cost of the borrowed funds (short-term interest rate) and what can be earned on the portfolio (intermediate and long-term interest rates). In practice these funds set a target yield they seek to achieve. Most of the taxable funds invest in high-yield corporate bonds. The tax-exempts typically invest in investment grade municipal bonds. Other than the use of leverage, these funds possess the same characteristics, advantages, and limitations of other bond funds.

Currently the taxable leveraged bond funds yield between 9 and 11 percent as compared with the tax-exempt yields of between 5 and 5.5 percent. The percent of this spread is close to the Andersons' 31 percent tax bracket. The higher-yielding taxable funds could be an attractive investment opportunity to the Andersons, who should keep in mind that the interaction of the leverage and the nature of the portfolios makes them riskier than similarly invested, nonleveraged funds.

Junk Bonds

Traditionally it was the default risk of either newly formed corporations or of troubled corporations or municipalities that caused the market to label certain debt instruments as junk bonds. Since these bonds receive ratings lower than investment grade, they provide relatively high rates of return to investors willing to accept the associated high risk.

In recent years a new crop of junk bonds has come to the market as a result of the numerous leveraged buyouts instigated either by existing management of publicly traded corporations or by outside interests (raiders). In either case a controlled corporation is formed for the purpose of acquiring the stock of a target corporation. Those individuals who directly own the equity interest in this controlled corporation put up a relatively small amount of the funds needed for the acquisition. The remainder of the funds for the stock tender offer is obtained through debt financing (bonds). Since these bonds represent perhaps as much as 90 percent of the capital raised by the acquiring firm, the firm is said to be highly leveraged. Despite actual profitability, if the acquired firm is unable to spin off sufficient cash flow for the servicing of the debt, default can occur. However, in this scenario the default is due to the high degree of financial leverage (debt). Regardless of whether the bond rating services rate these bonds as low or noninvestment grade, investors perceive them as high risk and thus require a high yield. An alternate scenario would involve the acquired corporation's issuing new debt and then repurchasing most of its stock from the controlled acquisition corporation. In this case the operating (acquired) corporation must have sufficient cash flow to service its own debt. When this pattern occurs, previously issued debt of the acquired corporation will be down-graded in its investment classification.

Junk bonds typically yield between 4 and 6 percent more than investment-grade bonds. Recent events have resulted in some of these bonds being sold at discounts of 35 percent or more from their face amount. This makes those bonds even more attractive provided the issuing corporations do not default. Dave could use a portion of his investable cash flow by diversifying an investment in these junk bonds through the mechanism of a mutual fund.

Real Estate

Dave currently rents the office space used for his medical practice and he indicated that the building might be sold (page 5.8). Since Dave has stated that direct ownership of rental real estate is his preferred investment vehicle, he might consider the purchase of the building in which his office is located.

The data in table 5-8 have been developed on the premise that the office building would be purchased at the estimated market price Dave obtained from the realtor and that rental income, operating income, and property taxes would all rise at an annual rate of 5 percent. Should Dave purchase the building, there would be a $16,284 operating loss in the first year. This loss would decrease by about $3,000 per year, and by the sixth year of ownership operating income should become positive. If Dave owned and managed the building personally, the losses would be passive losses for tax purposes, except for the portion attributable to Dave's own business use. These losses could be deducted against any passive income from Dave's other holdings. Otherwise, the losses would be suspended. Table 5-9 summarizes the passive income (loss) data for the years 1994–1998. Part A of the table shows how the passive income (losses) over the period affects Dave's suspended losses under the assumption that Dave does *not* purchase the office building. Beginning in 1995 the suspended losses begin to decline due to passive income being generated. If no more passive investments are acquired, the after-tax passive income flow can be placed in assets producing portfolio (investment) income. Part B of table 5-9 shows the effect on the Andersons' suspended losses under the assumption that the building is owned effective January 1996. When the data from ownership of the office building is added to that of their other passive activities, the Andersons' suspended losses will continue to increase over the period 1994–1998.

However, if Dave does purchase the building, the net cash flow picture appears attractive. Except for the first year in which a cash flow deficit of $2,688 occurs and the second year in which $188 is incurred, the building's cash flow—after all operating expenses, property taxes, interest expense, and principal payments—becomes positive in the third year.

Since the economics of the building appear attractive at this time, Dave could inform either the building's owner(s) or the realtor that he might be interested in purchasing it if it is placed on the market in 1995 or 1996.

TABLE 5-8
Financial Analysis of Office Building

Cost-revenue analysis for office building	1996		1997		1998	
Projected rental income		$60,000		$63,000		$66,150
Less expenses						
Operating expenses	$ 4,000		$ 4,200		$ 4,410	
Property taxes	6,000		6,300		6,615	
Depreciation	16,000	26,000	16,000	26,500	16,000	27,025
Operating income		34,000		36,500		39,125
Interest expense		50,284		50,011		49,727
Income before taxes		(16,284)		(13,511)		(10,602)
Principal reduction (first year)		2,404		2,677		2,961
Total suspended losses		16,284		29,795		40,397
Cash-flow analysis for office building						
Cash revenue		60,000		63,000		66,150
Less cash outgo (operating expenses, property taxes, interest, and principal)		62,688		63,188		63,713
Net cash flow		($ 2,688)		($ 188)		$ 2,437
Other data						
Acquisition cost						
Land cost		96,000				
Building cost		504,000				
Depreciation/year		16,000				
Depreciation period		31.5 years				
Interest rate		10.5 percent				
Mortgage amount		480,000				
Mortgage duration		30 years				
Monthly mortgage payment		4,390				

TABLE 5-9
Summary of the Andersons' Passive Income (Loss) and Suspended Losses for the Years 1994–1998

Part A	1994	1995	1996	1997	1998
Gate house	$ 600	$ 1,200	$ 1,800	$ 2,400	$ 3,000
Northbrook	(3,674)	(1,135)	2,020	3,000	3,800
Smokey River	(2,208)	(1,913)	(850)	700	1,800
Rental house	14	494	1,010	1,561	2,152
Total passive income (loss) for year	($ 5,268)	($ 1,354)	$ 3,980	$ 7,661	$10,750
Beginning of year suspended losses	($14,751)	($20,019)	($21,373)	($17,393)	($10,316)
Passive income (loss) for year	(5,268)	(1,354)	3,980	7,661	10,750
End of year suspended losses	($20,019)	($21,373)	($17,393)	($ 9,732)	$ 434

Part B	1994	1995	1996	1997	1998
Passive income (loss) for year from Part A	($ 5,268)	($ 1,354)	$ 3,980	$ 7,661	$10,750
Passive income (loss) from office building	–	–	(16,284)	(13,511)	(10,602)
Total passive income (loss) for year	($ 5,268)	($ 1,354)	($12,304)	($ 5,850)	$ 148
Beginning of year suspended losses	($14,751)	($20,019)	($21,637)	($33,677)	($39,527)
Passive income (loss) for year	(5,268)	(1,354)	(12,304)	(5,850)	148
End of year suspended loss	($20,019)	($21,373)	($33,677)	($39,527)	($39,379)

Ownership of the building has other beneficial considerations for the Andersons. As stated above, it not only meets Dave's (and to a lesser degree, Diana's) investment vehicle preference, but it can also provide a mechanism that meets two of their general personal financial goals—capital appreciation and inflation protection. Moreover, the opportunity to employ one or more of the children in a bona fide job maintaining the building as a means of shifting some income not subject to the kiddie tax is an additional plus from the Andersons' perspective.

Recommendations

In 1995 the Andersons should have approximately $43,000 of additional investable cash flow for the purpose of increasing their personal net worth. As shown in the cash-flow summary in case II projections, this surplus amount increases during each of the next few years.

The Andersons' portfolio diversification was noted in the section on repositioning of assets. Future surplus cash flows provide the opportunity for the Andersons to further diversify their investments and still meet their objectives.

Dave and Diana do have some differences as to the preferred investment vehicles each would select. Dave's preferences, in addition to direct ownership of real estate, are for growth mutual funds, growth common stock, and municipal bonds. His investment preferences are consistent with his personal financial concerns of long-term growth, inflation protection, and tax reduction/deferral.

Diana's investment preferences, on the other hand, are for collectibles, money market funds, income-oriented mutual funds, corporate bonds, and direct ownership of real estate. However, Diana's higher-ranked personal financial concerns are for safety of principal, inflation protection, and future income. On the surface there appears to be some inconsistency between her general financial concerns and her preferences for investment vehicles. However, a closer analysis shows that two of her investment preferences, collectibles and real estate, have the potential for inflation protection and future income. Diana's other preferences, money market mutual funds, corporate bonds, and income mutual funds, are compatible with her concern for safety of principal.

Prior recommendations for the Andersons included a money market fund for their emergency reserve, corporate bonds for the education trusts, and retention of the existing real estate investments. The first two of these recommendations are consistent with Diana's preferences for safety of principal and investment vehicles. The retention of the real estate satisfies both Dave's investment preferences and his financial concerns, as well as being within Diana's range of acceptability.

To meet the objective of wealth accumulation, the Andersons can select investments carrying greater inherent risk with both increased growth and return potentials. The annual surplus cash during the planning horizon could be allocated in the following manner:

Investment Vehicle	Percent of Investable Funds	Expected Return
Growth common stock mutual funds	25	10–12%; 2% current taxable
Growth common stocks	30	10–12%; 2% current taxable
Leveraged, closed-end bond fund or high-yield bond fund	10	9–11% taxable
Municipal bond funds	25	5–5.5%; nontaxable
Collectibles (coins and porcelain)*	10	16–19%; no current taxation
Office building	—	

*Annual allocation divided equally between coins and porcelain.

In 1995 about $10,700 can be divided between two or three growth mutual funds, $13,000 invested in two or three growth common stocks, $4,300 in one or two leveraged bond funds, and another $10,700 divided over two or three mutual bond funds. The $4,300 for collectibles is assumed to be divided equally between coins and porcelains. The final allocation for the collection should depend on the availability of suitable items.

The collectibles are definitely Diana's preference. They have potential for long-term growth and do not generate taxable income until sold.

The growth common stock mutual fund and the growth common stocks are recommended to provide long-term growth and inflation protection. Since these investments provide little current income, most of their expected total return is tax deferred, fulfilling another important objective of the Andersons. The growth mutual fund offers diversification within the fund itself.

The funds invested in growth common stock, if used to purchase two or three different corporate stocks each year, will create a relatively diversified portfolio within 4 or 5 years. In the short run having only a few common stocks does produce a somewhat risky situation for the Andersons. However, it is a relatively small portion of their total investment portfolio and would be consistent with Dave's preferences and financial concerns.

The leveraged, closed-end bond fund, despite producing taxable income, does have an attractive yield. A relatively small portion of the investable cash flow could be placed in one or two of these funds.

The municipal bond funds should be selected to produce tax-free investment income consistent with the tax-deferral/reduction objective. Also these municipal bond funds will provide safety since each holds a diversified portfolio.

The office building can provide an additional investment opportunity for some of their investable cash flow. At this time the building is not for sale, but, as stated above, Dave should monitor its availability. Should it actually be put on the market or be rumored to be coming to the market, Dave should rearrange his yearly cash investments to come up with the needed down payment. In a year or two, his cash flow will be sizable. Perhaps only a one- or two-year hiatus in the above investment recommendations will be all that is needed to have sufficient funds for the down payment.

Overall the portfolio components selected mesh with the Andersons' preferences, concerns, and objectives. One final portfolio consideration is how the assets should be titled. The collectibles could be placed in Diana's name if this is acceptable to Dave. Consideration should also be given to titling additional investment assets in her name. If collectibles are purchased and Diana accumulates significant assets in her name, a review of her estate plan may be needed, as discussed in the estate planning section.

PLANNING FOR THE SMALL FAMILY-OWNED BUSINESS AND ITS OWNERS

An important and very interesting aspect of financial planning is planning for the shareholder-employees of small family-owned businesses. These businesses usually represent both the client's largest asset and the family's primary source of income. The family in this instance may include the client, spouse, adult children who are employed by the business, and even nonactive children or other more peripheral family members who benefit from the business either directly or indirectly. It is vital in this type of case to recognize that the business and the client may have distinct legal and tax identities. While the needs of the business and the objectives of the client as an individual may sometimes appear to be adverse, the survival of the business and the improvement of the client's personal situation are very closely related. It is essential in these cases to seek solutions to problems and methods to achieve the client's personal objectives that will be acceptable compromises between the business and the individual and that will allow the survival and continuing vitality of the business. Naturally few owners of small family businesses wish to see their lifetime work placed in jeopardy or acquired by someone outside the family group.

CASE NARRATIVE

Personal Information

Lawrence (Larry) and Anne Miller are 62 and 59 respectively and live in a small Georgia town of approximately 30,000 people. They have been married 40 years and have three children. Steve, their oldest son, is 38, is married to Jennifer, and has two children, Alex, 10, and Tony, 7. Doug is 32, is divorced, and has one child, Maria, 8. Lisa is 28 and is married to Tom Hale, a career army officer. The Hales have three children, Kerry, 5, Katie, 4, and Andrew, 1. The Millers have given each grandchild on his or her first birthday a gift of $1,000 under the Uniform Gifts to Minors Act. The children's parents are designated custodians of the UGMA accounts. Larry and Anne do not plan further significant gifts to their grandchildren.

The Millers started their furniture business 37 years ago with money that he borrowed from Anne's father. In return for the loan Anne's father owned 33 percent of the company stock until his death 12 years ago, although the indebtedness had long since been repaid. When Anne's father died, he left her 23 percent of the company stock (57.5 shares). He left Steve the remaining 10 percent of the company stock (25 shares). Because of Larry's hard work the business has grown into a profitable enterprise and has provided a good living for him and Anne and their children. Steve, the oldest son, has been involved in the business on a full-time basis since he graduated from college. He is Larry's heir apparent in the management and ownership of the business.

Larry's basis in his Millers stock is approximately $160 per share. Anne and Steve's stock, which was inherited from Anne's father, has a basis of $1,000 per share in their hands.

The younger son, Doug, also worked in Millers and in another furniture store his father owned in a town about 45 miles away. Six years ago when Larry became uneasy about dividing his time between the two stores, Doug and a business associate purchased the stock of the second store, a separate corporation. The purchase price was $230,000 for 100 percent of the stock, and it was financed with a $20,000 cash down payment and an installment note for 15 years at 10 percent interest. From the sale Larry has annual income of $27,609. This $27,609 figure is made up of the following components for tax purposes: $10,833 return of basis, $4,500 capital gain, and $12,276 of ordinary income. Doug and his business associate still own the store and seem to be doing well.

Larry and Anne's daughter, Lisa, has never been involved in the business as she married immediately after college, and her husband's career requires that they relocate frequently.

Larry says his primary concern at this point is to assure that Steve can succeed him in both the management and the ownership of the corporation. At the same time he does not wish to deprive his other children of a part of their inheritance. He does not, however, believe that leaving the business to Steve, Doug, and Lisa equally will be the most efficient way to assure the continuity of Millers, which is very important to him. In addition, the bulk of his wealth is directly or indirectly tied up in Millers and he would like to explore ways to translate this investment into a secure retirement income for himself and Anne. Larry says he is too young to retire and has no definite plans to retire at 65. However, he would like to start cutting back on his day-to-day duties in the business and give Steve some time in a more direct management position before phasing himself out of the business. He has no idea when he would like to completely give up participation in the business and sees himself as continuing to participate at some level as long as his health permits.

He does, however, wish to be free to travel more extensively and to spend more time with Anne and their grandchildren. Larry thinks he is ready to transfer effective control of the management of the corporation to Steve. Although he is still heavily involved with Millers every day, he doesn't think it necessary or fair to wait until he dies for Steve to own a controlling interest in the business.

Anne has lived in their small town all her life. In addition to 23 percent of the stock of Millers her father also left her some other assets, most of which were blue-chip securities. She continues to have a portfolio of these investments that she enjoys trading. Anne considers that she has been quite successful in managing the portfolio under the supervision and with the advice of a stockbroker with whom she has been associated for many years.

Larry does not share his wife's interest in stocks and bonds; instead he has kept his excess cash in money market funds for the past 5 years.

Anne liquidated a portion of her stocks and bonds several years ago in order to buy a beach condominium in a neighboring state and financed the purchase with a 20 percent down payment and a 20-year loan at 7 3/4 percent interest. After 3 years she decided she was uncomfortable with "being in debt" and paid off the mortgage. Anne's beach condominium has potential as an income-producing property and in fact is rented for brief periods during the year, producing about $4,000 of net income annually. She prefers, however, not to treat the property as a money-making proposition because it requires her to give up too much of the flexibility she enjoys in taking the children and grandchildren to the beach for a week or a weekend whenever it is convenient for her to do so. Property taxes on the condominium were $1,000 last year and are expected to increase 6 percent annually.

The Millers are both uncomfortable with large amounts of debt and therefore have no significant liabilities. Their personal residence was purchased from Anne's grandfather in 1954 for $25,000. It is an older home, dating back to the 1890s, and they believe it is currently worth about $180,000 in their market. It would be expensive to replace; in fact, replacement cost would probably be in the $350,000 range. The house is completely paid for. Much of the furniture in the house was inherited from Anne's family. Larry considers that the remainder of the furniture has been gifted to her, as it has been acquired through the years. They estimate the value of the household furnishings at $60,000. Property taxes on their residence were $1,150 last year and are expected to increase at 3 percent annually. The Millers gave $3,000 to charity last year, and their nondeductible living expenses were $30,000. They expect these amounts to increase by about 6 percent annually.

Larry and Anne carry $150,000 of insurance coverage on their house under a homeowners form 3 that provides for replacement cost coverage. The personal liability coverage limit of the policy is $150,000. They also carry a personal auto policy on their automobiles with liability limits of $300,000 and physical damage coverage.

Larry has two personal life insurance policies, both of which are whole life policies. The face amount of the first policy is $83,500. It is owned by Larry with Anne as the beneficiary and has a present cash value of $19,293. The second policy has a face amount of $10,000 and a present cash value of $7,647. Larry is the owner, and his estate is the beneficiary.

Anne has only one insurance policy, the face amount of which is $10,000. There is $6,430 in accumulated dividends on deposit, making the death benefits available $16,430. The present cash value of the policy is $4,890. The insurance policy is owned by Anne and is payable to Larry as the beneficiary.

Both Larry and Anne realize that they are paying substantial income taxes, but they are not interested in any aggressive tax-planning techniques that might cause the IRS to audit them. They have never been audited and would rather pay the taxes than worry about any involvement with the IRS.

The following is a statement of net worth for Larry and Anne as of December 31, 1993.

LARRY AND ANNE MILLER
Statement of Net Worth
12/31/93

Assets	Owner	Value
Checking account	Joint	$ 3,000
Savings account	Anne	12,000
Money market fund	Larry	46,000
Stocks and bonds	Anne	103,000
Millers, Inc., stock	Larry	506,172
Millers, Inc., stock	Anne	173,760
Personal residence	Larry	180,000
Household furnishings	Anne	60,000
Resort home	Anne	150,000
Automobiles	Larry	16,000
Store building	Larry	330,000
Note receivable (second store)	Larry	159,000
Profit-sharing plan	Larry	65,800
Cash value (life insurance)	Larry	26,940
Cash value (life insurance)	Anne	4,890
Accumulated dividends (life insurance)	Anne	6,430
Total		$1,842,992

If Larry predeceases Anne, he would like her to be financially independent for the rest of her life. Although there is no friction between Anne and her children, she does not wish to depend on them for assistance and wishes to be able to pay for any household help or luxuries that she requires as she gets older. Larry wishes any assets remaining at Anne's death to be divided equally among his children and the share of any deceased child to be split equally among the deceased child's children.

Both Larry's parents are deceased, but Anne's mother is still living. Although she is in her late seventies, she continues to enjoy good health and a luxurious life-style. Anne's mother was the primary beneficiary under Anne's father's will, which left the bulk of his estate to her outright. Anne believes that she and her younger brother are the principal beneficiaries of their mother's will and that their inheritances from her could be at least $300,000 to $400,000 each.

Larry's and Anne's wills have not been updated for 16 years. Each leaves all his or her property to the other spouse, if surviving. If there is no surviving spouse, all property is left to their living children or children of a deceased child equally, per stirpes.

Business Information

Larry is proud of the business he has built and thinks he has accumulated a sufficient net worth to allow him a financially untroubled retirement. However, because so much of his accumulated wealth is tied up in Millers, he has requested advice on the implementation of some plan allowing those assets to be translated into a more liquid form so that they can provide retirement income for Anne and him. Larry also wants to be sure that his business interest is not burdensome for Anne at his death and that she can be assured of an income from his assets. At the same time he does not wish to have an estate plan or a business transition plan that will damage the continuing viability of Millers.

Larry feels that an orderly business transition of Millers to Steve during Larry's lifetime is only equitable, as Steve has spent many years working for the corporation, and that he should be able to have ownership or at least control of the company without waiting for Larry to die. Larry considers that the sale of the other corporation's stock to Doug has assured Doug of a secure source of income if he is willing to devote himself diligently to the business. He feels that the transition of Millers stock to Steve will achieve the same objective.

Millers is a regular (C) corporation. There are 250 shares of common stock authorized and issued. Of those shares Larry owns 167.5 shares (67 percent), Steve owns 25 shares (10 percent), and Anne owns 57.5 shares (23 percent). The corporation has never paid dividends. It uses a calendar-year accounting period and employs the specific-identification inventory accounting method. At year-end 1993 the net worth of the corporation was $755,480, and the book value of each of the 250 shares was $3,022, as shown on the corporate balance sheet on the next page.

The corporation employs 34 people, 26 of whom are full-time. Last year salaries were $686,000, of which Larry was paid $65,000 and Steve was paid $42,500. Larry expects his and Steve's salaries to increase at about 6 percent a year. In 1993 the corporation had sales of approximately $2,200,000 and taxable income of $175,000.

The corporation provides a profit-sharing plan for its employees. The plan requires that if corporate pretax profits reach $200,000 a year, a 10 percent contribution will be made to the plan. If corporate profits do not reach $200,000, there is no contribution to the profit-sharing plan. Therefore the plan has only been funded sporadically.

Larry is unhappy with the performance of the plan, which he feels the employees do not view as a motivator. He comments that perhaps this situation exists because most of his employees, except for 3 or 4 rank-and-file employees, are under 40 and consequently too young to be concerned about retirement. In addition, the plan's sporadic funding does not strongly motivate employees. Larry's account balance in the profit-sharing plan is $65,800, and he is fully vested.

CORPORATE BALANCE SHEET Millers, Inc. 12/31/93	
Assets	
Cash	$ 205,000
Accounts receivable	179,000
Inventory	486,000
Office equipment (net of depreciation)	20,000
Delivery vehicles (net of depreciation)	20,000
Leasehold improvements	42,000
Life insurance cash value	77,480
Total assets	$1,029,480
Liabilities and Net Worth	
Current liabilities	$ 274,000
Common stock ($160 par)	40,000
Retained earnings	715,480
Total liabilities and net worth	$1,029,480

Regarding other employee benefits, Millers provides its hourly employees with 7 days of sick leave per year and a week of vacation after a year of service. Vacation is increased to 2 weeks after 3 years of employment. Hourly employees are allowed to accumulate sick leave up to 21 days. Salaried staff are provided 2 weeks of vacation after a year of employment and 3 weeks of vacation after employment for 5 years. Sick leave for salaried employees is 10 days per year, and salaried employees may carry over unused sick leave up to a maximum of 60 days. Larry carries an excellent medical insurance plan for his employees that provides $1 million of lifetime coverage and, after a $100 deductible, provides coverage of 80 percent of the first $3,000 of covered benefits. After the $3,000 of covered benefits is reached, additional expenses are paid in full. The corporation provides employee coverage on a noncontributory basis. However, dependent coverage is available only if the employee will pay the additional amount. The corporation does not provide long-term disability income benefits or life insurance benefits for employees. The corporation, however, does carry a $200,000 whole life insurance policy on Larry's life that was acquired 20 years ago. The corporation is the owner and beneficiary of this policy, which has a current cash value of $77,480.

Larry individually, and not the corporation, owns the building that houses Millers. It was built 10 years ago and has been leased to the corporation since that time. The cost to construct the building was approximately $185,000. Larry estimates its present worth at $330,000 and assumes that it will increase in value at about 4 percent per year. At present it provides net rental income of $33,000 per year.

INSTRUCTIONS TO STUDENTS

Based on this information, prepare a working outline for the Millers. When this has been completed, it can be compared with the suggested solution that follows. After comparing the working outlines, go to page 6.11 for further instructions.

WORKING OUTLINE

I. Clients' objectives

    A. Lifetime objectives
       1. Assure that control of Millers goes to Steve during Larry's lifetime
       2. Enjoy a secure retirement and maintain some continuing involvement with Millers

    B. Dispositions at death
       1. Assure that Anne is well provided for and that Larry's accumulated assets are not burdensome to her at his death
       2. Divide any assets remaining at Anne's death equally among the children
       3. Achieve his other objectives without damaging Millers

II. Business planning

    A. Tax planning
       1. Present position
       2. Business transition
          a. Installment sales
- General requirements
- Avoiding the limitations on the deductibility of investment interest

          b. Using an S election to facilitate the transfer of a business interest
- The tax on built-in gains
- Practical considerations in planning for an S election
- Additional principles applicable to the taxation of installment sales

          c. Redemptions
- Requirements for favorable federal income tax treatment
- Sec. 318 attribution problems
- Sec. 302(c)(2) election—the waiver approach
- Sec. 303 redemptions

          d. Recapitalizations
- General requirements
- Restrictions

          e. Private annuity

       3. Shareholder-employee compensation planning
          a. Reasonable compensation for shareholder-employees
          b. Employment contracts
          c. Consulting contracts

       4. Employee benefits
          a. Qualified plans of deferred compensation
- Problems with present plans
- General requirements
- Recommendations

          b. Nonqualified deferred compensation
- Avoiding immediate inclusion in the employee's income
- Deductibility by the corporation
- Avoiding the imposition of federal estate tax

    B. Insurance planning
       1. Medical insurance plans
       2. Disability income plans

      3. Life insurance plans
      4. Property and liability coverage for the business—fundamental requirements

III. Personal planning

   A. Tax planning
      1. Present position
      2. Assuring a comfortable retirement with Larry continuing to have some involvement with Millers
      3. Dispositions at death
         a. Analysis of present plans
         b. Possible improvements in estate plan
         c. Concept of estate equalization
         d. Recommendations
         e. Life insurance placement
           • General discussion
           • Structuring the irrevocable life insurance trust
         f. Deferral of estate taxes under IRC Sec. 6166

   B. Insurance planning
      1. Personal life insurance coverage
      2. Personal property and liability coverage

   C. Investment planning
      1. Client profile
      2. Investment alternatives
         a. Certificates of deposit
         b. Municipal bond funds
         c. Municipal bonds
         d. Balanced mutual funds
         e. Convertible bonds or convertible bond funds
      3. Recommendations
      4. Preretirement planning
         a. Repositioning of assets
         b. Asset conservation
         c. Plan distribution options
         d. Retirement income estimation
         e. Potential dependent parent
         f. Recreation/health
         g. Personal asset acquisition
         h. Possible new career

INSTRUCTIONS TO STUDENTS

Now prepare a financial plan for the Millers. When you have completed your financial plan, you can compare it to the suggested solution that follows.

> Suggested Solution

PERSONAL FINANCIAL PLAN

for

LARRY AND ANNE MILLER

CLIENTS' OBJECTIVES

A. Lifetime objectives
   1. Assure that control of Millers goes to Steve during Larry's lifetime
   2. Enjoy a secure retirement and maintain some continuing involvement with Millers
B. Dispositions at death
   1. Assure that Anne is well provided for and that Larry's accumulated assets are not burdensome to her at his death
   2. Divide any assets remaining at Anne's death equally among the children
   3. Achieve Larry's other objectives without damaging Millers

BUSINESS PLANNING

TAX PLANNING

Present Position

Millers is not only the largest and most important single asset that Larry and Anne have accumulated, but it has also been the primary source of income to support their life-style and to allow them to accumulate other assets. Larry has a very strong desire to preserve the business for their oldest son, Steve, who has worked in the business for many years and who Larry thinks is capable of continuing to manage it profitably. Another corporation has already been sold to their younger son, Doug, and a business associate.

Larry has no present plan to retire completely from Millers but would like to cut back his day-to-day responsibilities there. He would like to transfer his responsibilities to Steve before planning to restrict severely the time he spends at the store. He thinks he is ready to pass management control of the business to Steve, since he is assured that Steve will succeed in a leadership role.

Larry presently owns 167.5 (67 percent) of the corporation's 250 authorized and issued shares. Anne owns 57.5 shares (23 percent) and Steve owns 25 shares (10 percent). The book value of Larry's shares at year end 1993 was $506,172, the book value of Anne's shares was $173,760, and the book value of Steve's shares was $75,548.

Larry wishes to accomplish the transition of control to Steve while assuring that his and Anne's interest in Millers will continue to produce income that will allow them to be secure during their later years. At the same time he does not want to implement techniques that will accomplish these personal objectives while compromising the continuing viability of the business. The following pages show the 5-year income statement, balance sheet, cash flow, and summary data of the Millers' present personal situation.

[text continues on page 6.30]

BASE CASE

CASE ASSUMPTIONS—BASE CASE

1. The checking account balance is maintained at $3,000 and is noninterest bearing.

2. The savings account earns 5 percent annually. Interest accumulates in the account.

3. Surplus cash earns 5 1/4 percent annually.

4. The money market funds earn 5 1/2 percent annually. Interest accumulates in the fund.

5. Larry's salary increases at 6 percent annually.

6. Anne's listed stocks and bonds will increase in value at 5 percent annually. Yields on these securities will average 4 percent annually.

7. Stock in Millers is based on 1993 year-end book value and will increase in value at 5 percent annually.

8. The personal residence will increase in value at 4 percent annually.

9. Property taxes on the residence will increase at 3 percent annually.

10. The resort condominium will increase in value at 8 percent annually.

11. Property taxes on the condominium will increase at 6 percent annually.

12. Increase or decrease in the value of household furnishings is ignored.

13. The value of the commercial building will increase at 4 percent annually. Net rental income from this property increases at 6 percent annually.

14. Nondeductible living expenses and charitable contributions increase at 6 percent annually.

15. The profit-sharing plan will earn 6 percent annually.

16. The cash values of the life insurance policies will grow at 8 percent annually.

1994   INCOME STATEMENT

LARRY & ANNE MILLER

BASE CASE	1994	1995	1996	1997	1998
Earned Income					
Salaries - Larry	68,900	73,034	77,416	82,061	86,985
	68,900	73,034	77,416	82,061	86,985
Interest/Dividends					
Notes Rec - Doug	15,508	14,296	12,958	11,479	9,845
Stocks/Bonds - Anne	4,326	4,542	4,769	5,008	5,258
Savings Acct - Anne	600	630	662	695	729
Money Market-Larry	2,530	2,669	2,816	2,971	3,134
Investable Cash	1,606	4,935	8,505	12,334	16,437
	24,570	27,072	29,710	32,487	35,403
Investments					
Rent-Commerc'l Bldg	33,000	34,980	37,079	39,304	41,662
Rent - Condo	4,000	4,000	4,000	4,000	4,000
	37,000	38,980	41,079	43,304	45,662
Other					
State Tax Refund	0	2	0	0	2
	0	2	0	0	2
Net Capital Gain	4,629	5,114	5,649	6,240	6,894
Adj Gross Income	135,099	144,210	153,854	164,092	174,953
Deductions					
Charitable 50%	3,000	3,180	3,371	3,573	3,787
State Tax Paid	6,942	7,441	7,971	8,534	9,130
Property Tax - Home	1,150	1,185	1,220	1,257	1,294
Property Tax -Condo	1,000	1,060	1,124	1,191	1,262
Reductn For High Inc	-792	-951	-1,122	-1,306	-1,506
Gross Deductions	11,300	11,914	12,564	13,248	13,968
Standard Deduction	6,200	6,400	6,600	6,850	7,100
Allowed Deductions	11,300	11,914	12,564	13,248	13,968
Pers Exemptions	4,700	4,900	5,100	5,200	5,400
Taxable Income	119,099	127,396	136,190	145,643	155,586
Fed Income Tax	29,310	31,597	34,036	36,666	39,441
Fed Tax Bracket	31.0	31.0	31.0	31.0	31.0

6.22

1994   **BALANCE SHEET**

LARRY & ANNE MILLER

BASE CASE	1994	1995	1996	1997	1998
LIQUID ASSETS					
Cash Balance	3,009	3,039	3,073	3,108	3,148
Cash Deposits					
Savings Acct - Anne	12,600	13,230	13,892	14,587	15,316
Investable Cash	62,782	130,134	202,380	279,806	362,786
Money Market-Larry	48,530	51,199	54,015	56,986	60,120
	123,912	194,563	270,287	351,379	438,222
Stocks & Bonds					
Stocks/Bonds - Anne	108,150	113,558	119,235	125,197	131,457
Miller Stock -Larry	531,481	558,055	585,957	615,255	646,018
Miller Stock - Anne	182,448	191,570	201,149	211,206	221,767
	822,079	863,183	906,342	951,659	999,242
Overpaid Taxes					
Overpaid State Tx	2	1	1	2	2
	2	1	1	2	2
Life Insurance					
Life Ins - Larry #1	20,836	22,503	24,304	26,248	28,348
Life Ins - Larry #2	8,259	8,919	9,633	10,404	11,236
Life Ins - Anne	5,281	5,704	6,160	6,653	7,185
	34,376	37,127	40,097	43,304	46,769
Liquid Assets	983,378	1,097,913	1,219,800	1,349,452	1,487,382

1994   **BALANCE SHEET**   (cont.)

LARRY & ANNE MILLER

BASE CASE	1994	1995	1996	1997	1998

NONLIQUID ASSETS

Benefit Plans

	1994	1995	1996	1997	1998
Profit Sharing Plan	69,748	73,933	78,369	83,071	88,055
	69,748	73,933	78,369	83,071	88,055

Receivables

Notes Rec - Doug	148,718	135,934	121,812	106,211	88,976
	148,718	135,934	121,812	106,211	88,976

Personal Property

Home	187,200	194,688	202,476	210,575	218,998
Condo	162,000	174,960	188,957	204,073	220,399
Commercial Bldg	343,200	356,928	371,205	386,053	401,495
Automobiles	13,600	11,560	9,826	8,352	7,099
Home Furnishings	60,000	60,000	60,000	60,000	60,000
	766,000	798,136	832,463	869,053	907,992
Nonliquid Assets	984,466	1,008,004	1,032,644	1,058,335	1,085,022
Total Assets	1,967,844	2,105,917	2,252,444	2,407,787	2,572,404
Net Worth	1,967,844	2,105,917	2,252,444	2,407,787	2,572,404

1994 CASHFLOW STATEMENT

LARRY & ANNE MILLER

BASE CASE	1994	1995	1996	1997	1998
BEGINNING OF YEAR					
Idle Cash On Hand	3,000	3,009	3,039	3,073	3,108
SOURCES OF CASH					
Cash Income					
Salaries - Larry	68,900	73,034	77,416	82,061	86,985
Interest+Dividends	19,834	18,838	17,727	16,487	15,103
Rents/Royalties	37,000	38,980	41,079	43,304	45,662
	125,734	130,852	136,222	141,852	147,749
Debt Recovered					
Notes Rec - Doug	11,572	12,784	14,122	15,601	17,235
	11,572	12,784	14,122	15,601	17,235
Tax Refund					
State Tax Refund	0	2	0	0	2
	0	2	0	0	2
Total Cash Inflow	137,306	143,638	150,344	157,453	164,986
Tot Cash Available	140,306	146,647	153,383	160,526	168,094

1994   **CASHFLOW STATEMENT** (cont.)

LARRY & ANNE MILLER

BASE CASE	1994	1995	1996	1997	1998
USES OF CASH					
Partly Deductible					
Charity Contrb-50%	3,000	3,180	3,371	3,573	3,787
	3,000	3,180	3,371	3,573	3,787
Not Tax Deductible					
Living Expenses	30,000	31,800	33,708	35,730	37,874
	30,000	31,800	33,708	35,730	37,874
Taxes Paid					
Fed Tax Paid	29,310	31,597	34,036	36,666	39,441
State Tax Paid	6,942	7,441	7,971	8,534	9,130
FICA/Soc Sec Tax	4,719	4,928	5,140	5,375	5,614
Real Estate Tax	2,150	2,245	2,344	2,448	2,557
	43,121	46,210	49,490	53,022	56,742
Purchase/Deposits					
Investable Cash	61,176	62,417	63,741	65,092	66,543
	61,176	62,417	63,741	65,092	66,543
Tot Cash Outflow	137,297	143,607	150,310	157,418	164,947
END OF YEAR					
Cash Balance	3,009	3,039	3,073	3,108	3,148

6.26

1994   SUPPORTING SCHEDULE

LARRY & ANNE MILLER

	JOINT 1994	JOINT 1995	JOINT 1996	JOINT 1997	JOINT 1998
BASE CASE	----	----	----	----	----
Income					
Earned Income	68,900	73,034	77,416	82,061	86,985
Adj Gross Income	135,099	144,210	153,854	164,092	174,953
Allowed Deductions	11,300	11,914	12,564	13,248	13,968
Pers Exemptions	4,700	4,900	5,100	5,200	5,400
Taxable Income	119,099	127,396	136,190	145,643	155,586
Capital Gains					
Notes Rec - Doug	4,629	5,114	5,649	6,240	6,894
Net Capital Gain	4,629	5,114	5,649	6,240	6,894
LTCG Txd At Max Rt	4,629	5,114	5,649	6,240	6,894
Notes Rec - Doug	-4,629	-5,114	-5,649	-6,240	-6,894
Federal Tax Liab					
Regular Tax	29,449	31,750	34,205	36,853	39,648
Max Tax On Cap Gn	29,310	31,597	34,036	36,666	39,441
Gross Fed Inc Tax	29,310	31,597	34,036	36,666	39,441
Fed Income Tax	29,310	31,597	34,036	36,666	39,441
Fed Tax Analysis					
Indexing Factor	46	51	56	62	68
Fed Tax Bracket	31.0	31.0	31.0	31.0	31.0
$ To Next Bracket	25,530	22,668	19,459	15,847	12,008
Next Bracket	36.0	36.0	36.0	36.0	36.0
Previous Bracket	28.0	28.0	28.0	28.0	28.0
$ To Prev Bracket	25,320	29,982	35,041	40,553	46,342
Alt Minimum Tax					
Adj Gross Income	135,099	144,210	153,854	164,092	174,953
State Tax Refund	0	-2	0	0	-2
Contributions	-3,000	-3,180	-3,371	-3,573	-3,787
Adjusted AMTI	132,099	141,028	150,483	160,519	171,164
Net Capital Gain	-4,629	-5,114	-5,649	-6,240	-6,894
AMT Exemptions	-45,000	-45,000	-45,000	-43,930	-41,432
AMT Taxable Inc	82,470	90,914	'99,834	110,348	122,838
Gross Alt Min Tx	21,442	23,638	25,957	28,691	31,938
Fed Tax Less FTC	-29,310	-31,597	-34,036	-36,666	-39,441

1994　　　　　　　　　　**SUPPORTING SCHEDULE**　(cont.)

LARRY & ANNE MILLER

	JOINT 1994	JOINT 1995	JOINT 1996	JOINT 1997	JOINT 1998
BASE CASE	----	----	----	----	----
Other Tax Liabs					
FICA/Soc Sec Tax	4,719	4,928	5,140	5,375	5,614
Adj Gross Inc	135,099	144,208	153,854	164,092	174,951
GA AGI Adjstmnts	0	-2	0	0	-2
GA Adj Grss Inc	135,099	144,206	153,854	164,092	174,949
GA Standard Ded	4,400	4,400	4,400	4,400	4,400
GA Itemized Ded	12,092	12,866	13,686	14,555	15,474
GA Exemptions	3,000	3,000	3,000	3,000	3,000
GA Taxable Inc	120,007	128,341	137,168	146,537	156,476
GA Regular Tax	6,940	7,440	7,970	8,532	9,128
GA Income Tax	6,940	7,440	7,970	8,532	9,128
Georgia Tax	6,940	7,440	7,970	8,532	9,128
Tot State/Local Tx	6,940	7,440	7,970	8,532	9,128
Total Inc Tax	40,969	43,965	47,146	50,573	54,183

1994   FINANCIAL SUMMARY

LARRY & ANNE MILLER

BASE CASE	1994	1995	1996	1997	1998
Gross Real Income					
Personal Earnings	68,900	73,034	77,416	82,061	86,985
Interest Income	20,244	22,530	24,941	27,479	30,145
Dividends Rcvd	4,326	4,542	4,769	5,008	5,258
Rent-Commerc'l Bldg	33,000	34,980	37,079	39,304	41,662
Rent - Condo	4,000	4,000	4,000	4,000	4,000
	130,470	139,086	148,205	157,852	168,049
Income & Inflation					
Gross Real Inc	130,470	139,086	148,205	157,852	168,049
Total Inc Tax	-40,969	-43,965	-47,146	-50,573	-54,183
Net Real Income	89,501	95,121	101,059	107,279	113,866
Cur Real Inc =	89,501	92,633	95,875	99,231	102,704
At Infltn Rate Of	4	4	4	4	4
Cash Flow					
Idle Cash On Hand	3,000	3,009	3,039	3,073	3,108
Norml Cash Inflow	137,306	143,638	150,344	157,453	164,986
Norml Cash Outflw	76,121	81,190	86,569	92,326	98,404
Cash Invested	61,176	62,417	63,741	65,092	66,543
Cash Balance	3,009	3,039	3,073	3,108	3,148
Net Worth					
Personal Assets	803,385	838,302	875,633	915,466	957,908
Investment Assets	1,164,457	1,267,612	1,376,810	1,492,320	1,614,495
Personal Net Worth	803,385	838,302	875,633	915,466	957,908
Investment Net Worth	1,164,457	1,267,612	1,376,810	1,492,320	1,614,495
Net Worth	1,967,844	2,105,917	2,252,444	2,407,787	2,572,404

Business Transition

Installment Sales

General Requirements. A simple method of transferring Larry's interest in Millers to Steve is an installment sale. Generally an installment sale occurs when property is disposed of in exchange for payments, at least one of which is to be received after the close of the taxable year in which the disposition occurs (IRC Sec. 453(a)).

The seller receives sale-or-exchange federal income tax treatment to the extent of gain realized on the transaction (selling price less adjusted basis = gain realized). When the installment method of reporting is used, the gain portion is recognized and reported as a percentage of each taxable year's payment. The interest portion of the installment payment is, of course, recognized as ordinary income in the year in which it is received. Use of the installment sale method can therefore spread a large gain over a number of years, with significant income tax deferral and possible overall tax savings.

Note, however, that for installment sales of depreciable property all recapture for depreciation must be treated as ordinary income in the year of the sale, regardless of whether any payment is received in that year (IRC Sec. 453(i), 453(i)(2)). However, stock in Millers is not depreciable property.

Installment sales of stock can also provide an important income stream for retirement years, particularly in cases such as this when many of the client's assets are wrapped up in a single business entity that is essentially nonliquid. The 5-year tax, net worth, and cash-flow results of an installment sale of Larry's entire interest in Millers to Steve at book value with a 9 percent interest rate for a term of 15 years are illustrated on the following pages.

[text continues on page 6.42]

CASE II
Installment Sale of Larry's
Entire Interest in Millers to Steve

CASE ASSUMPTIONS—CASE II

New Assumption

Steve purchases all of Larry's Millers stock on July 1, 1995, at a projected 1994 book value ($531,480) for no down payment at 9 percent interest for a term of 15 years. Larry remains active in the business for at least 4 years.

Continuing Assumptions

1. The checking account balance is maintained at $3,000 and is noninterest bearing.

2. The savings account earns 5 percent annually. Interest accumulates in the account.

3. Surplus cash earns 5 1/4 percent annually.

4. The money market funds earn 5 1/2 percent annually. Interest accumulates in the account.

5. Larry's salary increases at 6 percent annually.

6. Anne's listed stocks and bonds will increase in value at 5 percent annually. Yields on these securities will average 4 percent annually.

7. Stock in Millers is based on 1993 year-end book value and will increase in value at 5 percent annually.

8. The personal residence will increase in value at 4 percent annually.

9. Property taxes on the residence will increase at 3 percent annually.

10. The resort condominium will increase in value at 8 percent annually.

11. Property taxes on the condominium will increase at 6 percent annually.

12. Increase or decrease in the value of household furnishings is ignored.

13. The value of the commercial building will increase at 4 percent annually. Net rental income from this property increases at 6 percent annually.

14. Nondeductible living expenses and charitable contributions increase at 6 percent annually.

15. The profit-sharing plan will earn 6 percent annually.

16. The cash values of the life insurance policies will grow at 8 percent annually.

1994

INCOME STATEMENT

LARRY & ANNE MILLER

CASE II	1994	1995	1996	1997	1998
Earned Income					
Salaries - Larry	68,900	73,034	77,416	82,061	86,985
	68,900	73,034	77,416	82,061	86,985
Interest/Dividends					
Notes Rec - Doug	14,296	12,958	11,479	9,845	8,041
Notes Rec - Steve	0	23,757	46,315	44,590	42,706
Stocks/Bonds - Anne	4,326	4,542	4,769	5,008	5,258
Savings Acct - Anne	600	630	662	695	729
Money Market-Larry	2,530	2,669	2,816	2,971	3,134
Investable Cash	1,613	5,505	10,711	16,727	23,083
	23,365	50,061	76,752	79,836	82,951
Investments					
Rent-Commerc'l Bldg	33,000	34,980	37,079	39,304	41,662
Rent - Condo	4,000	4,000	4,000	4,000	4,000
	37,000	38,980	41,079	43,304	45,662
Other					
State Tax Refund	0	2	2	3	3
	0	2	2	3	3
Net Capital Gain	5,114	13,802	23,684	25,976	28,487
Adj Gross Income	134,379	175,887	218,941	231,192	244,099
Deductions					
Charitable 50%	3,000	3,180	3,371	3,573	3,787
State Tax Paid	6,901	9,235	11,656	12,332	13,045
Property Tax - Home	1,150	1,185	1,220	1,257	1,294
Property Tax -Condo	1,000	1,060	1,124	1,191	1,262
Reductn For High Inc	-770	-1,902	-3,075	-3,319	-3,580
Gross Deductions	11,281	12,758	14,296	15,033	15,808
Standard Deduction	6,200	6,400	6,600	6,850	7,100
Allowed Deductions	11,281	12,758	14,296	15,033	15,808
Pers Exemptions	4,700	4,606	3,264	3,016	2,916
Taxable Income	118,398	158,523	201,381	213,142	225,375
Fed Income Tax	29,079	40,986	55,088	58,594	62,238
Fed Tax Bracket	31.0	31.0	36.0	36.0	36.0

6.34

1994 **BALANCE SHEET**

LARRY & ANNE MILLER

CASE II

	1994	1995	1996	1997	1998
LIQUID ASSETS					
Cash Balance	3,007	3,042	3,030	3,094	3,000
Cash Deposits					
Savings Acct - Anne	12,600	13,230	13,892	14,587	15,316
Investable Cash	63,063	152,142	266,591	387,345	515,081
Money Market-Larry	48,530	51,199	54,015	56,986	60,120
	124,193	216,571	334,498	458,918	590,517
Stocks & Bonds					
Stocks/Bonds - Anne	108,150	113,558	119,235	125,197	131,457
Miller Stock-Larry	531,481	0	0	0	0
Miller Stock - Anne	182,448	191,570	201,149	211,206	221,767
	822,079	305,128	320,384	336,404	353,224
Overpaid Taxes					
Overpaid State Tx	2	2	3	3	3
	2	2	3	3	3
Life Insurance					
Life Ins - Larry #1	20,836	22,503	24,304	26,248	28,348
Life Ins - Larry #2	8,259	8,919	9,633	10,404	11,236
Life Ins - Anne	5,281	5,704	6,160	6,653	7,185
	34,376	37,127	40,097	43,304	46,769
Liquid Assets	983,658	561,870	698,012	841,723	993,513

1994 **BALANCE SHEET** (cont.)

LARRY & ANNE MILLER

CASE II

	1994	1995	1996	1997	1998
NONLIQUID ASSETS					
Benefit Plans					
Profit Sharing Plan	69,748	73,933	78,369	83,071	88,055
	69,748	73,933	78,369	83,071	88,055
Receivables					
Notes Rec - Doug	135,934	121,812	106,211	88,976	69,937
Notes Rec - Steve	0	522,893	504,521	484,424	462,443
	135,934	644,705	610,732	573,400	532,380
Personal Property					
Home	187,200	194,688	202,476	210,575	218,998
Condo	162,000	174,960	188,957	204,073	220,399
Commercial Bldg	343,200	356,928	371,205	386,053	401,495
Automobiles	13,600	11,560	9,826	8,352	7,099
Home Furnishings	60,000	60,000	60,000	60,000	60,000
	766,000	798,136	832,463	869,053	907,992
Nonliquid Assets	971,682	1,516,775	1,521,564	1,525,524	1,528,426
Total Assets	1,955,340	2,078,645	2,219,576	2,367,247	2,521,939
Net Worth	1,955,340	2,078,645	2,219,576	2,367,247	2,521,939

1994   CASHFLOW STATEMENT

LARRY & ANNE MILLER

CASE II	1994	1995	1996	1997	1998
BEGINNING OF YEAR					
Idle Cash On Hand	3,000	3,007	3,042	3,030	3,094
SOURCES OF CASH					
Cash Income					
Salaries - Larry	68,900	73,034	77,416	82,061	86,985
Interest+Dividends	18,622	41,257	62,563	59,443	56,005
Rents/Royalties	37,000	38,980	41,079	43,304	45,662
	124,522	153,271	181,058	184,808	188,651
Debt Recovered					
Notes Rec - Doug	12,784	14,122	15,601	17,235	19,039
Notes Rec - Steve	0	8,587	18,372	20,097	21,981
	12,784	22,709	33,973	37,332	41,020
Tax Refund					
State Tax Refund	0	2	2	3	3
	0	2	2	3	3
Total Cash Inflow	137,306	175,982	215,033	222,143	229,674
Tot Cash Available	140,306	178,989	218,075	225,173	232,768

1994   CASHFLOW STATEMENT (cont.)

LARRY & ANNE MILLER

CASE II	1994	1995	1996	1997	1998
USES OF CASH					
Partly Deductible					
Charity Contrb-50%	3,000	3,180	3,371	3,573	3,787
	3,000	3,180	3,371	3,573	3,787
Not Tax Deductible					
Living Expenses	30,000	31,800	33,708	35,730	37,874
	30,000	31,800	33,708	35,730	37,874
Taxes Paid					
Fed Tax Paid	29,079	40,986	55,088	58,594	62,238
State Tax Paid	6,901	9,235	11,656	12,332	13,045
FICA/Soc Sec Tax	4,719	4,928	5,140	5,375	5,614
Real Estate Tax	2,150	2,245	2,344	2,448	2,557
	42,849	57,393	74,228	78,749	83,453
Purchase/Deposits					
Investable Cash	61,450	83,574	103,738	104,027	104,653
	61,450	83,574	103,738	104,027	104,653
Tot Cash Outflow	137,299	175,947	215,045	222,079	229,768
END OF YEAR					
Cash Balance	3,007	3,042	3,030	3,094	3,000

1994   SUPPORTING SCHEDULE

LARRY & ANNE MILLER

	JOINT 1994	JOINT 1995	JOINT 1996	JOINT 1997	JOINT 1998
CASE II					

Income
Earned Income	68,900	73,034	77,416	82,061	86,985
Adj Gross Income	134,379	175,887	218,941	231,192	244,099
Allowed Deductions	11,281	12,758	14,296	15,033	15,808
Pers Exemptions	4,700	4,606	3,264	3,016	2,916
Taxable Income	118,398	158,523	201,381	213,142	225,375

Capital Gains
Notes Rec - Doug	5,114	5,649	6,240	6,894	7,616
Notes Rec - Steve	0	8,153	17,444	19,082	20,871
Net Capital Gain	5,114	13,802	23,684	25,976	28,487
LTCG Txd At Max Rt	5,114	13,802	23,684	25,976	28,487
Notes Rec - Doug	-5,114	-5,649	-6,240	-6,894	-7,616
Notes Rec - Steve	0	-8,153	-17,444	-19,082	-20,871

Federal Tax Liab
Regular Tax	29,232	42,078	56,983	60,672	64,516
Max Tax On Cap Gn	29,079	40,986	55,088	58,594	62,238
Gross Fed Inc Tax	29,079	40,986	55,088	58,594	62,238
Fed Income Tax	29,079	40,986	55,088	58,594	62,238

Fed Tax Analysis
Indexing Factor	46	51	56	62	68
Fed Tax Bracket	31.0	31.0	36.0	36.0	36.0
$ To Next Bracket	26,716	229	90,153	90,034	90,012
Next Bracket	36.0	36.0	39.6	39.6	39.6
Previous Bracket	28.0	28.0	31.0	31.0	31.0
$ To Prev Bracket	24,134	52,421	27,697	31,916	36,188

Alt Minimum Tax
Adj Gross Income	134,379	175,887	218,941	231,192	244,099
State Tax Refund	0	-2	-2	-3	-3
Contributions	-3,000	-3,180	-3,371	-3,573	-3,787
Adjusted AMTI	131,379	172,705	215,568	227,616	240,309
Net Capital Gain	-5,114	-13,802	-23,684	-25,976	-28,487
AMT Exemptions	-45,000	-42,774	-34,529	-32,090	-29,544
AMT Taxable Inc	81,265	116,129	157,355	169,549	182,278
Gross Alt Min Tx	21,129	30,193	40,912	44,083	47,538
Fed Tax Less FTC	-29,079	-40,986	-55,088	-58,594	-62,238

6.39

1994   SUPPORTING SCHEDULE   (cont.)

LARRY & ANNE MILLER

	JOINT 1994	JOINT 1995	JOINT 1996	JOINT 1997	JOINT 1998
CASE II	----	----	----	----	----
Other Tax Liabs					
FICA/Soc Sec Tax	4,719	4,928	5,140	5,375	5,614
Adj Gross Inc	134,379	175,885	218,939	231,189	244,096
GA AGI Adjstmnts	0	-2	-2	-3	-3
GA Adj Grss Inc	134,379	175,883	218,937	231,186	244,093
GA Standard Ded	4,400	4,400	4,400	4,400	4,400
GA Itemized Ded	12,051	14,660	17,371	18,353	19,389
GA Exemptions	3,000	3,000	3,000	3,000	3,000
GA Taxable Inc	119,328	158,224	198,566	209,833	221,705
GA Regular Tax	6,899	9,233	11,653	12,329	13,042
GA Income Tax	6,899	9,233	11,653	12,329	13,042
Georgia Tax	6,899	9,233	11,653	12,329	13,042
Tot State/Local Tx	6,899	9,233	11,653	12,329	13,042
Total Inc Tax	40,697	55,147	71,881	76,298	80,894

1994   FINANCIAL SUMMARY

LARRY & ANNE MILLER

CASE II	1994	1995	1996	1997	1998
Gross Real Income					
Personal Earnings	68,900	73,034	77,416	82,061	86,985
Interest Income	19,039	45,519	71,983	74,828	77,693
Dividends Rcvd	4,326	4,542	4,769	5,008	5,258
Rent-Commerc'l Bldg	33,000	34,980	37,079	39,304	41,662
Rent - Condo	4,000	4,000	4,000	4,000	4,000
	129,265	162,075	195,247	205,201	215,597
Income & Inflation					
Gross Real Inc	129,265	162,075	195,247	205,201	215,597
Total Inc Tax	-40,697	-55,147	-71,881	-76,298	-80,894
Net Real Income	88,568	106,928	123,365	128,902	134,704
Cur Real Inc =	88,568	91,668	94,877	98,197	101,634
At Infltn Rate Of	4	4	4	4	4
Cash Flow					
Idle Cash On Hand	3,000	3,007	3,042	3,030	3,094
Norml Cash Inflow	137,306	175,982	215,033	222,143	229,674
Norml Cash Outflw	75,849	92,373	111,307	118,052	125,115
Cash Invested	61,450	83,574	103,738	104,027	104,653
Cash Balance	3,007	3,042	3,030	3,094	3,000
Net Worth					
Personal Assets	803,384	838,305	875,590	915,451	957,760
Investment Assets	1,151,954	1,240,337	1,343,983	1,451,793	1,564,176
Personal Net Worth	803,384	838,305	875,590	915,451	957,760
Investment Net Worth	1,151,954	1,240,337	1,343,983	1,451,793	1,564,176
Net Worth	1,955,340	2,078,645	2,219,576	2,367,247	2,521,939

Another important advantage of installment sales in situations such as Larry and Anne's is that such sales are not subject to the tax problems in corporate redemptions that occur as a result of the attribution rules of IRC Sec. 318 when a business is wholly owned by one family. These problems will be discussed further in the section on redemptions.

Also an installment sale takes an appreciating asset out of Larry's estate and replaces it with one that has a fixed value. In fact, the value of the installment proceeds can actually decrease if the proceeds are consumed prior to Larry's death.

If Larry were to sell Steve his entire interest in Millers in 1995 for no down payment and monthly payments calculated at 9 percent interest for a term of 15 years, Steve's annual level payments of principal and interest would be $64,687 (in 12 monthly payments). Steve's present salary obviously would not allow him to afford such high payments. In fact, it would probably be difficult to raise Steve's salary in the near future to a level that would allow him to afford these payments and avoid an IRS challenge on the reasonableness of his compensation, particularly since Millers is a C corporation.

It would not, however, be difficult to raise Steve's salary to allow him to acquire some of Larry's stock immediately through an installment sale, especially in view of the additional duties Larry would like to see Steve undertake.

Steve could purchase 101 of Larry's 167.5 shares at a projected 1994 book value of $320,483 at 9 percent interest for a term of 15 years for annual principal and interest payments of $39,007. In the early years close to $35,000 of that amount would be interest. Since Millers is a C corporation, the interest payments would be an investment interest expense to Steve and therefore subject to the limitations on the deductibility of investment interest, discussed in the next section. If Steve purchased 101 shares, he would own 126 shares (101 + 25) and the controlling interest in the corporation.

The 5-year income statement, balance sheet, and cash flow results to Larry and Anne of such a sale are shown on the following pages.

[text continues on page 6.54]

CASE III
Installment Sale of 101 Shares
of Millers Stock to Steve

CASE ASSUMPTIONS—CASE III

New Assumption

Steve purchases 101 shares of Larry's Millers stock on July 1, 1995, at a projected 1994 book value ($320,483) for no down payment at 9 percent interest for a term of 15 years. Larry remains active in the business for at least 4 years.

Continuing Assumptions

1. The checking account balance is maintained at $3,000 and is noninterest bearing.

2. The savings account earns 5 percent annually. Interest accumulates in the account.

3. Surplus cash earns 5 1/4 percent annually.

4. The money market funds earn 5 1/2 percent annually. Interest accumulates in the account.

5. Larry's salary increases at 6 percent annually.

6. Anne's listed stocks and bonds will increase in value at 5 percent annually. Yields on these securities will average 4 percent annually.

7. Stock in Millers is based on 1993 year-end book value and will increase in value at 5 percent annually.

8. The personal residence will increase in value at 4 percent annually.

9. Property taxes on the residence will increase at 3 percent annually.

10. The resort condominium will increase in value at 8 percent annually.

11. Property taxes on the condominium will increase at 6 percent annually.

12. Increase or decrease in the value of household furnishings is ignored.

13. The value of the commercial building will increase at 4 percent annually. Net rental income from this property increases at 6 percent annually.

14. Nondeductible living expenses and charitable contributions increase at 6 percent annually.

15. The profit-sharing plan will earn 6 percent annually.

16. The cash values of the life insurance policies will grow at 8 percent annually.

1994   INCOME STATEMENT

LARRY & ANNE MILLER

CASE III	1994	1995	1996	1997	1998
Earned Income					
Salaries - Larry	68,900	73,034	77,416	82,061	86,985
	68,900	73,034	77,416	82,061	86,985
Interest/Dividends					
Notes Rec - Doug	14,296	12,958	11,479	9,845	8,041
Notes Rec - Steve	0	14,325	27,928	26,889	25,753
Stocks/Bonds - Anne	4,326	4,542	4,769	5,008	5,258
Savings Acct - Anne	600	630	662	695	729
Money Market-Larry	2,530	2,669	2,816	2,971	3,134
Investable Cash	1,613	5,289	9,870	15,054	20,544
	23,365	40,413	57,524	60,462	63,459
Investments					
Rent-Commerc'l Bldg	33,000	34,980	37,079	39,304	41,662
Rent - Condo	4,000	4,000	4,000	4,000	4,000
	37,000	38,980	41,079	43,304	45,662
Other					
State Tax Refund	0	2	0	2	2
	0	2	0	2	2
Net Capital Gain	5,114	10,566	16,760	18,400	20,201
Adj Gross Income	134,379	163,003	192,779	204,237	216,316
Deductions					
Charitable 50%	3,000	3,180	3,371	3,573	3,787
State Tax Paid	6,901	8,505	10,175	10,806	11,472
Property Tax - Home	1,150	1,185	1,220	1,257	1,294
Property Tax -Condo	1,000	1,060	1,124	1,191	1,262
Reductn For High Inc	-770	-1,515	-2,290	-2,511	-2,747
Gross Deductions	11,281	12,414	13,600	14,316	15,069
Standard Deduction	6,200	6,400	6,600	6,850	7,100
Allowed Deductions	11,281	12,414	13,600	14,316	15,069
Pers Exemptions	4,700	4,900	4,284	4,160	4,104
Taxable Income	118,398	145,689	174,895	185,760	197,144
Fed Income Tax	29,079	37,104	46,107	49,343	52,737
Fed Tax Bracket	31.0	31.0	36.0	36.0	36.0

1994   **BALANCE SHEET**

LARRY & ANNE MILLER

CASE III	1994	1995	1996	1997	1998
LIQUID ASSETS					
Cash Balance	3,007	3,041	2,943	2,997	3,052
Cash Deposits					
Savings Acct - Anne	12,600	13,230	13,892	14,587	15,316
Investable Cash	63,063	143,698	242,172	346,359	456,799
Money Market-Larry	48,530	51,199	54,015	56,986	60,120
	124,193	208,127	310,079	417,932	532,235
Stocks & Bonds					
Stocks/Bonds - Anne	108,150	113,558	119,235	125,197	131,457
Miller Stock -Larry	531,481	237,572	249,451	261,923	275,019
Miller Stock - Anne	182,448	191,570	201,149	211,206	221,767
	822,079	542,700	569,835	598,327	628,243
Overpaid Taxes					
Overpaid State Tx	2	1	2	2	3
	2	1	2	2	3
Life Insurance					
Life Ins - Larry #1	20,836	22,503	24,304	26,248	28,348
Life Ins - Larry #2	8,259	8,919	9,633	10,404	11,236
Life Ins - Anne	5,281	5,704	6,160	6,653	7,185
	34,376	37,127	40,097	43,304	46,769
Liquid Assets	983,658	790,995	922,956	1,062,562	1,210,302

1994   **BALANCE SHEET** (cont.)

LARRY & ANNE MILLER

CASE III	1994	1995	1996	1997	1998

NONLIQUID ASSETS

Benefit Plans
Profit Sharing Plan	69,748	73,933	78,369	83,071	88,055
	69,748	73,933	78,369	83,071	88,055

Receivables
Notes Rec - Doug	135,934	121,812	106,211	88,976	69,937
Notes Rec - Steve	0	315,305	304,226	292,108	278,854
	135,934	437,117	410,437	381,084	348,791

Personal Property
Home	187,200	194,688	202,476	210,575	218,998
Condo	162,000	174,960	188,957	204,073	220,399
Commercial Bldg	343,200	356,928	371,205	386,053	401,495
Automobiles	13,600	11,560	9,826	8,352	7,099
Home Furnishings	60,000	60,000	60,000	60,000	60,000
	766,000	798,136	832,463	869,053	907,992

Nonliquid Assets	971,682	1,309,187	1,321,269	1,333,208	1,344,837
Total Assets	1,955,340	2,100,182	2,244,225	2,395,770	2,555,139
Net Worth	1,955,340	2,100,182	2,244,225	2,395,770	2,555,139

6.48

1994 CASHFLOW STATEMENT

LARRY & ANNE MILLER

CASE III	1994	1995	1996	1997	1998
BEGINNING OF YEAR					
Idle Cash On Hand	3,000	3,007	3,041	2,943	2,997
SOURCES OF CASH					
Cash Income					
Salaries - Larry	68,900	73,034	77,416	82,061	86,985
Interest+Dividends	18,622	31,825	44,176	41,742	39,052
Rents/Royalties	37,000	38,980	41,079	43,304	45,662
	124,522	143,839	162,671	167,107	171,698
Debt Recovered					
Notes Rec - Doug	12,784	14,122	15,601	17,235	19,039
Notes Rec - Steve	0	5,178	11,079	12,118	13,254
	12,784	19,300	26,680	29,353	32,293
Tax Refund					
State Tax Refund	0	2	0	2	2
	0	2	0	2	2
Total Cash Inflow	137,306	163,141	189,351	196,462	203,993
Tot Cash Available	140,306	166,148	192,392	199,404	206,990

1994   **CASHFLOW STATEMENT** (cont.)

LARRY & ANNE MILLER

CASE III	1994	1995	1996	1997	1998

USES OF CASH

Partly Deductible
Charity Contrb-50%	3,000	3,180	3,371	3,573	3,787
	3,000	3,180	3,371	3,573	3,787

Not Tax Deductible
Living Expenses	30,000	31,800	33,708	35,730	37,874
	30,000	31,800	33,708	35,730	37,874

Taxes Paid
Fed Tax Paid	29,079	37,104	46,107	49,343	52,737
State Tax Paid	6,901	8,505	10,175	10,806	11,472
FICA/Soc Sec Tax	4,719	4,928	5,140	5,375	5,614
Real Estate Tax	2,150	2,245	2,344	2,448	2,557
	42,849	52,781	63,766	67,971	72,380

Purchase/Deposits
Investable Cash	61,450	75,346	88,604	89,133	89,896
	61,450	75,346	88,604	89,133	89,896

Tot Cash Outflow	137,299	163,107	189,449	196,408	203,938

END OF YEAR
Cash Balance	3,007	3,041	2,943	2,997	3,052

6.50

1994 SUPPORTING SCHEDULE

LARRY & ANNE MILLER
CASE III

	JOINT 1994	JOINT 1995	JOINT 1996	JOINT 1997	JOINT 1998
Income					
Earned Income	68,900	73,034	77,416	82,061	86,985
Adj Gross Income	134,379	163,003	192,779	204,237	216,316
Allowed Deductions	11,281	12,414	13,600	14,316	15,069
Pers Exemptions	4,700	4,900	4,284	4,160	4,104
Taxable Income	118,398	145,689	174,895	185,760	197,144
Capital Gains					
Notes Rec - Doug	5,114	5,649	6,240	6,894	7,616
Notes Rec - Steve	0	4,917	10,520	11,506	12,585
Net Capital Gain	5,114	10,566	16,760	18,400	20,201
LTCG Txd At Max Rt	5,114	10,566	16,760	18,400	20,201
Notes Rec - Doug	-5,114	-5,649	-6,240	-6,894	-7,616
Notes Rec - Steve	0	-4,917	-10,520	-11,506	-12,585
Federal Tax Liab					
Regular Tax	29,232	37,458	47,448	50,815	54,353
Max Tax On Cap Gn	29,079	37,104	46,107	49,343	52,737
Gross Fed Inc Tax	29,079	37,104	46,107	49,343	52,737
Fed Income Tax	29,079	37,104	46,107	49,343	52,737
Fed Tax Analysis					
Indexing Factor	46	51	56	62	68
Fed Tax Bracket	31.0	31.0	36.0	36.0	36.0
$ To Next Bracket	26,716	9,827	109,715	109,840	109,957
Next Bracket	36.0	36.0	39.6	39.6	39.6
Previous Bracket	28.0	28.0	31.0	31.0	31.0
$ To Prev Bracket	24,134	42,823	8,135	12,110	16,243
Alt Minimum Tax					
Adj Gross Income	134,379	163,003	192,779	204,237	216,316
State Tax Refund	0	-2	0	-2	-2
Contributions	-3,000	-3,180	-3,371	-3,573	-3,787
Adjusted AMTI	131,379	159,821	189,408	200,662	212,527
Net Capital Gain	-5,114	-10,566	-16,760	-18,400	-20,201
AMT Exemptions	-45,000	-45,000	-39,338	-36,935	-34,418
AMT Taxable Inc	81,265	104,255	133,310	145,327	157,908
Gross Alt Min Tx	21,129	27,106	34,661	37,785	41,056
Fed Tax Less FTC	-29,079	-37,104	-46,107	-49,343	-52,737

6.51

1994   SUPPORTING SCHEDULE   (cont.)

LARRY & ANNE MILLER

CASE III

	JOINT 1994	JOINT 1995	JOINT 1996	JOINT 1997	JOINT 1998
Other Tax Liabs					
FICA/Soc Sec Tax	4,719	4,928	5,140	5,375	5,614
Adj Gross Inc	134,379	163,001	192,779	204,235	216,314
GA AGI Adjstmnts	0	-2	0	-2	-2
GA Adj Grss Inc	134,379	162,999	192,779	204,233	216,312
GA Standard Ded	4,400	4,400	4,400	4,400	4,400
GA Itemized Ded	12,051	13,930	15,890	16,827	17,816
GA Exemptions	3,000	3,000	3,000	3,000	3,000
GA Taxable Inc	119,328	146,070	173,889	184,406	195,497
GA Regular Tax	6,899	8,504	10,173	10,804	11,469
GA Income Tax	6,899	8,504	10,173	10,804	11,469
Georgia Tax	6,899	8,504	10,173	10,804	11,469
Tot State/Local Tx	6,899	8,504	10,173	10,804	11,469
Total Inc Tax	40,697	50,536	61,420	65,522	69,820

1994   FINANCIAL SUMMARY

LARRY & ANNE MILLER

CASE III	1994	1995	1996	1997	1998
Gross Real Income					
Personal Earnings	68,900	73,034	77,416	82,061	86,985
Interest Income	19,039	35,871	52,755	55,454	58,201
Dividends Rcvd	4,326	4,542	4,769	5,008	5,258
Rent-Commerc'l Bldg	33,000	34,980	37,079	39,304	41,662
Rent - Condo	4,000	4,000	4,000	4,000	4,000
	129,265	152,427	176,019	185,827	196,105
Income & Inflation					
Gross Real Inc	129,265	152,427	176,019	185,827	196,105
Total Inc Tax	-40,697	-50,536	-61,420	-65,522	-69,820
Net Real Income	88,568	101,891	114,598	120,305	126,285
Cur Real Inc =	88,568	91,668	94,877	98,197	101,634
At Infltn Rate Of	4	4	4	4	4
Cash Flow					
Idle Cash On Hand	3,000	3,007	3,041	2,943	2,997
Norml Cash Inflow	137,306	163,141	189,351	196,462	203,993
Norml Cash Outflw	75,849	87,761	100,845	107,275	114,042
Cash Invested	61,450	75,346	88,604	89,133	89,896
Cash Balance	3,007	3,041	2,943	2,997	3,052
Net Worth					
Personal Assets	803,384	838,303	875,503	915,354	957,813
Investment Assets	1,151,954	1,261,877	1,368,720	1,480,414	1,597,324
Personal Net Worth	803,384	838,303	875,503	915,354	957,813
Investment Net Worth	1,151,954	1,261,877	1,368,720	1,480,414	1,597,324
Net Worth	1,955,340	2,100,182	2,244,225	2,395,770	2,555,139

Avoiding the Limitation on the Deductibility of Investment Interest. In an installment sale the purchaser's deductibility of interest payments can be a crucial issue when the purchaser's salary must be raised to make such a purchase possible. In Steve's case the inability to deduct a major portion of the interest would require a substantially greater salary increase. This would increase the likelihood of the IRS's characterizing the compensation as unreasonable and therefore nondeductible by the corporation.

Generally an individual taxpayer can deduct investment interest only up to the amount of the taxpayer's *net investment income,* which means the excess of *investment income* over investment expenses.

Investment income is income from interest, dividends, rents, royalties, and all capital gains arising from the disposition of assets that produce investment income. Under the facts of this case Millers pays no dividends. Thus there will be no investment income to Steve as a result of having acquired additional stock in Millers.

Investment expenses are deductible expenses other than interest that are directly connected with the production of investment income. Steve will not be incurring investment expenses as a consequence of this transaction.

The purchase of an ownership interest in a corporation (that is, stock) has traditionally been characterized as a purchase of an asset held for investment. This has resulted in the limitation of the deductibility of interest payments under the current investment interest expense rules.

However, in 1987 the Internal Revenue Service announced its intention to treat interest on a debt incurred to purchase an interest in an *S corporation* or a *partnership* as interest incurred in the conduct of a trade or business and *not* as investment interest (IRS Announcement No. 87-4), as long as the taxpayer purchasing the interest materially participates in the business.

This means that if a taxpayer uses the installment method to purchase an interest in an S corporation or a partnership, the interest payments will be fully deductible as a business expense and not subject to the investment interest expense limitations described above.

Although Steve is not a client of the planner at this time, his ability to deduct his interest payments in connection with the purchase of Larry's stock is very important to Larry in terms of making the transaction affordable for Steve.

Millers is presently operated as a regular (C) corporation. Therefore in order to have the interest payments on Steve's obligation fully deductible as business interest payments under current IRS thinking, Millers would have to make an S election. If the S election was in effect prior to the consummation of an installment sale, it is very likely that Steve could take advantage of the position taken by the IRS in Announcement 87-4 and deduct the full amount of his interest payments as a business expense.

However, the other effects of making an S election in this case must be explored.

Using an S Election to Facilitate the Transfer of a Business Interest

---

NOTE TO STUDENTS

To avoid repetition, background information on S corporations such as that contained on pages 3.23–3.26 has been omitted. In an actual plan this type of information should be presented to the client for completeness. In addition, if the student is not completely familiar with this material, it should be reviewed before proceeding through this suggested solution.

The Tax on "Built-in Gains"

Millers would qualify for an election to be taxed as an S corporation, since it meets the basic requirements for the election. However, qualification is not the only factor that must be considered.

First, a special income tax liability can result in the case of existing C corporations that make elections under Subchapter S. Briefly stated, this tax liability is designed to prevent taxpayers from using S elections to circumvent the corporate-level tax imposed on corporate liquidations under current federal income tax law. This tax that can result from an S election is referred to as the *built-in gains tax*.

A detailed explanation of these provisions is beyond the scope of this plan as there is a tremendous amount of complexity involved. In summary, however, Millers could be subject to both a corporate-level built-in gains tax and a shareholder-level tax upon the subsequent sale of any inventory that existed prior to the time of an S election that is sold within 10 years of the effective date of such election (IRC Sec. 1374(d)). The corporate-level tax in this situation is assessed at a rate of 34 percent on the amount of the inventory's untaxed gain existing at the time of the S election. The shareholder-level tax on the same gain is assessed at the marginal rate of each shareholder.

The inventory appears to be the only significant "ordinary income" type of asset that would be subject to the built-in gains tax if an S election were made in this case. Millers accounts receivable have already been "booked" for income tax purposes under the accrual method of accounting. Since the receivables have already been recognized for tax purposes, they are not subject to the built-in gains tax.

The built-in gains tax will also apply to the corporation's capital assets. Any capital assets sold by the corporation within 10 years of the S election will be subject to a 34 percent corporate-level tax (in addition to the tax on the shareholders) with respect to the amount of appreciation that was "built in" or existing at the time of the S election. However, since Larry owns the store building individually, only the property or improvements the corporation owns can be taxed under these rules. If the corporation waits 10 years after an S election before selling its capital assets, the tax will not be imposed. Also any capital assets sold before an S election became effective will be taxed at the corporation's marginal rate but will not be subject to the double tax that would result if the assets were sold after an S election.

As previously stated, sales of existing inventory *after* an S election will result in a built-in gains tax. One practical way to minimize this tax is to reduce inventory as much as possible just before the first day of the calendar year in which the S election becomes effective. If there is less inventory existing at the time an S election becomes effective, the built-in gains tax will be less of a problem.

Clearly these are sophisticated tax matters that the financial planner cannot single-handedly resolve. Larry's accountant and attorney must be consulted to determine the built-in gains tax liability that could result from an S election.

Larry's accountant would also have to examine how distributions by the corporation after an S election might be affected by the complex rules regarding previously taxed income of S corporations and the shareholders' "accumulated adjustment account" ("triple A account"). These matters are generally beyond the scope of this discussion.

However, it is significant to note that because Millers has substantial retained earnings, dividend treatment can still be applied to certain corporate distributions even after the time of an S election because Millers would still have substantial earnings and profits accumulated during its life as a C corporation. As a result the tax rules regarding redemptions (discussed in a later section) will still apply after an S election to determine whether dividend treatment would be applied to the proceeds of any proposed redemption. As discussed below, the treatment of a stock redemption as a dividend for federal income tax purposes is not a desirable result.

Practical Considerations in Planning for an S Election

At such time as Millers makes an S election, Larry and Steve will no longer be eligible for tax-favored fringe benefits. They will be taxed on the value of their medical coverage, for example. Also they will be prohibited from borrowing from their profit-sharing plan. Most significantly the shareholders will be taxed on their proportionate shares of the corporation's taxable income, regardless of whether the income is distributed. Therefore care must be taken that Larry and Anne will receive at least enough money from Millers in the form of distributed corporate taxable income to cover this additional tax liability.

If Steve is sold a controlling interest in Millers, he will basically have the authority to decide how much of the corporation's taxable income should be distributed to its shareholders. In this case it is unlikely that Steve will refuse to distribute enough to allow his father to pay the additional taxes. However, the contract for the sale of Larry's stock could include a provision requiring Steve to make such distributions if Larry is concerned over the issue. This should be further explored before any agreements are signed.

It should be noted that an S election could provide Larry and Anne with additional retirement income if a substantial portion of their share of corporate taxable income is distributed to them. In addition, such distributions are with respect to stock ownership and not made in exchange for performance of services. Therefore the issue of reasonableness of compensation is generally avoided. Such distributions could be made regardless of whether Larry is working for the corporation at the time.

The Treasury has recently issued regulations that deal with various aspects of operating as an S corporation. These regulations make operating as an S corporation additionally burdensome, since compliance with certain formalities becomes more important than ever. The most urgent illustration is the Treasury position dealing with the inadvertent issuance of a second class of stock. Although the latest treasury regulations dealing with the inadvertent issuance of a second class of stock are not as strict as earlier pronouncements, this issue is still a cause for concern and needs to be borne in mind. The issuance of certain debt instruments can be viewed by the IRS as a second class of stock, which would have the effect of invalidating the S election.

The possible problems associated with an S election have been noted. However, there appears to be no substantial disadvantage to Millers if they make an S election. The principal advantage would be to allow Steve to deduct interest payments on his installment obligation incurred to acquire S corporation stock. This would make such a purchase much more feasible in terms of its affordability to Steve. Another advantage would be the lower individual tax rates (as compared to corporate rates) imposed on taxable income of the corporation in excess of $75,000. Therefore subject to the agreement of Larry's attorney and accountant, our recommendation would be for Millers to make an election to be taxed as an S corporation, effective for the 1995 tax year. The election should be made in 1994 but in no event may it be made later than March 15, 1995, in order for it to be effective for taxable year 1995. The election must be made before Larry makes an installment sale of his stock to Steve.

In addition, if Anne's stock in Millers is redeemed immediately by the corporation (as will be discussed later), it will not be necessary for Steve to purchase 101 shares from Larry in order to acquire a controlling interest in the business. After Anne's stock is redeemed, Steve need only purchase 72 shares to own more than 50 percent of the total value of the stock then outstanding. This is preferable to Steve's purchasing additional shares because it will reduce his total installment obligation. Also the gain on Anne's shares will be treated in a tax-favored manner (as will also be discussed later), since dividend treatment to Larry and Anne can be avoided for this particular redemption.

A 15-year installment sale of 72 shares will cost Steve $28,342 per year in installment payments, of which close to $25,000 will be deductible interest in the early years. Steve should be able to service this debt through either a salary increase, a distribution of the S corporation taxable income, or a combination of both.

The following are the 5-year income statement, balance sheet, and cash flow results to Larry and Anne if Steve purchases 72 shares of Larry's stock at a 1994 book value of $228,463, payable over 15 years at an interest rate of 9 percent, and if the corporation also redeems Anne's 57.5 shares at a 1994 book value of $182,453, payable over 10 years at an interest rate of 9 percent. The projections do not show additional income from Millers as a result of an S election. Therefore the assumption is that Larry receives an annual distribution from Millers equal to his share of the tax liability arising from his stock ownership, resulting in no net cash effect.

[text continues on page 6.71]

CASE IV
Installment Sale of 72 Shares
of Millers Stock to Steve
and Redemption by Millers
of Anne's 57.5 Shares
of Millers Stock

CASE ASSUMPTIONS—CASE IV

New Assumptions

1. Steve purchases 72 shares of Larry's Millers stock on July 1, 1995, at a projected 1994 book value ($228,463) for no down payment at 9 percent interest for a term of 15 years. Larry remains active in the business for at least 4 years.

2. Millers redeems Anne's 57.5 shares on December 1, 1994, at a projected 1993 book value of $182,453, financed by an installment note for the total amount payable over 10 years at 9 percent interest.

Continuing Assumptions

1. The checking account balance is maintained at $3,000 and is noninterest bearing.

2. The savings account earns 5 percent annually. Interest accumulates in the account.

3. Surplus cash earns 5 1/4 percent annually.

4. The money market funds earn 5 1/2 percent annually. Interest accumulates in the account.

5. Larry's salary increases at 6 percent annually.

6. Anne's listed stocks and bonds will increase in value at 5 percent annually. Yields on these securities will average 4 percent annually.

7. Stock in Millers is based on 1993 year-end book value and will increase in value at 5 percent annually.

8. The personal residence will increase in value at 4 percent annually.

9. Property taxes on the residence will increase at 3 percent annually.

10. The resort condominium will increase in value at 8 percent annually.

11. Property taxes on the condominium will increase at 6 percent annually.

12. Increase or decrease in the value of household furnishings is ignored.

13. The value of the commercial building will increase at 4 percent annually. Net rental income from this property increases at 6 percent annually.

14. Nondeductible living expenses and charitable contributions increase at 6 percent annually.

15. The profit-sharing plan will earn 6 percent annually.

16. The cash values of the life insurance policies will grow at 8 percent annually.

1994 **INCOME STATEMENT**

LARRY & ANNE MILLER

CASE IV	1994	1995	1996	1997	1998
Earned Income					
Salaries - Larry	68,900	73,034	77,416	82,061	86,985
	68,900	73,034	77,416	82,061	86,985
Interest/Dividends					
Notes Rec - Doug	14,296	12,958	11,479	9,845	8,041
Notes Rec - Steve	0	10,212	19,909	19,169	18,358
Notes Rec - Miller	1,368	15,853	14,739	13,520	12,186
Stocks/Bonds - Anne	4,326	4,542	4,769	5,008	5,258
Savings Acct - Anne	600	630	662	695	729
Money Market-Larry	2,530	2,669	2,816	2,971	3,134
Investable Cash	1,655	5,778	11,079	16,908	23,075
	24,775	52,642	65,453	68,116	70,781
Investments					
Rent-Commerc'l Bldg	33,000	34,980	37,079	39,304	41,662
Rent - Condo	4,000	4,000	4,000	4,000	4,000
	37,000	38,980	41,079	43,304	45,662
Other					
State Tax Refund	0	0	2	2	3
	0	0	2	2	3
Net Capital Gain	5,760	17,292	22,641	24,833	27,238
Adj Gross Income	136,435	181,948	206,599	218,324	230,680
Deductions					
Charitable 50%	3,000	3,180	3,371	3,573	3,787
State Tax Paid	7,017	9,578	10,957	11,604	12,285
Property Tax - Home	1,150	1,185	1,220	1,257	1,294
Property Tax -Condo	1,000	1,060	1,124	1,191	1,262
Reductn For High Inc	-832	-2,083	-2,704	-2,933	-3,178
Gross Deductions	11,335	12,919	13,967	14,692	15,451
Standard Deduction	6,200	6,400	6,600	6,850	7,100
Allowed Deductions	11,335	12,919	13,967	14,692	15,451
Pers Exemptions	4,700	4,312	3,774	3,536	3,456
Taxable Income	120,400	164,717	188,858	200,096	211,773
Fed Income Tax	29,680	42,925	50,663	53,989	57,441
Fed Tax Bracket	31.0	36.0	36.0	36.0	36.0

6.63

1994   **BALANCE SHEET**

LARRY & ANNE MILLER

CASE IV	1994	1995	1996	1997	1998
LIQUID ASSETS					
Cash Balance	3,007	2,898	2,940	3,000	3,064
Cash Deposits					
Savings Acct - Anne	12,600	13,230	13,892	14,587	15,316
Investable Cash	64,699	161,204	271,945	389,069	513,050
Money Market-Larry	48,530	51,199	54,015	56,986	60,120
	125,829	225,633	339,852	460,642	588,486
Stocks & Bonds					
Stocks/Bonds - Anne	108,150	113,558	119,235	125,197	131,457
Miller Stock -Larry	531,481	329,592	346,072	363,375	381,544
	639,631	443,150	465,307	488,572	513,001
Overpaid Taxes					
Overpaid State Tx	1	2	2	3	3
	1	2	2	3	3
Life Insurance					
Life Ins - Larry #1	20,836	22,503	24,304	26,248	28,348
Life Ins - Larry #2	8,259	8,919	9,633	10,404	11,236
Life Ins - Anne	5,281	5,704	6,160	6,653	7,185
	34,376	37,127	40,097	43,304	46,769
Liquid Assets	802,845	708,810	848,198	995,522	1,151,323

1994   **BALANCE SHEET** (cont.)

LARRY & ANNE MILLER

CASE IV   1994   1995   1996   1997   1998
                        ----   ----   ----   ----   ----

NONLIQUID ASSETS

Benefit Plans
  Profit Sharing Plan   69,748   73,933   78,369   83,071   88,055
                        --------   --------   --------   --------   --------
                        69,748   73,933   78,369   83,071   88,055

Receivables
  Notes Rec - Doug   135,934   121,812   106,211   88,976   69,937
  Notes Rec - Steve   0   224,772   216,874   208,236   198,787
  Notes Rec - Miller   181,505   169,624   156,629   142,415   126,867
                        --------   --------   --------   --------   --------
                        317,439   516,208   479,714   439,627   395,591

Personal Property
  Home   187,200   194,688   202,476   210,575   218,998
  Condo   162,000   174,960   188,957   204,073   220,399
  Commercial Bldg   343,200   356,928   371,205   386,053   401,495
  Automobiles   13,600   11,560   9,826   8,352   7,099
  Home Furnishings   60,000   60,000   60,000   60,000   60,000
                        --------   --------   --------   --------   --------
                        766,000   798,136   832,463   869,053   907,992
                        ========   ========   ========   ========   ========
Nonliquid Assets   1,153,187   1,388,278   1,390,546   1,391,751   1,391,637
                        ========   ========   ========   ========   ========
Total Assets   1,956,032   2,097,088   2,238,744   2,387,273   2,542,960

Net Worth   1,956,032   2,097,088   2,238,744   2,387,273   2,542,960
                        ========   ========   ========   ========   ========

1994   **CASHFLOW STATEMENT**

LARRY & ANNE MILLER

CASE IV	1994	1995	1996	1997	1998
BEGINNING OF YEAR					
Idle Cash On Hand	3,000	3,007	2,898	2,940	3,000
SOURCES OF CASH					
Cash Income					
Salaries - Larry	68,900	73,034	77,416	82,061	86,985
Interest+Dividends	19,990	43,565	50,896	47,542	43,843
Rents/Royalties	37,000	38,980	41,079	43,304	45,662
	125,890	155,579	169,391	172,907	176,489
Debt Recovered					
Notes Rec - Doug	12,784	14,122	15,601	17,235	19,039
Notes Rec - Steve	0	3,691	7,898	8,638	9,449
Notes Rec - Miller	943	11,881	12,995	14,214	15,548
	13,727	29,694	36,494	40,087	44,036
Tax Refund					
State Tax Refund	0	0	2	2	3
	0	0	2	2	3
Total Cash Inflow	139,617	185,273	205,887	212,996	220,528
Tot Cash Available	142,617	188,280	208,785	215,936	223,529

6.66

1994   **CASHFLOW STATEMENT** (cont.)

LARRY & ANNE MILLER

CASE IV	1994	1995	1996	1997	1998
USES OF CASH					
Partly Deductible					
Charity Contrb-50%	3,000	3,180	3,371	3,573	3,787
	3,000	3,180	3,371	3,573	3,787
Not Tax Deductible					
Living Expenses	30,000	31,800	33,708	35,730	37,874
	30,000	31,800	33,708	35,730	37,874
Taxes Paid					
Fed Tax Paid	29,680	42,925	50,663	53,989	57,441
State Tax Paid	7,017	9,578	10,957	11,604	12,285
FICA/Soc Sec Tax	4,719	4,928	5,140	5,375	5,614
Real Estate Tax	2,150	2,245	2,344	2,448	2,557
	43,566	59,675	69,104	73,416	77,897
Purchase/Deposits					
Investable Cash	63,044	90,727	99,662	100,216	100,906
	63,044	90,727	99,662	100,216	100,906
Tot Cash Outflow	139,610	185,382	205,845	212,935	220,464
END OF YEAR					
Cash Balance	3,007	2,898	2,940	3,000	3,064

6.67

1994 **SUPPORTING SCHEDULE**

LARRY & ANNE MILLER

CASE IV	JOINT 1994	JOINT 1995	JOINT 1996	JOINT 1997	JOINT 1998
Income					
Earned Income	68,900	73,034	77,416	82,061	86,985
Adj Gross Income	136,435	181,948	206,599	218,324	230,680
Allowed Deductions	11,335	12,919	13,967	14,692	15,451
Pers Exemptions	4,700	4,312	3,774	3,536	3,456
Taxable Income	120,400	164,717	188,858	200,096	211,773
Capital Gains					
Notes Rec - Doug	5,114	5,649	6,240	6,894	7,616
Notes Rec - Steve	0	3,505	7,499	8,202	8,972
Notes Rec - Miller	646	8,138	8,902	9,737	10,650
Net Capital Gain	5,760	17,292	22,641	24,833	27,238
LTCG Txd At Max Rt	5,760	17,292	22,641	24,833	27,238
Notes Rec - Doug	-5,114	-5,649	-6,240	-6,894	-7,616
Notes Rec - Steve	0	-3,505	-7,499	-8,202	-8,972
Notes Rec - Miller	-646	-8,138	-8,902	-9,737	-10,650
Federal Tax Liab					
Regular Tax	29,853	44,308	52,475	55,976	59,620
Max Tax On Cap Gn	29,680	42,925	50,663	53,989	57,441
Gross Fed Inc Tax	29,680	42,925	50,663	53,989	57,441
Fed Income Tax	29,680	42,925	50,663	53,989	57,441
Fed Tax Analysis					
Indexing Factor	46	51	56	62	68
Fed Tax Bracket	31.0	36.0	36.0	36.0	36.0
$ To Next Bracket	25,360	111,325	101,633	101,937	102,365
Next Bracket	36.0	39.6	39.6	39.6	39.6
Previous Bracket	28.0	31.0	31.0	31.0	31.0
$ To Prev Bracket	25,490	2,475	16,217	20,013	23,835
Alt Minimum Tax					
Adj Gross Income	136,435	181,948	206,599	218,324	230,680
State Tax Refund	0	0	-2	-2	-3
Contributions	-3,000	-3,180	-3,371	-3,573	-3,787
Adjusted AMTI	133,435	178,768	203,226	214,749	226,890
Net Capital Gain	-5,760	-17,292	-22,641	-24,833	-27,238
AMT Exemptions	-45,000	-42,131	-37,354	-35,021	-32,587
AMT Taxable Inc	82,675	119,345	143,231	154,894	167,065
Gross Alt Min Tx	21,496	31,030	37,240	40,273	43,437
Fed Tax Less FTC	-29,680	-42,925	-50,663	-53,989	-57,441

6.68

1994   **SUPPORTING SCHEDULE** (cont.)

LARRY & ANNE MILLER

	JOINT 1994	JOINT 1995	JOINT 1996	JOINT 1997	JOINT 1998
CASE IV	----	----	----	----	----
Other Tax Liabs					
FICA/Soc Sec Tax	4,719	4,928	5,140	5,375	5,614
Adj Gross Inc	136,435	181,948	206,597	218,322	230,677
GA AGI Adjstmnts	0	0	-2	-2	-3
GA Adj Grss Inc	136,435	181,948	206,595	218,320	230,674
GA Standard Ded	4,400	4,400	4,400	4,400	4,400
GA Itemized Ded	12,167	15,003	16,672	17,625	18,629
GA Exemptions	3,000	3,000	3,000	3,000	3,000
GA Taxable Inc	121,268	163,946	186,923	197,695	209,046
GA Regular Tax	7,016	9,576	10,955	11,601	12,282
GA Income Tax	7,016	9,576	10,955	11,601	12,282
Georgia Tax	7,016	9,576	10,955	11,601	12,282
Tot State/Local Tx	7,016	9,576	10,955	11,601	12,282
Total Inc Tax	41,415	57,429	66,758	70,965	75,337

1994

FINANCIAL SUMMARY

LARRY & ANNE MILLER

CASE IV	1994	1995	1996	1997	1998
Gross Real Income					
Personal Earnings	68,900	73,034	77,416	82,061	86,985
Interest Income	20,449	48,100	60,684	63,108	65,523
Dividends Rcvd	4,326	4,542	4,769	5,008	5,258
Rent-Commerc'l Bldg	33,000	34,980	37,079	39,304	41,662
Rent - Condo	4,000	4,000	4,000	4,000	4,000
	130,675	164,656	183,948	193,481	203,427
Income & Inflation					
Gross Real Inc	130,675	164,656	183,948	193,481	203,427
Total Inc Tax	-41,415	-57,429	-66,758	-70,965	-75,337
Net Real Income	89,260	107,227	117,189	122,516	128,091
Cur Real Inc =	89,260	92,384	95,618	98,964	102,428
At Infltn Rate Of	4	4	4	4	4
Cash Flow					
Idle Cash On Hand	3,000	3,007	2,898	2,940	3,000
Norml Cash Inflow	139,617	185,273	205,887	212,996	220,528
Norml Cash Outflw	76,566	94,655	106,183	112,719	119,558
Cash Invested	63,044	90,727	99,662	100,216	100,906
Cash Balance	3,007	2,898	2,940	3,000	3,064
Net Worth					
Personal Assets	803,384	838,161	875,500	915,358	957,825
Investment Assets	1,152,647	1,258,923	1,363,242	1,471,912	1,585,133
Personal Net Worth	803,384	838,161	875,500	915,358	957,825
Investment Net Worth	1,152,647	1,258,923	1,363,242	1,471,912	1,585,133
Net Worth	1,956,032	2,097,088	2,238,744	2,387,273	2,542,960

Additional Principles Applicable to the Taxation of Installment Sales. As a general rule installment reporting of the income from an installment sale will be allowed even though the parties to the sale are closely related persons. However, abusive tax strategies have occurred in this area. These generally involve a person selling to a close relative on an installment basis and having the purchaser (who has received a step-up in basis on the sale) dispose of the asset at little or no gain by selling it again almost immediately for cash while still paying for the original purchase over many years. To combat such abuses the Code provides that a disposition of the property that is the subject of an installment sale between related parties cannot be made by the purchaser without the seller's being treated for tax purposes as if he or she has received the balance of the purchase price (subject to some limitations) regardless of whether the price has actually been paid to the original seller (IRC Sec. 453(e)).

Since this provision is aimed at abusive situations, it does not apply in many cases. In fact, unless the property that is the subject of the installment sale consists of marketable securities, the period during which a disposition of the property will trigger adverse consequences to the related seller expires 2 years after the initial sale.

Since the stock of Millers is not a marketable security, only the 2-year rule against dispositions will apply.

Under the current federal income tax laws there are additional rules regarding the tax treatment of certain installment sales. The installment tax treatment is no longer permitted for sales of publicly traded property such as marketable securities. In addition, installment sales of property such as inventory and certain real estate may subject the seller to the alternative minimum tax on the full amount of gain in the year of sale. However, there is currently no reason for concern that the alternative minimum tax will be applied to the full amount of gain in the case of an installment sale of closely held (nonpublicly traded) stock. However, developments in the tax law should be closely monitored before entering into any installment sale, given the uncertain tax climate.

One additional potential problem of an installment sale such as the one proposed here is a purely personal one and is not tax related. The undertaking of such a purchase by a younger-generation successor of a family business means that for a very long period of time, his or her life-style will be curtailed by the purchase. Since Steve's ability to purchase the stock depends on increasing his total income from Millers substantially, the business must expand somewhat in order to allow him substantially more income. This means that during the period when he is raising and educating his family, available cash flow may be limited. As long as Steve and his wife have thoughtfully considered this fact and are committed to the business, there may be no further problems. It is always advisable, however, to point out these implications to the seller as well as to the purchaser.

Redemptions

Few owners of closely held businesses who spend their working life in a small business realize that as a matter of federal income tax law, it may be very difficult to transform their investment in that corporation into another type of investment that may be more appropriate for their later years without paying a heavy price in taxes. Because of the family attribution rules of IRC Sec. 318, this is especially true when several members of a family own stock in the corporation.

The problem with redemptions arises from the rule that dividends are not deductible to the corporation when distributed to corporate shareholders and are taxable to the shareholders as ordinary income. In most small wholly owned or family-owned corporations, dividends are either never paid or are paid rarely and in small, often insignificant, amounts. This is usually not troubling to the shareholders of these corporations, who are most often also employees of the corporation and who depend on salaries rather than dividends for their livelihoods.

In the absence of statutory restraints on corporate redemptions, any time a shareholder of a wholly owned corporation wished to take money out of the corporation without subjecting these funds to dividend treatment (ordinary income to the recipient and nondeductibility to the corporation), the shareholder could simply sell some shares back to the corporation for cash and pay the federal income tax on the gain.

An example of such a transaction follows:

Mickey MacDonald owns 100 percent (300 shares) of M. M. Corporation, each share of which is worth $1,000. He causes M. M. Corporation, which has earnings and profits, to redeem 10 shares of his stock for $10,000. Result: Mickey still owns 100 percent of M. M. Corporation although he now owns only 290 shares of stock.

Mickey would like to treat the redemption as the sale of a capital asset and pay taxes only on the gain. Since the redemption is essentially the same as if a cash dividend had been paid to Mickey, the Internal Revenue Code provides that the entire $10,000 will be treated as ordinary income.

The question of whether a corporate redemption will qualify as a sale or exchange of a capital asset is still significant, even though there is no longer a 60 percent exclusion for long-term capital gains. Whether the redemption qualifies for capital-gains treatment determines whether the taxpayer will pay taxes on the entire amount of the money or other property distributed, if treated as a dividend, or only on the amount of the gain (amount distributed − basis = gain) the taxpayer realizes on the transaction, if treated as a capital gain. Furthermore, the capital-gains rate of tax is 28 percent. In terms of the example above this principle can be illustrated as follows:

If Mickey has a basis of $400 in each of his 300 shares of stock, and if he could effect a redemption of 10 shares that would qualify for treatment as a sale or exchange, he would only pay tax on the amount of his $6,000 gain ($600 per share x 10 shares). If, however, the redemption is treated as a dividend (as it inevitably would be in our example), the entire $10,000 distribution is taxable. Note that if the distribution is treated as a dividend, Mickey's basis in the 10 shares of redeemed stock is preserved by assigning it to his remaining 290 shares.

In addition, capital losses are fully deductible against capital gains but are deductible against ordinary income only up to $3,000 in a given year. Therefore in a situation in which a taxpayer has capital losses (such as stock sales in a down market), the losses can "shelter" capital gains fully. However, a taxpayer's capital losses cannot "shelter" dividend income, except to the extent of $3,000 per year.

Requirements for Favorable Federal Income Tax Treatment. Particularly as they get older, the shareholders of closely held businesses may wish to take some or all of their investment out of the corporation so that their lifetime accumulation of wealth will no longer be subject to the frailties and errors of new management—even if the new management is to consist of their own children.

If shareholders are willing to sell their stock either to their children or to an outsider, the problems with redemptions are avoided. A redemption is defined by the Internal Revenue Code as the acquisition by a corporation of its stock from a shareholder in exchange for money or other property (excluding stock in the corporation) (IRC Sec. 317).

The purchase of a substantial interest in a business may be difficult for a younger family member to finance without altering his or her life-style even if payments are made over a period of years. Therefore redemptions are often considered in business transition plans for family businesses.

The type of redemption attempted by Mickey in the example on the preceding page is clearly an attempt to take the earnings and profits out of the corporation without treating them as dividends. However, in attempting to prevent such abuses, the Internal Revenue Code has enacted provisions that require that as a general rule a corporation's purchase of its own stock will be treated as a dividend (to the extent of the earnings and profits of the corporation) (IRC Secs. 302(d), 301(c)). This general rule will apply regardless of whether an attempt is being made to transform dividends into capital gains unless the taxpayer can meet one of the exceptions in Sec. 302(b) that will guarantee capital-gains treatment.

The exceptions include the following:

- redemptions not essentially equivalent to a dividend (IRC Sec. 302(b)(1)). This is not a precise test but basically depends on whether there is a meaningful reduction of the shareholder's interest under all the facts and circumstances of the case. For this purpose the shareholder's constructive ownership under the attribution rules of IRC Sec. 318 (discussed below) will be considered. This is a very perilous exception on which to advise a client to rely.

- substantially disproportionate redemptions. A redemption qualifies for capital-gains treatment under this exception to the general rule provided that *immediately after the redemption* (a) the redeemed shareholder's proportion of ownership of both the outstanding *voting* stock and the *common* stock of the corporation must be less than 80 percent of his or her proportionate ownership before the redemption, and (b) the redeemed shareholder must own less than 50 percent of the total voting power of all classes of stock entitled to vote (IRC Sec. 302(b)(2)).

An example of a redemption that would qualify as substantially disproportionate is the following:

> X corporation has 100 shares of one class of voting common stock outstanding. A and B each own 50 of those shares. X redeems 20 of A's 50 shares. The corporation now has 80 shares of voting common stock outstanding, of which A owns 30 and B owns 50.
>
> A's proportion of ownership before the redemption was 50 percent (50 ÷ 100). Her proportion of ownership after the redemption is 37.5 percent (30 ÷ 80). Since 50 percent x 80 percent is 40 percent, and A now owns 37.5 percent, her proportion of ownership of voting and common stock after the redemption (37.5 percent) is less than 80 percent of her proportion of ownership before the redemption (40 percent). Since A also now owns less than 50 percent of the total voting power in the corporation, both the 80 percent and 50 percent tests are met and the redemption will qualify as substantially disproportionate.

- a redemption that is a complete termination of a shareholder's interest (IRC Sec. 302(b)(3))

For corporations whose stockholders are not subject to the attribution rules of IRC Sec. 318, these exceptions are relatively straightforward. However, when they are combined with the complexities of constructive ownership through these attribution rules, they can become quite difficult, so redemptions that qualify for capital-gains treatment can become virtually impossible to achieve in family-owned corporations.

Sec. 318 Attribution Problems. For purposes of determining the ownership of a corporation before and after a redemption, the redeemed stockholder is considered to own

- all the stock he or she actually owns
- all the stock the stockholder's spouse, children, grandchildren, or parents own
- stock owned by an estate or partnership of which the stockholder is a partner or beneficiary (in proportion to his or her interest in the partnership or estate)
- stock owned by a trust of which the stockholder is a beneficiary (in proportion to his or her actuarial interest in the trust)

- stock owned by another corporation in which the stockholder also owns directly or indirectly 50 percent or more of the outstanding stock (in proportion to his or her stock ownership in the other corporation)

The family and entity attribution rules are complex, and a full discussion of them would be more extensive than necessary for this financial plan. However, some time devoted to an explanation of the family attribution rules is important to Larry and Anne's situation.

When the family attribution rules of IRC Sec. 318(a)(1) are applied to the Millers' situation, the results show that Larry owns

directly	67%
constructively (Anne's)	23
constructively (Steve's)	10
Total ownership actually and constructively	100%

If Steve buys 40 percent of the stock from Larry, the result to Larry is unchanged. He then owns 27 percent of the stock directly, *but* he still owns Anne's 23 percent and Steve's 50 percent constructively under Sec. 318. The result is that Larry's ownership for purposes of the tax treatment of a redemption under Sec. 302 is still 100 percent.

Even if Larry sold all but one share of his stock to Steve, the results are unchanged in that Larry would then own

directly	.4%
constructively (Anne's)	23.0
constructively (Steve's)	76.6
Total ownership actually and constructively	100.0%

Because Larry will always be deemed to own the stock owned by his wife and son, he will not be able to effect a lifetime redemption that will enable him to both qualify for capital-gains treatment *and* still remain active in the business. The significance of remaining active in the business will be addressed in the next section.

Sec. 302(c)(2) Election—The Waiver Approach. The difficulties in redeeming shareholders in family-owned corporations without dividend treatment could force some shareholders into very difficult tax situations even though they are making no improper attempt to withdraw the earnings and profits of the corporation. Consequently the Internal Revenue Code provides a method that can be elected to waive the family attribution rules of IRC Sec. 318 and allow the redemption of a shareholder such as Larry to qualify as a complete termination of his interest (IRC Sec. 302(c)(2)).

In order to effect this result, the shareholder must dispose of all his or her stock. However, there is no requirement that all the stock must be redeemed, and combinations of sales and redemptions are not unusual. In addition, immediately after the redemption the shareholder must have no continuing interest (including an interest as an officer, director, or employee) in the corporation except that of a creditor and must agree not to acquire an interest in the corporation (except by inheritance) within 10 years from the date of the redemption. Furthermore, the employee must file an agreement with the Internal Revenue Service agreeing to notify them if an interest is acquired within the prohibited period.

Even if these conditions are met, the redemption will not qualify for capital-gains treatment if either (1) any portion of the stock that is being redeemed was acquired within 10 years of the date of the redemption from a person whose ownership of the stock would be attributable to the person whose stock is being redeemed, or (2) if any person whose stock would be attributable to the person whose stock is being redeemed has acquired that stock within a 10-year period directly or indirectly from the person whose stock is being redeemed, unless his or her stock is also redeemed. For example, a husband cannot have given a portion of his stock to his wife and have the corporation redeem the remainder of the stock he holds under a Sec. 302(c)(2) election and receive capital-gains treatment unless the gift took place more than 10 years prior to the redemption and Sec. 302(c)(2) election. Also he could not have been the recipient of a gift of Millers stock from his wife during that 10-year period.

Since Larry wishes to continue his involvement with Millers for the foreseeable future, it is unlikely that this election out (waiver approach) would appeal to him at present. As his involvement with Millers becomes less important to him, however, this type of a redemption may become viable.

Anne, on the other hand, could take advantage of this provision immediately to have her interest in Millers redeemed. This would be beneficial to Anne because she has a basis of $1,000 per share in Millers, which could be recovered tax free when the redemption proceeds are paid. In contrast, Larry's basis in his stock is $160.

If properly structured, the redemption does not have to drain the corporation of needed cash flow and can provide Anne and Larry with a steady income stream as well as an opportunity to spread the gain over a number of years. For example, Anne's shares could be surrendered and a Sec. 302(c)(2) election made in 1994 or 1995 in return for the corporation's obligation to pay the redemption price over a period of years at an appropriate interest rate. The interest should be deductible to the corporation. The principal payments, however, are not.

In conclusion, the recommendation would be that Anne's shares be redeemed with an appropriate Sec. 302(c)(2) election and that the corporation be allowed to spread payments by an installment payout, such as the 10-year installment payout illustrated in case IV. If the income picture of Millers requires a lower payment, the term of the obligation could be lengthened, thereby lowering the annual payment. As already noted, this redemption should be coordinated with the installment sale to Steve to allow him to acquire control of the business as a result of both transactions. Larry, on the other hand, can retain any of his shares not sold to Steve until he is ready to retire completely from Millers.

If he continues to be involved with Millers until his death, he may wish to leave his remaining shares to Steve with appropriate provisions that Steve's portion of Larry's residuary estate be adjusted to reflect the bequest of the stock.

Sec. 303 Redemptions. Many shareholders of family-owned businesses do continue to hold stock in their corporations until death with the result that their estates are illiquid. IRC Sec. 303 provides a method for assuring that sufficient stock can be redeemed without dividend treatment to pay estate taxes and deductible funeral and administrative expenses if certain requirements are met. Redemption proceeds in excess of the estate's funeral and administrative expenses cannot be treated under Sec. 303. The threshold test for utilizing a Sec. 303 redemption is that the value of the stock of the corporation owned by the decedent must exceed 35 percent of his or her adjusted gross estate for federal estate tax purposes.

Capital-gains treatment is particularly important in the case of a redemption from a decedent's estate, regardless of whether the redemption is treated under Sec. 302 or Sec. 303. Since the estate has received a stepped-up basis in the redeemed stock, capital-gains treatment will generally provide little or no income tax liability for the estate. If dividend treatment applies, the estate loses the benefit of the stepped-up basis, since the proceeds will be fully taxed assuming the corporation has sufficient earnings and profits.

It should be noted that Larry's shares are valued at $286,601 and his adjusted gross estate is assumed to be $1,395,102. Therefore the 35 percent test is not satisfactorily met.

In short, if Larry were to die with his present stock holdings, his estate would not qualify for a Sec. 303 redemption. Even if Larry's estate were to qualify today for Sec. 303 treatment, the planned sale of shares in Millers to Steve would reduce the stock ownership amount below the 35 percent threshold level.

Since Larry has indicated a strong desire not to force Steve to wait until Larry's death to take control of Millers, a Sec. 303 redemption would not be appropriate in any event.

Recapitalizations

General Requirements. The Internal Revenue Code provides for tax-free treatment of various corporate reorganizations (IRC Sec. 368). One type of reorganization is an "E" reorganization—a "recapitalization" (IRC Sec. 368(a)(1)(E)). The Code does not define a recapitalization and the regulations offer no definition, but they do contain some examples of transactions that would qualify as recapitalizations. The most frequently quoted general definition is from a 1942 United States Supreme Court decision that described a recapitalization as a "reshuffling of a capital structure within the framework of an existing corporation" (*Helvering v. Southwest Consolidated Corp.*, 315 U.S. 194 (1942)).

In the past a common type of such a reshuffling of capital was the exchange by older shareholders of all or a part of their common stock in the corporation for preferred stock. This technique was used for some or all of the following purposes: to transfer control to younger-generation management, to assure the older shareholder of an income stream from dividends on the preferred stock, or to attempt to freeze the value of the older shareholder's interest in the corporation for estate tax purposes.

In the typical recapitalization all the shareholders were offered the opportunity pursuant to a plan of reorganization to exchange their shares of common stock for preferred stock. Normally the older shareholders elected the exchange, while the younger shareholders chose to retain their shares of common stock.

In a recapitalization if the value of the preferred stock received is equal to the value of the common stock surrendered, the transaction is generally tax-free at the time of the transfer. If the value of the preferred is less than the common surrendered, the difference in value may be treated as a taxable gift to the other shareholders. To assure equivalency of value, the preferred shares must pay a reasonable dividend, dividends must be cumulative, and the preferred stock must have liquidation preferences. The question of valuation in recapitalizations has been one of the most troublesome parts of making a decision to recapitalize a corporation. Rev. Rul. 83-120, 1983-2 C.B. 170 provided valuable specific advice on the valuation question in recapitalizations. This revenue ruling approved the basic valuation devices described above and added further, more specific guidelines.

One particular guideline in Rev. Rul. 83-120 indicates in effect that preferred stock issued in a recapitalization that does not pay dividends at a rate approximating the prime rate at the date of issue has an actual value less than its par value.

Restrictions on the Use of Recapitalizations and on Other Estate-Freezing Techniques. Prior changes in the federal tax laws dealt a severe blow to recapitalizations and other techniques intended to freeze the estate tax value of an older-generation owner's interest in a family business. These changes have been codified in IRC Secs. 2701–2704, sometimes referred to as the chapter 14 estate-freeze provisions.

In essence IRC Secs. 2701–2704 are gift tax provisions that set forth rules for placing a value on a stock interest or a partnership interest transferred by gift or by sale to a family member. The prohibitions that Sec. 2701 sets forth are stringent and effectively remove the estate freeze as a viable estate planning technique.

Specifically Sec. 2701 provides rules for determining (a) whether the transfer of an interest in a *controlled* corporation or partnership to (or for the benefit of, such as through a trust) a *member of the family* of the transferor is a completed gift for this purpose or (b) whether the transferor has retained some interest. If the transferor has retained any interest, then a completed gift will be deemed not to have been made. The gift tax value of such gift, the value of certain *retained rights* with respect to an *applicable retained interest* held by the transferor or an *applicable family member* immediately after the transfer, is generally deemed to be zero.

This effectively means that there can be no valuation credit granted for the value of any proprietary interest that has been retained.

Sec. 2702 deals with transfers in trust and provides for the same type of prohibition with respect to transfers of interests in a controlled corporation or partnership to a member of the family.

The enactment of the new chapter 14 estate-freeze rules has made effective use of a recapitalization of a closely held corporation to shift future appreciation to family members exceedingly difficult.

Private Annuity

A private annuity is a contract for a private individual (not a commercial annuity company) to pay the purchase price for an asset over the actuarial life of the seller. If the seller does not live to his or her actuarial life expectancy, the purchaser's obligation ceases, and there is nothing of the obligation remaining to include in the deceased seller's estate. If the seller lives longer than his or her actuarially determined life expectancy, the purchaser must pay the predetermined payments for the seller's actual life.

To avoid inclusion in the seller's income in the year of the sale, the transaction must not be secured; that is, it must be a naked promise to pay.

Payments to the seller have more than one component for tax purposes. First, a portion of each payment will represent a nontaxable return of the seller's basis. Second, a portion will typically be taxed as the sale or exchange of a capital asset. The seller will pay a capital-gains tax on the portion of each payment that represents gain from the sale of the property. Third, there will be ordinary income tax on any portion in excess of the sum of the seller's return of basis and capital-gain portions. For purposes of determining gain to the seller, the sale price for the asset transferred is the present value of the total of annuity payments to be made over the seller's life expectancy.

There are some drawbacks to the private annuity arrangement. For example, the purchaser cannot deduct any part of the payment, including the portion taxed as ordinary income to the seller. In contrast, under an installment sale the interest portion of the payments may be deductible subject to the limitations already discussed.

The private annuity does not meet the Millers' needs, because the termination of the payment obligation at Larry's death could severely deplete Larry's estate if he died prematurely, depriving Anne of income Larry wishes to assure her and resulting in a windfall to Steve. Steve, on the other hand, could not afford to purchase any significant amount of his father's stock without the benefit of the interest deduction.

Shareholder-Employee Compensation Planning

Reasonable Compensation for Shareholder-Employees

The issue of unreasonable compensation is generally raised only in closely held corporations where there is a strong identity of interest between the role of employee and that of stockholder or where a member of the employee's family is a stockholder. The Internal Revenue Service's position is that an arm's-length transaction setting the value of personal services and effectively eliminating the unreasonable compensation issue cannot exist in most closely held corporations. Obviously the closer the identity of interest between the corporation and the employee, the more vulnerable to IRS scrutiny compensation becomes; for example, the most vulnerable situation occurs between an employee and his or her wholly owned corporation. Because of the identity of interests, the issue of unreasonable compensation is also frequently raised in family-owned corporations.

If Steve's salary, for example, was substantially raised in order to provide him with funds to buy Larry's stock, Millers might be denied a deduction for a portion of Steve's salary that the IRS deemed to be unreasonable.

However, if Millers elects Subchapter S status as previously recommended, the unreasonable compensation issue will not be a problem, as long as Larry is being paid a comparable salary based upon actual services rendered.

Steve and Larry will be taxed directly on their proportionate shares of corporate taxable income if Millers makes an S election. Therefore payments of such income to Steve will not be taxable as a dividend, as long as the taxable income distributed is attributable to activity of the corporation after the S election.

Employment Contracts

Employment contracts between unrelated employees and employers are often used to reduce misunderstandings about the rights and responsibilities of each party. In the case of a shareholder-employee of a closely held corporation employment agreements are often utilized not only to clarify the duties of the shareholder-employee but also to describe compensation arrangements in an effort to support the reasonableness of compensation in the event of an IRS challenge. The first consideration is very important for the Millers in this business transition period.

Another benefit of employment contracts is their ability to minimize shareholder dissension, which may be especially important to Larry and Steve as they work at transferring the management of the store to Steve. They should fully and thoughtfully discuss which duties are the responsibility of each, and their agreements on these issues should be included in their employment agreements.

Employment contracts can run for any period of time, but care should be taken to treat the contract as if it were being entered into between an employee and an unrelated employer, that is, as an arm's-length transaction. For this reason contract periods are usually quite short, although some contain options to renew for an additional specified period. These renewals can even be tailored to occur automatically, unless the employer gives appropriate and timely notice to the employee.

For the reasons indicated, employment contracts covering corporate duties and compensation agreements should be implemented for both Larry and Steve.

Consulting Contracts

Consulting contracts are merely specialized forms of employment contracts. As Larry substantially withdraws from daily participation in Millers, consulting contracts should be implemented to demonstrate the decrease in his duties and the new compensation arrangements. Since the primary issues that would need to be dealt with (for example, exact duties as well as amounts and methods of payment) may not be ascertainable for several years, it is only necessary to note that these contracts should be drawn at an appropriate time.

Employee Benefits

Qualified Plans of Deferred Compensation

Since Larry has noted that he is displeased with the performance of the profit-sharing plan of Millers, now would be a good time to see if the qualified plan could be improved and its performance enhanced instead of being terminated.

Problems with Present Plans. The utilization of appropriate corporate qualified plans not only reduces shareholder-employees' present tax burden but can also accumulate earnings tax free on the amount in the plans until distribution and can even allow them to borrow from the plans if that is necessary or desirable.

Even at the time of distribution there is favorable federal income tax treatment on the distribution of proceeds from qualified plans. The tax-free accumulation within the plan can obviously allow assets to increase at a much more rapid rate than if taxes were currently payable. All of this can be accomplished at absolutely no tax risk. In fact, the Internal Revenue Code specifically authorizes qualified plans, which are statutorily sanctioned tax shelters as a result. If there is a proper balance between corporate cost and present benefits to the employees, qualified plans can be good employee motivators.

The current profit-sharing plan of Millers is unnecessarily restrictive with its provision for mandatory contributions when corporate profits reach a certain level.

General Requirements. There are basically two types of qualified plans: defined-contribution plans and defined-benefit plans. Defined-benefit pension plans promise the recipient a specific benefit within statutory limits at retirement age, and the funding necessary to provide that benefit for the actuarial life of the recipient is contributed by the employer. As already noted, defined-benefit plans usually work best for funding retirement benefits for older shareholder-employees when there is only a short time left to provide significant retirement benefits. These plans can be very expensive to the funding corporation, and most have the additional disadvantage of being subject to regulation by the Pension Benefit Guaranty Corporation. Since defined-benefit plans are "pension plans" under the Internal Revenue Code, contributions to the plan are mandatory once the plan is in place.

Defined-contribution plans merely set a contribution level that the employer contributes into a tax-free trust. The funds are invested over the employee's working life, and the benefits available at retirement consist of the contributions that have been made to the plan, plus forfeitures that have been added to the account, plus earnings on the account assets. Defined-contribution plans are generally preferable to defined-benefit plans for a younger work force because the potential benefits are greater. The defined-contribution plans that small corporations most often utilize fall into two categories: profit-sharing plans and money-purchase pension plans.

Profit-sharing plans, as already noted, do not promise recipients a specified amount at retirement. All funds the employer contributes and their accumulated tax-free earnings, whatever the resulting amount, will be the benefit the retiring participant receives.

Recommendations. There is not enough information on the facts of the case to determine whether the Millers' plans would be top-heavy. Many, if not most, small plans will be subject to the top-heavy rules. However, the fact that Millers employs 34 people indicates that the plan is probably not top-heavy. The qualified retirement plan presently in place has not been perceived as performing well, and the recommendation would be to amend the plan to allow for purely discretionary contributions, which could be made regardless of whether pretax profits reach $200,000 per year. In addition, the plan must immediately comply with the eligibility and vesting requirements of the Internal Revenue Code.

NOTE TO STUDENTS

To avoid repetition of background material on qualified plans, that material has been omitted from this chapter. In an actual plan material such as that on pages 3.38–3.48 *and* pages 5.46–5.50 should be presented to the client. If the student is not totally familiar with the noted material from previous chapters, it should be reviewed prior to proceeding through this section of the suggested solution.

An appropriate vesting schedule might be 3- to-7-year vesting, which is an acceptable schedule under the current tax laws if the plan is not top-heavy. The schedule is as follows:

Years of Service	Vested Percentage
3	20%
4	40
5	60
6	80
7 or more	100

The plan will also have to meet the minimum coverage requirements. In essence a plan cannot discriminate in coverage or in the amount of contributions made. Several safe harbor design strategies could be recommended. Also an alternative vesting schedule would have to be included in case the plan becomes top-heavy.

An integrated money-purchase pension plan could also be instituted. Plan integration would allow a higher rate of contributions to be applied to compensation earned over specified levels. In effect it is a permitted form of discrimination that would skew plan contributions in favor of Larry Miller.

Since Larry has expressed satisfaction with the amount of assets he has already acquired, assuming they can provide liquidity for his retirement, this package of qualified plans is aimed at the younger employees (primarily Steve) and will benefit them most. The plans would not, however, exclude Larry, since qualified plans cannot exclude employees from participation based on age.

Nonqualified Deferred Compensation

Another important benefit that can be available to shareholder-employees of a closely held corporation on a discriminatory basis is a nonqualified deferred-compensation arrangement. These arrangements do not have to meet the funding, employee coverage, and other requirements necessary to satisfy the qualified plan definition under IRC Sec. 401(a), as ERISA exempts from almost all its requirements an unfunded arrangement maintained "primarily for the purpose of providing deferred compensation for a select group of management or highly compensated employees." (There are a few minor ERISA requirements, however, even for nonqualified deferred-compensation plans.)

While nonqualified plans of deferred compensation may involve compensation in the form of money or other property, many are salary continuation plans of various types.

Nonqualified salary continuation plans, for example, may provide significant disability or retirement income for shareholder-employees or death benefits for the spouse or beneficiaries of shareholder-employees. They may be particularly appropriate in the case of a corporation that wishes to provide such benefits to shareholder-employees but finds a qualified plan too costly because of ERISA requirements. Alternatively these plans may be used to provide benefits to shareholder-employees in addition to those allowable under qualified plans.

There are generally three fundamental hurdles in structuring a nonqualified deferred-compensation plan. The first is structuring the arrangement so that compensation is in fact deferred, thereby escaping immediate inclusion in the shareholder-employee's income. The second is the question of whether the deferred-compensation arrangement will be deductible to the employer corporation. The third is the question of whether an attempt should be made to structure the deferred-compensation plan to escape federal estate taxation at the employee's death.

Avoiding Immediate Inclusion in the Employee's Income. Initially the deferred amount must qualify as bona fide deferred compensation to escape immediate inclusion in the employee's income. The IRS can argue for inclusion in current income under either a constructive receipt or an economic benefit theory.

The concept of constructive receipt is explained by the Treasury Regulations as follows:

> Income although not actually reduced to a taxpayer's possession is constructively received by him in the taxable year in which it is credited to his account, set apart for him or otherwise made available so that he may draw upon it at any time, or so that he could have drawn upon it during the taxable year if notice of intention to withdraw had been given. However, income is not constructively received if the taxpayer's control of its receipt is subject to substantial limitations or restrictions. (Reg. 1.451-2(a)).

The economic benefit theory provides that if compensation is readily convertible into cash, it is not bona fide deferred compensation. The economic benefit theory has not generally been extended to tax the value of an employer's unsecured contractual obligation to pay deferred compensation. However, if the contractual obligation is (1) unconditional, (2) that of a solvent employer, (3) freely assignable or transferrable or immediately convertible into cash, and (4) of a type frequently transferred to banks or investors at a discount not greater than the prevailing premium for the use of money, the IRS position for immediate inclusion in income has been upheld by the courts (*Cowden v. Comm'r, Watson, Jones Co., Steen, Evans,* Rev. Rul. 68-606). It appears that the addition of a clause in the deferred-compensation agreement that prohibits the assignment, transfer, or pledging of the agreement would be sufficient protection against the inclusion of deferred compensation in present income under the economic benefit theory. It would be prudent to include such a provision.

The best guidance for avoiding immediate taxation under nonqualified deferred-compensation plans is contained in Rev. Rul. 60-31, 1960-1 C.B. 174. This revenue ruling sets forth the IRS position that when an employee receives an unfunded promise to pay an amount in the future, deferral of the promised amount will generally be allowed provided the amount of compensation to be delivered at a future date is not set apart in any type of special fund that would be protected from the employer's creditors.

Also deferred-compensation contracts or agreements entered into prior to performance of services appear to have the best chance to withstand IRS attack (Rev. Rul. 60-31, 1960-1 C.B. 174).

Prior to the issuance of Rev. Rul. 60-31 practitioners and commentators generally believed that the one safe way to keep an amount under a deferred-compensation contract from being currently taxable was to make the payment "subject to forfeiture." Forfeiture provisions often condition payment under a deferred-compensation arrangement on the employee's agreement to (1) work for the employer for a specified number of years or until retirement; (2) render advisory or consulting services after retirement at the request of the employee; (3) refrain from disclosing customer lists, trade secrets, or other information valuable to the employer's business; or (4) refrain from engaging in a competitive business as an owner, stockholder, partner, employee, or otherwise.

Although these forfeiture provisions may no longer be necessary to avoid current income taxation after Rev. Rul. 60-31, they often offer desirable protection for the employer for other business reasons and are therefore still found in many deferred-compensation arrangements. The maintenance of forfeiture provisions may again have taken on increased importance to prevent current withholding of income tax, FICA, and other employment taxes due to recent legislation that authorizes such withholding upon the lapse of the substantial risk of forfeiture to the employee.

Well-known private rulings issued by the IRS indicate that the employer may set aside funds in a so-called *rabbi trust* (PLR 8113107) without creating problems under the constructive receipt or economic benefit doctrines. Such trusts can provide additional assurance to the participants that funds will be available to pay benefits actually promised by the plan.

Such rabbi trusts involve a trust established by the employer in which contributions are periodically made to finance the promised benefits. The trust can be irrevocable in favor of the plan participants except that trust assets must be subject to claims of the employer's creditors. The employee-beneficiary must be prohibited from transferring or assigning any part of his or her interest in the trust assets. If these conditions are met, the funds will not be includible in the employee's income until the employee actually receives them; that is, the plan will be treated as an unfunded plan for tax purposes. The trust itself will be taxed as a grantor trust, which means that the employer will be taxed on any income the trust generates.

The deductibility of payments by the employer falls within the general rules for nonqualified arrangements discussed below.

Deductibility by the Corporation. To be deductible all compensation paid to an employee, including deferred compensation, must be reasonable and in fact paid purely for services (Treas. Reg. Sec. 1.162-7; Treas. Reg. Sec. 1.162-9). In determining reasonableness of compensation, the entire amount of compensation, present and deferred, is examined. Although various courts have enumerated factors that they feel are important in making a determination on the issue of reasonableness, no single factor appears decisive since each situation must be considered as a whole (*Mayson Mfg. Co. v. Comm'r*).

If a deferred-compensation agreement is reasonable and is intended to provide only retirement or disability benefits to the employee, generally the corporation is entitled to a deduction for a deferred-compensation payment in the year in which the payment is made (Treas. Reg. Sec. 1.404(a)-12).

If the employer is legally obligated to pay an employee's estate or specified beneficiaries under a death-benefit-only plan, the benefits paid to the surviving spouse or beneficiary will generally be deductible by the corporation in the year paid (Treas. Reg. Sec. 1.404(a)-12).

The deductibility of a death benefit payment to a surviving spouse or beneficiary may be called into question when such survivor is a shareholder in a closely held corporation. If, in fact, the employee has been adequately compensated during his or her lifetime and the corporation will be controlled by the surviving spouse or other members of the deceased's family, extreme care should be taken to enter into an agreement with the corporation at the earliest possible date. The contract must emphasize that certain payments that will be made to a surviving spouse or other beneficiary are deferred compensation to the employee.

Avoiding the Imposition of Federal Estate Tax. In order to escape the inclusion of the benefits of a salary continuation plan in the deceased employee's estate, it must be a death-benefit-only plan. If exclusion is not a primary concern, the plan can also provide for benefits to be paid to the employee upon retirement or disability. Such a nonqualified retirement or disability agreement can provide substantial amounts of income during retirement or prolonged disability in addition to providing income to a surviving spouse after the employee's death. The tax price one pays for this increased security is that the remaining value of the survivor's interest is includible in the estate of the deceased employee and is subject to estate tax (IRC Sec. 2039(a)).

Even if the plan is a death-benefit-only plan, the proceeds are not automatically excluded from estate taxation. This area involves some complexity. IRC Sec. 2039(a) requires that the value of any annuity or other payment (other than from a qualified plan) receivable by a decedent as the result of a contract or agreement be included in calculating the decedent's gross estate if the decedent had the right to receive such annuity or other payment in any of the following situations:

- for life
- for a period not ascertainable without reference to the decedent's death
- for a period that does not, in fact, end before the decedent's death

An annuity or other payment is not restricted to commercial annuity payments but includes any annuity or other payment that, according to the regulations, may be equal or unequal, conditional or unconditional, periodic or sporadic, and that may be one or more payments extending over any period of time (Treas. Reg. Sec. 20.2039-1(b)(1)).

In order for the proceeds of a death-benefit-only deferred-compensation plan to be included under Sec. 2039(a), the annuity or other payment must have been "payable to the decedent"; that is, the decedent must have been receiving payments at death, or the decedent must have possessed the right to receive such payment or annuity. In other words, inclusion in the employee's estate results if the employee possessed an enforceable right to receive payments at some time in the future, regardless of whether he or she was receiving payments at the time of death (Treas. Reg. Sec. 20.2039-1 (b)(1); *Estate of Bahen*).

The inclusion of plan proceeds in an employee's estate may not be such a poor result, considering that it is exchanged for an income stream during retirement. In addition, if the intended beneficiary is the employee's spouse, the proceeds may qualify for the marital deduction.

Note that even if a death-benefit-only plan is selected, other nonqualified plans (such as disability plans) will all be viewed together when determining whether the tests for includibility under Sec. 2039 are met (Reg. Sec. 20.2039-2). Benefits receivable under qualified plans of deferred compensation will not be included in determining whether the employee had the right to an annuity or other payment that meets the other criteria of Sec. 2039(a) and that would require inclusion of a death-benefit-only plan in the employee's gross estate (Rev. Rul. 76-380, 1976-2 C.B. 270).

Since Larry is concerned about providing Anne with a good income stream for her life, a death-benefit-only plan could be implemented to continue some portion of his salary to her for 5 to 7 years. Funding for this purpose could come from the insurance the corporation has on his life.

In this area it is worth noting that care should be taken to enlist a competent attorney to draft documents to implement these plans.

INSURANCE PLANNING

Medical Insurance Plans

Since the present medical insurance plan provides Millers employees with excellent benefits, no improvements appear necessary.

Disability Income Plans

As already noted, no disability income plan exists for Millers employees. It is questionable whether many of the rank-and-file employees would benefit materially from a long-term disability plan because of their modest average salaries. Most of the employees would probably have their disability benefits either eliminated or substantially reduced because of coordination with social security.

Disability income protection for Larry and Steve is a different matter entirely. The installment sale to Steve would provide income to Larry regardless of disability. In addition, a nonqualified deferred-compensation plan could continue Larry's salary if he became disabled before leaving Millers. As discussed in the section on nonqualified deferred compensation, a disability plan of this type would almost certainly cause inclusion of the death-benefit-only plan in Larry's estate. However, Steve should obtain the maximum amount of long-term disability income coverage that insurers are willing to underwrite. Since the S election will prevent tax-favored coverage through the corporation, Steve should obtain personal coverage. If he becomes disabled, he will need additional financial protection to complete payment for the purchase of Larry's stock.

Life Insurance Plans

The group insurance coverages of Millers are characterized by two extremes—an extremely broad medical expense plan and an obvious lack of anything else. In reviewing an employee benefit plan it is necessary to understand the objectives of a firm in providing employee benefits. Is it primarily to meet the needs of the employees or to meet the needs of the owners? The latter tends to be particularly true for many small firms such as Millers.

If the employees' needs are of concern, the lack of a group life insurance plan is noticeable. Most firms of this size with a relatively stable employment would provide some coverage, even if only a modest flat amount per employee, such as $5,000 or $10,000. In fact, with salespeople who are often paid on a commission basis, a flat amount of coverage may be appropriate. Salespeople could be provided with a level amount of insurance that is roughly equivalent to that provided to salaried personnel.

Millers should consider a group life insurance policy for its employees with coverage based on a multiple of salary. The multiple would depend on the corporation's ability and willingness to pay premiums. It is common for such plans to provide between one and two times salary for salaried employees.

It is significant to remember that Larry and Steve would have to include the value of this coverage in their gross incomes after an S election is made because of their stock ownership.

Larry has over $1 million in separately owned assets but only about $100,000 of this is in liquid assets. This liquidity and his present insurance coverage are currently adequate to cover the estate taxes and administrative costs at Larry's death. As long as Larry remains active in the corporation, group life insurance for him would provide additional contingency protection. Such coverage may be less expensive than individual coverage even though Larry cannot participate in a group plan on a tax-advantaged basis. The coverage could be assigned to an irrevocable life insurance trust to avoid inclusion of the proceeds in his estate (see pages 6.108–6.112 for estate planning). Group life coverage on Steve could help pay the installment contract in case Steve predeceases Larry.

Although Steve is not currently a planning client, some planning for Steve is important to Larry and Anne because of the possibility that Steve could die or become disabled before the installment sale is fully paid for. If this happened, the security of Larry and Anne's retirement could be imperiled because of Steve's inability to meet his obligations under the installment sale contract.

In addition, the corporation should consider a key person life insurance policy to cover Steve. Millers would be both owner and beneficiary of the policy. If Steve should die, especially after Larry has substantially withdrawn from Millers, the corporation will almost certainly have to hire someone else to replace Steve in order to keep the corporation viable. The corporation may also need to redeem Steve's shares in the corporation if he predeceases Larry. Planning for this redemption should be carefully considered and coordinated between Millers and Steve (and his family's personal objectives) to assure that Steve's estate will be able to qualify for exemption from the family attribution rules and to achieve capital-gains treatment.

The $200,000 policy owned by Millers insuring Larry can be left in place to provide funding for a salary continuation death-benefit-only plan or to fund the survivorship benefit portion to Anne of any salary continuation plan for Larry by the corporation. If necessary, Millers can always fall back on the cash value of the life insurance to help make the installment sale payments to Anne for the redemption of her stock.

Property and Liability Coverage for the Business—Fundamental Requirements

In analyzing the property and liability needs of a business, it is important to realize that the needs of businesses are much less uniform than those of individuals, and more flexibility is needed in designing their insurance coverages than in designing those of an average homeowner.

In general loss exposures of a business can be divided into four categories:

- damage to or destruction of property
- loss of possession of property
- loss of income or the imposition of extraordinary expenses
- liability for payment of damages to others

The first category is self-explanatory and includes loss or damage by fire, wind, flood, and many other perils. The second category includes loss of possessions resulting from criminal activities of others, including employee dishonesty. The third category includes such items as lost profits and additional expenses following the damage or destruction of business property. The last category includes obligations to reimburse others for legal injuries for which a business is liable.

Historically many separate policies had to be purchased to meet all a business's needs. However, in recent years package policies have been made available to most businesses so that these needs can be met with a minimum number of insurance contracts. It has also become common in situations like the one in this case (when the owner of a business also owns the real estate rented by the business) to insure the building and the business under a single package policy, with the owner of the building and the owner of the business both being named as insureds as their interests may appear.

Most of the needs of Millers (and Larry's needs for property and liability insurance on the building rented by Millers) can be met under a business owner's policy for small and medium-size businesses. The business owner's policy is standardized and is designed for small businesses that have little need for flexibility in insurance coverages. Based on the information in the case Millers has no unusual insurance exposures with regard to property and liability insurance and would be well suited for this contract.

The business owner's policy can now include coverage for automobiles. However, a separate workers' compensation policy will be necessary since this coverage is not included. In addition, the Millers may decide that a commercial excess-liability policy is needed to supplement the liability coverages available under the business owner's policy.

The typical business owner's policy (some variations exist among insurers) provides the following basic coverages, with the insured selecting the amount of insurance for each coverage:

- buildings. All buildings on the premises are covered on a replacement-cost basis. No coinsurance applies, but the amount of insurance must usually be equal to the full replacement cost of the property. The amount of insurance increases quarterly with inflation. Buildings can be insured on either a named-peril or an open-peril basis, with the latter providing broader protection at a slightly increased cost.
- business personal property. This is also on a replacement-cost basis without coinsurance. In addition to inventory and office equipment, it also covers tenants' improvements. There is limited coverage ($1,000) for goods away from the insured premises, such as those being delivered on the company's trucks. Additional coverage can be added if this exposure is significantly greater. Coverage also exists for the property of others in the care, custody, or control of the insured if the insured is legally liable. This coverage, for example, would cover the liability of Millers for damage to furniture that was being repaired or reupholstered for customers. One concern of a business such as Millers is to see that proper insurance is maintained on inventory that fluctuates in value. As long as the amount of insurance carried is equal to at least 100 percent of the average inventory during the 12 months prior to the loss, the amount of insurance can be increased automatically by up to 25 percent to cover peak season values.

- loss of income. Coverage for lost profits, continuing expenses, and extra expenses is provided for up to 12 months if a business suffers a loss resulting from an insured peril.
- optional property coverages. Numerous endorsements are available that provide coverage for many types of property and liability situations not adequately covered under other sections of the policy. These include employee dishonesty, plate glass, outdoor signs, earthquake, and boiler and machinery coverage.
- business liability. Coverage of up to $1 million is available for liability arising from the premises and operations. Personal injury coverage (for example, libel, slander, false arrest) is also provided.

PERSONAL PLANNING

TAX PLANNING

Present Position

Larry and Anne appear to have achieved a good deal of success in their lives both financially and personally. They have created a successful business that has provided the means for them to enjoy a comfortable life-style both in the past and, through proper planning, in future years. Their children are all grown and seem to have found careers in which they are content.

The primary objectives to be dealt with in Larry and Anne's personal plan are assuring that they are able to be secure during their retirement and that Anne is well provided for as long as she lives should Larry predecease her.

Assuring a Comfortable Retirement with Larry Continuing to Have Some Involvement with Millers

Most of the techniques for assuring that Larry and Anne will be guaranteed a comfortable retirement income have been discussed at length in the business plan. These techniques include (1) the installment sale of 72 shares of Millers stock to Steve for an installment obligation with a term of 15 years, (2) the redemption of Anne's Millers stock for an installment obligation with a term of 10 years, and (3) the possible later redemption of Larry's Millers stock if future circumstances warrant.

Steve's installment obligation will add approximately $28,340 per year to Larry and Anne's cash flow for a 15-year period. If the corporation redeems Anne's stock with a 10-year note at 9 percent, another $28,400 will be added to the Millers' cash flow for 10 years. However, if a 10-year note places too heavy a cash drain on Millers, a longer-term obligation would still provide the Millers with substantial cash payments well into their retirement years. In addition, there will also be retirement income available from the qualified plan. Since Larry is very concerned about providing income to Anne should he predecease her, he might consider electing a term certain or a joint and survivor annuity as the method of payment for benefits from the defined-contribution plan.

Dispositions at Death

Analysis of Present Plans

The Millers' present estate plan, in which each leaves everything to a surviving spouse and then to living children or children of a deceased child, *per stirpes,* may have been perfectly adequate 16 years ago when it was implemented. Since the Millers have acquired a substantial amount of additional assets, however, their present plan is unnecessarily expensive in terms of estate tax liabilities. This fact remains true despite the current availability of the unlimited marital deduction, because their current wills could result in all the assets of both Larry and Anne being taxed in her estate at marginal rates of up to 55 percent. Larry's unified credit is wasted. In cases such as this when the wife has substantial assets (and especially considering the fact that an outright inheritance from her mother could materially increase her taxable estate), an estate plan that uses only the unlimited marital deduction is not indicated.

Although Larry has expressed his desire that any assets Anne does not consume during her lifetime be divided equally among their three children, the present estate plan contains no provision for assuring this result.

In addition, the present placement of Larry and Anne's personal insurance results in the inclusion of the proceeds in their estates for estate tax purposes.

Possible Improvements in Estate Plan

Because Anne already owns a significant amount of assets, it is not advisable to add to her taxable estate unnecessarily. This can be avoided by structuring an estate plan to make the bulk of Larry's assets available to Anne but to shield them from federal estate taxation at the time of her subsequent death. The fact that she is the potential beneficiary of a significant sum from her mother complicates somewhat the issue of the exact amount. It does not, however, alter the fact that at least an amount sufficient to allow Larry to utilize his unified credit should be left in a trust that will not be taxed again at Anne's death.

The issue of whether to utilize a marital trust or to leave the marital deduction property to Anne outright is one that should be decided between Larry and Anne.

The marital portion of the bequest can be left in a trust and can still qualify for the marital deduction provided that the trust is required to pay all the income from the trust to the wife in annual or more frequent payments. The wife may be given a general power of appointment (the power to appoint the property to herself, her estate, her creditors, creditors of her estate, and any other appointee) exercisable either during her life or by specific reference to the power in her will, or both. In other words, the wife can either be allowed to appoint property as she sees fit to herself or others during her lifetime, or she can be effectively restricted from withdrawing the principal of the marital trust until the time of her death by the use of a testamentary power alone. Alternatively a trust that pays all the income to the spouse annually or more frequently but provides for no power of appointment for the spouse can be federal estate tax marital deduction property if the executor of the estate elects to treat the trust as qualified terminable interest property (a QTIP trust). Typically a QTIP trust will contain provisions governing the disposition of the property after the death of the surviving spouse. Many spouses, however, object to having all or most of their inheritance tied up in trusts, as they feel they must deal continuously with bank trust officers who may be less than sympathetic to their wishes.

The use of a marital trust does not seem indicated in this case, especially when considered in the light of Anne's investment experience. However, if such a trust is used, there are some assets, primarily the principal residence, that should not be included in the marital trust. If the residence is included in the marital trust, the non-recognition-of-gain provisions for the sale of the principal residence and the one-time $125,000 exclusion from capital-gains taxation upon the sale of a principal residence by a taxpayer who is 55 or older (IRC Sec. 121) will be lost unless the beneficiary seeking to take advantage of these provisions has the sole power to vest the trust property in himself or herself and is therefore treated as the owner of the trust for income tax purposes under the Internal Revenue Code. In addition, the management of a residence by a trustee may present practical administrative problems. For these reasons it may be advisable to convey the house as a separate item in the will, and such a bequest should be an outright bequest of all the decedent's interest to the spouse.

Concept of Estate Equalization

Some planners recommend that in addition to the utilization of the unified credit, an estate plan for clients such as the Millers should provide for the payment of some federal estate tax when the first spouse dies, instead of a complete deferral of estate tax liability to the surviving spouse's estate. This is accomplished by intentionally failing to fully use the federal estate tax marital deduction with respect to the taxable estate in excess of the unified credit exemption equivalent (currently $600,000) in order to achieve estate equalization. The potential benefit of estate equalization is a lower estate tax bracket applied to the portion of the estate that would otherwise be taxed in a higher estate tax bracket if the property passed to the surviving spouse under the marital deduction and thus increased the surviving spouse's estate. "Splitting" or "equalizing" the spouses' taxable estates can cause lower estate tax brackets to be utilized in each estate, instead of only in the surviving spouse's estate.

Such a technique may be desirable for older clients and may in fact result in a tax savings if both spouses die within a relatively short time of one another.

One problem with the equalization approach is the applicability of the time-value-of-money concept. The surviving spouse and the other family members lose the use of the money paid out for the "prepaid" estate tax. If the surviving spouse lives for many years, the future value of the tax paid may be greater than the higher tax that would be payable later if the equalization approach had not been used.

Another drawback of equalization is that the surviving spouse can employ other and sometimes better planning devices, such as gifts, to reduce his or her taxable estate after the first spouse's death, which in turn will reduce the ultimate tax liability.

A third drawback is that clients generally prefer to defer taxes when possible. When both spouses are in good health, it usually does not make sense to them to "prepay" federal estate taxes.

It should also be borne in mind that there is always the danger that the surviving spouse might dispose of these inherited assets in a manner not intended by the deceased spouse.

For these reasons it is recommended that the equalization approach not be used for the Millers. The assets in excess of $600,000 of the first spouse to die should pass to the surviving spouse under the marital deduction.

Recommendations

Our recommendations for Larry's estate plan would be an outright bequest of the cars and the residence to Anne, an outright bequest of a marital portion equal to the excess of Larry's taxable estate over the unified credit exemption equivalent, and a unified credit shelter residuary trust of which Anne is the primary beneficiary for her life. Anne could be the sole beneficiary of the residuary trust; however, it might be more prudent to allow the trustee to invade the trust for the benefit of Larry and Anne's children and grandchildren for specified purposes, such as education or catastrophic medical expenses. Since Anne has assets of her own and stands to inherit substantial assets from her mother, her estate plan should take the same approach (except for the specific bequests).

Whichever form the trust takes, the trustee should be empowered to pay income and to invade the corpus of the trust as necessary for Anne's benefit. If an independent trustee is used, the trustee can be instructed to pay income and invade the corpus for her comfort and happiness.

At Anne's death the trust will terminate, and the principal remaining in the trust will be divided equally among their three children, if living. If a child has died but leaves living children, the will should be designed so that the child's portion goes to his or her living children, *per stirpes*. If the child leaves no living children, the assets will be shared among Larry and Anne's remaining children.

The following computer illustrations show a comparison of the Millers' present estate plans with the proposed arrangement. The illustrations assume administration and funeral expenses of 7 percent of the gross estate. It is also assumed that Larry dies in 1994 before the sale of shares in Millers is finalized, and Anne dies in 1995. Assets are based on the clients' current situation and are assumed to appreciate at 5 percent annually (except for the note receivable from Doug). By reviewing the total costs figure on the "Comprehensive Estate Tax Report," a total savings under the revised plan of $281,277 is shown ($383,003 − $101,726).

(text continues on page 6.108)

COMPREHENSIVE ESTATE TAX REPORT

LARRY & ANNE MILLER
CURRENT ESTATE

	LARRY Predeceasing ANNE		ANNE Predeceasing LARRY	
Date: Dec 31, 1994 Under Present Will	LARRY's Estate	ANNE's Estate	ANNE's Estate	LARRY's Estate
Individually Held Assets	1,389,369	525,198	525,198	1,389,369
Share from Joint Assets	1,489	2,979	1,489	2,979
Life Insurance Proceeds	93,500	10,000	5,281	103,500
Assets Received from Spouse	0	83,500	0	0
Gross Estate	1,484,358	621,677	531,968	1,495,848
Administration Expenses	100,837	44,347	38,185	100,945
Adjusted Gross Estate	1,383,521	577,330	493,783	1,394,903
Marital Deduction	84,990	0	6,771	0
Taxable Estate	1,298,531	577,330	487,012	1,394,903
Total Taxable Amount	1,298,531	577,330	487,012	1,394,903
Fed Tax Before Credit	469,168	184,412	151,384	510,608
Unified Tax Credit	192,800	184,412	151,384	192,800
Net Federal Estate Tax	276,368	0	0	317,808
Net Federal + State Tax	276,368	0	0	317,808
Combined Tax	$276,368		$317,808	

ESTATE ANALYSIS
ASSET DISTRIBUTION

LARRY & ANNE MILLER
CURRENT ESTATE

Date: Dec 31, 1994
Under Present Will

	LARRY Predeceasing ANNE		ANNE Predeceasing LARRY	
	LARRY's Estate	ANNE's Estate	ANNE's Estate	LARRY's Estate
Liquid Assets	$870,611	$399,678	$304,688	$881,356
Non-liquid Assets	613,747	221,999	221,999	614,492
Total Assets	1,484,358	621,677	526,687	1,495,848
Passing to Spouse	84,990	0	1,490	0
Passing to Trust/Heirs	1,022,163	577,330	487,012	1,077,095
Estate Shrinkage	377,205	44,347	38,185	418,753

ESTATE ANALYSIS
LIQUIDITY SITUATION

LARRY & ANNE MILLER
CURRENT ESTATE

	LARRY Predeceasing ANNE		ANNE Predeceasing LARRY	
Date: Dec 31, 1994 Under Present Will	LARRY's Estate	ANNE's Estate	ANNE's Estate	LARRY's Estate
Debt	0	0	0	0
Administration Expenses	100,837	44,347	38,185	100,945
Estate Taxes	276,368	0	0	317,808
Charitable Contributions	0	0	0	0
Need for Liquid Capital	377,205	44,347	38,185	418,753
Liquid Capital Available	870,611	399,678	304,688	881,356
Addt'l Liquidity Needed	0	0	0	0

ESTATE ANALYSIS
MARITAL DEDUCTION

LARRY & ANNE MILLER
CURRENT ESTATE

	LARRY Predeceasing ANNE		ANNE Predeceasing LARRY	
Date: Dec 31, 1994 Under Present Will	LARRY's Estate	ANNE's Estate	ANNE's Estate	LARRY's Estate
Marital Deduction is--	Ok		Overqualified	
Best Deduction Amount	$459,154		$1,490	
Your Amount Exceeds by	$0		$5,281	
Resulting Additional Cost	$2,235		$0	
Total Family Assets	$2,021,046		$2,026,327	
Joint Estate Taxes	$276,368 14.00%		$317,808 16.00%	
Total Shrinkage	$421,552 20.86%		$456,938 22.55%	
Remaining for Heirs	$1,599,494 79.14%		$1,569,389 77.45%	

6.99

ESTATE DISTRIBUTION FLOWCHART

(LARRY Predeceasing ANNE on Dec 31, 1994)

The MILLERs

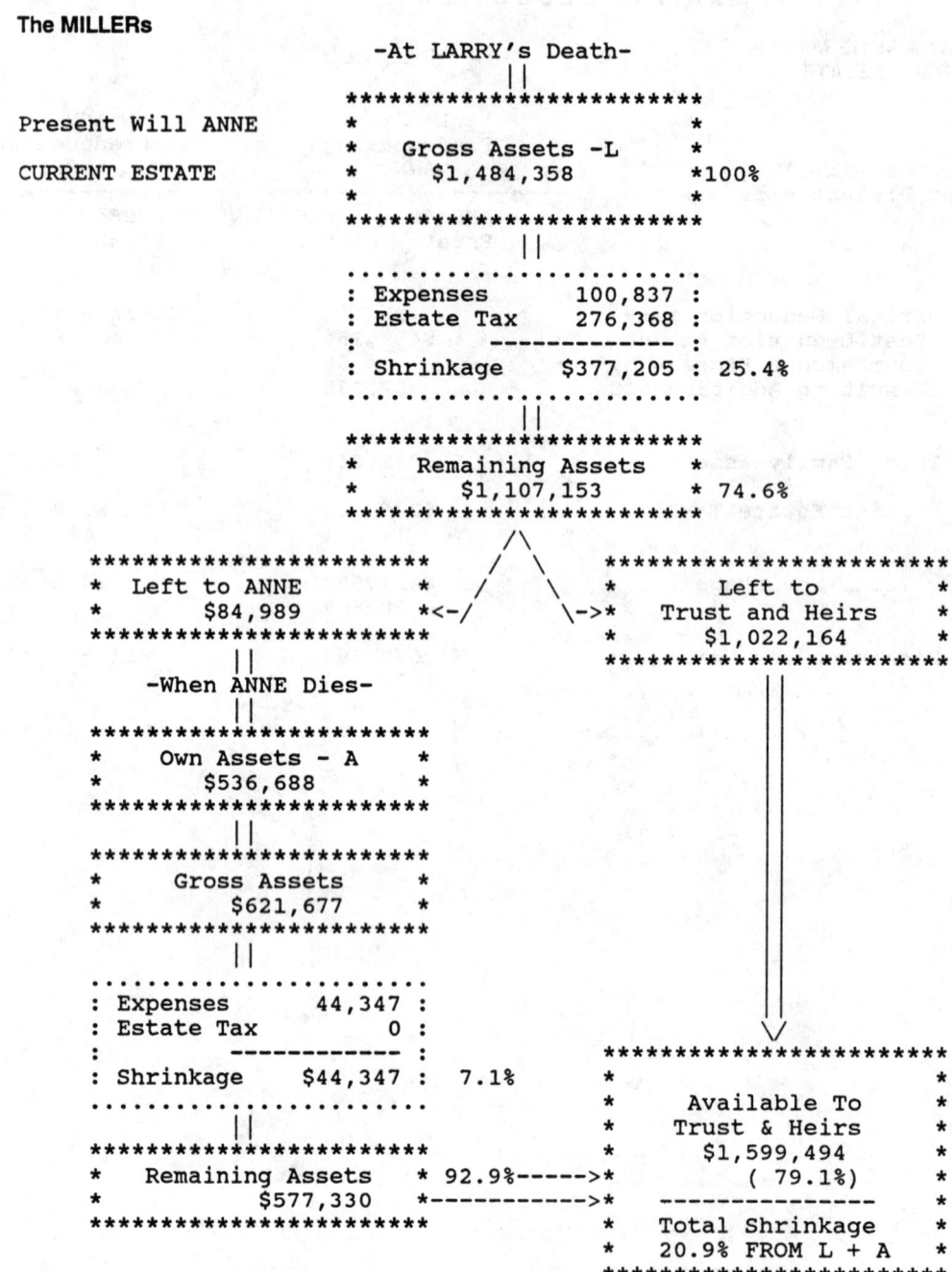

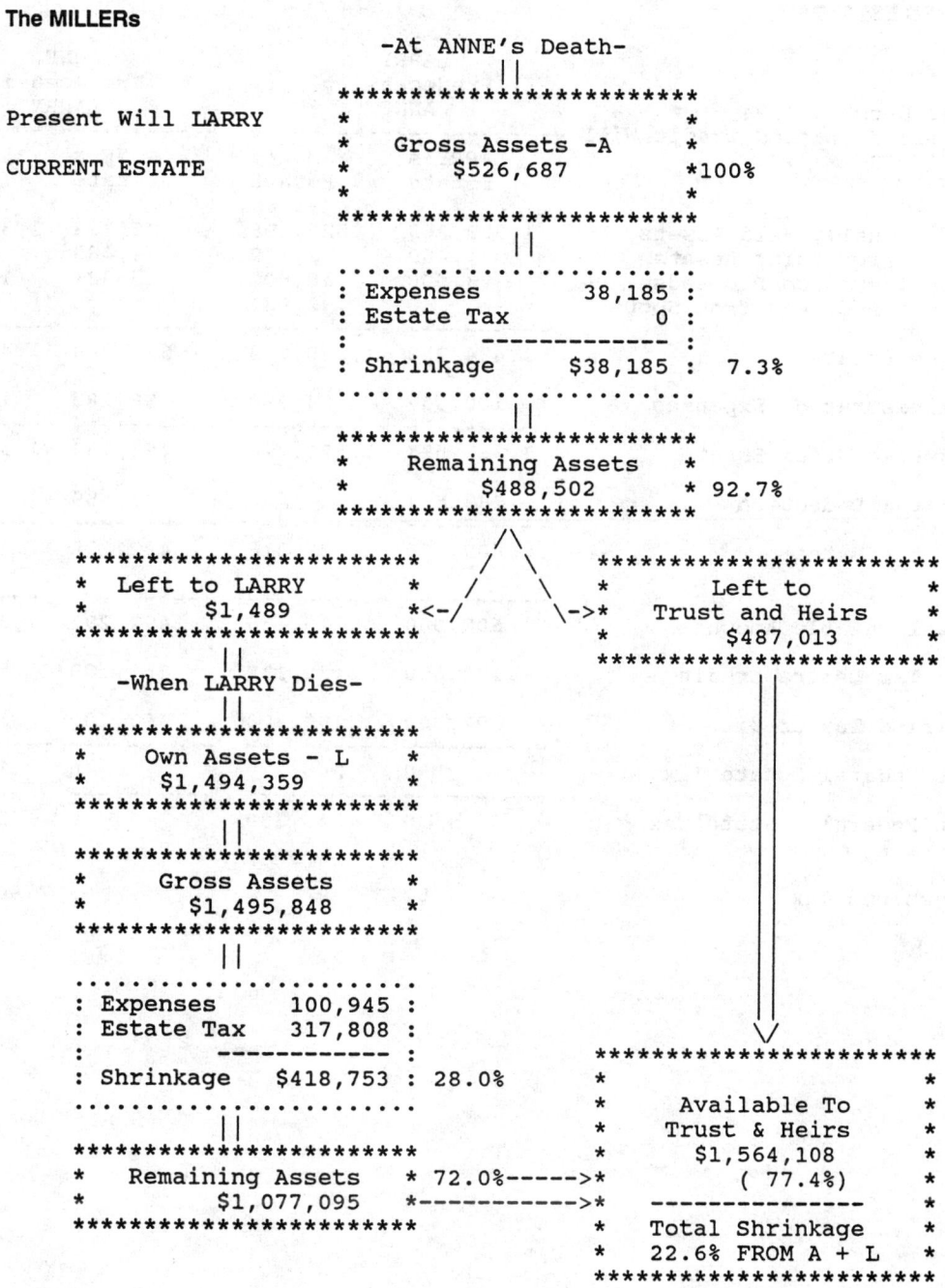

COMPREHENSIVE ESTATE TAX REPORT

LARRY & ANNE MILLER
REVISED ESTATE

	LARRY Predeceasing ANNE		ANNE Predeceasing LARRY	
Date: Dec 31, 1994 Maximized Unified Credit Will	LARRY's Estate	ANNE's Estate	ANNE's Estate	LARRY's Estate
Individually Held Assets	1,389,369	525,198	525,198	1,389,369
Share from Joint Assets	1,489	2,979	1,489	2,979
Life Insurance Proceeds	93,500	10,000	5,281	103,500
Assets Received from Spouse	0	782,031	0	0
Gross Estate	1,484,358	1,320,208	531,968	1,495,848
Administration Expenses	100,837	94,990	38,185	100,945
Adjusted Gross Estate	1,383,521	1,225,218	493,783	1,394,903
Marital Deduction	783,521	0	1,489	0
Taxable Estate	600,000	1,225,218	492,294	1,394,903
Total Taxable Amount	600,000	1,225,218	492,294	1,394,903
Fed Tax Before Credit	192,800	438,139	153,180	510,608
Unified Tax Credit	192,800	192,800	153,180	192,800
Net Federal Estate Tax	0	245,339	0	317,808
Net Federal + State Tax	0	245,339	0	317,808
Combined Tax	$245,339		$317,808	

6.102

ESTATE ANALYSIS
ASSET DISTRIBUTION

LARRY & ANNE MILLER
REVISED ESTATE

	LARRY Predeceasing ANNE		ANNE Predeceasing LARRY	
Date: Dec 31, 1994 Maximized Unified Credit Will	LARRY's Estate	ANNE's Estate	ANNE's Estate	LARRY's Estate
Liquid Assets	$870,611	$1,084,462	$304,688	$881,356
Non-liquid Assets	613,747	235,746	221,999	614,492
Total Assets	1,484,358	1,320,208	526,687	1,495,848
Passing to Spouse	783,521	0	1,490	0
Passing to Trust/Heirs	600,000	979,879	487,012	1,077,095
Estate Shrinkage	100,837	340,329	38,185	418,753

ESTATE ANALYSIS
LIQUIDITY SITUATION

LARRY & ANNE MILLER
REVISED ESTATE

	LARRY Predeceasing ANNE		ANNE Predeceasing LARRY	
Date: Dec 31, 1994 Maximized Unified Credit Will	LARRY's Estate	ANNE's Estate	ANNE's Estate	LARRY's Estate
Debt	0	0	0	0
Administration Expenses	100,837	94,990	38,185	100,945
Estate Taxes	0	245,339	0	317,808
Charitable Contributions	0	0	0	0
Need for Liquid Capital	100,837	340,329	38,185	418,753
Liquid Capital Available	870,611	1,084,462	304,688	881,356
Addt'l Liquidity Needed	0	0	0	0

ESTATE ANALYSIS

MARITAL DEDUCTION

LARRY & ANNE MILLER
REVISED ESTATE

	LARRY Predeceasing ANNE		ANNE Predeceasing LARRY	
Date: Dec 31, 1994 Maximized Unified Credit Will	LARRY's Estate	ANNE's Estate	ANNE's Estate	LARRY's Estate
Marital Deduction is--	Overqualified		Overqualified	
Best Deduction Amount	$459,154		$1,490	
Your Amount Exceeds by	$324,367		$0	
Resulting Additional Cost	$21,849		$0	
Total Family Assets	$2,021,046		$2,026,327	
Joint Estate Taxes	$245,339 12.00%		$317,808 16.00%	
Total Shrinkage	$441,166 21.83%		$456,938 22.55%	
Remaining for Heirs	$1,579,880 78.17%		$1,569,389 77.45%	

6.105

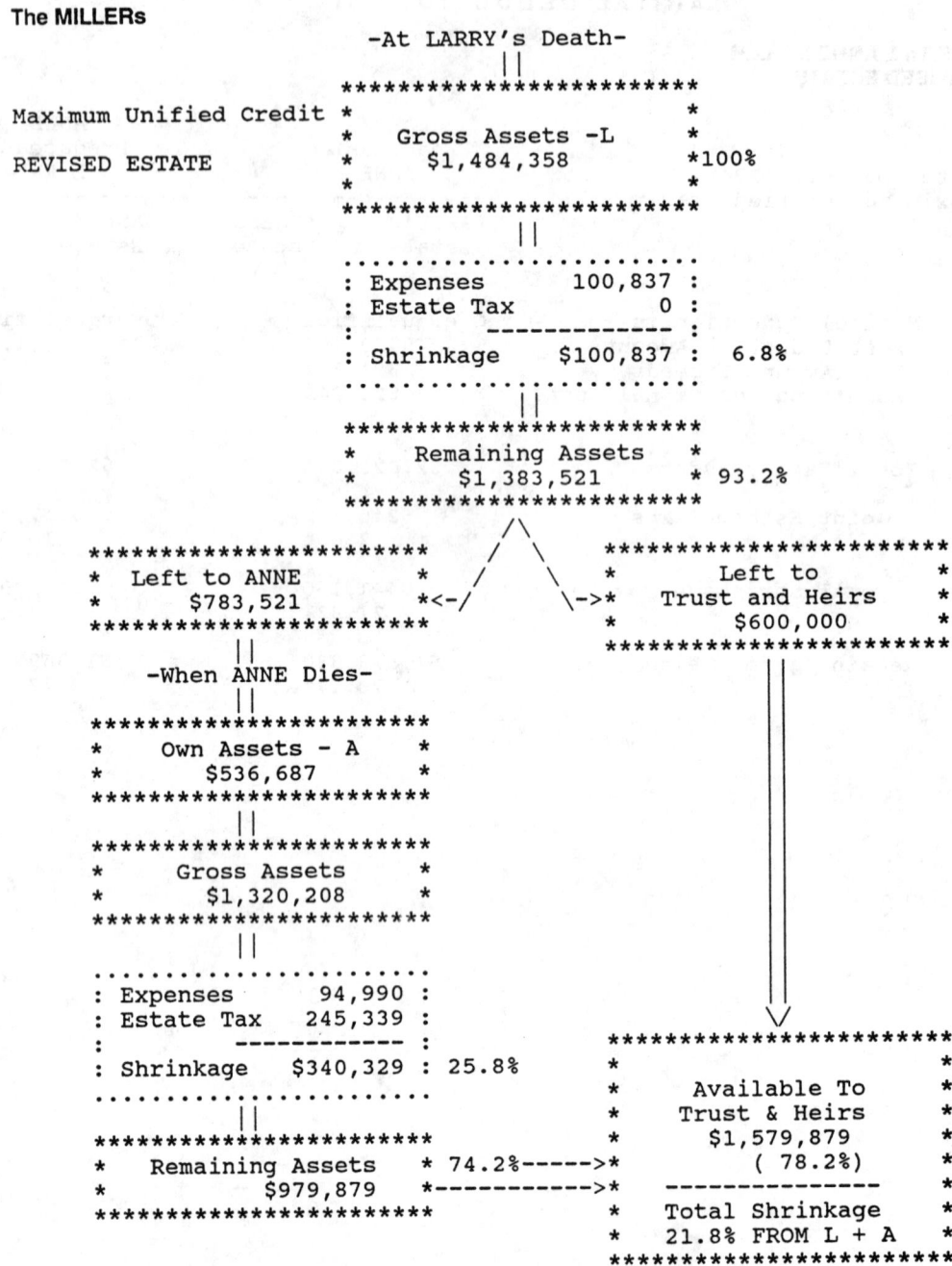

ESTATE DISTRIBUTION FLOWCHART

(LARRY Predeceasing ANNE on Dec 31, 1994)

The MILLERs

Maximum Unified Credit

REVISED ESTATE

ESTATE DISTRIBUTION FLOWCHART

(ANNE Predeceasing LARRY on Dec 31, 1994)

The MILLERs

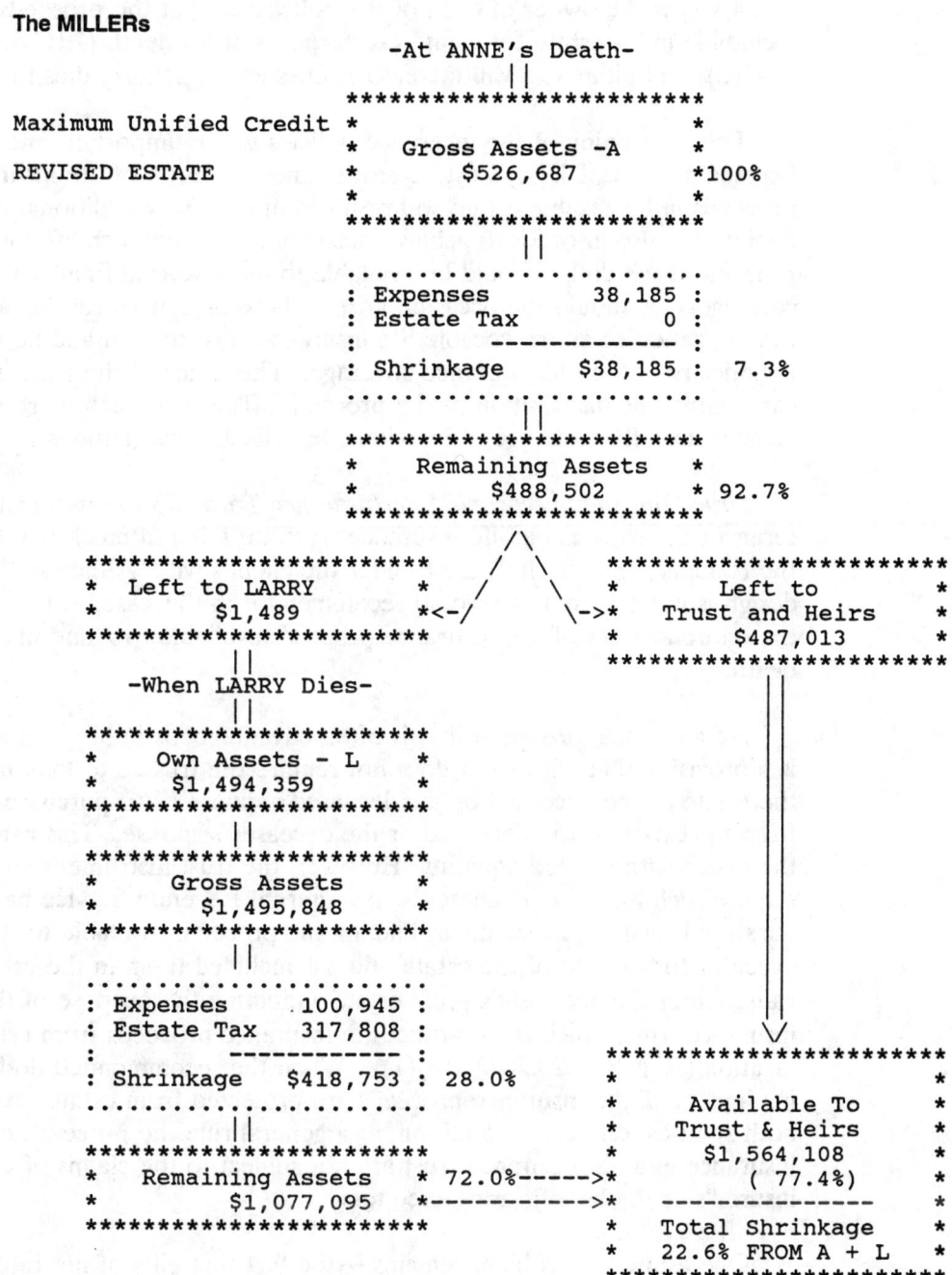

6.107

Life Insurance Placement

General Discussion. At present Larry has $93,500 in personal life insurance death benefits. The most significant problem with this coverage is that Larry is the owner of each of the policies so that the proceeds will be includible in his estate for estate tax purposes at his death (IRC Sec. 2042(2)) and ultimately will increase Anne's estate if Larry dies first.

The positioning of the insurance policies is very important and may become more so if Larry's estate grows, since inclusion of life insurance proceeds in his taxable estate will result in unnecessary additional estate tax liabilities. Also in order to achieve maximum economy with life insurance proceeds, each dollar should be available to meet several financial needs or contingencies should the occasion arise. These objectives can be achieved by the utilization of an irrevocable life insurance trust to own and be the beneficiary of the life insurance coverage. The terms of the trust instrument can control the distribution of the proceeds. This is a much more flexible arrangement than the use of individual beneficiary designations.

Structuring the Irrevocable Life Insurance Trust. In the usual case the terms of the irrevocable life insurance trust are tailored much like those in the residuary (nonmarital) trust under the client's will. Although this type of design is not required, we would recommend it in this case, as it would make the entire amount of the insurance proceeds available to Anne until her death.

An additional provision that is often advantageous in life insurance trusts is a provision that allows but does not require the trustee to loan money to the estate of the deceased or the deceased's spouse or to purchase assets from the estate of the deceased or the deceased's spouse. This can provide the estate with needed liquidity. However, the trust instrument must not require such loans or purchases. The Internal Revenue Service has construed such requirements as making the proceeds available to the executor for the use of the estate and has included them in the estate tax valuation of the decedent's gross estate, defeating the purpose of the insurance trust, which is to protect the insurance proceeds from estate taxation (Reg. Sec. 20.2042-1(b)(1)). When the recommended design is implemented, the insurance proceeds are protected from estate taxation in both spouses' estates. In addition, as a general rule the proceeds of life insurance in a life insurance trust are not subject to the claims of either the insured's or the beneficiaries' creditors.

One estate tax problem remains—the fact that gifts of life insurance policies within 3 years of death will result in taxation of the proceeds of the policy in the insured decedent's estate (IRC Sec. 2035(d)(2)).

If restrictions are placed on the beneficiaries' rights to exercise immediate ownership rights on the policies or the funds to pay premiums on the policies, the gift is a gift of a future interest and the $10,000 per-year-per-donee gift tax exclusion does not apply. The result is that an immediate gift tax liability arises. This problem can be avoided by giving the beneficiaries a withdrawal right called a *Crummey provision (Crummey v.*

Comm'r, which gives the trust beneficiaries the absolute right to demand payment to them of annual gifts to the trust. The right to withdraw such gifts usually lasts for only a short period of time and then lapses. The period of time must be reasonable—usually 30 to 60 days is sufficient—and there is some authority that notice of the withdrawal right must be given to the beneficiary. The fact that the beneficiary is a minor without an appointed guardian will not invalidate the Crummey provision. To ensure avoiding adverse federal gift tax consequences in the event of a lapse of the right, the annual amount subject to withdrawal should not exceed $5,000.

From a legal and statutory point of view the Crummey doctrine is based on the subsection of the Code that deals with the lapse of a general power of appointment. Secs. 2514(e) and 2041(b)(2) provide that the lapse of a general power of appointment (created after October 21, 1942) is a release of such power. The release of a general power of appointment is "deemed to be a transfer of property by the individual possessing such power." This concept of a release or transfer of a power, although technical and complex, is very important because it is limited to the greater of $5,000 or 5 percent of the value of the assets held by a trust. It is this "5-and-5 power" that applies to Crummey trusts. This means that the amount of the annual exclusion available under the Crummey doctrine can never exceed the greater of $5,000 or 5 percent of the value of the assets held by a trust.

Prior to the enactment of the Economic Recovery Tax Act of 1981 (ERTA), the 5-and-5 power was a moot point because the annual exclusion was $3,000 per donee. Since this was less than the $5,000 standard, a problem was never created. However, ERTA increased the annual exclusion from $3,000 per donee to $10,000 per donee. Did this now mean that the annual exclusion in the Crummey setting would be $10,000 per donee?

Since the Crummey doctrine is based on the 5-and-5 power and since Congress, although increasing the amount of the annual exclusion to $10,000, did not create a "10-and-5 power," the conclusion has been that there is still a limitation of $5,000 on the amount available for the annual exclusion. Although many articles and papers have been written in support of using the higher 10-and-5 approach, at this point there has been no ruling or court case supporting the higher standard. Therefore although the annual exclusion is now $10,000 per year per donee, the maximum amount that may be taken as part of the Crummey power is the greater of $5,000, or 5 percent of the trust corpus.

Because the Economic Recovery Tax Act of 1981 increased the annual exclusion from $3,000 to $10,000 and there was no corresponding increase in the lapse-of-powers provisions in the Internal Revenue Code, a lapse-of-demand powers in excess of the 5-and-5 ceiling creates a gift tax exposure, which is generally not what the donor wants. In the event that the beneficiary who possesses the withdrawal right has no other beneficiary interest in the trust, the lapse in excess of the 5-and-5 power may be treated as if the beneficiary had donated his or her own assets to the trust—also an undesirable result since a taxable gift is considered made, which will fail to qualify for the annual exclusion.

Determining whether a taxable gift has taken place will depend on the terms of the trust instrument itself. The astute estate planner, however, should be able to find a variety of ways to avoid creating a taxable lapse of a power of withdrawal.

- We know that if the property subject to the demand power does not exceed the greater of $5,000 or 5 percent of trust assets and the beneficiary fails to exercise the demand power, the 5-and-5 ceiling will effectively and successfully protect the beneficiary from the imposition of the federal gift tax. As mentioned previously, however, this does not allow the taxpayer to obtain the full amount of the annual exclusion—that is, $10,000 per spouse.
- One popular technique for avoiding this potential obstacle is commonly referred to as the *hanging power*. A hanging power permits the withdrawal powers regarding the property in excess of the 5-and-5 limitation to hang—that is, to continue in force from one year to the next. Therefore if a gift of $20,000, for example, is made to a trust, the demand power, if unexercised, will lapse with respect to the first $5,000, and no gift tax will be imposed on the unlapsed excess. The remaining $15,000 will be subject to the withdrawal power in the second calendar year and will lapse to the extent of the greater of $5,000 or 5 percent of the trust principal. At some time in the future the amount that hangs will be eliminated entirely because 5 percent of the trust corpus will be greater than the amount subject to the demand power.

In Letter Ruling 8901004, the IRS took the position that hanging powers are considered invalid and will therefore be ignored for federal gift tax purposes. The ruling concerned a trust for which each beneficiary had a noncumulative right to withdraw his or her pro rata share of such property within 30 days after receiving notice that property had been added to the trust. In addition, the trust provided as follows:

> Notwithstanding the above, if upon the termination of any power of withdrawal, the person holding the power will be deemed to have made a taxable gift for federal gift tax purposes, then such power of withdrawal will not lapse, but will continue to exist with respect to the amount that would have been a taxable gift and will terminate as soon as such termination will not result in a taxable gift.

The IRS pointed out that

> Here the trust provision will not be activated until after an addition to the trust has been made; notice has been given to a beneficiary and the beneficiary's right of withdrawal has lapsed. At that time, the power of withdrawal will be recharacterized as not subject to a set time limit and hence an incomplete gift, so as to avoid federal gift tax consequences of the lapse.

Accordingly the provision is a condition subsequent and is deemed not valid as tending to discourage enforcement of federal gift tax provisions by either defeating the gift or rendering examination of the return ineffective.

In the event that the courts uphold the IRS position with the result that a hanging power is ignored for federal gift tax purposes and the naming power approach proves ineffective, a powerholder will be deemed to have made a future gift to the other trust beneficiaries to the extent that the amount subject to the power exceeds the $5,000/5 percent limitation.

- An additional technique to avoid the application of the federal gift tax is to grant the beneficiary a testamentary power of appointment over the trust. In the event that the appointees of the beneficiary's testamentary power are not readily ascertainable, no completed gift will be considered to have taken place since the beneficiary retains the power to change the disposition of the trust assets.
- One last approach that is sometimes employed to successfully avoid a federal gift tax is to grant each beneficiary a special power of appointment over the excess. This approach will avoid the application of Sec. 2514(b) of the Internal Revenue Code, which applies only to general powers of appointment.

It should be noted that the most effective use of a Crummey trust for an insurable donor is the issuance of a new policy that the trust applies for and owns. In this way there is no possibility of an application of the 3-year contemplation-of-death rule. Furthermore, since there is no gift of a life insurance policy to the trust, only the funds to pay premiums are given.

If Larry's present life insurance coverage is transferred to the trust, there will be a taxable gift in the amount of the interpolated terminal reserve of the polices. Proper structuring of the Crummey provision ensures that this amount should not exceed the annual gift tax exclusion.

There are also income tax consequences to a grantor of a trust that is empowered to use the trust income to pay premiums on policies of insurance on the life of the grantor or the grantor's spouse (IRC Sec. 677(a)(3)). In this case since no assets other than an existing life insurance policy would be transferred to the trust, as in the case of most irrevocable insurance trusts, there is little or no trust income to be taxable to the grantor.

Under the revised plan the removal of the insurance proceeds from both Larry's and Anne's estates should ultimately produce an additional federal estate tax savings of approximately $39,000.

Deferral of Estate Taxes under IRC Sec. 6166

Sec. 6166 provides that if more than 35 percent of a decedent's adjusted gross estate consists of an interest in a closely held business, the executor may elect to pay the federal estate tax attributable to such stock over a period of up to 14 years and 9 months. You will recall that Larry's estate would not qualify for a Sec. 303 redemption after the recommended installment sale to Steve because it failed to meet the 35 percent test. For the same reason—failure to meet the 35 percent test—deferral of estate taxes under Sec. 6166 will not be available. Note that the availability of Sec. 6166 is not limited to corporations but applies to all closely held business interests as defined in IRC Sec. 6166(b). Sec. 303, on the other hand, applies specifically to redemptions of corporate stock.

INSURANCE PLANNING

Personal Life Insurance Coverage

Although Larry presently has life insurance and other liquid assets that are sufficient to pay his estate taxes and administrative expenses, he should at least participate in the corporation's group insurance plan as long as he remains an employee to give him an extra margin of protection. As his investment is withdrawn from Millers and becomes more liquid, his present coverage may be sufficient.

Personal Property and Liability Coverage

From the information given in the case, two questions can be raised about the Millers' personal property and liability needs. First, the amount of insurance on the Millers' residence is inadequate to satisfy the replacement-cost provision of their homeowners policy. Under homeowners form 3, property losses are settled on a full replacement-cost basis only if the amount of insurance carried at the time of loss is equal to 80 percent or more of the full replacement cost of the dwelling. However, loss settlements are limited to the amount of insurance carried, and an insured suffering a total loss will be fully indemnified only if insurance equal to 100 percent of the full replacement cost is carried. If the amount of insurance is less than 80 percent of the full replacement cost, the insurer's liability will be limited to the greater of (1) an amount calculated as if the policy contained an 80 percent coinsurance clause, based on the full replacement cost, or (2) the actual cash value of the damaged property. Thus the Millers will not have any losses to their house paid in full unless they carry an amount of insurance equal to at least $280,000 or 80 percent of the dwelling's $350,000 replacement cost. (Since the actual replacement value seems to be only an estimate, an appraisal is probably in order.)

Second, no mention is made of any insurance on the condominium in another state. It can be adequately insured under a homeowners form 6, which is specifically designed to meet the needs of condominium owners. In addition to providing liability protection, it insures the real property that comprises the individual condominium unit. It is, however, up to the condominium association to insure the shell of the building. The basic form applies only to owner-occupied units, and an endorsement will be necessary since the unit is occasionally rented to others. The charge for this endorsement reflects the increased exposure resulting from tenant-occupied property. In addition, an endorsement is also needed if the real property within the unit (for example, fixtures, improvements, and alternations) is valued at more than $1,000. Finally, the basic contract provides named-peril coverage but can be endorsed to all-risks coverage as exists for real property in homeowners form 3.

INVESTMENT PLANNING

Client Profile

Larry's current assets reflect his risk avoidance attitude and result in an investment program seeking stability of value and modest earnings. Other activities such as a modest home and avoidance of debt suggest that the Millers are quite conservative in their total outlook. Any recommendations for investments must recognize these views.

The projections over the next several years indicate that the Millers will have more than $90,000 available annually for investment purposes if the recommended solutions (the sale of 72 shares to Steve and the redemption of Anne's shares) are implemented. Larry's income from continued employment is almost sufficient to meet their cash needs. Unless the Millers drastically alter their life-style, most of their additional income is available for reinvestment. Any recommendations for specific investment assets should also recognize that convenience of reinvestment of income is a desirable characteristic.

Anne inherited some blue-chip stocks and bonds from her father. She has been managing the portfolio with the advice of her stockbroker, with whom she has been associated with for many years. She enjoys trading the portfolio and has been successful. Since Anne enjoys successfully managing her securities, no repositioning of her portfolio is appropriate. Larry, on the other hand, keeps his cash in money market mutual funds. The following investment recommendations are directed at the cash the Millers will be receiving in the future. These recommendations should be reviewed by Anne as well as Larry.

The bulk of the Millers' investable cash will come from the sale of Millers stock owned by Larry. A portion, however, will come from the redemption of Anne's stock.

Except for Anne's inheritance the Millers should consider dividing ownership of investment assets equally between them. This is preferable to joint ownership because it will assure that both Larry and Anne will be able to make full use of the unified credit for estate tax purposes. Jointly held assets, on the other hand, would pass under the marital deduction regardless of any estate planning documents.

Investment Alternatives

Certificates of Deposit

These are term deposits with either banks or savings and loan associations that are available with varying maturity dates and interest yields. Currently certificates of deposit (CDs) are yielding approximately 5 1/4 percent interest for 5-year maturities. Provided no more than $100,000 is in any one account at any one bank (or savings and loan), the account is insured by the FDIC—a desirable feature for this client's risk profile. Five-year maturities should reduce the likelihood of forced-sale problems since the Millers' annual cash flow is projected to be quite sizable. Another characteristic of CDs is that interest income can be either left to accumulate at the stipulated rate or withdrawn on a regular basis. Since the Millers will have a need for income reinvestment each year, the reinvestment feature is desirable. Furthermore, the Millers can later decide to take the current earnings on a regular basis if the return on newly issued CDs becomes higher than those already in their portfolio.

One disadvantage of CDs is that there is no growth in value other than through interest accumulations since CDs are a bank deposit. This lack of growth means CDs are subject to the inflation risk. There is also a form of the interest-rate risk. Higher earnings can be realized by having investable cash in a more liquid form if interest rates rise. If interest rates do rise after any CDs are purchased, the CDs can be turned in for early redemption, the early redemption penalty paid, and the proceeds reinvested in the then-higher rate being paid on newly issued CDs. Each rollover of this type should be analyzed to determine if the higher interest rate being earned justifies paying the redemption penalty. Some banks are now issuing CDs that do not have an early redemption penalty. However, those CDs carry a lower interest rate than those with the penalty.

The Millers should plan a schedule of purchasing some CDs each year as a means of reducing a portion of the potential interest-rate risk during the period of acquisition. Also they should not have all their CDs mature in the same year. This spreading of maturity dates avoids the possibility of having to reinvest large portions of their portfolio at a particularly low point in the interest-rate cycle.

Municipal Bond Funds

This form of fund acquires a portfolio of tax-exempt bonds. The fund can pass the federal tax exemption on municipal bond income to its shareholders. Under current law most municipal bonds issued on or before August 7, 1986, and bonds issued after that date that are deemed to be public-purpose bonds produce income that is fully exempt from federal income taxation. Bond funds that have a portfolio consisting totally of bonds issued by the states or their subdivisions in which the shareholder resides are typically free of that state's income tax. Although a state income tax exemption is a nice feature, the overriding consideration should be the quality of the bond portfolio held by the fund. For risk averters the bond fund portfolio should be high-investment grade with only a small or minor portion of the holdings having bond ratings less than AA. These funds are currently yielding approximately 6 percent on a tax-exempt basis, a yield that converts to an equivalent before-tax yield for clients in the 28 percent bracket of 8.3 percent (6%/1 − .28). Money market tax-exempt funds are currently yielding 4 percent aftertax, which is equivalent to a 5.5 percent before-tax yield.

Since these bond funds are solely invested in debt instruments, the interest-rate risk is a cause for concern. Should interest rates rise, the fund's per-share value will fall although the interest income stream might not be affected. In addition, as with all fixed-income securities, the purchasing-power risk is an inherent characteristic and will affect the buying power of the income stream.

Municipal Bonds

Direct ownership of municipal bonds can be a desirable investment for risk-averse clients provided sufficient diversification can be achieved. Newly issued investment grade municipal bonds have a tax-exempt yield of approximately 6 percent (8.3 percent before tax if the owner is in the 28 percent tax bracket) for 25- to 30-year maturity dates. The disadvantages are a lack of sufficient diversification if the portfolio consists of only one or two issues and also the same disadvantages that municipal bond funds have.

Balanced Mutual Funds

These funds distribute their portfolio among the various classes of securities: bonds, common stocks, and preferred stocks. The proportion of their assets in any one security can be either at the fund manager's discretion or specified in the prospectus. These funds are generally the most conservative of any mutual fund that invests in common stock. Their investment objectives in order of priority are to preserve capital, to generate income, and to obtain capital gains if possible. During declining markets the holding of different types of securities provides protection for the investor since typically not all markets—bond, preferred stock, and common stock—fall simultaneously.

In addition to the conservative nature of balanced funds, they, like all other funds, provide diversification and professional management, and they offer automatic reinvestment of dividends, all features desirable to the Millers. These funds provide minimal growth opportunities since only a portion of their assets is invested in common stocks. But this limited potential growth can nevertheless serve as a means of offsetting some effects of inflation.

Any investor using balanced funds, or any fund for that matter, must choose between load versus no-load funds and must also time acquisitions after the dividend date to avoid having a portion of the investment immediately returned as taxable income.

Convertible Bonds or Convertible Bond Funds

The unique feature of convertible bonds is the option the bond holder has to convert the bond, when desired, to common stock of the issuing corporation. For conservative investors these bonds provide a creditor status. However, should the common stock of the issuer rise substantially in price, the holder can convert and obtain the benefit of the increased market price of the stock. The conventional wisdom is that over long periods of time, common stocks in general tend to outperform inflation. If this holds true, this form of bond provides potential inflation protection while still spinning off interest income that is greater than the dividend flow on the underlying common stocks during the years immediately following the bond's issue. Also the bond never has to be converted. At maturity the face amount is returned to the bondholders.

Like all bonds, convertibles are subject to the interest-rate risk, and unless the underlying common stock rises faster than the price level so that conversion is desirable, they are also subject to the purchasing-power risk.

Risk-averse investors could well consider purchasing convertibles, either directly or through a convertible bond fund (with the usual fund advantages and disadvantages), provided the portfolio of these bonds (individually owned or through the bond fund) is of investment-grade quality. The yield will perhaps be one-eighth of a percent less than could be earned on nonconvertible debt of the same risk. It is the potential increase in the value of the underlying common to offset inflation that makes this form of debt attractive, particularly to investors like the Millers. They are nearing retirement, do not wish to take undue investment risks, but will probably experience inflation during the remainder of their lives.

Recommendations

Any and all the investments described above could be appropriate for the Millers. Other investments such as growth stocks or growth stock mutual funds, for example, entail risk that does not seem appropriate for these clients.

A recommended investment plan covering the next 5 years could distribute their investment funds as follows:

Investment	Percent of Annual Investment Funds
5-year CDs	25%
Municipal bond fund	45
Convertible bond fund	15
Balanced mutual fund	15

For 1995 when slightly more than $90,000 is available (based on the cash-flow summary in the case IV projections), the Millers could place about $22,500 (25 percent of $90,000) in CDs, $40,500 in perhaps two or three different municipal bond funds, $13,500 in one or two convertible bond funds, and $13,500 in one or two balanced mutual funds. A portfolio of this distribution matches their risk profile: safety of principal is paramount and level of income flow is secondary. These recommendations result in an investment portfolio that contains diversification, produces some tax-free income from the municipal bond funds, and also permits reinvestment of interest or dividend flows through the convenience of the CDs and mutual funds. The convertible bond fund and the balanced mutual fund provide some emphasis on growth and inflation protection. If inflation remains at current low levels, the Millers should have sufficient future income, given their modest expenditure patterns (relative to their income), to be essentially free of financial worries during their lifetime.

Preretirement Planning

At this point in their lives Anne and Larry should consider preretirement planning. They have devoted a major portion of their financial activities to the establishment and prosperity of their furniture business and are now nearing the conclusion of their peak wealth-accumulation years. Their efforts should focus on preparing the way for their actual retirement in a manner that will provide financial security during those years. Important factors for Larry and Anne to consider at this time include

- repositioning of assets
- asset conservation
- plan-distribution options
- retirement income estimation
- potential dependent parent
- recreation/health
- acquisition of personal assets (autos, home appliances, and so on)
- possible new career

Many of these factors have received some attention in the solution as presented up to this point. Each of these factors will now be examined for the Millers.

Repositioning of Assets

The recommendation is for Larry to sell a portion of his stock in Millers through an installment sale to their son, Steve. This sale will convert a portion of his ownership in Millers to an annual cash flow that will provide income for both himself and Anne during retirement. Larry will still have 95.5 shares in Millers that are not available for repositioning due to their general nonmarketability. At some time in the future consideration could be given to a disposition of Larry's remaining shares in Millers, possibly by means of a redemption.

Anne will have her stock redeemed by the corporation, thus producing a stream of income that will increase their cash flow.

An examination of the Millers' balance sheet discloses that they own few other assets that can be repositioned. Although the potential for repositioning Anne's portfolio of stock and bonds does exist, Anne enjoys managing these assets and has been successful in doing so. Any repositioning of these securities by the planner appears to be undesirable. However, this is a matter that should be explored with the client.

Another asset that might be repositioned is the store building. Again, in situations such as this the sale of the building to a third party could jeopardize much of this family's well-being. Steve would be at the mercy of an unsympathetic owner of the building and could have little option but to renew leases at the owner's terms. Although the asset is worth close to one-third of a million dollars, Larry would probably prefer to retain the ownership to protect both his installment sale, Anne's installment redemption, and Steve's livelihood from the furniture store. Larry should discuss with Steve the need for some long-term inflation protection from the rents that Steve will be paying. Perhaps the lease agreement should incorporate a form of escalator clause adjusting the rent either for some broad-based inflation measure or linked to increases in rents being paid in the town. Larry might consider doing this while he retains working control of Millers as part of his preretirement planning.

The beach condo Anne owns provides her with the satisfaction of being able to use it as she and the family desire. With approaching retirement promising to bring Anne and Larry more leisure time, it does not seem prudent to convert the condo into either a more full-time, rental real estate property or to sell it and use the proceeds to acquire additional income-producing securities. Under the current situation since the property is free of any debt, the modest rental income earned more than covers the annual cash drain for taxes and insurance. Continued ownership should enhance their retirement leisure time. Fortunately the Millers' financial position is such that the opportunity cost (forgone interest earnings) of the money invested in the condo does not affect their ability to meet their financial goals. Of course, the potential does exist for a subsequent sale should the need arise.

The remaining assets do not appear suited for repositioning. Perhaps the return being earned on Anne's accumulated life insurance dividends could be examined to determine whether a higher return could be obtained on the funds if placed elsewhere. The remaining assets, such as the checking and savings accounts, money market fund, automobiles, and life insurance cash values, need not be considered for repositioning at this time.

Asset Conservation

Asset conservation has two elements. The first is a relatively risk-free portfolio. The second is keeping the bulk of the assets available for the client's use should the need arise.

As is the case with many owners of small businesses, most of their wealth accumulation is in their family business, so these ventures typically involve high risk. Through the mechanisms of the installment sale to Steve and the installment payout of Anne's stock redemption the Millers will begin to move some of their wealth from the family business. However, their retirement income flow will depend on the ability of the furniture store to produce income to meet these obligations. Also Larry will continue to own some shares in Millers.

Only two of their existing assets—the store building and Anne's stock and bond portfolio—exhibit high-risk characteristics. The store building probably has alternative uses and in that sense is less risky than a special-purpose building would be. The composition of Anne's portfolio is not specifically stated, and perhaps a somewhat less risky mix of stocks and bonds could provide additional asset conservation.

The recommendations presented earlier for the Millers to employ for their investable cash flow during the next several years are relatively conservative in nature and are consistent with an asset-conservation objective.

Maintaining their accumulated assets for their use is the method recommended for the Millers (that is, the installment sale) in transferring ownership in Millers. In addition, their recommended estate plans provide the maximum protection to the surviving spouse. Thus their assets are being managed in a manner that will provide them with the desired economic benefits.

Plan Distribution Options

Larry presently has almost $66,000 in the profit-sharing plan of Millers. He plans to continue his employment for several years before withdrawing from any active involvement in the business. Even if no further contributions are made for his benefit, and assuming the plan earns about 8 percent annually over the next several years, Larry should have at least $90,000 of plan assets available for income-producing purposes. Since retirement is not imminent, there is no immediate need for Larry and Anne to choose between a lump-sum distribution and installment distribution or a joint and survivor annuity. Given their expected cash flows during the next few years, the Millers should continue deferring the removal of plan assets as long as is feasible without incurring penalties in order to obtain the maximum benefit of tax deferral.

Retirement Income Estimation

Table 6-1 projects the amount of cash inflow Larry and Anne will have during the first 5 years of their retirement under the assumption that Larry retires from Millers in 1999.

During the first 5 years of retirement the Millers' cash outflows will rise less than the increase in their cash inflows from sources presently available to them. The effect of this is shown on the net cash inflow line in table 6-1. Based on this data the Millers will be able to save a rather sizable sum each year, which, if invested in bonds yielding a 6 percent return, will result in a year-to-year increase in their income. The Millers should be financially secure during their years of retirement.

One important point to consider is that the $27,000 (approximate) annual cash inflow from the proposed redemption of Anne's stock in Millers will cease with the payment in 2004 (if a 10-year installment term is in fact implemented), so their income will be reduced beginning in 2005. The payments from Doug for the purchase of the second store will end in 2001. The combined effect of these two events is to reduce their annual saving by the aftertax cash inflow from these two installment transactions.

TABLE 6-1
Retirement Cash Inflow/Cash Expense Estimation

	1999	2000	2001	2002	2003
Cash Inflow					
Installment sale (Doug)	$ 27,080	$ 27,080	$ 27,080	$ 27,080	$ 27,080
Installment sale (Steve)	28,340	28,340	28,340	28,340	28,340
302 redemption	28,430	28,430	28,430	28,430	28,430
Social security	17,484	18,009	18,549	19,105	19,678
Pension plan	10,500	10,500	10,500	10,500	10,500
Building rental	44,000	46,640	49,438	52,405	55,549
Anne's portfolio	5,521	5,742	5,972	6,210	6,459
Investment portfolio (reinvested cash flow [12/31/98])	26,935	26,935	26,935	26,935	26,935
Interest on retirement savings	0	3,205	7,313	10,997	14,686
Total cash inflow	$187,054	$193,645	$201,320	$208,767	$216,421
Cash Outflow					
Expenses	47,000	49,820	52,809	55,978	59,336
Federal and state income taxes	69,000	72,000	75,000	78,000	81,000
Vacation/travel	10,000	11,000	12,100	13,310	14,641
Total cash outflow	$126,000	$132,820	$139,909	$147,288	$154,977
Net cash inflow (annual investable cash)	$ 61,054	$ 60,825	$ 61,411	$ 61,479	$ 61,444
Accumulated net savings during retirement	$ 61,054	$121,879	$183,290	$244,769	$306,213

The following assumptions were made with respect to the cash inflow and outflow of the Millers:

- The installment payments from Doug will cease at the end of 2003.
- The installment sale to Steve of some of Larry's stock will be completed in 1995 and will provide an annual cash inflow of $28,340 (approximately) for 15 years.
- The stock redemption by Millers of Anne's shares will be completed in 1994 and will provide a cash inflow of $28,430 (approximately) for 10 years.
- Social security benefits will commence in 1999 with Larry receiving the maximum benefit and Anne obtaining the 50 percent spousal benefit. It is assumed that social security benefits will grow at a rate of 3 percent each year.

- Larry will have about $90,000 in the profit-sharing pension at the end of 1998. This amount could be higher if Millers alters its plan or increases its profitability. The $90,000 could purchase a joint and survivor annuity of $10,500 per year (at current rates) for Larry and Anne (although the Millers might opt to take a lump-sum distribution or an installment payout at that time).
- The rental income from the store building is $33,000 annually and is anticipated to increase at a rate of 6 percent each year. It will be about $44,000 in 1999.
- The reinvested cash flow the Millers will have at the end of the planning period, 1998, will be $513,050. A 5 1/4 percent return will be earned after retirement.
- Anne's portfolio will continue to increase in value at a 5 percent annual rate. The yield on these securities will average 4 percent annually.
- It is assumed that Millers will be converted to S corporation status. Since Larry will retain 95.5 shares, a portion of the firm's net profits must be included in his income. It is assumed that Larry will receive distributions equal in amount to his income tax liability arising from his pro rata share of Millers's taxable income. These figures have not been entered into the table.
- Anne currently receives about $4,000 in rental income from the condo. Since this is a relatively small portion of the Millers' expected income and might well be reduced if they use the condo to a greater degree when in retirement, it is excluded from these projections.
- Their committed, discretionary, and property tax expenses are expected to be about $47,000 in 1999. Inflation will cause these to increase at an annual rate of 6 percent.
- Both federal and state income tax rates are assumed to remain at their current rates.
- Vacation/travel expenses will increase 10 percent each year.
- Any excess cash flow after January 1, 1999, will be accumulated. The yield is assumed to be 5 1/4 percent.

Potential Dependent Parent

Anne's mother, the sole surviving parent of either Anne or Larry, appears to be financially independent and in good health at this time. Unless serious medical problems or long-term nursing care deplete her assets, it is unlikely that the Millers will be called upon to provide financial support. Therefore they need not include any expenditure planning for the benefit of Anne's mother in their retirement plans. However, they might have to consider the possibility of providing some personal time to care for her should she experience a deterioration in health.

Recreation/Health

At this time both the Millers expect to travel and to use their condo to a greater degree when Larry either spends less time with Millers or fully retires. Fortunately the Millers enjoy good health, so these factors do not create any unique planning considerations at this time.

Personal Asset Acquisition

Since Larry is in the furniture business, it can be assumed that furniture for the home is not needed now nor will be at retirement. The Millers might wish to consider the purchase of a new car when Larry retires completely if their travel plans include lengthy car trips in this country. Other than the car, it does not appear they have any unfilled wishes in this category.

Possible New Career

Larry has not indicated any interest in possibly embarking on a different career upon retirement. His expressed desire to travel and to spend more time with Anne and their grandchildren is the extent of his expected use of his retirement time.

PLANNING FOR THE OFFICER OF A LARGE ORGANIZATION

In addition to the group of self-employed persons and small business owners, there is a rapidly growing group, the managers and officers of large organizations, who are becoming clients of professional financial planners. These clients often have a specialized set of benefits as a consequence of their employment, but they also have many of the same priorities and concerns that can benefit from a financial planner's expertise. With increasing awareness of the availability of comprehensive, well-trained financial planners, some large organizations offer personal financial counseling as an executive benefit. In other cases the relationship with the financial adviser is developed as an outgrowth of some single-purpose planning provided by an insurance agent, a securities banker, a CPA, or a lawyer.

In contrast to the young couple with only the potential to accumulate substantial assets, these clients, typically between 45 and 60 years of age, have reached or are nearing the peak of their careers. Hence a portfolio of investment assets is part of their current financial situation. In addition, the prospect of further significant accumulation exists, since children's education expenses are actually or almost completely paid. The clients can focus on the adequacy of their retirement planning. Although included in the upper ranks of their employer's management team, these clients lack the requisite clout to install benefit programs suited to their specific situation, and any desirable changes in employment-related benefits may be beyond their power or influence. Thus individual plans, although lacking some of the tax advantages found in corporate plans, provide the means to meet the clients' financial objectives.

Today medical advances and increased longevity enhance the likelihood that clients in this age bracket should consider their potential need for long-term care outside of their home for themselves and their spouses. Also some of these clients may need to provide financial assistance to care for a parent or to provide resources for the care of a disabled child over a long period. Once again, personal planning and funding techniques may provide the only adequate basis for a satisfactory course of action that will meet the objective.

CASE NARRATIVE

Personal Information

Edgar (Ed) and Amy Martinson are 54 and 45 respectively and reside in a suburb of Atlanta, Georgia. They have been married 24 years and have two children. Beatrice (Bea) is 22, single, and has been employed in the international division of a large bank since graduating from college 2 years ago. Their son, Scott, is 16 and attends high school.

Shortly after Amy and Ed were married in 1970 they had simple, reciprocal wills drafted in which each left all of his or her respective estate properties to the surviving spouse. No revisions have been made to these wills.

Ed joined Inc, Inc., in 1974 as an assistant to the plant superintendent. He has progressed to his current position of vice president of manufacturing, which became effective on December 1, 1992. Details of Ed's employment and benefits are described in the section titled "Employment Information."

Amy began a career in retailing as a buyer for a large department store but interrupted her career at their daughter's birth. When Scott entered kindergarten, she returned to her former employer. When their son was injured 7 years ago, Amy resigned to care for him and presently has no plans to continue her career.

Ed, Amy, and Bea all enjoy excellent health, but Scott has serious health problems. Seven years ago he fell from a tree, severely injuring his leg and hip. After a long hospital stay and months of rehabilitation therapy he appeared to be fully recovered. However, about 3 years ago Scott began to experience aches in the hip joint and eventually was unable to move about. Although he had a hip replacement at that time, it only slightly alleviated the pain and did little to improve his mobility. Ed's health insurance under Inc's plan has covered most of the medical expenses resulting from the accident, but the Martinsons are uncertain about Scott's future medical costs. In addition to any out-of-pocket medical expenses, Amy took several specialized courses at the local hospital so she could give Scott some care that would otherwise require hospitalization or semiskilled nursing experience.

As a result of these recent health problems Scott has become rather frail physically. Although he continues to attend school, he lacks a positive attitude toward education. Since his grades reflect this attitude, the Martinsons doubt that he will continue any education beyond high school. They worry that this lack of education beyond the high school level, combined with his physical condition, will make it impossible for him to support himself adequately.

By the time Bea started college, the Martinsons had accumulated about $25,000 for her educational expenses. These funds, plus some of their annual income, were sufficient to cover Bea's college expenses. Ed's mother, who was very fond of Bea, died when Bea was 4. Her will established a testamentary trust for Bea's benefit with Grass Roots Bank as the trustee. The terms of the trust permit each year's trust income to be paid out annually if Bea notifies the trustee, but Bea has not yet exercised her option to withdraw any trust income. The corpus and accumulated income, if any, can be invaded to fund an elaborate wedding or a down payment on a home. When Bea is 35, any funds remaining must be distributed to her. Trust assets have a current market value of $70,000.

Since Bea's prospective financial concerns appear to be largely taken care of, the Martinsons want to focus their attention on providing for Scott. Currently they have about $26,000 set aside for him. These funds are invested in conservative common stocks, and although Ed and Amy are the owners, the stocks are held in street name in a separate account maintained with a large brokerage firm. The stocks are increasing in value at a rate of 6 percent a year and are paying a dividend of 3 percent a year. All dividend income is automatically invested in the issuers' dividend reinvestment plans. Until Ed retires and perhaps for a few years thereafter, the Martinsons anticipate that they can provide for Scott's needs from their current income. However, by the time Ed retires they would like to have some provision in place for a life-long stream of income to supplement Scott's impaired earning capacity and to cover his continuing medical expenses. At today's prices the Martinsons' target is to provide Scott with an annual supplemental income of $3,000, adjusted for inflation. Ed planned to retire by age 62 but is now unsure whether this will be feasible in light of their objective to provide long-term support for Scott.

A further concern of Ed's is Amy's life expectancy. Not only is she a bit younger than he, but her family history indicates it is likely that she will have a longer than normal life expectancy. Although he doesn't need to make any decisions now about distributions from the corporate defined-benefit, noncontributory pension plan and the contributory 401(k) plan, Ed and Amy believe these decisions must be considered in conjunction with some retirement planning necessary to supplement the retirement benefits available from both Inc and social security.

Both of Amy's parents are in their 70s, and three of her four grandparents are still hale and hearty folk. Although some of Amy's elderly relatives may need support, Amy and Ed are not concerned about accumulating any funds for this contingency because fortunately Amy's father was very successful financially and is able to afford the support necessary at this time. He has been open with Amy about his finances and, barring unforeseen financial reverses, expects to provide economic assistance for Amy's grandparents as well as provide for his and his spouse's support. Amy has a brother, Bob, aged 48, who is a physician in a different state.

Ed's family does not include such long-lived ancestors, and both his parents died in their early 70s. Except for an unmarried brother, Jack, who is 10 years younger than he, Ed has no living relatives other than his spouse and children.

Four years ago, expecting that Ed would rise to the executive ranks of Inc, the Martinsons sold their home for $200,000 and purchased a newly built $325,000 home in an exclusive suburb. Their adjusted basis in the old home was $58,000. The Martinsons made a down payment of $200,000 and financed the remainder of the acquisition cost with a 25-year mortgage at a fixed interest rate of 10.8 percent. The estimated fair market value of their home is $355,000.

When Ed and Amy were married in 1970, Ed purchased a $50,000 whole life policy with an annual premium of $1,120. He is the owner and Amy is the primary beneficiary. He has since named Bea and Scott as the contingent beneficiaries, per stirpes. This policy has a current cash value of $18,100. Amy converted her group term life insurance to $5,000 face of whole life in 1972, naming Ed as the primary beneficiary. The children are the contingent beneficiaries, per stirpes. The policy has a $120 annual premium and a cash value of $1,800. Ed has two $25,000 policies with combined premiums of $1,215 and a total cash value of $16,325. Each of these policies was purchased when a child was born. Each child is the named primary beneficiary on a policy, and Amy is the contingent beneficiary for both policies.

Over the years the Martinsons have invested their excess income in several different instruments. First, during the years that the IRA window permitting fully tax deductible contributions of up to $2,000 annually was open for participants in qualified pension plans without an income limitation, Ed funded an IRA and a spousal IRA at the local savings and loan when their finances permitted. CDs were used as the investment instrument. The blended current return based on differing maturity dates of the CDs is 8.1 percent. When the contributions ceased being tax deductible, Ed discontinued adding additional money to the IRA. Overall he put $9,800 into his IRA, which now has an accumulated value of $21,200. The spousal IRA for Amy, with $1,250 invested, has an accumulated value of $2,200. Its current return is about the same as Ed's.

They maintain a regular joint checking account that currently has a $10,000 balance. They also have a money market deposit account at the same bank. The account typically has a target average balance of about $25,000 and currently earns 4.75 percent. Their monthly mortgage payment and other large bills are paid by drafts drawn on this account. If the deposit account becomes too large, the excess is divided between investments in a balanced mutual fund and a growth mutual fund. In both funds all dividends and capital gains have been reinvested. Their basis is $15,000 in the balanced fund, which now has a current value of $28,000. His investment in the growth fund is worth $40,000 and has a basis of $19,000. The estimated annual return on these funds has averaged 9.5 percent and 13 percent respectively over the last 5 years.

The taxable portion of the total return from the balanced fund averages 4.3 percent and from the growth fund it is 1.5 percent. The remainder of each fund's return is unrealized capital gains on the portfolio and increases in the net asset value of their shares.

Amy has furnished their new home with $30,000 worth of additional purchases, which were partially financed over 2 years. Furnishings and other personal property they own increase the value of the contents to about $75,000.

Ed's auto was purchased in December 1993 and is being financed with 42 monthly payments of $440. Currently the vehicle is worth about $20,000. Amy's station wagon is fully paid for and has a value of $12,000.

Until the additional problems with Scott began to drain some of their potential savings, Ed and Amy anticipated having Scott's education fully funded before he entered college. They then expected to establish a side fund for their retirement. Their target was and still is to have an additional $5,000 of annual income beginning at the expected retirement date. This additional income, they thought, would enable Ed to retire at age 62, the earliest date permitted under Inc's pension plan. They felt the side fund was needed due to both the difference in their ages and to Amy's potential long life.

Employment Information

Ed's job requires him to spend about 30 percent of his time on visits to Inc's facilities in North America and Europe. Inc plans to commence building at least one manufacturing operation in an Asian country during the next 2 years. Whenever Ed is traveling on company business, he is covered with accidental death insurance that is double his annual base salary. This is in addition to other employment-related life insurance described below.

In his new position Ed's salary is $95,000 per year, and he is now eligible for Inc's executive bonus plan that over the past several years has distributed an annual bonus equal to 10 percent of each participating executive's salary. The total bonus distributed by the plan is directly related to corporate profits. The percentage of corporate profits distributed by the bonus plan has remained constant over the past several years. Each plan participant's potential share of next year's profits is determined by Inc's board at its December meeting. Inc uses the calendar year for financial statement and income tax purposes.

Coverage for 100 percent of lost salary for short-term disability (maximum of 6 months) is provided under a nonfunded sick-pay plan. Salary lost due to a disability preventing a return to employment status after a period of 6 months is replaced at 75 percent, including social security disability benefits, for the duration of the disability or until normal retirement age, whichever comes first. This amounts to almost $6,000 a month. Inc will continue to credit years of employment for pension plan coverage and make both the employer and the employee contributions to the 401(k) plan. In addition, coverage will be continued under the company's insured medical plan at no cost to the disabled employee. The Martinsons stated that they would want to have the equivalent of Ed's current salary of almost $8,000 a month should he become disabled. Therefore they have a shortfall of $2,000 a month.

Inc's qualified noncontributory defined-benefit pension plan will provide a maximum retirement income of 1.5 percent of the average of an employee's highest 5 years of income times the number of years of service, with the maximum number of years of service for the purpose of the plan being 25 years. The pension benefit is not offset by retirement income provided under social security. The value of the future pension benefit, reduced to present value, is approximately $180,000.

Six years ago Inc instituted a voluntary-participation, salary reduction type 401(k) plan for its employees. About 85 percent of Inc's employees participate in the plan. For employee contributions up to 5 percent of salary, Inc will contribute 50 percent of the employee's contribution during the first 5 years of service and 75 percent until 10 years of service are achieved. At that point Inc will match the employee's contribution. The plan permits lump-sum withdrawals upon retirement or severance from the employer. The 401(k) plan is self-directed; plan participants may choose the investment instruments and may shift invested funds within a limited set of alternatives. Investment options include Inc's common stock, which is traded on a national exchange; a no-load family of mutual funds that includes a money market, a U.S. government bond, a corporate bond, a balanced, a growth, and an international fund as its "family"; and Series EE U.S. government savings bonds. Ed has participated in the plan since its inception and divides both his and Inc's contributions equally between the U.S. government bond fund and Inc's stock. At the end of last year Ed's account in the bond fund was $25,000, and Inc's stock had a market value of $37,000. He anticipates contributing 5 percent of salary each year until retirement.

As a result of Ed's promotion last December he became a participant in Inc's nonqualified deferred-compensation plan. Assuming that Ed remains with Inc until normal retirement age (65), the plan will provide a benefit of $1,500 per month for a period of 10 years provided Ed does not engage in activities deemed to be in direct competition with Inc. Should Ed die before the end of the 10-year period, the plan will continue the payments to Amy for the unpaid period of time. If Amy fails to live until the end of the 10-year period, the remaining payments will be made to Ed's estate. Although Inc is placing funds into a separate account earmarked to fund the deferred-compensation obligation, these funds are part of Inc's assets and are available to its creditors.

Inc provides noncontributory group term life insurance in the amount of 1.5 times annual base salary for all employees. Ed has named Amy as the primary beneficiary of the policy and Bea and Scott, per stirpes, as the contingent beneficiaries. Upon retirement the insurance protection decreases to $10,000 and then declines over the next 5 years to a face amount of $5,000.

Inc's comprehensive medical insurance plan provides $500,000 of lifetime coverage for each family member. Each year after a $250 per-person deductible, the insurance provides coverage for 80 percent of the first $5,000 of each year's covered benefits for the family. After the $5,000 of covered benefits is incurred in any one year, additional medical expenses are paid in full. The plan is noncontributory for employee coverage, but dependent coverage is available only if the employee contributes $10 monthly to the cost of coverage. Scott is covered under the plan until graduation from high school and coverage would be continued if he were a full-time, post-high-school student until age 23. When Scott's qualification as a student for participation in the health plan ends, the COBRA rules permit coverage to extend for 36 months as long as the premium is properly paid.

When an employee retires at normal retirement age, 65, Inc pays the full cost of medical insurance to supplement medicare for both the employee and the employee's spouse. If the joint and survivor option is selected under Inc's pension plan, Inc will continue to pay the supplemental premium for the surviving spouse. If the retired or deceased employee's spouse is not eligible for medicare, then Inc provides a group supplemental plan that will pay 80 percent of the surviving spouse's medical expenses in excess of a spouse's basic Blue Cross/Blue Shield plan until such time as the spouse is eligible for medicare. Before medicare coverage is available, the spouse pays the premium for the basic insurance, and Inc pays for the supplemental insurance. When medicare coverage becomes available, the spouse is provided the medicare supplemental insurance as described above.

Because of the latest Financial Accounting Standards Board requirement that the present value of retirees' medical expenses must be reported in a company's annual financial report and because of the rapid inflation of medical costs, Inc is currently studying the possibility of (1) discontinuing its payments for the supplemental medicare insurance, (2) having the retired employee pay for the coverage under a group plan, or (3) having the employee make contributions during his or her employment years toward the retirement medical insurance. If the first two options were implemented, Inc would make some improvements in its pension plan to partially compensate for the loss of the full payment of the supplemental medical insurance. Whatever changes are made will only affect future retirees, such as Ed.

The Martinsons' property tax assessment is $60,000 for the land and $300,000 for home improvements, although they anticipate that the property would sell for no more than $355,000. They carry an HO-3 homeowners policy that insures the dwelling for $300,000, which is the amount they anticipate it would cost to replace the structure. The contents are insured for one-half the limit on the dwelling. The policy provides $500,000 of liability coverage and what they believe is adequate additional living expense coverage should a loss occur that preludes living in their home. Although the homeowners policy would provide some coverage, the Martinsons have opted to insure Amy's jewelry and furs for scheduled values on a separate policy.

The automobiles are covered under one policy that has a liability limit of $500,000 and medical expense coverage of $10,000. In addition, the policy includes uninsured motorists, towing, collision, and other-than-collision coverages (comprehensive). The latter coverages have $500 deductibles.

To further protect themselves, the Martinsons carry a $1 million umbrella policy that requires liability insurance for both the home and the automobile in the amount of $500,000.

FIGURE 7-1
Inventory of Assets

Assets	Cost or Basis	Fair Market Value	Current Return %	Current Return $	Form of Owner-ship[1]	Available for Liquidity	Collater-alized	Location
Checking account	$10,000	10,000	--	--	JT	Yes	No	Bank
Money market deposit account	25,000	25,000	4.75	1,188	JT	Yes	No	Bank
Residence	183,000	355,000	--	--	JT	No	Yes	--
Life ins. cash value	18,100	18,100	--	--	S(H)	Yes	No	Safe-deposit box
Life ins. cash value	1,800	1,800	--	--	S(W)	Yes	No	Safe-deposit box
Life ins. cash value	16,325	16,325	--	--	S(H)	Yes	No	Safe-deposit box
IRA	9,800	21,200	8.1	1,720	S(H)	No	No	Safe-deposit box
IRA	1,250	2,200	8.1	180	S(W)	No	No	Safe-deposit box
Balanced fund	15,000	28,000	4.3	1,204	S(H)	Yes	No	Mutual fund
Growth fund	19,000	40,000	1.5	600	S(H)	Yes	No	Mutual fund
401(k) bond fund	--	25,000	--	--	S(H)	No	No	Mutual fund
401(k) stock	--	37,000	--	--	S(H)	No	No	Mutual fund
Group term life	--	142,500[2]	--	--	S(H)	Yes	No	Employer
Nonqualified deferred compensation	--	52,000[2]	--	--	S(H)	No	No	Employer
Vested pension benefit	--	180,000	--	--	S(H)	Yes	No	Employer
Common stock	15,000	26,000[2]	3.0	910	S(H)	Yes	No	Safe-deposit box
Household furnishings	75,000	75,000	--	--	JT	No	No	--
Auto	28,000	20,000	--	--	S(H)	Yes	Yes	--
Auto	20,000	12,000	--	--	S(W)	No	No	--

[1] JT = joint tenants with right of survivorship; S = single ownership; H = husband; W = wife
[2] Value of plan benefits

INSTRUCTIONS TO STUDENTS

Based on this information, prepare a working outline for the Martinsons' financial plan. When this has been completed, it can be compared with the suggested solution that follows. After comparing your working outline to the suggested solution, turn to page 7.13 for further instructions.

WORKING OUTLINE

I. Client's objectives

   A. For lifetime planning
      1. Accumulate sufficient wealth to assure that current life-style continues following retirement
      2. Address the retirement planning issues stemming from the fact that Amy's family has a history of longevity and therefore Amy will probably survive Ed by many years
      3. Accumulate a fund that will assure an adequate stream of income to Scott for purposes of maintenance and medical costs
      4. Provide current medical insurance coverage for Scott both while he is covered by Inc's plan and after he is no longer covered by the plan
      5. Assess current insurance coverage and restructure such coverages optimally

   B. For disposition at death
      1. Provide for Amy since she is likely to outlive Ed
      2. Construct the estate plan so that Scott's disability is adequately addressed should Ed and/or Amy predecease him
      3. Equalize eventual inheritances in some equitable manner to allow Bea to receive an equal benefit and an equal amount of estate property
      4. Ensure that the entire family will have sufficient assets to maintain their life-style if Ed should die prematurely
      5. Provide for estate liquidity at death
      6. Avoid unnecessary taxes at the death of either Ed or Amy

II. Personal planning

   A. Tax planning
      1. Present situation
      2. Choosing the appropriate method of distribution from qualified plans
         a. Lump-sum distribution
         b. Annuity payout approach
      3. Treatment of distributions from nonqualified deferred-compensation plan
      4. Creation of fund for Scott
         a. Outright gifts
         b. 2503(b) trust
         c. 2503(c) trust
         d. UGMA gifts
      5. Reduction of federal income tax burden—accomplishment of personal objectives through income-shifting devices to reduce cost
      6. Dispositions at death
         a. Revision of estate plan
         b. Analysis of present situation
         c. Recommendations
         d. Modification of present plan to consider concept of "equity of inheritance"
         e. Considerations stemming from Amy's family's history of longevity
         f. Use of irrevocable life insurance trust

   B. Insurance planning
      1. Long-term care protection for Scott

2. Long-term care protection for Amy
3. Current life insurance coverage
4. Equalization of benefit for Bea
5. Review of accidental death and dismemberment coverage to determine its necessity
6. Review of disability insurance situation
7. Comprehensive review of all medical coverages for Ed, Amy, and Scott
8. Evaluation of existing personal property and liability coverages for scope and amounts

C. Investment planning
   1. Review on a comprehensive basis the existing assets and evaluate the desirability of repositioning such assets
   2. Determine funding needs for pension supplement
   3. Determine funding needs for Scott and recommend strategy and investments for achievement of this objective
   4. Examine alternate investment vehicles and recommend investment plans for current and future available funds

INSTRUCTIONS TO STUDENTS

Now prepare a financial plan for the Martinsons. When you have prepared your solution, you can compare it to the suggested solution that follows.

Suggested Solution

PERSONAL FINANCIAL PLAN

for

EDGAR AND AMY MARTINSON

CLIENTS' OBJECTIVES

A. For lifetime planning
1. Accumulate sufficient wealth to assure that current life-style continues following retirement
2. Address the retirement planning issues stemming from the fact that Amy's family has a history of longevity and therefore Amy will probably survive Ed many years
3. Accumulate a fund that will assure an adequate stream of income to Scott for purposes of maintenance and medical costs
4. Provide current medical insurance coverage for Scott both while he is covered by Inc's plan and after he is no longer covered by the plan
5. Assess current insurance coverage and restructure such coverages optimally

B. For disposition at death
1. Provide for Amy since she is likely to outlive Ed
2. Construct the estate plan so that Scott's disability is adequately addressed should Ed and/or Amy predecease him
3. Equalize eventual inheritances in some equitable manner to allow Bea to receive an equal benefit and an equal amount of estate property
4. Ensure that the entire family will have sufficient assets to maintain their life-style if Ed should die prematurely
5. Provide for estate liquidity at death
6. Avoid unnecessary taxes at the death of either Ed or Amy

PERSONAL PLANNING

TAX PLANNING

Present Situation

There are eleven separate issues stemming from the Martinsons' current situation that need to be addressed within the framework of tax planning. Each of the following current situations contains some financial and/or tax considerations that will affect their ability to achieve their objectives:

- the corporate defined-benefit noncontributory pension plan
- the contributory 401(k) plan
- the tax implications of the purchase of the new residence
- the $50,000 whole life insurance policy
- the individual retirement account (IRA)
- the money market deposit account
- the capital-gain reinvestments in the mutual fund
- the current salary of $95,000
- the nonqualified deferred-compensation plan
- the group term life insurance
- the refinancing of their residence

[text continues on page 7.31]

BASE CASE

CASE ASSUMPTIONS—BASE CASE

1. The checking account balance is maintained at $10,000; the account is noninterest bearing.

2. Ed's salary is increased at 5 percent annually.

3. The money market deposit account earns 4 3/4 percent annually.

4. Investable cash is invested and earns 5 percent annually.

5. Expenditures for food, clothing and cleaning, utilities, phone, vacations, and charitable contributions will increase annually at 3 percent.

6. Expenditures for transportation will increase 4 percent annually.

7. Expenditures for entertainment will increase 5 percent annually.

8. Expenditures for medical insurance and other medical expenses will increase at 6 percent annually.

9. Decreases in the value of furniture have been ignored.

10. Automobiles decrease in value at a rate of 15 percent annually.

11. The value of the home will increase at 1 percent annually.

12. The common stock portfolio will increase at 9 percent annually.

13. Dividends from the common stock portfolio are currently $850, will increase 4 percent annually, and are reinvested in the portfolio.

14. IRAs will earn 8.1 percent annually over the next 4 years.

1994   **INCOME STATEMENT**

EDGAR & AMY MARTINSON

BASE CASE	1994	1995	1996	1997	1998
Earned Income					
Compensation-C1	95,000	99,750	104,738	109,974	115,473
Company Bonus	9,500	9,975	10,474	10,997	11,547
401(K)-Ed's Contr	-4,750	-4,988	-5,237	-5,499	-5,774
	99,750	104,737	109,974	115,473	121,246
Interest/Dividends					
Money Market Fund	1,188	1,188	1,188	1,188	1,188
Stock Portfolio	827	877	929	985	1,044
Investable Cash	567	1,776	3,142	4,749	6,665
Growth Mutual Funds	1,115	1,278	1,465	1,678	1,924
Balnced Mutual Fund	1,182	1,299	1,428	1,571	1,727
	4,879	6,418	8,152	10,171	12,548
Other					
State Tax Refund	0	0	0	2	0
	0	0	0	2	0
Adj Gross Income	104,629	111,155	118,127	125,654	133,794
Deductions					
Charitable 50%	2,000	2,060	2,122	2,185	2,251
State Tax Paid	4,410	4,781	5,179	5,608	6,074
Property Tax--Home	3,000	3,090	3,183	3,278	3,377
Home Mortgage	12,893	12,713	12,511	12,286	12,038
Reductn For High Inc	0	0	-50	-153	-271
Gross Deductions	22,303	22,644	22,944	23,204	23,468
Standard Deduction	6,200	6,400	6,600	6,850	7,100
Allowed Deductions	22,303	22,644	22,944	23,204	23,468
Pers Exemptions	7,050	7,350	7,650	7,800	8,100
Taxable Income	75,276	81,161	87,532	94,650	102,226
Fed Income Tax	16,280	17,756	19,358	21,164	23,110
Fed Tax Bracket	28.0	28.0	28.0	28.0	28.0

1994 　　　　　　　　　　　　　**BALANCE SHEET**

EDGAR & AMY MARTINSON

BASE CASE	1994	1995	1996	1997	1998
LIQUID ASSETS					
Cash Balance	9,991	10,005	10,005	10,025	10,034
Cash Deposits					
Investable Cash	23,251	49,580	79,236	115,474	157,803
IRA (CD's) - Ed	22,917	24,773	26,780	28,949	31,294
IRA (CD's) - Amy	2,378	2,571	2,779	3,004	3,247
Money Market Fund	25,000	25,000	25,000	25,000	25,000
	73,546	101,924	133,795	172,427	217,344
Stocks & Bonds					
Stock Portfolio	28,340	30,891	33,671	36,701	40,004
Growth Mutual Funds	45,843	52,540	60,215	69,011	79,093
Balnced Mutual Fund	30,787	33,851	37,219	40,923	44,996
	104,970	117,281	131,105	146,636	164,093
Overpaid Taxes					
Overpaid State Tx	1	1	2	1	1
	1	1	2	1	1
Life Insurance					
LifeInsCashValu-Ed	34,425	34,425	34,425	34,425	34,425
LifeInsCashValu-Amy	1,800	1,800	1,800	1,800	1,800
	36,225	36,225	36,225	36,225	36,225
Liquid Assets	224,733	265,436	311,132	365,314	427,696
NONLIQUID ASSETS					
Retirement Plans					
401(K) Plan	67,270	72,988	79,192	85,923	93,226
401(K)-Ed's Contr	4,750	9,738	14,975	20,474	26,248
401(K)-Emplyr Contr	4,750	9,738	14,975	20,474	26,248
Vested Pension	149,625	157,106	164,961	173,209	181,869
	226,395	249,570	274,103	300,080	327,591
Personal Property					
Home	346,430	349,894	353,393	356,927	360,496
Ed's Car	17,000	14,450	12,283	10,440	8,874
Amy's Car	10,200	8,670	7,370	6,264	5,324
Home Furnishings	75,000	75,000	75,000	75,000	75,000
	448,630	448,014	448,045	448,631	449,695
Nonliquid Assets	675,025	697,584	722,148	748,711	777,286
Total Assets	899,758	963,020	1,033,280	1,114,025	1,204,982

7.25

1994 **BALANCE SHEET** (cont.)

EDGAR & AMY MARTINSON

BASE CASE	1994	1995	1996	1997	1998

LIABILITIES

Mortgage Loans
Home Mortgage	118,505	116,733	114,759	112,560	110,113
	118,505	116,733	114,759	112,560	110,113

Notes Payable
Ed's Car Loan	11,429	6,998	2,151	0	0
	11,429	6,998	2,151	0	0
Total Liabilities	129,934	123,731	116,910	112,560	110,113
Net Worth	769,824	839,289	916,370	1,001,465	1,094,869

1994   CASHFLOW STATEMENT

EDGAR & AMY MARTINSON

BASE CASE	1994	1995	1996	1997	1998
BEGINNING OF YEAR					
Idle Cash On Hand	10,000	9,991	10,005	10,005	10,025
SOURCES OF CASH					
Cash Income					
Compensation-Cl	95,000	99,750	104,738	109,974	115,473
Company Bonus	9,500	9,975	10,474	10,997	11,547
Interest+Dividends	2,015	2,065	2,117	2,173	2,232
	106,515	111,790	117,328	123,145	129,252
Tax Refund					
State Tax Refund	0	0	0	2	0
	0	0	0	2	0
Total Cash Inflow	106,515	111,790	117,328	123,147	129,252
Tot Cash Available	116,515	121,781	127,333	133,152	139,277
USES OF CASH					
Fully Tax Deductible					
401(K)-Ed's Contr	4,750	4,988	5,237	5,499	5,774
Home Mortgage	12,893	12,713	12,511	12,286	12,038
	17,643	17,701	17,748	17,785	17,812
Partly Deductible					
Med Ins Premium	240	254	270	286	303
Other Medical Expen	2,800	2,968	3,146	3,335	3,535
Charity Contrb-50%	2,000	2,060	2,122	2,185	2,251
	5,040	5,282	5,538	5,806	6,089
Not Tax Deductible					
Ed's Car Loan	1,228	849	433	49	0
Food	8,000	8,240	8,487	8,742	9,004
Clothing	3,000	3,090	3,183	3,278	3,377
Entertainment	2,000	2,100	2,205	2,315	2,431
Vacations	3,000	3,090	3,183	3,278	3,377
Transportation	1,000	1,040	1,082	1,125	1,170
Home Insurance Prem	500	510	520	531	541
Prop/Liab Ins Prem	100	102	104	106	108
Auto Insurance Prem	1,000	1,040	1,082	1,125	1,170
Ed's Life Ins Prems	2,335	2,335	2,335	2,335	2,335
Amy's Life Ins Prem	125	125	125	125	125
Home Improvements	1,000	1,030	1,061	1,093	1,126
Utility/Phone	2,000	2,060	2,122	2,185	2,251
Personal Care Items	1,300	1,339	1,379	1,421	1,463
	26,588	26,950	27,300	27,708	28,477

7.27

1994   CASHFLOW STATEMENT (cont.)

EDGAR & AMY MARTINSON

BASE CASE	1994	1995	1996	1997	1998
Taxes Paid					
Fed Tax Paid	16,280	17,756	19,358	21,164	23,110
State Tax Paid	4,410	4,781	5,179	5,608	6,074
FICA/Soc Sec Tax	5,235	5,460	5,688	5,939	6,194
Real Estate Tax	3,000	3,090	3,183	3,278	3,377
	28,925	31,087	33,408	35,989	38,755
Purchase/Deposits					
Investable Cash	22,684	24,553	26,514	31,489	35,664
	22,684	24,553	26,514	31,489	35,664
Liability Liquidation					
Home Mortgage	1,592	1,772	1,974	2,199	2,447
Ed's Car Loan	4,052	4,431	4,847	2,151	0
	5,644	6,203	6,821	4,350	2,447
Tot Cash Outflow	106,524	111,776	117,328	123,127	129,244
END OF YEAR					
Cash Balance	9,991	10,005	10,005	10,025	10,034

1994   SUPPORTING SCHEDULE

EDGAR & AMY MARTINSON

BASE CASE	JOINT 1994	JOINT 1995	JOINT 1996	JOINT 1997	JOINT 1998
Income					
Earned Income	99,750	104,737	109,974	115,473	121,246
Adj Gross Income	104,629	111,155	118,127	125,654	133,794
Allowed Deductions	22,303	22,644	22,944	23,204	23,468
Pers Exemptions	7,050	7,350	7,650	7,800	8,100
Taxable Income	75,276	81,161	87,532	94,650	102,226
Federal Tax Liab					
Regular Tax	16,280	17,756	19,358	21,164	23,110
Gross Fed Inc Tax	16,280	17,756	19,358	21,164	23,110
Fed Income Tax	16,280	17,756	19,358	21,164	23,110
Fed Tax Analysis					
Indexing Factor	46	51	56	62	68
Fed Tax Bracket	28.0	28.0	28.0	28.0	28.0
$ To Next Bracket	13,874	11,139	7,968	4,200	124
Next Bracket	31.0	31.0	31.0	31.0	31.0
Previous Bracket	15.0	15.0	15.0	15.0	15.0
$ To Prev Bracket	38,376	42,961	47,982	53,700	59,876
Alt Minimum Tax					
Adj Gross Income	104,629	111,155	118,127	125,654	133,794
State Tax Refund	0	0	0	-2	0
Contributions	-2,000	-2,060	-2,122	-2,185	-2,251
Home Mortgage	-12,893	-12,713	-12,511	-12,286	-12,038
Adjusted AMTI	89,736	96,382	103,494	111,181	119,505
AMT Exemptions	-45,000	-45,000	-45,000	-45,000	-45,000
AMT Taxable Inc	44,736	51,382	58,494	66,181	74,505
Gross Alt Min Tx	11,631	13,359	15,208	17,207	19,371
Fed Tax Less FTC	-16,280	-17,755	-19,358	-21,164	-23,110
Other Tax Liabs					
FICA/Soc Sec Tax	5,235	5,460	5,688	5,939	6,194
Adj Gross Inc	104,629	111,155	118,127	125,652	133,794
GA AGI Adjstmnts	0	0	0	-2	0
GA Adj Grss Inc	104,629	111,155	118,127	125,650	133,794
GA Standard Ded	4,400	4,400	4,400	4,400	4,400
GA Itemized Ded	22,303	22,644	22,995	23,357	23,740
GA Exemptions	4,500	4,500	4,500	4,500	4,500
GA Taxable Inc	77,826	84,011	90,632	97,793	105,555
GA Regular Tax	4,409	4,780	5,177	5,607	6,073
GA Income Tax	4,409	4,780	5,177	5,607	6,073
Georgia Tax	4,409	4,780	5,177	5,607	6,073
Tot State/Local Tx	4,409	4,780	5,177	5,607	6,073
Total Inc Tax	25,924	27,996	30,223	32,710	35,377

1994   FINANCIAL SUMMARY

EDGAR & AMY MARTINSON

BASE CASE	1994	1995	1996	1997	1998
Gross Real Income					
Personal Earnings	104,500	109,725	115,211	120,972	127,020
Interest Income	1,755	2,964	4,330	5,937	7,853
Dividends Rcvd	3,124	3,454	3,822	4,234	4,695
	109,379	116,143	123,364	131,143	139,568
Income & Inflation					
Gross Real Inc	109,379	116,143	123,364	131,143	139,568
Total Inc Tax	-25,924	-27,995	-30,223	-32,710	-35,377
Net Real Income	83,455	88,147	93,141	98,433	104,191
Cur Real Inc =	83,455	86,376	89,399	92,528	95,766
At Infltn Rate Of	4	4	4	4	4
Cash Flow					
Idle Cash On Hand	10,000	9,991	10,005	10,005	10,025
Norml Cash Inflow	106,515	111,790	117,328	123,147	129,252
Norml Cash Outflw	83,840	87,223	90,814	91,638	93,580
Cash Invested	22,684	24,553	26,514	31,489	35,664
Cash Balance	9,991	10,005	10,005	10,025	10,034
Net Worth					
Personal Assets	494,846	494,244	494,275	494,881	495,954
Investment Assets	404,911	468,775	539,003	619,143	709,028
Personal Liabilities	-129,934	-123,731	-116,910	-112,560	-110,113
Personal Net Worth	364,912	370,513	377,365	382,321	385,841
Investment Net Worth	404,911	468,775	539,003	619,143	709,028
Net Worth	769,824	839,289	916,370	1,001,465	1,094,869

7.30

The Corporate Defined-Benefit Noncontributory Pension Plan

Ed's employer, Inc, established a qualified noncontributory defined-benefit pension plan that provides a maximum retirement income benefit of 1.5 percent of the average of an employee's highest 5 years of income times the number of years of service, with the maximum number of years of service for the purpose of the plan being 25 years. The plan benefit is not offset by retirement income provided under social security.

The 401(k) Plan

Inc also established a voluntary participation salary reduction type 401(k) plan for its employees 6 years ago. At this point almost 85 percent of Inc's employees participate in the plan. For employee contributions up to 5 percent of salary, Inc will contribute 2.5 percent of salary during the first 5 years of service and 3.75 percent until 10 years of service are achieved. After that time Inc will match the employee's 5 percent contribution. The plan further stipulates that employee contributions in excess of 5 percent are permitted but that no increased contribution on the part of Inc shall be made. The 401(k) plan does permit lump-sum withdrawals upon retirement or severance from the employer. Further features of the plan are that it is self-directed so that plan participants may choose the investment instruments, and that they may shift invested funds within a limited set of alternatives.

Tax Implications of the Residential Real Estate Purchase

When the Martinsons sold their house for $200,000 4 years ago, they paid $325,000 for their newly built house, which today has a fair market value of $355,000. The Martinsons' basis in the first house was $58,000. Since a new principal residence was purchased within a 2-year period following the sale of the prior principal residence, the Martinsons' gain on any such sale will not currently be recognized for purposes of federal income taxation. However, the original basis in the prior principal residence must be carried over. Therefore if the Martinsons were to sell their new home today for $355,000, the cost basis to be used for purposes of determining the capital gain would be $58,000 plus any additional after-tax funds added to the purchase price.

The $50,000 Whole Life Insurance Policy

When Ed and Amy were married in 1970, Ed purchased a $50,000 whole life policy. He is the owner of the policy, and Amy is the primary beneficiary.

Under federal law if an insured has any "incidents of ownership" in a life insurance policy at the date of death, the face amount of the policy will have to be included in the insured's gross estate for federal estate tax purposes. Since Ed is the policyowner, if he dies today the face amount of the life insurance policy, $50,000, will be included in his gross estate.

The Individual Retirement Account (IRA)

The Martinsons have continuously invested their excess income in several different instruments. During the years that the individual retirement account (IRA) provisions under IRC Sec. 408 permitted fully tax-deductible contributions of up to $2,000 annually for everyone, including those who were also participating in other qualified plans without limitation, Ed funded a personal IRA at the local savings and loan. Although Ed can no longer make deductible contributions to an IRA, the funds that were previously contributed to the plan will continue to generate interest income on a tax-deferred basis until distributions are taken from the plan. (Because Ed is a participant in a corporate pension plan and because his adjusted gross income exceeds the allowable amount, he is prevented under current tax law from making deductible contributions to an individual retirement account.)

Taxability of Money Market Account Income

The Martinsons own a money market deposit account jointly at the local savings and loan. The account typically has an average balance of about $25,000. Since these funds are not invested in tax-exempt vehicles, the interest income generated by the money market deposit account is currently taxable as ordinary income.

The Reinvestment of Income and Capital Gains in the Mutual Fund

The Martinsons monitor the money market account and if the balance grows too large, the excess is divided between investments in a balanced mutual fund and a growth mutual fund. In both these funds, all dividends and capital gains are being reinvested. As a matter of federal income taxation the capital gains and dividend reinvestments will have to be recognized currently as part of the Martinsons' gross income.

The Current Salary of $95,000

Currently Ed's salary is $95,000 per year. This amount is taxable as ordinary income and will translate into a sizable federal income tax liability each year. Unfortunately, there is little that can be done when a taxpayer/client is an employee of a large corporation and does not have the power or influence to determine the internal salary/benefit structure.

The Nonqualified Deferred-Compensation Plan

When Ed was promoted in December 1992, he became a participant in Inc's nonqualified deferred-compensation plan. During the years that Ed works at Inc, the firm will earmark funds in a separate account to fulfill the deferred-compensation obligation. It should be remembered, however, that these funds are part of Inc's assets and are available to its creditors and not to Ed. Of course, Ed would not have to recognize any current income tax on these assets.

The Group Term Life Insurance

Inc provides noncontributory group term life insurance in the amount of 1.5 times annual base salary for all employees. IRC Sec. 79 permits the cost of the first $50,000 worth of coverage on an insured-employee to be free of federal income tax. Furthermore, the excess coverage will be taxable to the insured-employee on a tax-favored basis because of the IRS approved-rate-of-insurance tables.

Treatment of Distributions from the Nonqualified Deferred-Compensation Plan

Nonqualified deferred compensation has become an extremely popular employee benefit over the last few years. The key points of the nonqualified deferred-compensation plan are as follows:

- Nonqualified deferred compensation is an employee benefit that allows an employee to defer from federal income taxation compensation that has been earned currently and that would therefore be taxed currently if not for the protection from current income taxation afforded by the plan.
- The properly structured plan will permit the employee's salary to be continued over a period of years following retirement. The fact that it is *nonqualified* will permit the employer to escape the strict nondiscrimination and reporting and disclosure requirements that ERISA imposes on qualified plans.
- The employee who participates in the plan enters into an agreement with his or her employer providing that specific payments are to be made to the employee or beneficiaries named by the employee in the event of death, disability, or retirement. Because certain standards must exist in the employer-employee relationship before federal income tax may be effectively deferred, the agreement must contain a clause establishing a contingency that can cause the employee to forfeit rights to future payments.

There are several federal income tax overtones of nonqualified deferred compensation that must be considered. It is appropriate to divide our analysis into federal tax implications affecting the employer and those affecting the employee.

The Employer

- Usually the employer funds the nonqualified deferred-compensation plan with life insurance acquired on the life of the employee. The employer pays the premiums, but they are not deductible for federal income tax purposes.
- To fund the retirement obligation when the employee reaches retirement age, the employer frequently uses one of the settlement options available under the terms of the life insurance policy. A part of each installment payment the employer receives will be taxable income under the annuity rules. Sometimes, however, the employer will choose to surrender the policy and receive a lump-sum payment.

In this case the amount that exceeds the employer's cost will be taxed as ordinary income.
- Any death proceeds the employer receives at the employee's death are free of federal income tax by reason of Sec. 101.
- The employer will have a federal income tax deduction when the benefits are actually paid out either to the employee or to the employee's family at death.

The Employee

- While employed, the plan participant is not required to include in gross income the portion of compensation that is effectively covered by the deferred-compensation plan.
- Any benefit the employee or the employee's named beneficiaries receive will be taxed as ordinary income when received.
- If the employee dies prior to retirement, $5,000 of any benefit paid to the employee's surviving spouse may be excluded from the recipient's gross income as an employee's death benefit.

Finally there are the federal estate tax implications stemming from being a participant in a nonqualified deferred-compensation plan. Under the federal estate tax laws the present value of the future benefits of a nonqualified deferred-compensation benefit payable to an employee or an employee's named beneficiary will be includible in the employee's gross estate for federal estate tax purposes. This result is based on a position taken by the IRS that during his or her life the decedent-employee had an interest in the benefit payable at some future time.

Creation of the Fund for Scott

Because of Scott's medical situation the Martinsons should begin to fund a separate account for Scott's benefit. The following approaches may be considered:

- outright gifts
- 2503(b) trusts
- 2503(c) trusts
- UGMA gifts

Each of these vehicles will be explored separately.

Outright Gifts

Under federal law IRC Sec. 2503(b) provides that the donor of a gift may exclude $10,000 worth of value of such gift from the computation of the federal gift tax for federal gift tax purposes. To the extent that the donor of the gifted property is married, the spouse can participate in the gift, doubling the amount of the allowable annual exclusion to $20,000. This annual exclusion applies to each donee of the gifted property and applies per calendar year. Since Scott will need funds for the balance of his life, it would be a prudent planning step for Ed and Amy to begin a continuous and concerted gifting effort. However, making outright gifts to Scott would not be wise under these facts in that there would be no control imposed on Scott's spending.

The Sec. 2503(b) Trust

Given Amy and Ed's objective to provide Scott with a lifetime supplemental income, they should consider either now, during lifetime, or at death to transfer assets into a trust so that Scott will be provided for after Ed and Amy's death. However, it is advisable for Ed and Amy to begin to transfer assets now to a trust for Scott's benefit, since some of the assets that will ultimately be transferred for his benefit could appreciate in value. From a planning perspective it is prudent to pay a federal gift tax on the current value of the asset being transferred rather than having the asset included in Ed and/or Amy's gross estate and subjected to the federal estate tax at a higher value and then transferred to the desired recipient.

Ed and Amy could now transfer assets to a trust. IRC Sec. 2503(b) provides that $10,000 ($20,000 for a married couple) worth of property may be transferred free of federal gift taxation as long as the gift is a completed gift and as long as it is a "gift of a present interest." Because this annual exclusion is such a valuable technique, steps must be taken to assure its availability and integrity.

The Sec. 2503(b) trust permits the donor to enjoy an annual exclusion for property transferred into the trust. The trust *requires* income to be distributed at least annually to (or for the use of) the minor beneficiary. The trust agreement states to whom income is to be distributed and allows the trustee no discretion as to its use. The minor beneficiary receives possession of the trust principal whenever the trust agreement specifies. A distribution of principal does not have to be made by age 21; corpus may be held for as long as the beneficiary lives—or for any shorter period of time. As a practical matter the principal can actually bypass the income beneficiary and go directly to other individuals whom the grantor—or even the named beneficiary—has specified. The trust instrument itself can also control the pattern of asset distribution in the event that the minor dies prior to receiving the corpus of the trust. It is not necessary that trust assets be paid to the minor's estate or appointees.

Many feel that obligatory payment of income to (or in behalf of) beneficiaries will become quite burdensome—especially while the beneficiary is still a minor. However, it should be remembered that such income could be deposited in a custodial account and used for the minor's benefit or left to accumulate in a custodial account until the minor attains majority—at which time the unexpended amount would be turned over to the beneficiary. As long as the trust qualifies as a Sec. 2503(b) trust, the annual exclusion will be available. Ed and Amy should create such a trust at this time for Scott's benefit. The main advantage of using the Sec. 2503(b) trust is that principal need not be distributed when the minor reaches age 21.

The Sec. 2503(c) Trust

As described in the preceding section, the Sec. 2503(b) trust has the primary advantage of not requiring distribution of principal when the minor reaches age 21, and it does require a current distribution of income on at least an annual basis. However, the Sec. 2503(c) trust requires that income and principal be distributed when the minor attains age 21 but does not require the trustee to distribute income currently.

It is possible to receive the benefit of the Sec. 2503(b) annual exclusion for a gift of a present interest while using the Sec. 2503(c) trust. Certain requirements make it possible for a donor to obtain the exclusion for a gift placed into a trust for the benefit of a minor. The requirements are that

- income and principal must be expended by or on behalf of the beneficiary
- to the extent that it is not so expended, income and principal must pass to the beneficiary at age 21 or
- if the beneficiary dies prior to that time, income and principal will go to the beneficiary's estate or to appointees under a general power of appointment

It should be understood that one of the main advantages of using the Sec. 2503(c) trust is the significant degree of flexibility that can be built into the arrangement. Income that has been accumulated, in addition to any principal in the trust, can be paid to the donee when he or she attains age 21. However, Ed and Amy will probably want the trust to continue to age 25, 30, or even longer. It is possible to provide continued management of the trust assets and at the same time avoid forfeiting the annual exclusion by giving the donee, at age 21, a right for a limited period to require immediate distribution by giving written notice to the trustee. If the beneficiary fails to give written notice, the trust can continue automatically for whatever period the donor provided when he or she created the arrangement. This is a technique that Ed and Amy will want to consider.

To summarize, Ed and Amy anticipate that because of their son's unfortunate medical situation, he will need financial assistance throughout his life. Rather than having assets pass through Ed and/or Amy's estate and having federal estate tax imposed at what will be a higher tax liability (if the assets appreciate in value), the assets should be gifted into either a Sec. 2503(b) or 2503(c) trust. The annual exclusion will be available in both types of trusts and to the extent that the value of the property transferred into the trust exceeds the annual exclusion amount, a gift tax will be payable but the unified credit will eliminate the need to actually pay any gift tax. As a practical matter it is prudent to pay federal transfer tax generated by the transfer of assets valued at today's lower values than to have such assets pass through an estate, at which time the value of the assets could be higher, thus triggering a higher federal transfer tax.

Uniform Gifts to Minors Act

The Uniform Gifts to Minors Act (and Uniform Transfers to Minors Act) provides an alternative to the Sec. 2503(c) trust. The UGMA (and UTMA) is frequently used for smaller gifts because of its simplicity and because it offers the benefits of management, income and estate shifting, and the investment characteristics of a trust with little or none of the start-up costs that are so frequently regarded as burdensome with the use of trusts.

As a practical matter the Uniform Gifts to Minors Act has been adopted in every state. In essence the statute provides that during lifetime an adult may make a gift of a security, money, a life insurance or annuity policy, or other property (which differs on a state-by-state basis) to an individual who is a minor on the date of the gift.

Because Scott is 16 and already in high school, he will attain majority in a few short years and have ready access to the accumulated funds. Therefore the use of the UGMA approach is not recommended in this case.

Improving the Martinsons' Cash Flow and Reducing the Federal Income Tax Burden

The federal income tax can have a detrimental effect on the accomplishment of the Martinsons' objectives. An integral component of the financial planning process is a consideration of possible income reductions or shifting techniques.

Many of the traditional techniques that planners employed for years as methods to shift the imposition of federal income taxation have now been removed from the Internal Revenue Code. Examples include the elimination of the 10-year trust (sometimes referred to as a Clifford trust or a short-term reversionary trust) and the imposition of the kiddie tax (which would not apply here because Scott is 16). The 1993 Internal Revenue Code changes reduced the income tax savings heretofore available from Sec. 2503(c) accumulation trusts. The maximum tax rate of 39.5 percent applies to trust income that exceeds $7,500.

Dispositions at Death

Thus far in the analysis the focus has been primarily on lifetime planning concerns. The nature of this case dictates that the Martinsons address these types of issues as soon as possible. In addition, another integral component of the comprehensive financial planning process will be estate planning considerations.

Revision of Estate Plan

The Martinsons have wills they have not updated since 1970 that no longer address their estate planning needs. At this time revision is needed to reflect their changed personal and financial situation. By virtue of the existence of the unlimited federal estate tax marital deduction, many tax advisers encourage the full use of the unlimited marital deduction of the estate by the first spouse to die. This approach will assure a deferral (but not a total forgiveness) of all federal estate taxation at the first death. Of course, the tax will subsequently be imposed at the death of the second spouse. However, the unified credit should be used in combination with the federal estate tax marital deduction in estates that, when merged, are greater than the amount of a single unified credit exemption equivalent, that is, $600,000.

The most important objective within the estate planning framework is to plan not only the estate of the first spouse to die but also to anticipate the surviving spouse's subsequent death. In any situation in which the unlimited federal estate tax marital deduction is utilized (as it is here because of the Martinsons' use of their respective "simple wills" that leave all estate assets to the surviving spouse), the unified credit of the first spouse to die is wasted by having never been used before the marital deduction applies. The result is that the entire value of marital deduction assets will end up being taxed in the estate of the surviving spouse.

By reason of this situation, the Martinsons must have an appropriate set of wills drafted. These revised wills must properly direct the integration of the unified credit exemption equivalent with the marital deduction amount. This way, there will be no overqualification of the marital deduction as there is under the current scenario. Further, the unified credit will not have been "wasted."

An alternative approach would be an estate plan in which the amount of assets equal to the unified credit equivalent can be directed by an appropriate will to a trust that provides the surviving spouse with full access to the funds without the trust's being included in the surviving spouse's gross estate for purposes of the federal estate tax. Such access may be totally unrestricted, or it may be restricted if that is the Martinsons' wish.

Assuming Ed predeceases Amy, a portion of his estate assets should be placed into a testamentary trust for the benefit of Scott. Of course, a sufficient amount of assets would need to pass for the benefit of Amy in order to qualify such assets for the estate tax marital deduction.

Analysis of Present Situation

Under the federal estate tax laws all property a decedent owns at the date of his or her death is included in the gross estate of the individual decedent. In general the larger the taxable estate is, the larger the estate tax liability will be. Therefore we must first firmly establish the size of the gross estate. Once this has been accomplished, we can then make recommendations to help reduce the amount of projected federal estate tax liability.

The ownership of the life insurance policies is a problem because Ed possesses incidents of ownership over such policies. Under IRC Sec. 2042(2) the face amount of these policies will be required to be included in Ed's gross estate for federal estate tax purposes.

We also know from the facts that Ed is a participant in several qualified plans. Under IRC Sec. 4980A there will be a federal excise tax imposed to the extent that the value of the plan exceeds certain limits.

For quite some time before 1986 there was a growing sentiment in both the IRS and Congress that taxpayers should not be permitted to accumulate excessive wealth in qualified retirement plans in a manner that resulted in too much of a tax-favored status. In response to this the Tax Reform Act of 1986 added Sec. 4981A (renumbered Sec. 4980A by the Technical and Miscellaneous Revenue Act of 1988), which imposed a 15 percent excise tax on excess distributions and excess retirement accumulations. This excise tax applies to excess accumulations in or distributions from any qualified plan, tax-sheltered annuity, or personal retirement plan. As a practical matter Sec. 4980A carves out two separate excise taxes in this area: a 15 percent excise tax imposed on "excess retirement distributions" received during lifetime and/or a 15 percent excise tax imposed at the date of death on "excess retirement accumulations." The 15 percent excess distributions tax is basically a federal levy payable by a taxpayer during lifetime. The 15 percent excise tax imposed on excess accumulations is imposed at the time of death and should be thought of as an additional federal tax.

Imposition of the Excise Tax

The 15 percent excise tax on excess retirement accumulations will apply to all excess retirement accumulations in existence at the date of death of the decedent/plan participant. The Internal Revenue Code states that an excess retirement accumulation is the value for federal estate tax purposes of the decedent/participant's interest in all plans, less the present value of a hypothetical life annuity in the amount of the "applicable annual exemption" for the decedent's attained age, using the interest rate and mortality assumptions that the IRS accepts for valuing life annuities. The Internal Revenue Code further clarifies the situation by defining the *applicable annual exemption* as the greater of (a) $150,000 or (b) $112,500 and then indexed for inflation with October 1, 1986, as the base period. The 15 percent excise tax is to be assessed as an additional federal estate tax, which is computed independently of the regular federal estate tax. Therefore the unified credit, other credits, the federal estate tax marital deduction, the federal estate tax charitable deduction, and other federal estate tax deductions cannot be used to reduce the imposition of this 15 percent excise tax.

Concept of "Equity of Inheritance"

Ed and Amy are fair and caring parents who love both their children equally. They believe that favoritism is wrong, and they have been extremely careful to see that this basic philosophy is carried out. However, Scott's accident and subsequent medical problems have made it difficult to reconcile their philosophy of equity with the fact that Scott will need more financial aid than Bea.

One vexing issue that Ed and Amy have discussed is the favorable treatment that Bea has already received. First, they paid her college education expenses, and her degree has enabled her to begin a promising career with the potential for a high income. In addition, Bea was the sole recipient of Ed's mother's largesse (Scott was not born at the time of her demise) and now has a nice nest egg of her own. Because of these two considerations, Ed and Amy believe that their objective to fund a program designed to provide a lifetime income for Scott tends to equalize the financial benefits bestowed upon both children. This view of equity also includes any unequal distributions from their estates.

Should the funding for Scott result in any inequitable treatment for Bea, Ed and Amy could acquire some life insurance on their lives at a later date, naming Bea as the beneficiary.

Considerations Stemming from Amy's Family History of Longevity

Because of their age difference the chances are quite good that Amy will outlive Ed by a long time. An integral part of the planning process for the Martinsons involves accepting this likelihood and initiating steps to resolve the problems stemming from this factor. It is clear that supplemental coverage will be necessary to add to the retirement benefits available from Inc and from social security.

The Use of the Irrevocable Life Insurance Trust

The case narrative indicates that the face amount of certain life insurance policies will be included in Ed's gross estate for federal estate tax purposes at the date of his death. Specifically the $50,000 whole life policy will be included in Ed's gross estate because he will own the policy on his life at the time of his death and because IRC Sec. 2042(2) will require inclusion of the policy proceeds of any life insurance policy owned by the decedent-insured at the date of death. For the same reason the two $25,000 policies will also be included in his estate. It is incumbent upon the financial services professional to reduce the size of the client's gross estate so that federal estate tax liability can be reduced. Removal of the life insurance from Ed's gross estate is an easy yet effective step in the right direction.

IRC Sec. 2042 addresses the issue of includibility of life insurance proceeds in the insured's gross estate. IRC Sec. 2042(1) provides that the face amount of the policy will be included in the insured's gross estate if the estate is named as the beneficiary of the life insurance policy. Nothing in the facts indicates that this is the case here. IRC Sec. 2042(2) provides that to the extent that the decedent-insured possesses any incidents of ownership in the policy, the proceeds will likewise be included in the insured's gross estate. Incidents of ownership not only include situations in which the insured is named as the owner but also include the right on the part of insured to borrow against the policy, change the beneficiary, pledge the policy against a loan, and so on. If Ed has an incident of ownership in a policy, he must relinquish ownership of the policy to remove the policy proceeds from his gross estate.

Ed could transfer the three whole life insurance policies that he currently owns to Amy, which would clearly remove all policy proceeds from Ed's gross estate since he would no longer possess any incidents of ownership over the policy. However, cross-ownership of life insurance policies between spouses is not the best approach since the transferee-spouse could predecease the transferor. Also because divorce is so prevalent in this country, cross-spousal ownership is often unwise.

The preferable approach would be to use an irrevocable life insurance trust. Ed should create such a trust and transfer the three life insurance policies that he currently owns to the trust. Amy and the two children should be named as beneficiaries of the trust. Upon Amy's death, her share of the trust assets are to be distributed to the children equally, share and share alike, per stirpes. Because of Scott's medical situation his portion of the policy proceeds should remain in trust for the balance of his life with the named trustee directed to apply income (and principal if necessary) for Scott's benefit. Upon Scott's death, the trust is to terminate, with the trust assets to be distributed to Scott's heirs, if any, and if none, to Bea if living, and if Bea has predeceased Scott, to her heirs, if any, and if none, to a named charity. Bea's portion could be distributed to her outright. The whole life policy would name the irrevocable life insurance trust as the beneficiary of the policy.

IRC Sec. 2035 provides that if a decedent-insured transfers a life insurance policy and fails to live 3 years following this transfer, the policy proceeds will still be required to be included as part of the insured's gross estate. Therefore Ed should be advised that if he fails to live 3 years following the creation of the irrevocable life insurance trust and the transfer of the policy into the trust, the policy proceeds will still be included in Ed's gross estate for federal estate tax purposes.

ACCUMULATION PLANNING

Amy and Ed have stated a desire to accumulate additional funds so they will have an adequate income during their retirement. Until Scott's accident and subsequent medical expenses they anticipated that between Scott's graduation from high school and Ed's retirement they would be able to concentrate their asset accumulation to meet this objective, which they stated as having accumulated sufficient funds to provide an additional $5,000 annual income (in current prices) during their retirement. Considering Scott's failure to recover fully from the accident, they feel they have an obligation to provide a source of income for him for life, apart from any income sources they might develop for themselves. A target of $3,000 per year in current prices is their goal. They estimate that prices will rise an average of 4 percent per year over the entire planning period; therefore the 4 percent inflation rate will apply before and after retirement.

Ed is now 54, and both Amy and he wonder how meeting these two accumulation goals will affect their cash flow. In addition, they are concerned about the impact of these accumulation goals on the possibility of Ed's retiring when he reaches age 62 in 8 years. Their target annual income for each of these income supplements, allowing for 4 percent inflation, is $6,842 for their supplement at age 62 and $7,696 at age 65. For Scott's funding the target annual income is $4,105 if Ed retires at age 62 and $4,618 at age 65. They have indicated that the retirement supplement should be sufficient to provide an annual income stream for 40 years and that the funds available for Scott should be sufficient to provide him an income stream for 50 years. In both cases the time period begins with an age 62 retirement, but Ed does not want to reduce the payout time if retirement is delayed.

Table 7-1 shows the estimated accumulation and annual funding needed for retirement at both age 62 and age 65. A 4 percent rate of inflation is assumed for both the preretirement and postretirement periods. Also a 6 percent after-tax rate of return is used for both periods. The funds will be liquidated over the 40-year period as stated above.

Table 7-2 shows the estimated accumulation and annual funds needed to achieve their goal of having funds set aside for Scott's benefit. Again the assumptions are made that Ed retires at age 62 and at age 65. The after-tax earnings assumption is 6 percent, and the payout period for liquidating the accumulation is 50 years.

TABLE 7-1
Funding for Retirement Income Supplement

Ed's Age	Target Annual Income	Lump Sum at Target Age	Annual Funding Level	Annual Funding Rising at 5 Percent Each Year
62	$6,842	$193,378	$16,381	$14,016
65	7,696	217,514	13,705	11,437

TABLE 7-2
Funding for Scott's Income Supplement

Ed's Age	Target Annual Income	Lump Sum at Target Age	Annual Funding Level	Annual Funding Rising at 5 Percent Each Year
62	$4,105	$133,632	$13,337	$10,831
65	4,618	150,332	9,472	7,547

The Martinsons have $22,000 set aside for Scott's education and doubt that these funds will be used for that purpose. If these funds were integrated into their funding plans, the $22,000 would grow to $35,064 during the next 8 years and to $41,762 during the next 11 years. Using the accumulated educational funds in this manner will reduce their annual contributions to those shown in table 7-3.

TABLE 7-3				
Annual Funding for Scott's Income Supplement Using the Accumulated Educational Funds					
			Annual Funding
Ed's Age	Target Annual Income	Lump Sum at Target Age (in Addition to $22,000 Already Accumulated)	Level	Rising at 5 Percent Each Year
62	$4,105	$ 98,568	$9,395	$7,989
65	4,618	108,569	6,841	5,449

Table 7-4 consolidates the annual funding needed for these twin objectives, assuming the $22,000 education fund set aside for Scott is used as part of his target amount.

Table 7-5 consolidates the information developed for the annual funding (both level and at a 5 percent rising amount) with the amount of their cash flow as shown in the base case on pages 7.26–7.27 over years 1995–1998.

If the Martinsons were to fund these objectives with an annual contribution that increases by 5 percent each year over an 8-year period, their annual cash flow would be sufficient to meet the amount needed.

TABLE 7-4 Total Annual Funding		
	At Age 62 (8-Year Funding)	
	Level	Rising
Amy and Ed	$16,381	$14,016
Scott	9,395	7,989
Total	$25,776	$22,005
	At Age 65 (11-Year Funding)	
	Level	Rising
Amy and Ed	$13,705	$11,437
Scott	6,841	5,449
Total	$20,546	$16,886

TABLE 7-5
Comparison of Annual Cash Flow and Needed Annual Funding

Year	Investable Cash Flow (Base Case)	Annual Funding Increasing 8-Year	Annual Funding Increasing 11-Year	Level Funding 8-Year	Level Funding 11-Year
1995	$24,553	$22,005	$16,886	$25,776	$20,546
1996	26,514	23,105	17,709	25,776	20,546
1997	31,489	24,161	18,594	25,776	20,546
1998	35,664	24,473	19,524	25,776	20,546

However, the Martinsons have the following other objectives that require attention and use of their cash flow:

- long-term care protection for Scott
- long-term care protection for Amy
- life insurance protection against reduction in income should Ed die first and the pension benefit be reduced
- life insurance protection against estate shrinkage due to loss of the marital deduction

Until the annual costs of these other dimensions of their financial planning are determined, the final recommendation for these two accumulation objectives will be postponed.

INSURANCE PLANNING

Long-Term Care Protection for Scott

Scott's medical condition is probably the most critical component of the Martinsons' overall financial plan. Since it is likely that Scott will require some form of long-term care protection, the Martinsons must take steps to be sure that this virtually certain development is appropriately addressed as part of the financial planning process.

Unfortunately most insurance carriers that underwrite long-term care policies will not insure individuals under age 45, and even if they did, Scott could be considered uninsurable due to the preexisting medical condition. Therefore the Martinsons must be prepared to provide funding for long-term care for Scott's benefit without the assistance of long-term care coverage.

Long-Term Care Protection for Amy

Since we know that Amy has a family history of longevity, the Martinsons should acquire long-term care protection for her. Unlike the situation with Scott, the Martinsons will have no problem acquiring this coverage on Amy.

Because approximately 30 million people over the age of 65 face a significant risk of requiring nursing home services sometime during their remaining years, the insurance industry has begun to make long-term care policies available. The Martinsons should seriously consider acquiring one on Amy as soon as possible.

Long-term care policies contain many differing attributes, and they also differ from one insurance company to another. There are over 100 insurance companies offering long-term care coverage, and the specific range of coverage goes from very limited protection on one hand to total and complete protection on the other. The Martinsons need to address the following issues before the appropriate policy can be selected:

- preexisting conditions
- elimination periods
- exclusions
- premium structure
- underwriting
- benefit provisions
- renewability
- inflation protection
- long-term care added to an existing life insurance policy

Preexisting Conditions

Long-term care insurance policies often contain preexisting condition provisions that exclude any benefit payments for a preestablished time after the policy has been issued for causes stemming from conditions that existed and for which the insured has previously received medical advice and treatment within a specified period of time before the policy was issued. Of course, the rationale behind the presence and use of a preexisting condition clause in a long-term care policy is to prevent adverse selection against the specific insurance company issuing the policy.

The National Association of Insurance Commissioners (NAIC) developed a model providing among other things that the preexisting-condition provisions should not exclude benefits for more than 6 months after policy issue and that specific exclusions should not be predicated on conditions that initially showed up more than 6 months prior to the date the policy was issued. Although most of the long-term care policies available today have incorporated and accepted the NAIC model concerning the 6-month standard, some states still permit long-term care policies to adopt a longer preexisting-condition provision. Some insurance companies will require a preexisting-condition provision of longer than 6 months for long-term care policies being issued to persons under the age of 65.

Not all insurance companies have adopted this rather strict posture on the preexisting-condition issue; some will demonstrate a more liberal attitude on this subject. Since Amy is in good health, the preexisting-condition issue will not be a problem for the Martinsons.

Elimination Period

All long-term care policies contain a provision for an elimination or waiting period. The elimination period may be thought of as a form of deductible that establishes the specific time at which the benefits will begin. In essence the elimination or waiting period is the amount of time that will elapse following the point when an insured can satisfy benefit eligibility but when no benefit will be paid. For example, if a long-term care policy contains a 120-day elimination period, the insured would have to be in the medical facility for 120 days before the policy benefits would be payable. There would be 120 days of long-term care with no benefits paid, but on the 121st day the payment of benefits would begin.

It is a fundamental principle that the length of the elimination period affects the premium owed. The longer the elimination period under the terms of the policy, the lower the premium. The Martinsons will need to make a decision about elimination period and its impact on premium payments.

The actual length of elimination periods in long-term care policies can vary dramatically. It is possible for the Martinsons to acquire a long-term care policy with no elimination period (which would be very expensive), with an elimination period of 730 days (with a much lower premium), or with some time period in between. Since this decision involving the elimination period will directly affect costs, it will have to be considered very carefully.

Exclusions

All insurance policies that provide any form of health care coverage will contain provisions dealing with exclusions. Although the actual exclusions in long-term care insurance policies are usually not very extensive, it is possible that a single exclusion might eliminate benefit payments for a cause for which other carriers could conceivably provide full coverage. Consequently the Martinsons must "shop" very carefully when choosing the appropriate coverage for Amy's long-term care.

Premiums

How the Martinsons pay for the long-term care coverage is of paramount importance. Although the immediate acquisition of this insurance is vital, the premiums can be relatively expensive, so care will have to be devoted to selecting the most cost-effective package. Most long-term care policies have level premiums for the balance of the insured's life, although some insurance carriers structure costs of long-term care products as increasing premiums. In this type of situation premiums will increase on an annual basis or at 2-, 3-, or 5-year intervals with level steps between adjustment points.

Regardless of whether the long-term care premium is level or increasing, the amount of the premium will be determined by the age of the insured at the time the policy is issued. Historically premium increases are only significant after age 40, and they are very steep after age 65.

One last point on the subject of premiums is that insurance carriers will not guarantee premium levels because the concept of long-term care policies is a new one, and to date there are very few statistics on experience available to carriers. Long-term care policies are presently "guaranteed renewable," which effectively means that the carrier can only increase premium rates for all policyowners in an entire class of policies and even then only on the basis of claims experience rather than on the basis of changes in an insured's age or health. This arrangement is basically in response to the fact that since long-term care policies are so new, there is no experience data yet, so all insurance companies could have computed premium levels at too low a figure. If so, in the future the industry might be forced to increase premium levels for existing policies as well as for newly issued products.

Some representative premiums are as follows:

Female Aged 45

$110/Day Benefit	Yearly Premium No Inflation Protection	Inflation Protection
3-year benefit period, 20-day waiting period	$247	$413
6-year benefit period, 20-day waiting period	294	491
Lifetime benefit period, 20-day waiting period	N/A	594

Underwriting Principles

The underwriting process has always been a complex aspect of any insurance company's internal operation. Because long-term care policies deal with the health of the insured and because these types of policies are sometimes issued through the older ages, a series of specialized underwriting principles is often necessary. Most carriers that currently market long-term care products have adopted a single classification approach for purposes of underwriting, which means that the insurance carrier will either accept or reject the application for the insurance coverage. However, a few of the carriers who are more involved in the marketing of long-term care products have begun rating policies. As long-term care products continue to grow in popularity and use, it is likely that additional underwriting classifications will be developed.

Benefits

When the Martinsons choose the right long-term care policy for Amy, they will need to be concerned primarily with the issue of benefits. Issues to be concerned about are the maximum duration of the benefits provided, the types and levels of care for which benefits will be provided, prerequisites for benefit eligibility, and the actual level of benefits payable.

With respect to duration the Martinsons will consider the fact that some long-term care policies provide unlimited benefit periods that would allow the insured to enjoy coverage for any length of stay required in a nursing home. The Martinsons will also learn, however, that some long-term care policies specify a maximum benefit duration such as 3 years or 5 years. Some policies will provide coverage for as short a period as one year. The Martinsons will need to select the appropriate coverage realizing, of course, that the longer the benefit period is, the more comprehensive the policy's level of protection will be.

With respect to the benefit payable, most long-term care policies will set forth the benefit as a specified dollar amount per day of benefit eligibility. The Martinsons must be especially cautious to select an adequate benefit level to provide the necessary protection for Amy.

Inflation Protection

Almost all long-term care policies contain some form of inflation protection or offer an inflation rider. Such protection will come in the form of either an automatic increase in the benefit each year on a formula basis linked to measure of inflation or a guarantee that the insured will have the opportunity to purchase additional increments of coverage at certain specified, preestablished intervals. Which approach is used is not too critical. The important thing is that the Martinsons must be sure to have some form of inflation protection.

Renewability

From the perspective of renewability there are two different types of long-term care policies currently available in the marketplace. Some insurance carriers market a long-term care product that is *conditionally renewable*. This type of policy sets forth specified, preestablished conditions that authorize the carrier either to refuse to renew the policy or to cancel the in-force protection. The Martinsons should be sure to avoid this type of policy. The other, referred to as *guaranteed renewable,* provides that the insured will be able to maintain the coverage in force as long as the premiums are paid when they come due. The insurance carrier that has issued the long-term care policy will be unable to refuse to renew the insurance protection or otherwise terminate the coverage for any reason whatsoever other than for nonpayment of premiums. Although this is the type of coverage that the Martinsons should select, it should be noted that it is somewhat more costly.

Studies have shown that the average stay in a full-service care facility is less than 3 years. Many carriers are currently offering policies that have either a 3-year coverage period, a 6-year coverage, or lifetime coverage.

Benefit Period

Insurers commonly offer 3-year, 6-year, and lifetime benefit periods on long-term care policies. Since the average stay in a full-service care facility is less than 3 years, it is tempting for clients to select a 3-year benefit period.

In Amy's case purchasing a policy with a $110-per-day benefit, a 3-year benefit, a 20-day elimination period, and inflation protection represents an approximate annual savings of $181 per year when compared to a similar policy with a lifetime benefit—$594 versus $413. However, the major purpose of insurance is to protect against the worst-case financial scenario, not the average case. Thus Amy should select lifetime coverage, especially because of her family history of longer-than-average lives.

Medicaid Spend-down Strategy

Some planners advise clients to select a short benefit period as part of a so-called "spend-down" strategy designed to maximize benefits available from medicaid. One of medicaid's programs provides financial assistance for individuals who need long-term care and whose income and nonexempt assets fall below state-specified levels. For individuals whose income or assets are above these levels, this spend-down strategy circumvents the restrictions so that the government, rather than the client, foots the bill for long-term care.

The spend-down approach usually involves the client's gifting assets to his or her adult children sufficient to reduce the individual's nonexempt assets below the state's threshold level. Assets exempt under federal guidelines include a primary residence if the spouse or a minor or disabled child still lives there, household effects, an automobile, and a prepaid burial contract. Each state has its own rules regarding other exemptions such as life insurance and securities.

Since social security payments and pension income are included in the maximum income threshold and cannot be gifted, it is critical to verify whether these income flows will preclude the client from qualifying for medicaid.

Gifts must be irrevocable with no strings attached, and the client must refrain from filing for medicaid coverage until at least 36 months after gifting the assets. If the client files before 36 months pass, medicaid will deny benefits under its look-back provision according to the following formula:

$$\text{Number of months ineligible for medicaid benefits} = \frac{\text{total value of all assets transferred during look-back period}}{\text{average monthly cost of private nursing homes}}$$

Example: An incapacitated client applies for admission to a high-quality, medicaid-approved care facility. He or she retains assets until admitted in case the facility questions the ability to pay the monthly bill. The client then gifts assets to his or her adult children. The client retains an amount of nonexempt assets sufficient to make 36 months of care facility payments plus just enough additional nonexempt assets to stay below the medicaid asset threshold. Thirty-six months after gifting the money, the client applies for medicaid to pay for his or her care in the facility. Since the care facility is medicaid-approved, it must accept medicaid's compensation as payment in full and cannot evict the client even though the payment may be below market rates.

If the spend-down strategy is designed in advance of the client's incapacitation, he or she can purchase long-term care insurance with a benefit period equal to or slightly greater than the medicaid look-back period. Thus, instead of paying out-of-pocket for 36 months while in the facility, the client receives insurance benefits.

Problems associated with the spend-down approach are numerous. First, many clients oppose the strategy on moral or ethical grounds. Second, many clients are unwilling to give up control of their assets. Third, the strategy does not lend itself well to the typical husband-wife family since the spouse's income and assets are included to determine medicaid eligibility. Even if the couple's income qualifies, the nonincapacitated spouse must give up assets without benefit of medicaid compensation for his or her living expenses. Fourth, care facility operators are aware of this strategy and recognize the devastating effect that below-market compensation from medicaid can have on their financial viability. Many high-quality facilities simply choose not to seek medicaid approval or seek to give up medicaid approval. Fifth, the facility could fail for reasons that are independent of medicaid, forcing the client to enter a medicaid-approved facility that is much less comfortable. Sixth, the client may recover his or her health and no longer qualify for long-term care. Having transferred almost everything to the children, the client must then rely on the children's largesse, assuming that the children haven't spent everything. Seventh, and most ominous, future legislative or judicial action may render the strategy disastrous by changing the income or asset threshold, by modifying the look-back period (which was already lengthened by the Omnibus Budget Reconciliation act of 1993), or by eliminating the program, possibly as a part of large-scale reform in the health care system.

Any planning for medicaid spend-down must be done with extreme caution and only by individuals who are both knowledgeable and experienced in the technical aspects of the relevant laws and regulations.

In Amy and Ed's case, even if they were comfortable with the ethics, complexity, and viability of the medicaid spend-down strategy, their current situation does not match the optimal conditions for that approach. One alternative is simply to do nothing now, anticipating use of the strategy later when their situation changes. For example, if Ed dies first and Amy subsequently requires long-term care, she can initiate the strategy at that time.

Unfortunately, if medicaid rules change in the future, making the spend-down strategy impossible, any financial planning that anticipates using the strategy could be disastrous. A future need for extended long-term care could consume the entire estate, even if Amy owns a long-term care policy with a 3-year benefit period. Although she may be able to purchase additional coverage later, it is possible that she will become uninsurable or that policies available in the market in the future will not meet her needs.

A more efficient approach for the Martinsons to insulate themselves from potential financial disaster resulting from long-term care is to purchase a long-term care insurance policy with a lifetime benefit period. The additional expense relative to a 3-year benefit is relatively small, and owning such a policy eliminates the need for a strategy that may prove counterproductive.

Long-Term Care Added to Existing Life Insurance Coverage

Thus far we have looked at long-term care policies that are issued for a specific, one-dimensional purpose. However, the Martinsons should be advised that there are some insurance carriers that have combined life insurance coverage with long-term care protection. This is accomplished administratively by adding a rider to the existing life insurance policy.

This rider accelerates the payment of a previously established portion of the death benefit to the insured when the insured becomes critically ill, requires custodial care, and is not expected to recover. In this situation a percentage of the face amount will be paid each year for a specified number of years.

In the Martinsons' situation the use of this accelerated death benefit is not appropriate for two reasons. First, when life insurance proceeds are distributed in this manner, the payments to the insured are currently treated as ordinary income for federal income tax purposes. When a separate long-term care policy is used, the annual premium qualifies as a potential medical deduction, and any proceeds when paid are treated as nontaxable income for federal income tax purposes. Second, at this time there is not sufficient life insurance coverage on Amy's life to make this a feasible rider to add to an existing policy.

Current Life Insurance Coverage: Comparison of Present Status with Estimated Needs and Recommendations for Needed Coverage as well as Form of Ownership

The case narrative explains Ed and Amy's current life insurance situation. We know that when Ed and Amy were married in 1970, Ed acquired a $50,000 whole life insurance policy with an annual premium of $1,120. He is the owner of the policy, and he named Amy as the primary beneficiary. He has since named his two children—Bea and Scott—as the contingent beneficiaries, per stirpes. We also know that Amy converted her group term life insurance to $5,000 face of whole life in 1972 and named Ed as the primary beneficiary. Given the current situation, it is recommended that the children be named as primary beneficiaries and that a charity be named as successor beneficiary. The two children have been named as contingent beneficiaries, per stirpes. Finally we know that Ed has two $25,000 policies with combined premiums of $1,215 and a total cash value of $16,325. A $25,000 policy was acquired when each of the Martinson children was born. Each child is the named primary beneficiary on one policy, and Amy is the contingent beneficiary for both policies.

The financial services professional must determine whether the current coverage is adequate. Our starting point will be to compute the approximate "cost of dying." Such expenditures as costs of administration, paying off debts, federal estate tax, and state inheritance tax (if any) need to be considered. Next the amount of available liquid assets will be ascertained. Finally a decision about the adequacy of the current life insurance coverage can then be reached.

Ed and Amy's gross estates are $904,200 and $251,700 respectively, determined as follows:

	Ed's Gross Estate	Amy's Gross Estate
Checking account	$ 5,000	$ 5,000
Money market deposit account	12,500	12,500
Residence	177,500	177,500
Life insurance—whole life	50,000	
Life insurance	25,000	
Life insurance	25,000	
Life insurance		5,000
IRA	21,200	
IRA		2,200
Balanced fund	28,000	
Growth fund	40,000	
401(k) bond fund	25,000	
401(k) stock fund	37,000	
Group term life insurance	142,500	
Nonqualified deferred compensation	52,000	
Vested pension benefit	180,000	
Common stock	26,000	
Household furnishings	37,500	37,500
Auto	20,000	
Auto		12,000
Gross estate	$904,200	$251,700

The case narrative states that Ed and Amy have simple, reciprocal wills. This type of will leaves all of the deceased's respective estate properties to the surviving spouse.

Based on the data above, Ed's gross estate is $904,200, and his total costs at the date of death will be as follows:

At Ed's death:

	Ed's Estate Computations	Ed's Estate Shrinkage
Gross estate	$904,200	
Less costs of administration (8 percent)	72,336	$ 72,336
Adjusted gross estate	831,864	
Less federal estate tax marital deduction	831,864	
Taxable estate	–0–	
Federal estate tax	–0–	
Less unified credit	N/A	
Federal estate tax owed	–0–	–0–
State inheritance tax	–0–	–0–
Total estate shrinkage at Ed's death		$ 72,336

At Amy's subsequent death:

	Amy's Estate Computations	Amy's Estate Shrinkage
Gross estate*	$1,083,564	
Less costs of administration	86,685	$ 86,685
Adjusted gross estate	996,679	
Less federal estate tax marital deduction	–0–	
Taxable estate	996,679	
Federal estate tax	344,583	
Less unified credit	192,800	
Federal estate tax owed	151,783	151,783
State inheritance tax	–0–	–0–
Total estate shrinkage at Amy's death		$238,468
Total shrinkage at both deaths		$310,804

*Assumes no increase in value of assets in her name.

In a simple will arrangement, all estate property passes to the surviving spouse. Therefore, all of Ed's property passes to Amy. In essence, this means that although the full federal estate tax marital deduction is enjoyed by Ed's estate at his (the first) death, too much estate property passes to Amy and is taxed at her subsequent death. A marital deduction that integrates the benefits of the unified credit with the marital deduction concept would be more prudent.

If the marital deduction trust approach is adopted, the computations are as follows:

At Ed's death:

	Ed's Estate Computations	Ed's Estate Shrinkage
Gross estate	$904,200	
Less costs of administration (8 percent)	72,336	$ 72,336
Adjusted gross estate	831,864	
Less federal estate tax marital deduction	231,864	
Taxable estate	600,000	
Federal estate tax	192,800	
Less unified credit	192,800	
Federal estate tax owed	–0–	–0–
State inheritance tax	–0–	–0–
Total estate shrinkage at Ed's death		$ 72,336

At Amy's subsequent death:

	Amy's Estate Computations	Amy's Estate Shrinkage
Gross estate	$483,564	
Less costs of administration	38,685	$ 38,685
Adjusted gross estate	444,879	
Less federal estate tax marital deduction	–0–	
Taxable estate	444,879	
Federal estate tax	137,059	
Less unified credit	137,059	
Federal estate tax owed	–0–	–0–
State inheritance tax	–0–	–0–
Total estate shrinkage at Amy's death		38,685
Total estate shrinkage at both deaths		$111,021

There is a total of $534,000 available in liquid assets at the time of Ed's death (including the present value of the future benefit of the vested pension). Therefore from an estate liquidity perspective there is no need for additional life insurance.

However, there are several reasons why additional life insurance coverage on Ed's life may be necessary:

- to fund Scott's income supplement
- to fund retirement income supplements for Ed and Amy
- to provide funds to pay estate obligations at the death of Ed and Amy
- to supplement loss of income when Ed dies
- possibly to equalize Bea's inheritance

Insurance to Fund Income Supplements for Ed and Amy's Retirement and for Scott

To achieve Ed's desire to retire at age 62, the Martinsons will need to accumulate approximately $200,000 ($193,378 from table 7-1). An additional $100,000 ($98,568 from table 7-3 on page 7.36 for Scott's benefit must also be accumulated. This combined amount of $300,000 will be in jeopardy if Ed dies before funding is completed. If an after-tax rate of return of 6 percent can be earned, then the present value of the $300,000 is about $190,000. This is the amount of life insurance needed on Ed's life. Since this insurance need is temporary, term insurance would be appropriate. Level term would have the Martinsons paying an annual premium for more insurance than they need for this purpose. The additional premium needed to pay for the level term is a relatively small cost that the Martinsons should be able to afford. Should inflation or other unforeseen events occur, the added protection could be worth the extra cost. This insurance will cost approximately $800 per year.

Due to the cost saving in having only one policy in the amount of $190,000 rather than two separate policies, a single policy should be purchased. The Martinsons' interests will be best served if Ed does not have any incidents of ownership in this policy because at his death the face amount of the policy will be included in his estate. An irrevocable life insurance trust containing a Crummey provision can be established that will apply for and own the policy. Ed will contribute sufficient money each year to pay the premium, and at his death the trust will use the proceeds to complete the funding for Scott and Amy.

Equalization of Benefit for Bea

Scott's unfortunate medical condition means that more of Ed and Amy's estate assets will probably pass to him so that after his parents' deaths he will be more assured of being adequately cared for. Bea may have mixed feelings about this situation. Surely she understands that she is more fortunate than her brother and does not actually fault her parents for leaving more assets to Scott than to her. After all, Bea is healthy, self-sufficient, and better able to take care of herself. Despite Bea's understanding attitude about the situation, at some time she might feel that an inequity has transpired.

Ed and Amy are good parents as well as perceptive individuals. They know that a form of inequity would take place if Scott received more of the estate assets. To prevent any perceived inequity of treatment, the use of life insurance is recommended. Ed should acquire a life insurance policy on his own life with a face amount equal to the excess value of assets that will ultimately pass to Scott. In order to avoid inclusion of the policy proceeds in Ed's gross estate for federal estate tax purposes, Bea should be named as owner of the policy. More significantly, however, Bea should also be named as the primary beneficiary of the policy. At Ed's death Bea will receive policy proceeds in an amount that will eliminate what would otherwise be an inequity between her and her brother regarding the receipt of valuable estate assets.

Since the Martinsons want to treat both children in an equitable manner, they feel that some specific assets should become available to Bea to balance the funds being accumulated for Scott's benefit. The total accumulation for Scott will be about $122,000. Since the Martinsons spent about $60,000 for Bea's education, an additional $60,000 would be a reasonable amount to give Bea to achieve their desire for equalization.

A $60,000 whole life insurance policy on Ed's life should be acquired for this purpose. An interest-sensitive insurance product would place too much risk on the Martinsons, given their age. As with the previous insurance recommendation, the same life insurance trust would be the appropriate vehicle. The premium would then be a gift of a present interest for federal gift tax purposes, and the proceeds, *if* the trust applied for and owned the policy, would not be included in Ed's estate.

This insurance need, as well as the insurance need described in the next section, should be purchased as one policy. The trustee can be directed to distribute $60,000 of the total proceeds to Bea.

Additional Income for Amy Should Ed Die First

Should Ed predecease Amy, there will be a reduction in the amount of the social security benefits payable to her. Indeed, there may be a period of years when her age prevents her from receiving a surviving spouse's benefit, and this gap must be provided for. In addition, if Ed and Amy choose a joint and 50 percent survivor pension, there will be a sizable setback due to the age difference. This is part of the reason why the Martinsons want to set up the fund that will provide them with the additional $5,000 income each year. Also if Ed dies first, Amy will have a reduction in the benefit for Inc's pension plan, so some additional provision for the social security and pension reductions should be part of their overall financial plan.

If Amy was old enough to receive social security benefits as Ed's surviving spouse, there would be a reduction in these benefits of approximately $400 per month ($4,800 per year). Ed's pension based on $100,000 as his estimated 5-year average salary under the plan would be $37,500 before applying the plan's setback for both early retirement at age 62 and for the age differential. The combined effect of these setbacks reduces the pension by $12,000 to $25,500 yearly. At Ed's death this amount would be further reduced by 50 percent. It is this subsequent reduction for which the Martinsons must make some provision.

Although the social security benefit will decline, it is not necessary for the Martinsons to replace this income for Amy except for the few years during which she might not qualify for the benefit if she is under age 60. A fund of about $50,000 should be adequate. For the pension reduction the replacement need is $12,500 annually. If this annual total reduction of $17,300 for the social security gap and pension-reduced benefits is capitalized at 7.2 percent, then $240,000 of income-producing assets will be needed to provide the income replacement for Amy. Since the Martinsons' excess cash flow will be used to fund the supplemental income streams for their retirement and for Scott's need, they will also need insurance to fund Amy's need for income replacement.

However, there is an existing $50,000 of insurance on Ed's life, which can be used to reduce the amount of insurance protection needed for meeting Amy's need. Therefore an additional $190,000 ($240,000 − $50,000) of insurance is needed to achieve the necessary target. Ed should be the insured, and the life insurance trust should apply for and own the policy. The annual cost for one participating whole life policy in the amount of $250,000 ($190,000 + $60,000) is $8,800.

Review of Accidental Death and Dismemberment Coverage

Ed has an accidental death and dismemberment policy as an employee benefit from Inc. The policy carries a death benefit of double Ed's annual base salary. This coverage is in addition to other employment-related life insurance. Because Ed travels frequently on business, such a benefit is a good one and is adequate. There seems to be no need for Ed to have any additional accidental death coverage on an individual basis. To the extent that Ed does decide to acquire more coverage, whole life or universal life would be more appropriate than additional accidental death coverage.

Review of the Disability Insurance

The case narrative indicates that Ed receives short-term disability benefits as part of his benefits package from Inc. Specifically coverage for 100 percent of lost salary for short-term disability (maximum of 6 months) is provided under a nonfunded wage contribution plan. Salary lost due to a disability that is serious enough to prevent a return to work after a 6-month period is replaced at 75 percent (including social security disability benefits) for the duration of the disability or until normal retirement age, whichever comes first. In the event of disability Inc will continue to credit years of service for purposes of coverage in the qualified pension plan and will make both the employer and the employee contributions to the 401(k) plan. Also the facts indicate that coverage will be continued under Inc's medical insurance plan at no charge to the disabled employee.

The issue is whether the employer-sponsored disability benefit is ample or whether Ed should purchase additional coverage on an individual basis. We know from the facts that Ed estimates a need of an additional $2,000 per month if he becomes disabled. It is therefore clear that the current employer-provided disability package is inadequate. One strong recommendation in the insurance planning portion of the financial plan is for

Ed to purchase individual disability insurance coverage that pays $2,000 a month until age 65 and has an annual cost of $1,220. Having the insurance until age 65 protects Ed should he not retire at age 62 as planned.

Review of Medical Coverage for Both Ed and Amy

Under the current arrangement Ed is covered by Inc's comprehensive medical insurance plan. Such coverage provides $500,000 of lifetime coverage for each family member. Each year after a $250 per-person deductible the insurance provides coverage for 80 percent of the first $5,000 of covered benefits for the family. After $5,000 of covered benefits is reached, additional covered medical expenses are paid in full under the terms of the policy.

The plan is noncontributory for employee coverage. Dependent coverage is available only if the employee will contribute to the cost of the coverage, for which the employee will pay $110 monthly. When an employee retires at normal retirement age, 65, Inc pays the full cost of the medicare supplemental insurance for both the employee and the employee's spouse. Inc is currently studying the possibility of (1) discontinuing its payments for the supplemental medicare insurance, (2) having the retired employee pay the coverage under a group plan, or (3) having the employee make contributions during his or her employment years toward the retirement medical insurance. Ed would be affected as a future retiree and may need to review expected postretirement medical coverage should Inc change its existing plan.

Property and Liability Coverages

The information in the case indicates that the homeowners policy and the automobile policies are appropriate for the clients' needs.

Summary of Insurance Needs

Table 7-6 summarizes the Martinsons' insurance needs, which total $11,780.

Recommendations for the Martinsons

Table 7-7 combines data for the Martinsons' cash flow and the dollar amount for funding their supplemental income needs (table 7-5) and the cost of the recommended insurance (table 7-6).

Comparison of their cash inflow and cash outflow over the 4-year period shows that the Martinsons currently have sufficient cash to either provide the supplemental income funding or acquire their needed insurance. Since they are unable to do both until 1998 when their cash inflow exceeds their cash outflow, they must make some choices at this time.

In family situations where the financial success depends on the earnings of one family member—in this case Ed—adequate life and disability income insurance to provide the future income stream of the surviving family

TABLE 7-6
Recommended Insurance for the Martinsons

Purpose	Policy Type	Cost Per Year
Disability income protection for Ed	Disability income	$1,220
Income supplements for Scott and the Martinsons	Yearly renewable term	800
Income supplement for Amy when Ed dies	Whole life	8,800
Long-term care for Amy	Long-term care	594

TABLE 7-7
Martinsons' Projected Cash Inflows and Outflows to Meet Objectives

		Cash Outflow		
Year	Investable Cash Inflow (Base Case)	8-Year Increasing Annual Funding	Projected Insurance Costs	Cash Inflow Minus Cash Outflow
1995	$24,553	$22,005	$11,414	($8,866)
1996	26,514	23,105	11,414	(8,005)
1997	31,489	24,161	11,414	(4,086)
1998	35,664	24,473	11,414	(223)

members normally takes precedence over competing uses for scarce dollars. For the Martinsons, then, the recommendation is that they acquire the following insurance in the amounts previously stated on pages 7.44 to 7.58 in the insurance section:

- whole life insurance on Ed for the purpose of protecting Amy in case he should die before her
- level-term life insurance on Ed to assure completion of the accumulation funding for their retirement years and for Scott
- disability income insurance to provide income equal to what would have been earned until age 65

The long-term care insurance covering Amy could be deferred for several years without significantly increasing the current annual premium. The amount of this premium is included in the insurance cost column of table 7-7, and it is assumed that the coverage will be purchased at this time.

One point to note with this recommended insurance package is that Ed is slightly overprotected with the level-term insurance used to fund the income supplements. Should Ed die, these excess insurance proceeds can be channeled to provide additions to the income stream being provided for Amy.

These recommendations specify that the remainder of their cash flows—for example, almost $12,775 in 1995—be channeled into investment assets as outlined in the investment section. In addition, if Ed's income from Inc increases more than anticipated over the 4-year planning horizon, then every effort should be made to add this income to the after-tax fund. Most likely their net cash flow will become positive in 1999. At that time, these additional funds should be used to begin eliminating the shortfalls that started in 1995.

Although Ed expressed a desire to retire early, he did not make a firm commitment to retiring at age 62. Subsequent evaluations of the progress toward goal achievement might reveal that age 62 is feasible or perhaps that retirement at age 63 would best serve their aggregate goal achievement if sufficient funds have not been accumulated.

INVESTMENT PLANNING

Refinancing the Home

Because of the decline in mortgage rates, the Martinsons should consider refinancing their home to lower the current monthly payment of $1,207.11, of which $1,080.00 is interest. When questioned, they revealed that they prefer a fixed-rate mortgage since they want to avoid the risk associated with mortgages that have an adjustable rate. The Martinsons also specified that they are willing to finance the existing $120,097 balance of their loan. However, they do not want to remove any of their equity in their home by refinancing more than the unpaid balance.

Because of a trend in standardization in the secondary mortgage market, most lenders offer fixed-rate mortgages only with 15- and 30-year maturities. A review of local rates has revealed that a 15-year mortgage at a rate of 7 1/4 percent with three points is available for a monthly principal-plus-interest payment of $1,096.32.

If the Martinsons choose a 30-year mortgage, the rate rises to 7 1/2 percent with three points, but the payment drops to $839.74, of which $750.61 is interest. Of course, this means that they have to make payments for 9 years longer than the current mortgage requires.

An alternative approach involves obtaining a 30-year mortgage and then making payments using a 21-year amortization schedule to match the current loan. This appeals to many clients since they often prefer not to extend the payment period beyond their original obligation. This calculation results in a planned payment of $947.76, but the required payment remains at $839.74.

The Martinsons' home mortgage interest is tax deductible. The interest payment in the 49th (current) month of the existing loan is $1,080.88. The after-tax mortgage payment for the 28 percent tax bracket is $904.46, calculated as follows: $1,207.11 − ($1,080.88 x 0.28). (Note that if mortgage interest is deductible at the state and/or local level, those marginal rates should be added to the federal marginal rate for this calculation.) Of course, interest on the mortgage declines every month, so the after-tax cost rises every month. At the time of the last mortgage payment, the after-tax cost will be within $5 of the mortgage payment. For the 30/21 year approach, the initial monthly after-tax cash outflow is $737.59, calculated as follows: $947.76 − ($750.61 x 0.28).

Both the 15-year mortgage and the 30-year mortgage require an immediate payment of three discount points to the lender ($3,602.92). Under current regulations, this is deductible but must be amortized over the life of the loan. (The original loan had no discount points.) Each of the proposed loans will also require other fees, including legal expenses, appraisal fees, and title insurance, totaling $2,850, which are not deductible.

The Martinsons should evaluate the proposed refinancing carefully. First, they must decide if the changes in cash flows caused by the new loan are affordable since discount points plus other fees total $6,452.92. Fortunately, the Martinsons have the ability and willingness to commit the funds. Second, they should analyze the proposals in greater detail, including the use of discounted cash-flow techniques.

An intuitively appealing comparison of the old loan to a new loan is the break-even point in months. This approach, which does not consider the time value of money, divides the initial outflow associated with the new loan by the change in the monthly after-tax cash flow. Assume the 30/21 year mortgage is the approach favored by the Martinsons:

$$\text{break-even in months} = \frac{\text{discount points plus other fees}}{\text{current after-tax payment} - \text{new after-tax payment} + \text{monthly tax savings from amortization of points}}$$

$$= \frac{\$3{,}602.92 + \$2{,}850}{\$904.46 - \$737.59 + [(\$3{,}602.92/360 \times 0.28)]}$$

$$= \frac{\$6{,}452.92}{\$169.67}$$

$$= 38 \text{ months}$$

Based on the foregoing, it will be 38 months before the monthly savings of the new loan total the costs associated with obtaining that loan. (It should be noted that the break-even would have been shorter if payments were made on a 30-year amortization, but the Martinsons' monthly payments would continue for 9 additional years.) If the Martinsons plan to move within that period, refinancing would not make sense.

Another approach to analyzing the proposed refinancing is to use the concept of time value of money. Two methods that consider the time value of money are the net present value approach and the after-tax internal rate of return approach. Each is theoretically sound, but the after-tax internal rate of return approach is more understandable. Both methods reach the same conclusion but the after-tax internal rate of return is easier to explain and will be used to analyze the refinancing.

Calculating the internal rate of return is a job for specialized computer software or a custom spreadsheet package. Again, there are outflows and inflows, although we handle them differently. For the existing loan the inflow is simply the current balance of the loan, and the outflows are the monthly after-tax mortgage payments. (Recall that the after-tax mortgage payment rises over the life of the loan due to the reduction in interest.) The annual rate that discounts the future outflows back to the present to equal the inflows is the after-tax internal rate of return.

For the new loan the process is more complicated. The inflow consists of the current balance of the loan reduced by any points and fees that are required. Outflows for the new loan are the after-tax monthly payments on the loan reduced by the monthly tax savings from the allocation of discount points on the new loan. However, since the Martinsons would be paying a 30-year mortgage over 21 years, they would have received only 70 percent (21/30) of the tax savings due to them from the allocation of discount points. Thus we reduce the last monthly cash outflow by an amount equal to the discount points times 30 percent times a projected tax rate of 28 percent (assumed to equal their current rate).

Our calculations reveal that the after-tax rate on the old loan is 8.06 percent, while the after-tax rate on the new loan is 6.14 percent. This implies that the new loan, even when we consider points and fees, is the better option.

Since the Martinsons have no intention of moving from their house, refinancing makes sense. They can obtain the funds necessary for refinancing, and the break-even point is only 38 months. A 30-year mortgage gives the flexibility of a much lower monthly house payment, and using a 21-year amortization period makes the time frames of both loans identical. Most important, the after-tax financing rate over the intended holding period is better for the new mortgage than for the old mortgage.

The new mortgage will be in place so that the first payment will be in January 1995.

Portfolio

The investment instruments that a client will use depend on the following variables:

- the client's risk profile
- the relative importance of the objective
- the possibility of postponing the date when the funds are needed

- the purpose for which the income from the accumulated assets or the assets themselves will be used

In light of the Martinsons' current situation, the first of these variables would suggest that relatively conservative investment instruments should be their choice. Their existing portfolio of common stocks and mutual funds is not overly aggressive and implies that the Martinsons are not high risk takers. Some of their investment is in Inc common, which could be doubly risky if Inc's fortunes decline, since both Ed's position and the value of the stock could be affected. Also their age, especially Ed's, would indicate that their portfolio should not be incurring higher and higher risk each year as Ed approaches his retirement date. The portfolio should slowly be restructured to move away from investments stressing capital appreciation, thus reducing its overall risk and increasing its income stream.

The Martinsons consider their two accumulation objectives, their retirement supplement and the income supplement for Scott, extremely important. Therefore placing any of these future savings funds into high-risk instruments could jeopardize their situation. (The extra retirement supplement, outside of the qualified and nonqualified pension plans, also accomplishes Ed's vital objective of providing for Amy.) When the funds accumulated are for achieving highly rated objective(s), appropriate investments typically include only those having a relatively low risk of loss.

Although Ed has expressed a desire to retire at age 62 if the needed funds can be accumulated within the next 8 years, the retirement date can be postponed until he reaches 65 and perhaps beyond if he is not considered an executive or employee in a high policy-making position as specified in the federal Age Discrimination in Employment Act. The fact that the date by which the funds will be needed can be deferred would make the use of investments with a somewhat higher risk/return profile appropriate.

The objective that these accumulations will seek to meet is an income stream over a long period. Once the long-term income stream begins, inflation starts its continual eroding of the dollar's buying power. Although the accumulation amounts and target sums specified in table 7-4 are adjusted for 4 percent inflation during the accumulation and payout periods, inflation can exceed that rate, making the buying power of the income stream diminish for both the Martinsons and their son. One way to offset this effect would be to place part of the funds in investments that would tend to provide after-tax returns in excess of the anticipated 4 percent inflation rate. The remainder of the funds would use relatively low-risk investment instruments.

A second aspect of this long-term income flow is the erratic behavior of investment returns. Some financial experts suggest that the direction of interest rates over the next several years will be downward. If this should transpire and if the Martinsons are planning to use only conservative, fixed-income instruments, the likelihood of achieving the estimated 6 percent after-tax return used in developing tables 7-1 to 7-5 might not be realized. However, periods of declining interest rates during the past 20 years have been associated with a buoyant and rising stock market.

> **INSTRUCTIONS TO STUDENTS**
>
> To avoid repetition of background material on the various investment risks, investor profiles, the need to match the risk-return tradeoff associated with the investment instruments, suggestions for matching investments in the general risk category with financial objectives, and selected investments appropriate for accumulation funding, that material has been omitted from this chapter. In an actual plan material such as that on pages 3.97–3.107, 3.109–3.115, 4.72–4.74, 5.119–5.121, 5.129–5.136, and 6.113–6.116 should be presented to the client. If the student is not familiar with the noted material from the previous chapters, it should be reviewed before proceeding through this section of the suggested solution.

Recommended Portfolio

Since both accumulation objectives are similar except for the income recipients, the same portfolio design can be appropriate for both. Based on the previous discussion of these objectives, the funds set aside for each portfolio could be allocated as follows:

U.S. government 5-year notes	25 percent
No-load corporate bond fund	25 percent
No-load balanced fund	30 percent
Individual common stock investments (such as Inc or conservative, defensive stocks)	20 percent

The government notes should not have more than a 5-year duration at this time due to the uncertainty of the direction of long-term interest rates. Currently they are lower than during the past few years, and they continue to move downward. If this direction should change, the Martinsons could end up in the unfortunate position of owning low-yield investments for their long-term purpose if they purchased 25- or 30-year bonds at this time. The government bonds do provide safety and a base of stability for their portfolio.

For the various mutual funds that comprise a sizable portion of the proposed portfolio, no-load funds are recommended, assuming that the returns are comparable. The amount of funding shown in tables 7.1–7.5 is the gross amount that must be invested at the assumed, blended, after-tax return of 6 percent. If load funds are used, the net amount the Martinsons will have working for them will be less. Thus a higher return would be needed from the load fund, for an equivalent risk, to achieve their targets.

Like the government notes, the bond fund provides stability but with a slightly higher rate of return. The balanced fund, with its slightly increased risk, provides some degree of potential growth due to this type of fund's being partially invested in common stock. Usually a balanced fund has safety of principal and current income as its primary investment objective, which blends with the Martinsons' situation.

The last two categories, a growth stock fund and direct ownership of common stocks, provide the somewhat higher risk section of the portfolio and over the long term should also offer somewhat higher returns that can compensate for unexpected variations in interest rates or inflation.

Additional Considerations

Maximizing the Use of Inc's 401(k) Plan

Ed participates in Inc's 401(k) plan by contributing 5 percent of salary, a contribution of approximately $5,000 this year. Although the Internal Revenue Code permits a maximum employee contribution of $8,400 each year subject to a possible lower limit due to rules in other sections of the Code, Ed has been unable to verify that Inc permits contributions in excess of 5 percent of salary. If the plan permits additional contributions, Ed should further reduce his salary by making larger, tax-deferred contributions that Inc does not match through the plan. Sufficient cash flow in excess of his additional insurance premiums permits him to take advantage of this feature, if permissible, in the 401(k) plan and still have after-tax cash flow available to make individual investments outside the qualified plan.

Several of the investment choices in Inc's plan are consistent with the recommendations made earlier regarding the composition of the Martinsons' portfolio for this accumulation objective. Allocating a portion of their 401(k) contribution to the corporate bond or balanced mutual fund and then investing the remaining cash flow in other investment instruments as recommended previously will meet their objective.

Taking advantage of the favorable tax treatment currently afforded 401(k) plans will reduce the underfunding of the supplemental income streams that they plan to fund.

Family of Funds

Many sponsors of mutual funds offer a variety of funds referred to as a *family of funds*. The reasons for doing this are twofold. First, investors who might want to allocate their portfolio in funds with different objectives and risk/return characteristics can do so without seeking a competing firm's product. Second, many investors prefer to switch their holdings, essentially those practicing market-timing, as economic conditions have changed or are expected to change.

Most authorities recommend investors using common stocks or stock-invested mutual funds within a portfolio to have a planning horizon of a minimum of 3–5 years for these securities and not to let short-run market fluctuations influence investment choices or decisions to buy or sell. But should fundamental conditions in the economic or securities spheres change, then portfolio restructuring can be desirable. For the convenience of making changes within their portfolio and not for the purpose of short-term trading, the Martinsons could consider selecting such a family of funds.

Ownership Considerations

Retirement Income Supplement. The age disparity between Ed and Amy plus Amy's family history suggests she will outlive him. In addition, she currently owns few assets. For these two reasons the best recommendation for the Martinsons to follow would be to title the assets being acquired in Amy's name. The advantages of this course of action would be as follows:

- No gift tax would be incurred due to the unlimited deduction for gifts between spouses.
- Should Amy predecease Ed, she would have assets that could be shielded from estate taxation by using the $192,800 estate tax credit ($600,000 exemption). To continue Ed's retirement income supplement for which these funds were accumulated, she could set up a testamentary trust that would give Ed the trust income for life and at his death have the corpus pass equally to the children, per stirpes.

One disadvantage of this ownership recommendation is that should Ed predecease Amy, his assets that pass to her could create estate tax liabilities and shrinkage before the net estate passes to the children. At the current time it is recommended that Ed's estate be structured so that most of his income-producing assets are placed in a bypass trust for Amy's benefit. Thus the total estate assets passing to Amy would not create major estate tax liabilities at her subsequent death.

Scott's Income Supplement. Using a trust for this objective would give the Martinsons the assurance that the funds they set aside would be used solely for Scott's benefit and that prudent supervision of trust assets and their disposition would take place over a long period.

The funding for this objective will continue past the time that Scott reaches age 21. Since the 2503(b) trust requires the annual distribution of trust income, no funds could be accumulated over the next few years that would provide the necessary long-term income flow to Scott. Therefore a 2503(c) trust would meet the Martinsons' needs because it would have two desirable features. First, the trust can accumulate income. Second, gifts made to the trust qualify for the annual $10,000 individual (or $20,000 joint) gift tax exclusion. A disadvantage is that the trust corpus must be distributed when Scott attains age 21. At that time, 5 years from now, the Martinsons will not have completed the funding for this purpose. In addition, the corpus, when Scott receives it, could be dissipated rather quickly.

To permit using the 2503(c) trust, the instrument should contain a Crummey provision that will allow Scott to withdraw trust income for a period of 20 consecutive days each year. With this clause in the document the life of the trust will extend beyond the time that Scott reaches age 21. In addition, whether the Martinsons fund the trust over the next 8 or 11 years (or some intermediary time), their annual contributions will continue to qualify for the annual gift tax exclusion because Scott has this withdrawal power.

Of course, if he makes any withdrawals, the total amount needed at the end of the funding period will not be available for his long-term income supplement. Hopefully Ed and Amy will be able to convince him of the need for restraint during the funding period. They will also need to stress the importance of his withdrawing only the amount of the annual income after the funding is completed each year so the desired income stream will not be jeopardized.

Since the possibility exists that Scott might not live as long as the 50 years for which the trust income stream is designed to provide the supplemental income, one or more corpus beneficiaries should be named. Since Ed has indicated that providing for Amy is his primary objective, Amy should be the corpus beneficiary if she survives Scott. Should Amy predecease Scott, Bea and her issue, per stirpes, would become the corpus beneficiaries. If Bea also predeceases Scott and leaves no issue, the corpus could be given to a qualified charity, such as Ed's college.

Finally, although Ed can retire anytime between age 62 and age 65 or perhaps later, he may not prefer this course of action. Indeed, instead of staying with Inc until the normal retirement age, 65, he has expressed a preference to leave at 62. Depending on the Martinsons' ability to achieve the necessary accumulation, based on their available cash flow and the direction of interest rates, Ed might be able to meet his targeted retirement age of 62.

CASE II
Acquisition of Additional Insurance
Beginning in 1994

CASE ASSUMPTIONS—CASE II

New Assumptions

1. Beginning in 1995, $11,414 will be spent on the additional insurance.

2. The investable cash flow for the years 1995–1998 inclusive will be allocated for the accumulation objectives and will earn a before-tax return of 8.35 percent.

3. The residence will be refinanced for a period of 30 years with a fixed interest rate of 7 1/2 percent with 3 points being paid.

Continuing Assumptions

1. The checking account balance is maintained at $5,000; the account is noninterest bearing.

2. Ed's salary is increased at 5 percent annually.

3. The money market deposit account earns 4 3/4 percent annually.

4. Expenditures for food, clothing and cleaning, utilities, phone, vacations, and charitable contributions will increase annually at 3 percent.

5. Expenditures for transportation will increase 4 percent annually.

6. Expenditures for entertainment will increase 5 percent annually.

7. Expenditures for medical insurance and other medical expenses will increase at 6 percent annually.

8. Decreases in the value of furniture have been ignored.

9. Automobiles decrease in value at a rate of 15 percent annually.

10. The value of the home will increase at 1 percent annually.

11. The common stock portfolio will increase at 9 percent annually.

12. Dividends from the common stock portfolio are currently $850, will increase 4 percent annually, and are reinvested in the portfolio.

1994   INCOME STATEMENT

EDGAR & AMY MARTINSON

CASE II	1994	1995	1996	1997	1998
Earned Income					
Compensation-Cl	95,000	99,750	104,738	109,974	115,473
Company Bonus	9,500	9,975	10,474	10,997	11,547
401(K)-Ed's Contr	-4,750	-4,988	-5,237	-5,499	-5,774
	99,750	104,737	109,974	115,473	121,246
Interest/Dividends					
Money Market Fund	1,188	1,188	1,188	1,188	1,188
Stock Portfolio	827	877	929	985	1,044
Investable Cash	753	2,196	3,715	5,650	8,119
Growth Mutual Funds	1,115	1,278	1,465	1,678	1,924
Balnced Mutual Fund	1,182	1,299	1,428	1,571	1,727
	5,065	6,838	8,725	11,072	14,002
Adj Gross Income	104,815	111,575	118,700	126,545	135,248
Deductions					
Charitable 50%	2,000	2,060	2,122	2,185	2,251
State Tax Paid	4,663	5,037	5,439	5,882	6,374
Property Tax--Home	3,000	3,090	3,183	3,278	3,377
Home Mortgage	8,617	8,497	8,366	8,227	8,076
Amortization-Points	0	120	120	120	120
Reductn For High Inc	0	0	-67	-180	-315
Gross Deductions	18,280	18,804	19,162	19,512	19,883
Standard Deduction	6,200	6,400	6,600	6,850	7,100
Allowed Deductions	18,280	18,804	19,162	19,512	19,883
Pers Exemptions	7,050	7,350	7,650	7,800	8,100
Taxable Income	79,485	85,421	91,887	99,233	107,266
Fed Income Tax	17,456	18,946	20,576	22,463	24,669
Fed Tax Bracket	28.0	28.0	28.0	31.0	31.0

7.72

1994 **BALANCE SHEET**

EDGAR & AMY MARTINSON

CASE II	1994	1995	1996	1997	1998
LIQUID ASSETS					
Cash Balance	9,998	10,011	10,036	10,040	10,057
Cash Deposits					
Investable Cash	18,800	36,002	56,688	84,291	118,296
IRA (CD's) - Ed	22,917	24,773	26,780	28,949	31,294
IRA (CD's) - Amy	2,378	2,571	2,779	3,004	3,247
Money Market Fund	25,000	25,000	25,000	25,000	25,000
	69,095	88,346	111,247	141,244	177,837
Stocks & Bonds					
Stock Portfolio	28,340	30,891	33,671	36,701	40,004
Growth Mutual Funds	45,843	52,540	60,215	69,011	79,093
Balnced Mutual Fund	30,787	33,851	37,219	40,923	44,996
	104,970	117,281	131,105	146,636	164,093
Overpaid Taxes					
Overpaid State Tx	1	1	1	1	1
	1	1	1	1	1
Life Insurance					
LifeInsCashValu-Ed	34,425	34,425	34,425	34,425	34,425
LifeInsCashValu-Amy	1,800	1,800	1,800	1,800	1,800
	36,225	36,225	36,225	36,225	36,225
Liquid Assets	220,289	251,864	288,614	334,146	388,213
NONLIQUID ASSETS					
Retirement Plans					
401(K) Plan	67,270	72,988	79,192	85,923	93,226
401(K)-Ed's Contr	4,750	9,738	14,975	20,474	26,248
401(K)-Emplyr Contr	4,750	9,738	14,975	20,474	26,248
Vested Pension	149,625	157,106	164,961	173,209	181,869
	226,395	249,570	274,103	300,080	327,591
Investments					
Points Paid	0	3,480	3,360	3,240	3,120
	0	3,480	3,360	3,240	3,120
Personal Property					
Home	346,430	349,894	353,393	356,927	360,496
Ed's Car	17,000	14,450	12,283	10,440	8,874
Amy's Car	10,200	8,670	7,370	6,264	5,324
Home Furnishings	75,000	75,000	75,000	75,000	75,000
	448,630	448,014	448,045	448,631	449,695
Nonliquid Assets	675,025	701,064	725,508	751,951	780,406
Total Assets	895,314	952,928	1,014,122	1,086,097	1,168,619

7.73

1994   **BALANCE SHEET**   (cont.)

EDGAR & AMY MARTINSON

CASE II	1994	1995	1996	1997	1998

LIABILITIES

Mortgage Loans
Home Mortgage	117,973	116,237	114,370	112,364	110,207
	117,973	116,237	114,370	112,364	110,207

Notes Payable
Ed's Car Loan	11,429	6,998	2,151	0	0
	11,429	6,998	2,151	0	0

Total Liabilities	129,402	123,235	116,521	112,364	110,207
Net Worth	765,912	829,693	897,601	973,733	1,058,412

1994   CASHFLOW STATEMENT

EDGAR & AMY MARTINSON

CASE II	1994	1995	1996	1997	1998
BEGINNING OF YEAR					
Idle Cash On Hand	10,000	9,998	10,011	10,036	10,040
SOURCES OF CASH					
Cash Income					
Compensation-Cl	95,000	99,750	104,738	109,974	115,473
Company Bonus	9,500	9,975	10,474	10,997	11,547
Interest+Dividends	2,015	2,065	2,117	2,173	2,232
	106,515	111,790	117,328	123,145	129,252
Total Cash Inflow	106,515	111,790	117,328	123,145	129,252
Tot Cash Available	116,515	121,788	127,339	133,181	139,292
USES OF CASH					
Fully Tax Deductible					
401(K)-Ed's Contr	4,750	4,988	5,237	5,499	5,774
Home Mortgage	8,617	8,497	8,366	8,227	8,076
	13,367	13,485	13,603	13,726	13,850
Partly Deductible					
Med Ins Premium	240	254	270	286	303
Other Medical Expen	2,800	2,968	3,146	3,335	3,535
Charity Contrb-50%	2,000	2,060	2,122	2,185	2,251
	5,040	5,282	5,538	5,806	6,089
Not Tax Deductible					
Ed's Car Loan	1,228	849	433	49	0
Food	8,000	8,240	8,487	8,742	9,004
Clothing	3,000	3,090	3,183	3,278	3,377
Entertainment	2,000	2,100	2,205	2,315	2,431
Vacations	3,000	3,090	3,183	3,278	3,377
Transportation	1,000	1,040	1,082	1,125	1,170
Home Insurance Prem	500	510	520	531	541
Prop/Liab Ins Prem	100	102	104	106	108
Auto Insurance Prem	1,000	1,040	1,082	1,125	1,170
Ed's Life Ins Prems	2,335	2,335	2,335	2,335	2,335
Amy's Life Ins Prem	125	125	125	125	125
Additionl Insurance	0	11,414	11,414	11,414	11,414
Home Improvements	1,000	1,030	1,061	1,093	1,126
Home Refinance Cost	2,850	0	0	0	0
Utility/Phone	3,000	3,000	3,000	3,000	3,000
Personal Care Items	1,300	1,339	1,379	1,421	1,463
Points Paid	3,603	0	0	0	0
	34,041	39,304	39,592	39,936	40,640

7.75

1994   **CASHFLOW STATEMENT** (cont.)

EDGAR & AMY MARTINSON

CASE II	1994	1995	1996	1997	1998
Taxes Paid					
Fed Tax Paid	17,456	18,946	20,576	22,463	24,669
State Tax Paid	4,663	5,037	5,439	5,882	6,374
FICA/Soc Sec Tax	5,235	5,460	5,688	5,939	6,194
Real Estate Tax	3,000	3,090	3,183	3,278	3,377
	30,354	32,533	34,886	37,562	40,613
Purchase/Deposits					
Investable Cash	18,047	15,006	16,971	21,953	25,886
	18,047	15,006	16,971	21,953	25,886
Liability Liquidation					
Home Mortgage	1,616	1,736	1,867	2,006	2,157
Ed's Car Loan	4,052	4,431	4,847	2,151	0
	5,668	6,167	6,714	4,157	2,157
Tot Cash Outflow	106,517	111,777	117,303	123,141	129,235
END OF YEAR					
Cash Balance	9,998	10,011	10,036	10,040	10,057

7.76

1994 SUPPORTING SCHEDULE

EDGAR & AMY MARTINSON

CASE II	JOINT 1994	JOINT 1995	JOINT 1996	JOINT 1997	JOINT 1998
Income					
Earned Income	99,750	104,737	109,974	115,473	121,246
Adj Gross Income	104,815	111,575	118,700	126,545	135,248
Allowed Deductions	18,280	18,804	19,162	19,512	19,883
Pers Exemptions	7,050	7,350	7,650	7,800	8,100
Taxable Income	79,485	85,421	91,887	99,233	107,266
Federal Tax Liab					
Regular Tax	17,456	18,946	20,576	22,463	24,669
Gross Fed Inc Tax	17,456	18,946	20,576	22,463	24,669
Fed Income Tax	17,456	18,946	20,576	22,463	24,669
Fed Tax Analysis					
Indexing Factor	46	51	56	62	68
Fed Tax Bracket	28.0	28.0	28.0	31.0	31.0
$ To Next Bracket	9,665	6,879	3,613	56,017	53,434
Next Bracket	31.0	31.0	31.0	36.0	36.0
Previous Bracket	15.0	15.0	15.0	28.0	28.0
$ To Prev Bracket	42,585	47,221	52,337	383	4,916
Alt Minimum Tax					
Adj Gross Income	104,815	111,575	118,700	126,545	135,248
Contributions	-2,000	-2,060	-2,122	-2,185	-2,251
Home Mortgage	-8,617	-8,497	-8,366	-8,227	-8,076
Amortization-Points	0	-120	-120	-120	-120
Adjusted AMTI	94,198	100,898	108,092	116,013	124,801
AMT Exemptions	-45,000	-45,000	-45,000	-45,000	-45,000
AMT Taxable Inc	49,198	55,898	63,092	71,013	79,801
Gross Alt Min Tx	12,791	14,533	16,404	18,463	20,748
Fed Tax Less FTC	-17,456	-18,945	-20,576	-22,463	-24,669
Other Tax Liabs					
FICA/Soc Sec Tax	5,235	5,460	5,688	5,939	6,194
Adj Gross Inc	104,815	111,575	118,700	126,545	135,248
GA Adj Grss Inc	104,815	111,575	118,700	126,545	135,248
GA Standard Ded	4,400	4,400	4,400	4,400	4,400
GA Itemized Ded	18,280	18,804	19,230	19,692	20,198
GA Exemptions	4,500	4,500	4,500	4,500	4,500
GA Taxable Inc	82,035	88,271	94,970	102,353	110,551
GA Regular Tax	4,662	5,036	5,438	5,881	6,373
GA Income Tax	4,662	5,036	5,438	5,881	6,373
Georgia Tax	4,662	5,036	5,438	5,881	6,373
Tot State/Local Tx	4,662	5,036	5,438	5,881	6,373
Total Inc Tax	27,353	29,442	31,702	34,283	37,236

1994   FINANCIAL SUMMARY

EDGAR & AMY MARTINSON

CASE II	1994	1995	1996	1997	1998
Gross Real Income					
Personal Earnings	104,500	109,725	115,211	120,972	127,020
Interest Income	1,941	3,384	4,903	6,838	9,307
Dividends Rcvd	3,124	3,454	3,822	4,234	4,695
	109,565	116,563	123,937	132,044	141,022
Income & Inflation					
Gross Real Inc	109,565	116,563	123,937	132,044	141,022
Total Inc Tax	-27,353	-29,441	-31,702	-34,283	-37,236
Net Real Income	82,212	87,121	92,235	97,761	103,786
Cur Real Inc =	82,212	85,089	88,067	91,149	94,340
At Infltn Rate Of	4	4	4	4	4
Cash Flow					
Idle Cash On Hand	10,000	9,998	10,011	10,036	10,040
Norml Cash Inflow	106,515	111,790	117,328	123,145	129,252
Norml Cash Outflw	88,470	96,771	100,332	101,188	103,349
Cash Invested	18,047	15,006	16,971	21,953	25,886
Cash Balance	9,998	10,011	10,036	10,040	10,057
Net Worth					
Personal Assets	494,853	494,250	494,306	494,896	495,977
Investment Assets	400,460	458,677	519,815	591,200	672,641
Personal Liabilities	-129,402	-123,235	-116,521	-112,364	-110,207
Personal Net Worth	365,451	371,015	377,785	382,532	385,770
Investment Net Worth	400,460	458,677	519,815	591,200	672,641
Net Worth	765,912	829,693	897,601	973,733	1,058,412

After refinancing their residence and acquiring the recommended insurance, the Martinsons' cash flow for the two accumulation objectives (supplementary retirement income for Ed and Amy and lifetime income stream for Scott) are shown in table 7.8. For the next 3 years the available cash is not sufficient to meet their funding needs as brought forward from table 7.7. A shortfall will exist for 3 years, after which time catch-up funding becomes feasible as their available cash flow improves.

TABLE 7-8
Martinson's Cash Inflow and Outflow to Meet Funding Objectives after Acquiring Insurance and Refinancing Their Residence

Year	Investable Cash Flow (Case II)	8-Year Increasing Annual Funding	Cash Inflow Minus Cash Outflow
1995	$15,006	$22,005	($6,999)
1996	16,971	23,105	(6,134)
1997	21,953	24,161	(2,208)
1998	25,886	24,473	1,413

8

PLANNING FOR A SURVIVING SPOUSE

Frequently a financial services professional may be called upon to counsel the soon-to-be- or already-widowed spouse. In the event that such a client is affluent, many complex, sophisticated, and challenging issues need to be addressed by the financial planner. Are there unusual federal income tax and estate tax issues that need to be considered for the first time now that the client will soon be widowed? Are the current insurance policies still appropriate, or must the insurance program be adjusted in accordance with the change in personal status? Is the existing investment picture still viable in light of the new situation? These are some issues that the practitioner will have to deal with.

Clearly the financial planner should allow the client time to adjust to a changed personal situation, but in some cases immediate action must be taken to deal with the impending death of a spouse and to marshall resources to provide for long-term financial needs arising from changes in health or marital status. Widowed status, either actual or impending, means many changes from the tax, estate, insurance, and investment points of view, and the client must take appropriate steps in these areas in a timely fashion. One factor that may be helpful in motivating the client to act is that the spouse's impending or actual death triggers planning regarding federal estate tax, state inheritance tax, insurance, and investments. Clients may feel that this situation is a learning experience and that failure to consider and develop effective plans harms the family's or the survivors' financial future. The financial planner may find clients in such a situation to be very cooperative.

Often the planner has been recently sought out. A debilitating illness, a comment of a friend or confidant, or the client's own recognition of the need for advice can lead to using a planner's service.

CASE NARRATIVE

Present Situation

Curtis Kelley, aged 63, and Constance Kelley, aged 60, live in western Pennsylvania in the city in which they were born and in which Constance attended high school and college. She met her husband, Curtis, while in her senior year at college. Curtis, now a chemist for a local concern, was a graduate student and teaching assistant in the chemistry department when they met. They have been married for 36 years. The Kelleys have four children—Pat, aged 34; Peggy, 32; Margie, 29; and Glenn, 26. Three of the four children reside in western Pennsylvania. None are married at this time, although Peggy and Margie are both divorced and have three children each. Margie's three children—Adam, aged 2; Scott, 4; and Jennifer, 7—all live with their mother in Erie. Peggy's three children—Kimberly, aged 6; Rachel, 4; and Heather, 18 months—all live with their mother in Corona, California.

A year ago, Curt became incapacitated after contracting a rare liver disorder. He has been totally disabled for 3 months now and has been declared terminally ill by his team of physicians. He is covered by his employer's short-term disability plan and is receiving payments each month. Medical reports indicate that Curtis has approximately 12 weeks to live.

Curt has been employed by Galaxy Pharmaceuticals, Inc., a large international drug company, for 31 years. At the time of Curt's disability, he was senior vice president in charge of research and development and was earning an annual salary of $229,000. Curt has participated in the firm's qualified profit-sharing plan every year since its inception (1975) and has accumulated $694,940 in the plan.

Employee Benefit Package

Since Galaxy provides a 26-week salary continuation (short-term disability) plan for Curtis, the Kelleys' income has not yet been reduced. The benefit coincidentally will terminate near the doctor's approximation of Curtis's date of death. Should Curtis live beyond that date, company-paid long-term disability income insurance benefits will begin, since the elimination period—the contractually specified period of disability that must pass before benefits begin—matches the salary continuation plan's benefit period.

Curtis also owns an individual disability policy with the following provisions: "own occupation" coverage, lifetime benefits, and a 180-day elimination period. Own occupation coverage requires that the insurer pay the full benefit if the disability renders the individual incapable of performing his own occupation even though he or she may be able to earn a substantial living in another occupation.

Current Residence

The Kelleys' current residence was acquired in 1987 at a cost of $375,000. They used the proceeds from the sale of their former primary residence and a mortgage of $100,000 to purchase this property. They have $225,000 of rolled-over, untaxed capital gains from previously owned primary residences. Like other homes they owned, this property and its furnishings are jointly owned.

Jewelry and Automobiles

Since Connie enjoys wearing fine jewelry, Curt has used occasions such as holidays and birthdays to give her additional pins, rings, and earrings set with precious or semiprecious stones. The jewelry was recently appraised at

$50,000 and is insured as scheduled property. Curt and Connie each own an automobile, valued at $25,000 and $10,000 respectively.

Individual Life Policies

The individual life insurance policies on Curt's life, of which he is the owner, have cash values as follows: $18,000 for a $100,000 universal policy and $56,400 for a $150,000 whole life policy. Curt has paid all the premiums on these two policies and there are no outstanding loans against the cash values. The group term policy, fully paid for by Galaxy, is two and one-half times his salary, or $572,500. Connie is the primary beneficiary of all the policies, and their four children, per stirpes, are the contingent beneficiaries.

Other Assets

During their lifetime, the Kelleys have acquired a significant amount of other assets. Curt's salary rose somewhat steadily until he was promoted to vice president. Initially the Kelleys used savings to acquire a base of secure assets consisting of U.S. Treasury bonds, corporate bonds, Series EE bonds, and money market funds.

Investment History

Then, since their main income flow was stable, the Kelleys decided to take above-average investment risks for a major portion of their holdings and began to place funds directly into individual securities with the potential for capital appreciation. Most of these investments were made during the last decade, when Curt's income increased sharply as a consequence of his promotion. Curt believed that through his knowledge of the drug industry he could select drug company common stocks, in addition to Galaxy's, with the potential for above-average growth. To this end an aggressive portfolio consisting primarily of drug company stocks has been accumulated. To decrease their dependence on this industry, the Kelleys have added an aggressive growth fund and an international fund, again with the intention of capturing above-average returns. Several years ago Connie used the inheritance she received to purchase a utility fund and an index fund that were recommended by her then son-in-law. These were acquired with the objectives of current income (utility fund) and modest stock market risk (index fund).

Need for Estate Planning

Recently Connie attended a local chapter meeting of the American Association of University Women, of which she is an active member, on the need for appropriate estate planning as means of marshalling and conserving personal assets. Given Curt's serious medical problem, they wonder if their wills, executed many years ago, properly serve their current needs. Both wills leave the deceased's assets to the surviving spouse, if living, and if the spouse is not living, the assets are distributed to their children, per stirpes. The meeting Connie attended suggested as a first step to prepare a list of assets and then prepare a separate list for each spouse. After preparing tables 8-1 and 8-2, the Kelleys realized that some planning might be needed.

TABLE 8-1
Inventory of Assets

	Cost or Basis	Fair Market Value	Current Return %	Current Return $	Form of Ownership[1]	Available for Liquidity	Collateralized	Location
Checking accounts	$ 70,000	$ 70,000	3.1	$ 2,325	JT	Yes	No	First National
Money market funds	75,000	75,000	5.0	1,000	JT	Yes	No	First National
Certificates of deposit	20,000	20,000	6.0	3,000[2]	JT	Yes	No	First National
EE bonds	15,000	50,000			S(H)	Yes	No	Safe-deposit box
Life insurance cash value		74,400			S(H)	?	No	Insurance company
Treasury bonds	110,000	125,000	7.2	9,000	S(H)	Yes	No	Safe-deposit box
Corporate bonds	85,000	100,000	7.3	7,300	JT	Yes	No	Safe-deposit box
Aggressive growth mutual fund	65,000	125,000	1.5	1,875	S(H)	Yes	No	Safe-deposit box
International fund	110,000	150,000	1.2	1,800	JT	Yes	No	Safe-deposit box
Galaxy Pharmaceutical Co. stock, 10,000 shares	200,000	500,000	1.5	7,500	JT	Yes	No	Safe-deposit box
Acme Drug Co. stock, 2,000 shares	40,000	70,000	1.8	1,260	JT	Yes	No	Safe-deposit box
Zenith Drug Co. stock, 3,000 shares	30,000	40,000	2.0	800	JT	Yes	No	Safe-deposit box
Utility fund	125,000	150,000	5.0	7,500	S(W)	Yes	No	Safe-deposit box
Index fund	150,000	200,000	2.5	5,000	S(W)	Yes	No	Safe-deposit box
Qualified retirement plan	0	694,940	--	--	S(H)	?	No	Galaxy
Residence	150,000	400,000	--	--	JT	No	$76,230	At home
Furnishings	125,000	125,000	--	--	JT	No	No	At home
Jewelry/furs	50,000	50,000	--	--	S(W)	No	No	At home
Autos								
Curt	38,000	25,000	--	--	S(H)	Maybe	No	Garage
Connie	20,000	10,000	--	--	S(W)	No	No	Garage

[1] JT = joint tenants with right of survivorship; S = single ownership; H = husband; W = wife.
[2] Interest deferred until redemption

8.4

TABLE 8-2

Asset	Curt	Connie
Checking account	$ 35,000	$ 35,000
MMMF	37,500	37,500
CDs	10,000	10,000
Series EE bonds	50,000	-----
Treasury bonds	125,000	-----
Corporate bonds	50,000	50,000
Aggressive growth fund	125,000	-----
International fund	75,000	75,000
Galaxy drug	250,000	250,000
Acme drug	35,000	35,000
Life insurance	822,000	-----
Zenith drug	20,000	20,000
Retirement plan	694,940	-----
Residence	200,000	200,000
Household furnishings	62,500	62,500
Jewelry/furs	-----	50,000
Automobiles	25,000	10,000
Utility fund	-----	150,000
Index fund	-----	200,000
Total	$2,616,821	$1,185,000

Life Insurance Portfolio

Connie has no life insurance but is in excellent health. She now sees how useful the coverage on her husband will be and wants to acquire some insurance on her life, if appropriate in her situation.

Charitable Giving

Curt and Constance both hope to make charitable gifts. Curt wishes to make a generous contribution to his alma mater but is not sure whether the gift should be made prior to his death or afterward. Connie's interest is in assisting organizations that care for abused children, and she would like to make some charitable gifts during her lifetime as well as at the time of her death.

Qualified Plan Guidance

The Kelleys need guidance on how to make best use of the profit-sharing plan assets. When Curt was in good health, they were willing to take investment risk. Since his illness, Connie has become more concerned about the risks of their portfolio.

Final Planning

The Kelleys know that Curt has only a short time to live, and they want to be sure that their financial planning is up-to-date and proper before Curt's death. They know that they have some serious problems and they have retained the services of a financial planner to review their financial affairs on an integrated basis. Curt is primarily concerned with providing for all of his heirs. In addition, Constance wants to be very sure that at Curt's death and at her subsequent death, the proper financial planning will have been undertaken so that the children and grandchildren can receive as much of the family assets as possible per stirpes, free of federal estate tax, state inheritance tax, and other burdens.

WORKING OUTLINE

I. Clients' Objectives

   A. Lifetime objectives
      1. Devise a proper estate plan prior to Curt's death
      2. Reduce federal income tax liability
      3. Maintain comfortable lifestyle for Connie
      4. Make appropriate decisions concerning distribution of husband's qualified plan proceeds
      5. Settle Curt's estate promptly
      6. Make charitable contributions to organizations that care for abused children

   B. Dispositions at death
      1. Minimize estate shrinkage
      2. Provide generously and equitably for Constance's children and grandchildren
      3. Make charitable contributions for maximum benefit to the charitable organization and for maximum federal tax benefit
      4. Minimize the effect of the generation-skipping transfer tax

II. Personal Planning

   A. Tax planning
      1. Unlimited marital deduction and unified credit
         a. IRS Sec. 2056
         b. Unified credit amount of $600,000
         c. Integration of marital deduction with unified credit
      2. Generation-skipping transfer tax (GSTT)
         a. Taxable distributions
         b. Taxable terminations
         c. Direct skips
      3. Charitable giving
         a. Inter vivos charitable gifts
         b. Testamentary charitable gifts
         c. Outright basis
         d. Use of a trust to make charitable gifts
         e. Split-interest arrangements
            - IRC Sec. 170(f)(2)(A)
            - Charitable remainder annuity trust
            - Charitable remainder unitrust
            - Pooled-income fund
      4. Present situation
         a. Curtis is terminally ill
         b. The current estate plan is ill-conceived
         c. Curtis has a simple will
         d. The majority of Curt's assets are jointly titled with Connie
         e. The unified credit is wasted
         f. At Connie's subsequent death, her estate tax liability will be very large
         g. The life insurance
            - Death benefits for life insurance on Curt's life will be taxed as part of his estate
            - Policy proceeds need to be removed from Curt's gross estate

- Possible use of life insurance trust
- Use of trust with sprinkle provision
- GSTT implications
- Charitable gift of insurance policy
- Election to annuitize the policy proceeds
- Lump-sum distribution with proceeds invested
- Accelerated benefits under the life policies
   h. The EE bonds
   - Charitable contribution
   i. The qualified retirement plan
   - Defined contribution
   - QPSA (Qualified Preretirement Survivor Annuity)
   j. The family residence
   - Sale of the residence while both spouses are alive, the property held as joint tenants with right of survivorship
   - Sale of the residence when only one spouse is alive, the property having been held as joint tenants with right of survivorship
   - Other factors influencing the decision to sell
   k. Aggressive Growth Mutual Fund
   l. The Treasury bonds
   m. The securities and bank accounts held as joint tenants with right of survivorship
   5. Connie's income needs
      a. Current cash flow income from the portfolio
      b. Expected growth rate in dividends
      c. To annuitize or to retain the principal?

B. Initial planning for Connie's income flow and adjustments to Curt's estate plan
   1. Connie's final status following Curt's death, having received all jointly owned property only
      a. Portfolio revision

C. Further planning of Connie's finances
   1. Decisions and the reasons for them
      a. Qualified pension plan
      b. Aggressive Growth Mutual Fund
      c. Social security
      d. Curt's car

D. Effects on Connie's finances
   1. Connie's gross income
      a. The pension lump-sum distribution
      b. Curt's car

E. Further planning decisions and reasons
   1. GSTT/credit shelter
      a. Assure optimum use of the federal estate tax marital deduction
      b. Use of bypass trust
      c. Taxable termination under IRC Sec. 2612(a)(2)
      d. Availability of $1 million exemption
   2. Qualifying Terminable Interest Property Trust (QTIP)
   3. The life insurance and life insurance trust

4. The Series EE bonds
5. The Treasury bonds

F. Effect of these changes on Curt's and Connie's estates
1. Curt's estate size
2. Estate tax reduction techniques
   a. Sell some of the Treasury bonds and make a charitable gift
   b. Instruct the trustee to use any estate assets remaining after deducting the amount of all debts, administration costs, state inheritance taxes, marital deduction, and $600,000 (for bypass trust) for the charitable gift
   c. Specify an amount to be given as a charitable gift from the estate
3. Connie's will
4. Connie's financial status
5. Revised estate costs

G. Combined effect of all decisions on Connie's financial situation
1. Income
2. Possible changes in portfolio
3. Connie's expressed interest for life insurance
4. Connie's checking account balance

INSTRUCTIONS TO STUDENTS

Now prepare a financial plan for the Kelleys. When you have prepared your solution, you can compare it to the suggested solution that follows.

Suggested Solution

PERSONAL FINANCIAL PLAN

for

CURTIS AND CONSTANCE KELLEY

CLIENTS' OBJECTIVES

A. Lifetime objectives
   1. Devise a proper estate plan prior to Curt's death
   2. Reduce federal income tax liability
   3. Maintain comfortable lifestyle for Connie
   4. Make appropriate decisions concerning distribution of husband's qualified plan proceeds
   5. Settle Curtis's estate promptly
   6. Make charitable contribution to organizations that care for abused children
B. Dispositions at death
   1. Minimize estate shrinkage
   2. Provide generously and equitably for Connie's children and grandchildren
   3. Make charitable contributions for maximum benefit to the charitable organization and for the maximum federal tax benefit
   4. Minimize the effect of the generation-skipping transfer tax

PERSONAL PLANNING

TAX PLANNING

Unlimited Marital Deduction and Unified Credit

The estate of every married individual may take advantage of the federal estate tax marital deduction. Internal Revenue Code Sec. 2056 provides that as long as an estate owner is married at the date of death and a nonterminable interest in estate property passes from the decedent to the surviving spouse at death, the estate property will pass free of any federal estate tax liability.

In addition, every individual or his or her estate is entitled to take advantage of the unified credit for taxable gifts during lifetime or through bequests at death. If taxable gifts are made during life, the unified credit must be used. (However, gifts between spouses are not considered taxable gifts, and there is no need to use any of the unified credit when making these gifts.) Whatever unified credit is left will be used at death. The unified credit amount is $192,800, which translates into an equivalent amount of $600,000 of estate assets. If the unified credit is not used, it is wasted, as it cannot be carried forward in any manner or transferred to another individual.

For a married client a properly drafted will should integrate the unified credit with the federal estate tax marital deduction. Since a taxable estate of $600,000 triggers no federal estate tax liability, this is the minimum taxable estate that should be created from the client's assets. In general, any overage should pass to the spouse in a manner that qualifies for the marital deduction. However, in certain cases effective estate planning dictates that the taxable estate exceed $600,000.

[text continues on page 8.29]

BASE CASE

CASE ASSUMPTIONS—BASE CASE

1. The checking account balance is maintained at $70,000; the account is non-interest-bearing.

2. Curt's salary is increased at 5 percent annually, assuming that Curt lives and continues to be employed for the next 5 years.

3. The money market deposit account earns 3.1 percent annually.

4. Investable cash is invested and earns 5 percent annually.

5. Expenditures for food, clothing and cleaning, utilities, phone, vacations, and charitable contributions will increase annually at 3 percent.

6. Expenditures for transportation will increase 4 percent annually.

7. Expenditures for entertainment will increase 5 percent annually.

8. Expenditures for medical insurance and other medical expenses will increase at 6 percent annually.

9. Decreases in the value of furniture have been ignored.

10. Automobiles decrease in value at a rate of 15 percent annually.

11. The value of the home will increase at one percent annually.

12. The various securities will increase at rates shown in table 8.3.

13. Income from the securities portfolio equals $44,360 and will grow at rates shown in table 8.3 below.

TABLE 8-3
Expected Growth Rate in Dividends and Market Value for Securities Owned by the Kelleys

Security	Dividend Growth Rate %	Market Price Growth Rate %
Aggressive Growth Fund	5.0	10.2
International Fund	3.0	7.0
Galaxy Pharmaceutical	2.0	9.0
Acme Drug	3.0	6.5
Zenith Drug	1.5	9.0
Utility Fund	3.0	3.0
Index fund	2.5	9.0

1994

INCOME STATEMENT

CURTIS & CONSTANCE KELLEY

BASE CASE	1994	1995	1996	1997	1998
Earned Income					
Salary - Curt	229,000	240,450	252,473	265,096	278,351
	229,000	240,450	252,473	265,096	278,351
Interest/Dividends					
Money Market Fund	2,325	2,325	2,325	2,325	2,325
Corporate Bonds	7,300	7,300	7,300	7,300	7,300
U S Treasury Bonds	9,000	9,000	9,000	9,000	9,000
Galaxy Pharmceutcal	7,500	7,650	7,803	7,959	8,118
Acme Drug Company	1,260	1,298	1,337	1,377	1,418
Zenith Drug Company	800	812	824	837	849
Aggrssve Grwth Fund	1,875	1,969	2,067	2,171	2,279
International Fund	1,800	1,854	1,910	1,967	2,026
Utility Fund	7,500	7,725	7,957	8,195	8,441
Index Fund	5,000	5,150	5,305	5,464	5,628
CDs	1,000	1,050	1,103	1,158	1,216
Overall Investmnt	2,755	8,443	14,535	21,091	28,140
	48,115	54,576	61,465	68,843	76,740
Adj Gross Income	277,115	295,026	313,937	333,939	355,091
Deductions					
Charitable 50%	2,000	2,060	2,122	2,185	2,251
State Tax Paid	7,507	8,009	8,538	9,098	9,691
Home - Property Tax	3,500	3,640	3,786	3,937	4,095
Home Mortgage	7,173	6,695	6,174	5,601	4,976
Reductn For High Inc	-4,938	-5,357	-5,802	-6,276	-6,780
Gross Deductions	15,242	15,047	14,818	14,545	14,233
Standard Deduction	6,400	6,600	6,850	7,100	7,350
Allowed Deductions	15,242	15,047	14,818	14,545	14,233
Pers Exemptions	588	102	0	0	0
Taxable Income	261,285	279,877	299,120	319,394	340,858
Fed Income Tax	79,727	86,255	93,012	100,155	107,732
Fed Tax Bracket	39.6	39.6	39.6	39.6	39.6

8.22

1994

BALANCE SHEET

CURTIS & CONSTANCE KELLEY

BASE CASE	1994	1995	1996	1997	1998
LIQUID ASSETS					
Cash Balance	68,790	68,832	68,903	68,937	68,975
Cash Deposits					
Overall Investmnt	112,945	233,218	362,698	502,019	651,731
CDs	21,000	22,050	23,153	24,311	25,527
Money Market Fund	75,000	75,000	75,000	75,000	75,000
	208,945	330,268	460,851	601,330	752,258
Stocks & Bonds					
U S Treasury Bonds	125,000	125,000	125,000	125,000	125,000
Series EE Bonds	50,000	53,000	56,180	59,551	63,124
Corporate Bonds	100,000	100,000	100,000	100,000	100,000
Galaxy Pharmceutcal	540,000	583,200	629,856	680,245	734,664
Acme Drug Company	74,550	79,396	84,556	90,053	95,906
Zenith Drug Company	43,600	47,524	51,801	56,463	61,545
Aggrssve Grwth Fund	137,750	151,801	167,284	184,347	203,151
International Fund	160,500	171,735	183,756	196,619	210,383
Utility Fund	154,500	159,135	163,909	168,826	173,891
Index Fund	218,000	237,620	259,006	282,316	307,725
	1,603,900	1,708,410	1,821,349	1,943,421	2,075,388
Life Insurance					
UnivLifePrem - Curt	18,000	19,080	20,225	21,438	22,725
WhlLifePrem - Curt	56,400	58,656	61,002	63,442	65,980
	74,400	77,736	81,227	84,881	88,705
Liquid Assets	1,956,036	2,185,246	2,432,331	2,698,568	2,985,326
NONLIQUID ASSETS					
Retirement Plans					
VestedPensionBeneft	694,940	789,489	893,549	1,007,978	1,133,710
	694,940	789,489	893,549	1,007,978	1,133,710
Personal Property					
Home	404,000	408,040	412,120	416,242	420,404
Car - Curt	25,000	21,250	18,063	15,353	13,050
Car - Connie	10,000	8,500	7,225	6,141	5,220
Home Furnishings	125,000	125,000	125,000	125,000	125,000
Jewelry & Furs	50,000	50,000	50,000	50,000	50,000
	614,000	612,790	612,408	612,736	613,675
Nonliquid Assets	1,308,940	1,402,279	1,505,957	1,620,715	1,747,384
Total Assets	3,264,976	3,587,525	3,938,288	4,319,283	4,732,710
LIABILITIES					
Mortgage Loans					
Home Mortgage	76,327	70,802	64,756	58,137	50,893
	76,327	70,802	64,756	58,137	50,893
Total Liabilities	76,327	70,802	64,756	58,137	50,893
Net Worth	3,188,649	3,516,723	3,873,532	4,261,146	4,681,817

8.23

1994   **CASHFLOW STATEMENT**

CURTIS & CONSTANCE KELLEY

BASE CASE	1994	1995	1996	1997	1998
BEGINNING OF YEAR					
Idle Cash On Hand	70,000	68,790	68,832	68,903	68,937
SOURCES OF CASH					
Cash Income					
Salary - Curt	229,000	240,450	252,473	265,096	278,351
Interest+Dividends	44,360	45,083	45,827	46,594	47,384
	273,360	285,533	298,299	311,690	325,735
Total Cash Inflow	273,360	285,533	298,299	311,690	325,735
Tot Cash Available	343,360	354,323	367,131	380,593	394,673
USES OF CASH					
Fully Tax Deductible					
Home Mortgage	7,173	6,695	6,174	5,601	4,976
	7,173	6,695	6,174	5,601	4,976
Partly Deductible					
Medical Ins Premium	500	530	562	596	631
Charity Contrb-50%	2,000	2,060	2,122	2,185	2,251
	2,500	2,590	2,684	2,781	2,882
Not Tax Deductible					
Food	8,000	8,240	8,487	8,742	9,004
Clothing	7,000	7,350	7,718	8,103	8,509
Entertainment	6,000	6,300	6,615	6,946	7,293
Vacations	8,000	8,240	8,487	8,742	9,004
Transportation	1,000	1,040	1,082	1,125	1,170
Home - Ins Premium	700	714	728	743	758
Auto - Ins Premium	1,200	1,248	1,298	1,350	1,404
Jewlry&Furs-InsPrem	1,000	1,020	1,040	1,061	1,082
Disability Ins-Curt	1,500	1,560	1,622	1,687	1,755
UmbrellaPolicy Prem	185	191	196	202	208
UnivLifePrem - Curt	2,200	2,200	2,200	2,200	2,200
WhlLifePrem - Curt	2,100	2,100	2,100	2,100	2,100
Home - Repair/Maint	3,000	3,090	3,183	3,278	3,377
Utility/Phone	4,000	4,120	4,244	4,371	4,502
Other Persnl Expnse	6,000	6,180	6,365	6,556	6,753
	51,885	53,593	55,365	57,206	59,118
Taxes Paid					
Fed Tax Paid	79,727	86,255	93,012	100,155	107,732
State Tax Paid	7,507	8,009	8,538	9,098	9,691
FICA/Soc Sec Tax	7,041	7,355	7,678	8,029	8,388
Home - Property Tax	3,500	3,640	3,786	3,937	4,095
	97,775	105,259	113,014	121,219	129,905

8.24

1994   **CASHFLOW STATEMENT** (cont.)

CURTIS & CONSTANCE KELLEY

BASE CASE	1994	1995	1996	1997	1998
Purchase/Deposits					
Overall Investmnt	110,190	111,830	114,945	118,230	121,572
	110,190	111,830	114,945	118,230	121,572
Liability Liquidation					
Home Mortgage	5,047	5,525	6,046	6,619	7,244
	5,047	5,525	6,046	6,619	7,244
Tot Cash Outflow	274,570	285,491	298,228	311,656	325,698
END OF YEAR					
Cash Balance	68,790	68,832	68,903	68,937	68,975

1994   SUPPORTING SCHEDULE

CURTIS & CONSTANCE KELLEY

	JOINT 1994	JOINT 1995	JOINT 1996	JOINT 1997	JOINT 1998
BASE CASE	----	----	----	----	----
Income					
Earned Income	229,000	240,450	252,473	265,096	278,351
Adj Gross Income	277,115	295,026	313,937	333,939	355,091
Allowed Deductions	15,242	15,047	14,818	14,545	14,233
Pers Exemptions	588	102	0	0	0
Taxable Income	261,285	279,877	299,120	319,394	340,858
Federal Tax Liab					
Regular Tax	79,727	86,255	93,012	100,155	107,732
Gross Fed Inc Tax	79,727	86,255	93,012	100,155	107,732
Fed Income Tax	79,727	86,255	93,012	100,155	107,732
Fed Tax Analysis					
Indexing Factor	51	56	62	68	73
Fed Tax Bracket	39.6	39.6	39.6	39.6	39.6
Previous Bracket	36.0	36.0	36.0	36.0	36.0
$ To Prev Bracket	11,285	21,127	31,270	42,194	53,958
Alt Minimum Tax					
Adj Gross Income	277,115	295,026	313,937	333,939	355,091
Contributions	-2,000	-2,060	-2,122	-2,185	-2,251
Home Mortgage	-7,173	-6,695	-6,174	-5,601	-4,976
Adjusted AMTI	267,942	286,271	305,641	326,153	347,864
AMT Exemptions	-15,514	-10,932	-6,090	-962	0
AMT Taxable Inc	252,428	275,338	299,552	325,191	347,864
Gross Alt Min Tx	67,180	73,595	80,375	87,554	93,902
Fed Tax Less FTC	-79,727	-86,255	-93,012	-100,155	-107,732
Other Tax Liabs					
FICA/Soc Sec Tax	7,041	7,355	7,678	8,029	8,388
PA Taxable Inc	268,115	286,026	304,937	324,939	346,091
PA Regular Tax	7,507	8,009	8,538	9,098	9,691
PA Income Tax	7,507	8,009	8,538	9,098	9,691
Pennsylvania Tax	7,507	8,009	8,538	9,098	9,691
Tot State/Local Tx	7,507	8,009	8,538	9,098	9,691
Total Inc Tax	94,275	101,619	109,228	117,282	125,811

1994   FINANCIAL SUMMARY

CURTIS & CONSTANCE KELLEY

BASE CASE	1994	1995	1996	1997	1998
Gross Real Income					
Personal Earnings	229,000	240,450	252,473	265,096	278,351
Interest Income	22,380	28,118	34,263	40,874	47,981
Dividends Rcvd	25,735	26,458	27,202	27,969	28,759
	277,115	295,026	313,937	333,939	355,091
Income & Inflation					
Gross Real Inc	277,115	295,026	313,937	333,939	355,091
Total Inc Tax	-94,275	-101,619	-109,228	-117,282	-125,811
Net Real Income	182,840	193,407	204,709	216,657	229,281
Cur Real Inc =	182,840	189,240	195,863	202,719	209,814
At Infltn Rate Of	4	4	4	4	4
Cash Flow					
Idle Cash On Hand	70,000	68,790	68,832	68,903	68,937
Norml Cash Inflow	273,360	285,533	298,299	311,690	325,735
Norml Cash Outflw	164,380	173,661	183,283	193,426	204,126
Cash Invested	110,190	111,830	114,945	118,230	121,572
Cash Balance	68,790	68,832	68,903	68,937	68,975
Net Worth					
Personal Assets	757,191	759,358	762,539	766,554	771,354
Investment Assets	2,507,785	2,828,167	3,175,749	3,552,729	3,961,356
Personal Liabilities	-76,327	-70,802	-64,756	-58,137	-50,893
Personal Net Worth	680,864	688,556	697,783	708,417	720,461
Investment Net Worth	2,507,785	2,828,167	3,175,749	3,552,729	3,961,356
Net Worth	3,188,649	3,516,723	3,873,532	4,261,146	4,681,817

If estate property is jointly titled between husband and wife, the ultimate disposition of such property will be unaffected by will provisions, as this property will pass from the decedent to the surviving spouse by operation of law. This property would qualify for the marital deduction.

If an estate owner's will is improperly drafted or does not effectively operate to pass estate property from a decedent to the surviving spouse, the unfortunate result may be that too many assets qualify for the federal estate tax marital deduction, leaving insufficient assets in the estate to make use of the unified credit. For example, if all of an estate owner's property is titled jointly with his or her spouse, it will pass by operation of law at the estate owner's death. Nothing will remain to make use of the $600,000 exclusion, and the will provisions will be ineffective. Even if the will had been structured to integrate the unified credit amount ($600,000 exclusion) with the federal estate tax marital deduction, it would be inoperative and the unified credit would be wasted.

Generation-Skipping Transfer Tax (GSTT)

Not long ago that a comprehensive consideration of federal transfer tax implications included only the federal estate tax and the federal gift tax. However, under the current Internal Revenue Code, there is a third transfer tax to consider—the generation-skipping transfer tax. This tax may be assessed against each of the three different generation-skipping distributions.

One such taxable distribution is any distribution of either income or principal from a trust to a person two or more generations below the transferor's generation who is not otherwise subject to an estate or gift tax. Individuals who receive property as part of such an arrangement are referred to as skip beneficiaries.

The second form of distribution is taxable termination that occurs if there is a termination of an existing arrangement by reason of death, lapse of time, or release of a power, or if the property interest held in trust passes to a skip beneficiary. Internal Revenue Code Sec. 2612(a)(2) provides that upon the termination of an interest in property that is held by a trust, if a specific portion of the trust assets is distributed to skip beneficiaries who are lineal descendants of the holder of such interest, this termination is considered a taxable termination with respect to that portion of the trust property.

The final type of distribution that is subject to the imposition of the generation-skipping transfer tax is the direct skip. In effect, outright transfers of property that skip a generation trigger the application of the generation-skipping transfer tax. It should be noted that direct skips may take place either during lifetime or at death by virtue of law or will.

Regardless of whether assets are transferred to grandchildren outright or through trust arrangements, the GSTT would be imposed on all such transfers but for the exemption written into the Internal Revenue Code. Specifically, the law provides that every individual or the individual's estate is permitted to make aggregate transfers of up to $1 million, either during lifetime or at death, that will be wholly exempt from imposition of the generation-skipping transfer tax. It should also be noted that under current law, the $10,000 ($20,000 for gifts from married couple) annual exclusion of IRC Sec. 2503(b) does not apply to the generation-skipping transfer tax.

Charitable Giving

Donors may make charitable contributions in several ways. Gifts may be made during the donor's lifetime of the donor's (inter vivos charitable gifts), or they may be made after the donor's death (testamentary charitable gifts). Gifts may be made outright or through a trust. If a donor uses a trust, the charitable beneficiary may receive some benefit at once, or there may be a split-interest arrangement, with both a charitable and a noncharitable beneficiary.

When assets are transferred to a trust with a qualifying charitable organization named as the sole and immediate beneficiary, it makes sense that a federal income tax deduction is triggered. Sometimes the donor wants both charitable and noncharitable beneficiaries to enjoy the property. If a charity receives a portion of estate property directly, either as a gift or as an immediate beneficiary of a trust, the federal estate tax deduction is equal to the fair market value of the property on the date of death (or on the alternate valuation date). But if there are noncharitable beneficiaries before the property passes to the charitable organization, how is the tax deduction computed?

Split-Interest Arrangements

Such cases are referred to as *split-interest arrangements*. The Code [Sec. 170(f)(2)(A)] provides that gifts of a remainder interest in trust are deductible for tax purposes only if the trust is a charitable remainder annuity trust, a charitable remainder unitrust, or a pooled-income fund. Treasury Department tables are to be consulted to ascertain the actual amount of the deduction available. Such tables, derived from actuarial data, use the life expectancy of the noncharitable beneficiaries. The value of the gift in this type of arrangement is its fair market value on the date of the transfer. This, in essence, is the basis of the gift. No other value is used.

The various split-interest vehicles are (1) the charitable remainder annuity trust, (2) the charitable remainder unitrust, and (3) the pooled-income fund.

A **charitable remainder annuity trust** provides either the taxpayer (if still living) or the other noncharitable trust beneficiaries with a lifetime income interest in the property transferred to the trust, with the charitable organization receiving the remainder interest. Since an estate could effectuate this arrangement, for example, with a university, on a testamentary basis, the estate would receive a federal estate tax charitable deduction based on the life expectancy of the noncharitable beneficiaries. The amount of the federal estate tax charitable deduction is limited to the actuarial value of the remainder interest deemed passing to the university. The family members receive the right to the income from the property for the rest of their lives (or for a term of specified years), and at their deaths (or upon the expiration of the term), the remainder interest will pass to the university. The charitable remainder annuity trust must provide for an annual payout of a "sum certain" that is not less than 5 percent of the initial net fair market value of the trust property. This amount may be expressed as a specified dollar amount or as a percentage or fraction of the initial fair market value of the trust assets. The amount of each payment is fixed initially; thus the annual payouts are the same.

A **charitable remainder unitrust** must provide for a payout each year of a fixed percentage of at least 5 percent of the annually determined net fair market value of its assets. Therefore, the amount of the annual payment will be different each year depending on the value of the trust principal.

A **pooled-income fund** is operated directly by the charitable organization and is made up of assets donated by multiple contributors and commingled into one fund. A donor retains the right either to receive a share of the fund's income for life or to select one or more individuals living at the time the contribution is made to receive the income.

Present Situation

All estate owners should be certain that their estate planning is current and tailored to their individual needs, especially when death may be imminent. Unfortunately, Curt is terminally ill, and to make matters even worse (if that is possible under the circumstances), the estate plan as currently constituted is ill-conceived and essentially nonresponsive to the family's needs.

As shown in table 8-2 (p. 8.5) Curt's gross estate would be $2,616,821 should he die today. Because his current will is a "simple will," all of his assets will pass to Constance at his death. As a practical matter, many of Curt's assets are jointly titled with his wife, and upon his death these assets will pass automatically to her by operation of law. In conjunction with the beneficiary status for the life insurance policies and the simple will approach for the remainder of the assets, the entire estate passes to Connie outright and results in an overqualification of the federal estate tax marital deduction.

	At Curt's Death	Computations	Actual Expenses Incurred
Gross estate		$2,616,821	
Less: Debts[1]		(76,327)	76,327
Less: Costs of administration[2]		(196,262)	196,262
Adjusted gross estate		$2,344,232	
Federal estate tax marital deduction[3]		2,344,232	
Taxable estate		-0-	
Federal estate tax owed		-0-	
Less unified credit[4]		N/A	-0-
State inheritance tax		44,841	$ 44,841
Total costs at first death			$317,430
At Connie's Subsequent Death			
Gross estate[5]		$3,529,232	
Less: Debts		-0-	-0-
Less: Costs of administration[2]		(264,692)	264,692
Adjusted gross estate		$3,264,540	
Federal estate tax marital deduction[6]		-0-	
Taxable estate		3,264,540	
Federal estate tax		1,436,297	
Less unified credit		192,800	
Federal estate tax owed		$1,243,497	1,243,497
State inheritance tax			195,872
Total costs at second death			$1,704,061
Total combined costs at both death			$2,021,491

Notes

[1] Curt's estate will pay off the mortgage on the residence.

[2] Assumed to be 7.5 percent of gross estate

[3] Pursuant to current simple wills, entire estate passes from Curt to Constance

[4] There is no federal estate tax liability because of the application of the unlimited federal estate tax marital deduction; thus the unified credit is wasted.

[5] This figure represents $2,344,232 passing from Curt's estate to Connie *plus* $1,185,000, which is the sum of Connie's share of the jointly titled property

and her separate property. This assumes no change in the value of her estate.

[6]There is no federal estate tax marital deduction available, as Connie is assumed to be unmarried at date of her death.

Connie's Estate Tax Liability

As the wills and property ownership are set up, there is no federal estate tax liability at the time of Curt's death, since all his property ownership interests pass to his surviving spouse in a manner that qualifies for the marital deduction. This results in an additional $2,344,232 of assets being owned by Connie and, when added to her assets, creates an estate in the amount of $3,529,232. At her death the estate will not have the benefit of the marital deduction, and a portion of the estate assets will be subject to the 55 percent tax rate. Even if her will makes use of the unified credit, the result is a very sizable shrinkage of the estate. Effective estate planning while Curtis is alive will reduce some of this shrinkage and also enable the Kelleys to achieve some of their goals.

At this point there should be an examination of the problems and of how Curt's assets, both separate and joint, can be most effectively used for the family's benefit. However, before reaching any decision concerning the use or disposition of these assets, the amounts and sources of income that Connie will require after Curt's death must be determined. Then plans and provisions maximizing the benefits from Curt's estate must be developed so that Connie's income needs are met.

The Life Insurance

The largest single amount that will pass to Connie from Curt is the $822,000 of death benefits from his life insurance. The Kelleys should explore the possibility of removing these policy proceeds from Curt's gross estate. Under current law if a life insurance policy is gifted, the policy proceeds will be included in the donor's estate if the gift was made within 3 years of death. Since Curtis is expected to live for but a short time, the opportunity to transfer ownership of any of the policies and thereby remove the proceeds from his estate does not really exist. In other circumstances a trust could be established and policies given to the trust. If the donor survives at least 3 years after the date of transfer, the proceeds are removed from the estate. Most likely little chance exists that this course of action would succeed in Curt's case because of his medical prognosis.

Use of Trust with Sprinkle Provision. Even if the proceeds of these policies that are in a trust are included in his estate, Curt could specify Connie and the grandchildren as the trust's income beneficiaries. The trustee could be granted a "sprinkle provision" that would permit the use of the trustee's discretion as to what percentage of trust income each beneficiary would receive each year. The trust instrument could also grant the trustee the power to accumulate income, a valuable planning technique if integrated with the grandchildren's parents' tax status. Curt might desire to have the income accumulated until each child attains majority. The grandchildren would be the corpus beneficiaries of the trust when Connie dies or when the youngest grandchild-beneficiary of the trust attains majority, whichever occurs last. Using the trust in this manner enables Curt to provide for both Connie and the grandchildren.

Generation-Skipping Transfer Tax Implications. Such a trust falls under the provisions of the generation-skipping transfer tax (GSTT) rules as a taxable termination. Curt has not used any of his $1 million exemption. At the time the trust is distributed, any amount of trust assets in excess of $1 million distributed to Curt's grandchildren would be subject to the generation-skipping tax. For any life insurance proceeds (or policies) placed in such a trust, the amount does not qualify for the marital deduction, since Connie does not have the power to appoint the trust corpus to herself or her estate. However, Curt's $600,000 estate tax exemption would offset most of the proceeds, and if this is the only portion of his estate subject to the unified estate and gift taxes, the tax paid by his estate would be at a lower rate than if the proceeds were taxed in Connie's estate at a later date.

Charitable Gift of the Insurance Policy. Since Curt is interested in making charitable gifts, one or more of the policy ownership interests could be gifted to a qualified charity while Curt is still alive. If the whole life policy were given, the amount gifted for income tax purposes is the amount of the terminal reserve. Should Curt die before the end of 3 years, the policy proceeds would be brought back and included in his estate. However, the proceeds would then be a charitable deduction for the estate; thus the Kelleys would receive both an income tax deduction and an estate tax deduction for the gift of an insurance policy. Whether one or more of the policies can be used in this manner depends on Connie's income needs and the Kelleys' other objectives.

Election to Annuitize Proceeds. Taking a different approach, since Connie is the named beneficiary of these policies, she could elect to annuitize the entire proceeds. The following table is an example of the cost to purchase $10 of monthly income with different annuity options and the resulting total annual income that Connie would receive if she took this course of action after Curt's death.

TABLE 8-4 Annual Income from Different Life Insurance Annuity Options from Insurance Proceeds of $822,500 for a Female Aged 60		
Annuity Option	Cost per $10 Monthly Income	Annual Income
Pure life annuity	$1,344	$73,437
10-year certain	$1,373	$71,886
Full refund	$1,402	$70,399

Lump-Sum Distribution with Proceeds Invested. Connie could take the lump sum and invest the proceeds in long-term government or corporate bonds with staggered maturities and earn an average return of 7.5 percent. This action would provide her with an annual income, without annuitizing the proceeds, of $61,687.

Accelerated Benefits. Another life insurance alternative especially relevant for the Kelleys (because of Curt's terminal illness) concerns accelerated benefits. Many policies and policy riders available in today's market offer payment of the death benefit or a large percentage of that benefit when the insured is diagnosed with a terminal illness. This payment is made in lieu of the actual death benefit. The definitions and requirements for collecting the benefit differ significantly among policies. Many insurers now offer riders to existing policies, although proof of insurability is required. Federal tax regulations do not address the taxation of accelerated benefits. However, the Treasury Department has proposed that accelerated benefits received within 12 months of the insured's death be treated the same as normal death benefits.

An option available to the terminally ill whose life insurance policies do not offer accelerated benefits is a *viatical settlement.* This relatively new concept involves a third party—the viatical settlement company—which pays a reduced accelerated benefit either to buy the policy or to become the beneficiary of the policy. The amount of reduction in the benefit depends on the viatical settlement company's required rate of return and its perception of the insured's life expectancy. Viatical settlement is so new to the market that there are few providers and no standardization. Only a handful of states have promulgated regulations regarding viatical settlements. Also, proceeds in excess of the policy basis are currently subject to income taxation, although legislation to eliminate the tax is pending.

For the Kelleys, even if the policies had accelerated benefits features, there would be no compelling reason to exercise them since there is no immediate need for cash and since Curt's life expectancy is so short. Likewise, viatical settlement is unnecessary.

The Series EE Bonds

This separate property of Curt's provides a unique planning opportunity for the Kelleys. Since Curt deferred any recognition of interest on these bonds, at his death, when the bonds are redeemed, this deferred interest must be included for income tax purposes. In addition, their total accumulated value will flow into his estate. If Curt were to specify that these bonds were to be a charitable contribution from his estate, or if he should make a lifetime gift of them to a qualified charity, the accumulated interest would not be part of either his estate or the Kelleys' income for income tax purposes. The same income and estate tax deductions explained for the lifetime gift of a life insurance policy would apply to a similar gift of the EE bonds.

Since Curt owns the Series EE bonds as separate property, another course available is to convert them to Series HH bonds, from which the owner receives semiannual interest. The tax-deferred, accumulated interest on the EE bonds would be rolled into the face amount of the HH bonds, with no income tax due on this deferred EE bond interest until the HH bonds are redeemed. That interest will reflect the total amount converted, that is, the original cost of the EE bonds plus the accumulated interest. If these EE bonds are converted into HH bonds as Curt's separate property, the bonds would be redeemed after his death and the EE bonds' deferred interest would then be taxable. However, Curt could have the HH bonds issued to them as joint tenants with right of survivor, thereby making a gift to Connie, and at his death Connie could have the bonds titled in her name, as survivor, and the deferred interest would not have to be recognized as taxable income at that time.

The Qualified Retirement Plan

Curt participates in a defined-contribution retirement plan that permits participants to make lump-sum withdrawals at retirement. The plan also permits these withdrawals if the participant elects early retirement. Curtis, being on disability, can elect to take early retirement and receive a lump-sum distribution.

If no change in Curt's status is made and he should die while on long-term disability, then the Qualified Preretirement Survivor Annuity (QPSA) provisions would come into play; that is, Connie would receive the survivor's portion of a joint and 50 percent survivor annuity. A check with Galaxy determined that Connie's QPSA benefit would be $33,001, since the joint and 50 percent survivor benefit would have been $66,002. A better course of action would be for Curt to retire immediately and elect a joint and 100 percent survivor annuity, which under Galaxy's plan would produce a total annual benefit of $58,377 for as long as both or either of the Kelleys lived.

A lump-sum distribution from the plan of Curt's benefit of $694,940 is also a possibility. Curt would qualify for the 10-year averaging instead of being eligible for only 5-year averaging since his birth date predates January 1, 1936. But, because of the use of the pre-1986 tax rates and the amount that Curt has in the plan, 10-year averaging would result in an income tax of $232,939 on the distribution under the 1994 tax rates. Under 5-year averaging and 1994 tax rates, the total income tax would be $198,375, or a saving of $34,564. (Author's note: To have the 5-year averaging result in a reduction in the amount of this tax, the plan distribution must exceed $387,968. For any lesser amount, a retiree who qualifies would have a lower tax by using 10-year averaging.) The 15 percent excise tax that applies to certain periodic and lump-sum distributions would not be assessed in this situation. Under 1994 tax law, the tax is assessed on annual distributions that exceed $150,000 and on lump-sum distributions that are five times that amount, or $750,000 ($150,000 x 5), which exceeds Curt's benefit.

In addition to the lump-sum distribution made directly to Curt, another option is a trustee-to-trustee lump-sum distribution to an IRA that Curt creates for this purpose, naming himself and Connie as the IRA's beneficiaries. By making the trustee-to-trustee distribution, the 20 percent income tax withholding is avoided. As long as Curt has not started taking periodic withdrawals from the IRA, mandatory withdrawals can be based on her age rather than his. Connie need not begin withdrawing from this IRA for more than a decade.

The Family Residence

At some point, the family residence will probably be sold, either while Curt or Connie or both are alive or by the estate of the last to die. The tax consequences of such a sale are somewhat different in each of these situations.

Sale of the Residence While Both Spouses Are Alive, the Property Held as Joint Tenants with Right of Survivorship. An individual taxpayer who is at least 55 years of age can take the one-time $125,000 exclusion from income taxation on the capital gain realized from the sale of his or her primary residence. This exclusion also applies to married taxpayers; however, a couple has only a single $125,000 exclusion, not a $125,000 exclusion for each. Based on the facts in this case, the Kelleys have a basis of $150,000 in the home that they jointly own. Should they decide to sell the home while Curtis is alive and realize the estimated value of $400,000 net of selling expenses, they will have a taxable gain of $125,000 [$400,000 − ($150,000 basis + $125,000 lifetime exclusion)]. With a maximum capital gain tax of 28 percent, the Kelleys would pay an income tax of $35,000 on the realized gain.

Sale of the Residence When Only One Spouse Is Alive, the Property Having Been Held as Joint Tenants with Right of Survivorship. When property is held as joint tenants with right of survivorship, each spouse is assumed to own one-half of the property and to have contributed one-half of its basis. At the death of the first spouse, the surviving spouse obtains ownership of the jointly held property unless a qualified disclaimer is made. However, the ownership interest of the deceased spouse receives a step-up in basis for which no income tax is levied on the capital gain. Should Curt Kelley die before their primary residence is sold, Connie will obtain full ownership of Curt's interest. Curt's interest had a basis of $75,000 ($150,000 ÷ 2), but his estate's basis would be $200,000 ($400,000 ÷ 2). By operation of law (the property having been held as joint tenants with right of survivorship) the property will become Connie's, and she will pick up Curt's basis of $200,000 to add to hers ($75,000) for a total basis of $275,000. As Curt's spouse, Connie can receive his $200,000 stepped-up basis free of any estate taxation (through the unlimited marital deduction for property passing between spouses). If Connie then sells the property for a net realized price of $400,000, she has a $125,000 [$400,000 − ($75,000 + $200,000)] realized capital gain. Since Connie has not used the one-time exclusion, she can exclude the full amount of the gain, and no capital gain tax would be paid on the residence's appreciation in value.

From a financial and tax view, it seems that any sale of the Kelleys' jointly held residence should not occur prior to Curt's death.

Other Factors Influencing the Decision to Sell. Widowed clients often are reluctant to sell the family home and move to a new and different physical environment. Indeed, this action is stressful under the best of circumstances.

When moving to a new house or location occurs along with the upcoming or recent death of a spouse (which is, according to psychologists, a person's most stressful event), the cumulative effect of the stress can affect the survivor's ability to cope. Consequently many advisers recommend that a surviving spouse not make a hasty decision to sell the family residence immediately but rather to wait, perhaps a year or more if personal factors and finances permit, before offering the property for sale. On the other hand, some widowed individuals are anxious to leave the residence to hasten their transition to a new phase of life.

Additional personal factors influence this decision, including the desire to remain in the family residence to provide a base for other family members to consider home, preference, enjoyment, the ability or financial wherewithal to manage the necessary upkeep and maintenance needs of the property, and—on the other hand—a fear of making an incorrect choice of new residence, particularly without the benefit of the spouse's input in the decision. In situations such as the Kelleys', the planner must be aware that factors other than solely financial ones are highly important to the client and may well be the deciding factor(s) in whether to sell or keep the property.

One further matter about the residence concerns property on which there is a debt and that is held as joint tenants with right of survivorship. In this situation, the full amount of the unpaid mortgage can be taken as a debt of the first to die, namely Curt. This was the procedure followed in determining the amount of Curt's estate as shown on p. 8.32. Connie thus can inherit the residence free of any mortgage payments, which affects the amount of annual income she will need during widowhood. However, she will not have any income tax deduction for any interest that would have been paid during those years.

After giving due consideration to both tax and other factors involved in a sale, it appears that the sale of the Kelleys' residence is not an appropriate course of action at this point.

Aggressive Growth Mutual Fund

The total return earned on this mutual fund has been more than satisfactory during the time it has been held in the Kelleys' portfolio. However, most of the return has been in the form of appreciation in the value of the fund shares not in the form of current dividends. While Curt is employed, his salary provides them with a very comfortable standard of living and the current return (dividends) is of little importance. When this separate asset of Curt's passes to either his estate or Connie, then it might be a candidate for sale and the proceeds used to acquire securities (stocks or bonds) that will produce a higher annual stream of income to augment Connie's income.

The Treasury Bonds

Other than his automobile, Curt's remaining separate property is the Treasury bonds. These will receive a step-up in basis upon his death, and under the terms of his current will they pass to Connie in a qualifying manner. They are liquid and could be used to pay some of the expenses, debts, and state inheritance taxes of the estate.

Earlier a discussion of using the Series EE bonds for a charitable contribution described the income and estate tax consequences of lifetime gifts. These Treasury bonds could also be used for charitable contributions.

The Securities and Bank Accounts Held as Joint Tenants with Right of Survivorship

Curt's share of these assets will pass to Connie by virtue of the form of ownership. Some consideration could be given to changing the ownership to separate property for some of these assets so that there would be sufficient liquidity should a decision be made to fund a trust with the life insurance proceeds. Separate property could also be used either to make charitable contributions (with tax considerations as described for life insurance, EE bonds, or Treasury bonds) or to provide for the grandchildren.

Connie's Income Needs

Now that some of the alternative ways Curt's property can be used to provide for Connie have been examined, the next phase of the planning for the Kelleys is to determine the amount of income she will need after Curt's death. Then choices must be made as to how best to achieve this and other goals.

The Kelleys' current income from their portfolio is shown in table 8.5. This excludes the deferred interest on the Series EE bonds. Adding Curt's salary of $229,000 to their $45,360 of portfolio income, they have a total income of $274,360.

TABLE 8-5 Curt and Connie's Portfolio Income				
	Ownership		
Income Source	Jointly Titled	Curt	Connie
Money market fund	$2,325		
CDs	1,000		
EE bonds		No current	
Treasury bonds		$9,000	
Corporate bonds	7,300		
Aggressive Growth Fund		1,875	
International Fund	1,800		
Galaxy Pharmaceuticals	7,500		
Acme Drug	1,260		
Zenith Drug	800		
Utility Fund			$ 7,500
Index fund			5,000
Income Totals	$21,985	$10,875	$12,500

Unfortunately no precise formula exists for ascertaining the exact amount of income Connie should have or would need to maintain the same lifestyle as a widow as she currently enjoys. However, the Kelleys' assets can provide ample income for her needs, both currently and for the rest of her life. The question is how best to use the assets. Examination of some of the Kelleys' personal finance and income tax records, discussions with the Kelleys, and consideration of Connie's expected lifestyle point to a targeted annual income of $105,000, in current dollars, as sufficient for providing Connie with a lifestyle such as she has been recently enjoying with Curt. This income should also permit Connie to purchase any major assets such as a car when needed and to give meaningful sums on an annual basis to either charities, children, or grandchildren as she desires.

Estimates were made of her itemized deductions (charitable contributions, property and state income taxes, etc.) and expected federal income taxes. With about $7,000 of itemized deductions, income taxes would be about $28,000, leaving Connie with an income in excess of $85,000 after state and federal taxes. Since the mortgage on the home can be treated as a debt of Curt's and can be deducted from his gross estate, Connie's income will be free of any mortgage payments, which on their 15-year, 9 percent $100,000 mortgage are nearly $12,200 a year.

In addition, the deployment of the assets that will provide this level of income now must be such that the income will rise to offset the effects of long-term inflation without regularly liquidating securities to make up shortfalls.

With particular emphasis on maximizing the use of Curt's assets to provide Connie with this income as well as providing for the other objectives, several alternative courses of action exist. Most plans begin with a base income of $35,164 for 1995 of dividends and interest from securities she owns in her own name and the full value of those owned jointly with Curt. The dividend income from some of these stocks is rather low. This income flow could be increased by repositioning some of these investments, either now or at some time in the future.

The two major assets in Curt's estate, the life insurance proceeds and the qualified retirement plan distribution, can provide more than the additional income needed by Connie—$69,836 ($105,000 − $35,164)—either as an annuity or, if lump-sum distributions are taken, from the investment income. Annuitizing either the life insurance proceeds or the lump-sum distribution from the pension plan will achieve the target.

A major decision that clients such as the Kelleys face, as a retired couple or as a surviving spouse, is whether to annuitize the principal over an expected lifetime or to retain the principal and use the return earned on the principal as the source of their income. Choosing between these two alternatives is not easy, particularly since the annuity decision tends to be final whereas taking the lump sum keeps open the option to acquire an annuity later. Of course, the lump-sum approach results in the individual, rather than the insurance company, bearing the investment risk.

Furthermore, the desire to distribute accumulated assets to children and grandchildren and to make capital contributions to charities, and the awareness that if income needs exceed the annual flow, some of the assets could be liquidated may make clients who have a large amount of accumulated assets reluctant to use up the assets despite the fact that the life annuity provides an income that cannot be outlived. The Kelleys, and particularly Connie, know that annuitizing the life insurance proceeds, even with a full refund option, would provide her with sufficient additional income to meet her current target of $105,000. Their decision is to not include the annuitization of the insurance proceeds in their plans designed to provide income for Connie. The proceeds could, if invested at 8 percent, produce annual income in excess of $64,000 so that her income would approach the target amount.

Since Curt is permitted to take both early retirement and a lump-sum distribution under the terms of Galaxy's pension plan, a rollover, trustee-to-trustee IRA could be established for Curt with Connie as the beneficiary. This would allow Connie to receive more than the QPSA benefit from Galaxy's plan. When Curt dies, Connie could commence distributions from the IRA that probably would be sufficient to enable her to receive the annual targeted income. This, however, would be an annuitization and does not mesh with their preferences. Alternatively, Curt could take a lump-sum distribution, pay the appropriate income tax with 5-year averaging, and then use the proceeds, if invested at 8 percent, to produce about $40,000 additional income each year without eating into the principal sum.

However, both courses of action require early retirement and, obviously, a cessation of income to the Kelleys from Galaxy's disability plan. If the medical prognosis proves to be correct, the Kelleys could use some of their existing assets as income sources until Curt dies. For the relatively short period, this would not use up very much of their assets. Should Curt retire, the Kelleys would be covered by Galaxy's fully paid health plan for retirees, which has the same benefits as for Galaxy's employees until a retiree or the spouse is eligible for medicare. As each becomes eligible for medicare, the retiree or spouse would be part of the medicare supplemental health insurance plan provided by Galaxy.

Social security benefits can be an additional source of income, both to the Kelleys at this time and for Connie after Curt's death. Curt's income has exceeded the social security base for a sufficient number of years so that his PIA at age 65 will be the maximum benefit of $1,184, or about $14,000 yearly. If Connie were to take the widow's benefit at age 60, the $14,000 benefit would be reduced to about 71 percent, making the annual benefit a little less than $10,000.

Based on the above analysis and preferences of the Kelleys, a course of action must be developed that will do the following:

- provide Connie with the desired income without liquidating any principal
- use some of Curt's estate to provide for grandchildren
- make a sizable charitable contribution

[text continues on page 8.51]

CASE II
Connie's Portfolio Income Beginning in 1995

CASE ASSUMPTIONS—CASE II

New Assumptions

1. Curt dies on December 31, 1994.

2. All jointly owned property passes to Connie.

3. Income from portfolio owned by Connie will grow at rates shown in table 8.3.

Continuing Assumptions

1. The checking account balance is maintained at $70,000; the account is non-interest-bearing.

2. The money market deposit account earns 3.1 percent annually.

3. Investable cash is invested and earns 5 percent annually.

4. Expenditures for food, clothing and cleaning, utilities, phone, vacations, and charitable contributions will increase annually at 3 percent.

5. Expenditures for transportation will increase 4 percent annually.

6. Expenditures for entertainment will increase 5 percent annually.

7. Expenditures for medical insurance and other medical expenses will increase at 6 percent annually.

8. Decreases in the value of furniture have been ignored.

9. Automobiles decrease in value at a rate of 15 percent annually.

10. The value of the home will increase at 1 percent annually.

Deleted Assumptions

1. Income from the portfolio equals $44,360 and will grow at rates shown in table 8.3.

2. Curt's salary is increased at 5 percent annually.

1995

INCOME STATEMENT

CONSTANCE KELLEY

CASE 2

	1995	1996	1997	1998	1999
Interest/Dividends					
Money Market Fund	2,325	2,325	2,325	2,325	2,325
Corporate Bonds	7,300	7,300	7,300	7,300	7,300
Galaxy Pharmceutcal	7,650	7,803	7,959	8,118	8,281
Acme Drug Company	1,298	1,337	1,377	1,418	1,461
Zenith Drug Company	812	824	837	849	862
International Fund	1,854	1,910	1,967	2,026	2,087
Utility Fund	7,725	7,957	8,195	8,441	8,695
Index Fund	5,150	5,305	5,464	5,628	5,796
CDs	1,050	1,103	1,158	1,216	1,276
	35,164	35,863	36,582	37,321	38,082
Adj Gross Income	35,164	35,863	36,582	37,321	38,082
Deductions					
Charitable 50%	2,060	2,122	2,185	2,251	2,319
State Tax Paid	985	1,004	1,024	1,045	1,066
Home - Property Tax	3,640	3,786	3,937	4,095	4,258
Gross Deductions	6,685	6,912	7,146	7,391	7,643
Standard Deduction	3,700	3,850	3,950	4,100	4,250
Allowed Deductions	6,685	6,912	7,146	7,391	7,643
Pers Exemptions	2,350	2,450	2,550	2,600	2,700
Taxable Income	26,129	26,501	26,886	27,331	27,739
Fed Income Tax	4,442	4,443	4,437	4,452	4,454
Fed Tax Bracket	28.0	28.0	28.0	28.0	28.0

1995   **BALANCE SHEET**

CONSTANCE KELLEY

CASE 2	1995	1996	1997	1998	1999
LIQUID ASSETS					
Cash Balance	56,034	41,137	25,272	8,370	-9,600
Cash Deposits					
CDs	22,050	23,153	24,311	25,527	26,803
Money Market Fund	75,000	75,000	75,000	75,000	75,000
	97,050	98,153	99,311	100,527	101,803
Stocks & Bonds					
Corporate Bonds	100,000	100,000	100,000	100,000	100,000
Galaxy Pharmceutcal	583,200	629,856	680,245	734,664	793,437
Acme Drug Company	79,396	84,556	90,053	95,906	102,140
Zenith Drug Company	47,524	51,801	56,463	61,545	67,084
International Fund	171,735	183,756	196,619	210,383	225,110
Utility Fund	159,135	163,909	168,826	173,891	179,108
Index Fund	237,620	259,006	282,316	307,725	335,420
	1,378,610	1,472,885	1,574,522	1,684,114	1,802,299
Liquid Assets	1,531,694	1,612,175	1,699,105	1,793,011	1,894,501
NONLIQUID ASSETS					
Personal Property					
Home	408,040	412,120	416,242	420,404	424,608
Car - Connie	8,500	7,225	6,141	5,220	4,437
Home Furnishings	125,000	125,000	125,000	125,000	125,000
Jewelry & Furs	50,000	50,000	50,000	50,000	50,000
	591,540	594,345	597,383	600,624	604,045
Nonliquid Assets	591,540	594,345	597,383	600,624	604,045
Total Assets	2,123,234	2,206,520	2,296,488	2,393,635	2,498,546
Net Worth	2,123,234	2,206,520	2,296,488	2,393,635	2,498,546

8.47

1995   C A S H F L O W   S T A T E M E N T

CONSTANCE KELLEY

CASE 2	1995	1996	1997	1998	1999
BEGINNING OF YEAR					
Idle Cash On Hand	70,000	56,034	41,137	25,272	8,370
SOURCES OF CASH					
Cash Income					
Interest+Dividends	34,114	34,760	35,424	36,105	36,806
	34,114	34,760	35,424	36,105	36,806
Total Cash Inflow	34,114	34,760	35,424	36,105	36,806
Tot Cash Available	104,114	90,794	76,561	61,377	45,176
USES OF CASH					
Partly Deductible					
Medical Ins Premium	530	562	596	631	669
Charity Contrb-50%	2,060	2,122	2,185	2,251	2,319
	2,590	2,684	2,781	2,882	2,988
Not Tax Deductible					
Food	5,000	5,150	5,305	5,464	5,628
Clothing	5,000	5,250	5,513	5,788	6,078
Entertainment	6,000	6,300	6,615	6,946	7,293
Vacations	5,000	5,150	5,305	5,464	5,628
Transportation	1,040	1,082	1,125	1,170	1,217
Home - Ins Premium	714	728	743	758	773
Auto - Ins Premium	1,248	1,298	1,350	1,404	1,460
Jewlry&Furs-InsPrem	1,020	1,040	1,061	1,082	1,104
UmbrellaPolicy Prem	191	197	203	209	215
Home - Repair/Maint	3,090	3,183	3,278	3,377	3,478
Utility/Phone	4,120	4,244	4,371	4,502	4,637
Other Persnl Expnse	4,000	4,120	4,244	4,371	4,502
	36,423	37,741	39,111	40,533	42,011
Taxes Paid					
Fed Tax Paid	4,442	4,443	4,437	4,452	4,454
State Tax Paid	985	1,004	1,024	1,045	1,066
Home - Property Tax	3,640	3,786	3,937	4,095	4,258
	9,067	9,232	9,398	9,592	9,778
Tot Cash Outflow	48,080	49,657	51,289	53,007	54,777
END OF YEAR					
Cash Balance	56,034	41,137	25,272	8,370	-9,600

1995   **SUPPORTING SCHEDULE**

CONSTANCE KELLEY
	SINGLE	SINGLE	SINGLE	SINGLE	SINGLE
CASE 2	1995	1996	1997	1998	1999
Income					
Adj Gross Income	35,164	35,863	36,582	37,321	38,082
Allowed Deductions	6,685	6,912	7,146	7,391	7,643
Pers Exemptions	2,350	2,450	2,550	2,600	2,700
Taxable Income	26,129	26,501	26,886	27,331	27,739
Federal Tax Liab					
Regular Tax	4,442	4,443	4,437	4,452	4,454
Gross Fed Inc Tax	4,442	4,443	4,437	4,452	4,454
Fed Income Tax	4,442	4,443	4,437	4,452	4,454
Fed Tax Analysis					
Indexing Factor	46	51	56	62	68
Fed Tax Bracket	28.0	28.0	28.0	28.0	28.0
$ To Next Bracket	27,371	28,899	30,464	32,019	33,661
Next Bracket	31.0	31.0	31.0	31.0	31.0
Previous Bracket	15.0	15.0	15.0	15.0	15.0
$ To Prev Bracket	4,029	3,601	3,186	2,781	2,339
Alt Minimum Tax					
Adj Gross Income	35,164	35,863	36,582	37,321	38,082
Contributions	-2,060	-2,122	-2,185	-2,251	-2,319
Adjusted AMTI	33,104	33,741	34,397	35,070	35,763
AMT Exemptions	-33,750	-33,750	-33,750	-33,750	-33,750
AMT Taxable Inc	0	0	647	1,320	2,013
Gross Alt Min Tx	0	0	168	343	523
Fed Tax Less FTC	-4,442	-4,442	-4,436	-4,452	-4,453
Other Tax Liabs					
PA Taxable Inc	35,164	35,863	36,582	37,321	38,082
PA Regular Tax	985	1,004	1,024	1,045	1,066
PA Income Tax	985	1,004	1,024	1,045	1,066
Pennsylvania Tax	985	1,004	1,024	1,045	1,066
Tot State/Local Tx	985	1,004	1,024	1,045	1,066
Total Inc Tax	5,427	5,447	5,461	5,497	5,520

1995   FINANCIAL SUMMARY

CONSTANCE KELLEY

CASE 2	1995	1996	1997	1998	1999
Gross Real Income					
Interest Income	10,675	10,728	10,783	10,841	10,901
Dividends Rcvd	24,489	25,135	25,799	26,480	27,181
	35,164	35,863	36,582	37,321	38,082
Income & Inflation					
Gross Real Inc	35,164	35,863	36,582	37,321	38,082
Total Inc Tax	-5,427	-5,446	-5,460	-5,497	-5,519
Net Real Income	29,737	30,416	31,121	31,824	32,562
Cur Real Inc =	29,737	30,778	31,855	32,970	34,124
Purch Power Drop	0	361	734	1,145	1,561
At Infltn Rate Of	4	4	4	4	4
Cash Flow					
Idle Cash On Hand	70,000	56,034	41,137	25,272	8,370
Norml Cash Inflow	34,114	34,760	35,424	36,105	36,806
Norml Cash Outflw	48,080	49,657	51,289	53,007	54,777
Cash Balance	56,034	41,137	25,272	8,370	-9,600
Net Worth					
Personal Assets	647,574	635,483	622,655	608,994	594,445
Investment Assets	1,475,660	1,571,038	1,673,833	1,784,641	1,904,102
Personal Net Worth	647,574	635,483	622,655	608,994	594,445
Investment Net Worth	1,475,660	1,571,038	1,673,833	1,784,641	1,904,102
Net Worth	2,123,234	2,206,520	2,296,488	2,393,635	2,498,546

INITIAL PLANNING FOR CONNIE'S INCOME FLOW AND ADJUSTMENTS TO CURT'S ESTATE PLAN

Connie's Financial Status Following Curt's Death, Having Received All Jointly Owned Property Only

Case II that appears on pages 8.45–8.50 presents a preliminary picture of Connie's finances under the assumption that only the jointly owned property passes to her. Although the income statement (page 8.46) reveals that Connie's income will be considerably short of their desired goal of $105,000, this statement provides little insight into the effect of her receiving only the jointly held property. Both the balance sheet and the cash-flow statement provide greater information about her financial affairs.

The cash-flow statement provides the analysis of what will happen to Connie's financial status over the next few years. First, she will experience a negative cash flow each year, with the result that her ending cash balance, which started at $70,000 at the end of December 1994 (page 8.23), will fall to a negative value. Given that their plans were for her to have an income of about $105,000 after Curt's death, this result is not unexpected even though some reductions in her cash expenses have occurred. The result of this decline in Connie's cash balance appears as the first item on her balance sheet (page 8.47). Obviously she would not be in a negative financial situation since some assets could be sold. But a year-to-year practice of selling assets to meet cash needs would not be consistent with the Kelleys' objective of not using up principal.

A second observation from the balance sheet is that the interest earned on the CDs accumulates at the bank with no cash received by Connie despite the fact that this income creates an annual cash drain for the amount of the income tax due on the earnings. The amount is small, but if the bank permits, this income can be converted into quarterly payments to Connie.

Third, Connie holds more than $1,300,000 of financial assets (bank deposits, stocks, and bonds) and yet has only an income stream from these assets of $35,164, since most of these assets are in stocks whose primary characteristic is long-term growth with little current income. This was an appropriate investment focus as long as Curt was employed. Now a revision of the portfolio's objective could enhance Connie's financial well-being.

Portfolio Revision

An investment objective that focuses more heavily on producing current income could be pursued. This would entail shifting a portion of the common stocks from their emphasis on the pharmaceutical industry to either stocks that provide higher annual income, bonds, or some combination thereof. The particular securities that could be used for this restructuring are Curt's former ownership interests in the jointly owned stocks. After his death these will receive a step-up in basis and can be sold with little or no capital gain. The sale of one-half of the pharmaceutical stocks and the international fund would provide more than $400,000 of cash that can be repositioned so that this portion of the portfolio would earn between 3 and 6 percent more than it does currently, depending on the particular assets acquired.

Consequences of this restructuring are, first, that the portfolio will experience a lower growth rate and might not provide sufficient inflation protection for Connie's future income needs. Second, no consideration has yet been made as to the asset ownership and income flows available from two of Curt's major assets—the life insurance proceeds and the pension plan. Until the effects of any decisions concerning these two assets are examined in light of Connie's financial situation, it is somewhat premature to consider any portfolio revision solely for the purpose of enhancing current income.

There is a need for some portfolio revision for meeting other investment objectives, such as reduction of dependence on one specific industry. The same securities that were identified for sale to produce income, as well as some of Connie's holdings in the pharmaceutical stocks, can constitute some of those to be reinvested in securities that provide greater diversification and hence less risk to the portfolio. Stock and bond mutual funds are alternatives that would provide diversification and increase her current cash flow from investments. She would also benefit from professional management. After the determination of the consequences of the decisions concerning Curt's remaining assets, then recommendations as to the portfolio restructuring can be made.

Lastly, the balance sheet shows the residence as an asset of Connie's. As was discussed earlier concerning the residence, the prudent course of action from a tax standpoint is to retain the property and benefit from the step-up in basis. Following Curt's death the property can be sold and the proceeds used to acquire either a portfolio of securities should Connie move to an apartment or a less expensive and less costly to operate residence, with the remaining proceeds available for investments. Whether this course of action is needed for cash-flow purposes, as with the portfolio restructuring, depends on the remaining cash flows available to her.

At this point an examination of the assumptions and resulting financial statements for Connie should be made to determine the effects of some of the remaining decisions the Kelleys can make to provide for her income needs and their other objectives.

FURTHER PLANNING OF CONNIE'S FINANCES

Based on the information contained in the financial statements of Case II, the Kelleys made several decisions as to the treatment of the assets that would be included in Curt's estate.

Decisions and the Reasons for Them

Qualified Pension Plan

Consistent with their desire not to use up assets, the Kelleys elected to take a lump-sum distribution from the pension plan and to use 5-year forward averaging for federal income tax purposes. The net amount received, after taxes and other expenses, is $496,565. They will then establish a jointly owned account at a brokerage firm and, following the account executive's recommendations, acquire a portfolio of corporate bonds that will earn an average of 8.12 percent. This results in an additional annual income flow to Connie of $40,000. After the account is established, Curt intends to gift his half to Connie to remove the asset from his estate.

Under the terms of the Galaxy plan, the full amount of Curt's vested pension benefit will be paid if Curt dies before the effective date of his early retirement.

Aggressive Growth Mutual Fund

The shares in the Aggressive Growth Mutual Fund will be distributed to Connie from Curt's estate. This provides further inflation protection, if needed, and also slightly increases her income.

Social Security

Connie will begin receiving social security payments as a surviving spouse as soon as possible after Curt's death. Since Curt experienced such a sudden decline in his health, the Kelleys feel that life is precarious and that a similar misfortune could befall Connie. If so, she might never receive any retirement benefits from social security. In addition, the marginal amount of income that is forgone by taking early benefits does not seem important to someone with Connie's financial wherewithal, and, if really needed, it could be made up from other sources.

Curt's Car

Curt's car is much more luxurious than Connie's and they prefer that she obtain that as a distribution from the estate and then dispose of hers. They questioned their children, none of whom expressed any interest in her car. If she finds that using his car affects her emotionally, she will use the proceeds from the sale of her car, the trade-in value of Curt's, and any cash needed to acquire a replacement without the emotional ties.

[text continues on page 8.65]

CASE III
Addition of Pension Plan Income, Social Security Benefits,
and Aggressive Growth Mutual Fund Dividends
to Connie's Projected Income

CASE ASSUMPTIONS—CASE III

New Assumptions

1. Curt arranges to take early retirement on December 31, 1994. All paperwork for a lump-sum distribution to be effective that day has been completed, and the Kelleys decide to pay the income tax using 5-year averaging. (Note that the assumption that Curt will die on this date still applies.)

2. The net proceeds of approximately $496,565 were placed into a jointly owned investment account on that date and used to acquire a bond portfolio earning 8.12 percent. Curt died before he could make a gift of his half of the account balance.

3. The Aggressive Growth Mutual Fund will pass to Connie as part of her distribution from his estate.

4. Social security benefits in the amount of $10,000 annually, will begin in January 1995 and will have an annual inflation increase of 3.5 percent.

5. Connie will sell her car, receive Curt's from his estate, and reduce her automobile insurance by 50 percent.

Continuing Assumptions

1. Curt dies on December 31, 1994.

2. All jointly owned property passes to Connie.

3. Income from portfolio owned by Connie will grow at rates shown in table 8.3.

4. The checking account balance is maintained at $70,000; the account is non-interest-bearing.

5. The money market deposit account earns 3.1 percent annually.

6. Investable cash is invested and earns 5 percent annually.

7. Expenditures for food, clothing and cleaning, utilities, phone, vacations, and charitable contributions will increase annually at 3 percent.

8. Expenditures for transportation will increase 4 percent annually.

9. Expenditures for entertainment will increase 5 percent annually.

10. Expenditures for medical insurance and other medical expenses will increase at 6 percent annually.

11. Decreases in the value of furniture have been ignored.

12. Automobiles decrease in value at a rate of 15 percent annually.

13. The value of the home will increase at 1 percent annually.

Deleted Assumptions

1. Income from the portfolio equals $44,360 and will grow at rates shown in table 8.3.

2. Curt's salary is increased at 5 percent annually.

1995

INCOME STATEMENT

CONSTANCE KELLEY

CASE 3	1995	1996	1997	1998	1999
Interest/Dividends					
Money Market Fund	2,325	2,325	2,325	2,325	2,325
Corporate Bonds	7,300	7,300	7,300	7,300	7,300
Bond Portfolio	40,321	40,321	40,321	40,321	40,321
Galaxy Pharmceutcal	7,650	7,803	7,959	8,118	8,281
Acme Drug Company	1,298	1,337	1,377	1,418	1,461
Zenith Drug Company	812	824	837	849	862
Aggrssve Grwth Fund	1,969	2,067	2,171	2,279	2,393
International Fund	1,854	1,910	1,967	2,026	2,087
Utility Fund	7,725	7,957	8,195	8,441	8,695
Index Fund	5,150	5,305	5,464	5,628	5,796
CDs	1,050	1,103	1,158	1,216	1,276
Overall Investmnt	824	2,237	3,421	4,615	5,819
	78,278	80,488	82,494	84,537	86,615
Other					
Txbl Social Sec	8,500	8,798	9,105	9,424	9,754
	8,500	8,798	9,105	9,424	9,754
Adj Gross Income	86,778	89,286	91,600	93,961	96,369
Deductions					
Charitable 50%	2,060	2,122	2,185	2,251	2,319
State Tax Paid	2,192	2,254	2,310	2,367	2,425
Home - Property Tax	3,640	3,786	3,937	4,095	4,258
Gross Deductions	7,892	8,162	8,432	8,713	9,002
Standard Deduction	3,700	3,850	3,950	4,100	4,250
Allowed Deductions	7,892	8,162	8,432	8,713	9,002
Pers Exemptions	2,350	2,450	2,550	2,600	2,700
Taxable Income	76,536	78,674	80,618	82,648	84,667
Fed Income Tax	19,245	19,743	20,185	20,634	21,098
Fed Tax Bracket	31.0	31.0	31.0	31.0	31.0

1995   **BALANCE SHEET**

CONSTANCE KELLEY

CASE 3	1995	1996	1997	1998	1999
LIQUID ASSETS					
Cash Balance	69,986	70,002	70,012	70,037	70,030
Cash Deposits					
Overall Investmnt	33,776	57,937	82,328	106,902	131,673
CDs	22,050	23,153	24,311	25,527	26,803
Money Market Fund	75,000	75,000	75,000	75,000	75,000
	130,826	156,090	181,639	207,429	233,476
Stocks & Bonds					
Corporate Bonds	100,000	100,000	100,000	100,000	100,000
Bond Portfolio	496,565	496,565	496,565	496,565	496,565
Galaxy Pharmceutcal	583,200	629,856	680,245	734,664	793,437
Acme Drug Company	79,396	84,556	90,053	95,906	102,140
Zenith Drug Company	47,524	51,801	56,463	61,545	67,084
Aggrssve Grwth Fund	151,801	167,284	184,347	203,151	223,872
International Fund	171,735	183,756	196,619	210,383	225,110
Utility Fund	159,135	163,909	168,826	173,891	179,108
Index Fund	237,620	259,006	282,316	307,725	335,420
	2,026,975	2,136,734	2,255,435	2,383,829	2,522,736
Liquid Assets	2,227,788	2,362,827	2,507,085	2,661,295	2,826,242
NONLIQUID ASSETS					
Personal Property					
Home	408,040	412,120	416,242	420,404	424,608
Car - Curt	21,250	18,063	15,353	13,050	11,093
Car - Connie	8,500	7,225	6,141	5,220	4,437
Home Furnishings	125,000	125,000	125,000	125,000	125,000
Jewelry & Furs	50,000	50,000	50,000	50,000	50,000
	612,790	612,408	612,736	613,674	615,138
Nonliquid Assets	612,790	612,408	612,736	613,674	615,138
Total Assets	2,840,578	2,975,235	3,119,821	3,274,969	3,441,380
Net Worth	2,840,578	2,975,235	3,119,821	3,274,969	3,441,380

1995   CASHFLOW STATEMENT

CONSTANCE KELLEY

CASE 3	1995	1996	1997	1998	1999
BEGINNING OF YEAR					
Idle Cash On Hand	70,000	69,986	70,002	70,012	70,037
SOURCES OF CASH					
Cash Income					
Soc Security Inc	10,000	10,350	10,712	11,087	11,475
Interest+Dividends	76,404	77,148	77,915	78,706	79,520
	86,404	87,498	88,628	89,793	90,996
Sale/Withdrawals					
Car - Connie	10,000	0	0	0	0
	10,000	0	0	0	0
Total Cash Inflow	96,404	87,498	88,628	89,793	90,996
Tot Cash Available	166,404	157,485	158,630	159,805	161,032
USES OF CASH					
Partly Deductible					
Medical Ins Premium	530	562	596	631	669
Charity Contrb-50%	2,060	2,122	2,185	2,251	2,319
	2,590	2,684	2,781	2,882	2,988
Not Tax Deductible					
Food	5,000	5,150	5,305	5,464	5,628
Clothing	5,000	5,250	5,513	5,788	6,078
Entertainment	6,000	6,300	6,615	6,946	7,293
Vacations	5,000	5,150	5,305	5,464	5,628
Transportation	1,040	1,082	1,125	1,170	1,217
Home - Ins Premium	714	728	743	758	773
Auto - Ins Premium	624	649	675	702	730
Jewlry&Furs-InsPrem	1,020	1,040	1,061	1,082	1,104
UmbrellaPolicy Prem	191	197	203	209	215
Home - Repair/Maint	3,090	3,183	3,278	3,377	3,478
Utility/Phone	4,120	4,244	4,371	4,502	4,637
Other Persnl Expnse	4,000	4,120	4,244	4,371	4,502
	35,799	37,092	38,436	39,831	41,281
Taxes Paid					
Fed Tax Paid	19,245	19,743	20,185	20,634	21,098
State Tax Paid	2,192	2,254	2,310	2,367	2,425
Home - Property Tax	3,640	3,786	3,937	4,095	4,258
	25,077	25,782	26,432	27,096	27,781
Purchase/Deposits					
Overall Investmnt	32,952	21,924	20,970	19,959	18,952
	32,952	21,924	20,970	19,959	18,952
Tot Cash Outflow	96,418	87,482	88,618	89,768	91,002
END OF YEAR					
Cash Balance	69,986	70,002	70,012	70,037	70,030

1995   **SUPPORTING SCHEDULE**

CONSTANCE KELLEY

CASE 3	SINGLE 1995	SINGLE 1996	SINGLE 1997	SINGLE 1998	SINGLE 1999
Income					
Adj Gross Income	86,778	89,286	91,600	93,961	96,369
Allowed Deductions	7,892	8,162	8,432	8,713	9,002
Pers Exemptions	2,350	2,450	2,550	2,600	2,700
Taxable Income	76,536	78,674	80,618	82,648	84,667
Federal Tax Liab					
Regular Tax	19,245	19,743	20,185	20,634	21,098
Gross Fed Inc Tax	19,245	19,743	20,185	20,634	21,098
Fed Income Tax	19,245	19,743	20,185	20,634	21,098
Fed Tax Analysis					
Indexing Factor	46	51	56	62	68
Fed Tax Bracket	31.0	31.0	31.0	31.0	31.0
$ To Next Bracket	38,464	40,376	42,582	44,902	47,333
Next Bracket	36.0	36.0	36.0	36.0	36.0
Previous Bracket	28.0	28.0	28.0	28.0	28.0
$ To Prev Bracket	23,036	23,274	23,268	23,298	23,267
Alt Minimum Tax					
Adj Gross Income	86,778	89,286	91,600	93,961	96,369
Contributions	-2,060	-2,122	-2,185	-2,251	-2,319
Adjusted AMTI	84,718	87,164	89,415	91,710	94,050
AMT Exemptions	-33,750	-33,750	-33,750	-33,750	-33,750
AMT Taxable Inc	50,968	53,414	55,665	57,960	60,300
Gross Alt Min Tx	13,252	13,888	14,473	15,070	15,678
Fed Tax Less FTC	-19,245	-19,743	-20,185	-20,634	-21,098
Other Tax Liabs					
PA Taxable Inc	78,278	80,488	82,494	84,537	86,615
PA Regular Tax	2,192	2,254	2,310	2,367	2,425
PA Income Tax	2,192	2,254	2,310	2,367	2,425
Pennsylvania Tax	2,192	2,254	2,310	2,367	2,425
Tot State/Local Tx	2,192	2,254	2,310	2,367	2,425
Total Inc Tax	21,437	21,997	22,495	23,001	23,523

1995   FINANCIAL SUMMARY

CONSTANCE KELLEY

CASE 3	1995	1996	1997	1998	1999
Gross Real Income					
Interest Income	51,820	53,286	54,525	55,777	57,041
Dividends Rcvd	26,458	27,202	27,969	28,760	29,574
Soc Security Inc	10,000	10,350	10,712	11,087	11,475
	88,278	90,838	93,207	95,624	98,091
Income & Inflation					
Gross Real Inc	88,278	90,838	93,207	95,624	98,091
Total Inc Tax	-21,437	-21,997	-22,495	-23,001	-23,523
Net Real Income	66,841	68,842	70,712	72,623	74,568
Cur Real Inc =	66,841	69,181	71,602	74,108	76,702
Purch Power Drop	0	339	890	1,485	2,134
At Infltn Rate Of	4	4	4	4	4
Cash Flow					
Idle Cash On Hand	70,000	69,986	70,002	70,012	70,037
Norml Cash Inflow	96,404	87,498	88,628	89,793	90,996
Norml Cash Outflw	63,466	65,558	67,648	69,809	72,050
Cash Invested	32,952	21,924	20,970	19,959	18,952
Cash Balance	69,986	70,002	70,012	70,037	70,030
Net Worth					
Personal Assets	682,776	682,410	682,748	683,711	685,168
Investment Assets	2,157,801	2,292,824	2,437,074	2,591,258	2,756,212
Personal Net Worth	682,776	682,410	682,748	683,711	685,168
Investment Net Worth	2,157,801	2,292,824	2,437,074	2,591,258	2,756,212
Net Worth	2,840,578	2,975,235	3,119,821	3,274,969	3,441,380

EFFECTS ON CONNIE'S FINANCES

Connie's Gross Income

With these two changes implemented into the Kelleys' plans, we find that Connie's gross income for tax purposes, as shown on the income statement on page 8.59, will rise by $50,469 for 1995. This comes from the following sources:

- $40,000 of interest income from the bond portfolio
- $8,500 of taxable social security benefits
- $1,969 of dividend income from Aggressive Growth Mutual Fund

Her gross cash income will increase by a total of $53,019, comprised of the three increases just listed above plus the 15 percent of the social security, or $1,500, that is not subject to income taxation and the $1,050 interest on the CD that has been recognized as income but not received in cash. The effect is to improve her cash flow by this amount and her total income by $51,969 ($53,019 − $1,050). This increase, plus her dividend and interest income results in Connie's having a gross income of $87,133, a figure still below their $105,000 target. At this point no portfolio restructuring is recommended, since decisions must yet be made with respect to the life insurance proceeds.

Further analysis of the cash-flow statement shows that in 1995 Connie will have an excess of cash inflow over cash outflow of approximately $32,000, although this amount will decline somewhat during the following 4 years. As stated in the earlier discussion concerning her income needs, her targeted income following Curt's death was to be sufficient not only to maintain her current lifestyle but also to enable her to make charitable gifts and provide any needed assistance to children and grandchildren. This goal appears satisfied with the existing income level. Because of uncertainties the Kelleys want to overprovide for Connie and therefore stay with the income target of $105,000.

The Pension Lump-Sum Distribution

The decision to take the lump-sum distribution and for Curt to have the distribution immediately placed in a joint account means that he has made a gift of one-half of the net distribution to Connie. The effect, as a consequence of this gift and the income tax on the distribution, is to reduce the amount in Curt's estate to $248,283. Since the bonds are now jointly owned, they will pass to Connie as part of the marital deduction.

As stated above, the amount to be invested from this distribution, $496,565, will be used to acquire a portfolio of corporate bonds. This portfolio will be divided so that one-third of the portfolio will mature every 3 years for the next 9 years. At the first maturity, bonds with a 9-year maturity will be acquired with the proceeds. This strategy, known as laddering, enables the investor to obtain an average of expected bond interest rates over the next 9 years. In addition, the portion of the portfolio that matures within 3 years will hold most of its value should interest rates drastically rise and a portion of the portfolio need to be liquidated.

Curt's Car

For many years the Kelleys have owned two cars, and both have driven both cars. The fact that each owns one of the cars is more for convenience rather than a way to determine who drives which one. For these reasons, Connie is quite comfortable with Curt's car and will dispose of hers.

FURTHER PLANNING DECISIONS AND REASONS

At this point, Connie's income still falls short of the target but not by a large amount. In addition, no decisions have been made as to the use of the life insurance proceeds, nor has any thought been given to Curt's objectives of providing for the grandchildren and making substantial charitable contributions.

GSTT/Credit shelter

On page 8.31 it was observed that the current estate plan of the Kelleys—the use of simple wills that pass all of Curt's estate assets to Connie (and all of Connie's estate assets to Curt)—forgoes valuable federal estate tax-sheltering opportunities. The proper way to structure the Kelleys' wills is to assure the optimal use of the federal estate tax marital deduction. To take maximum advantage of this marital deduction and in turn to reduce estate tax liability, a credit-shelter bypass trust should be created under the terms of the will.

The bypass trust should empower the trustee to accumulate income or to sprinkle income among income beneficiaries in accordance with the trustee's discretion. At Connie's death, the trust will terminate and the trust corpus will be distributed to the Kelley grandchildren, assuming the youngest grandchild has attained majority. The Kelley children would not be named beneficiaries of Curt's credit-shelter trust, as they would be provided for under the terms and provisions of Connie's revised will.

It should be noted that when the Kelley grandchildren receive the trust corpus from Curt's credit-shelter bypass trust, a generation-skipping transfer will be deemed to have taken place under the tax rules. In essence, when the trust terminates and the trust corpus is distributed to the Kelley grandchildren, a taxable termination under Sec. 2612(a)(2) will occur. This section provides that upon the termination of an interest in property held in trust, if a specified portion of the trust assets is distributed to skip persons who are lineal descendants of the holder of such interest, such termination constitutes a taxable termination with respect to such portion of the trust property. Therefore, when Curt's credit-shelter trust terminates and the corpus passes to the Kelley grandchildren, a generation-skipping transfer will take place. However, the exemption created by Sec. 2631 makes this an academic point only. Under this section of the Code, every individual, including a trust, is permitted to make aggregate transfers of up to $1 million that will be exempted from the imposition of the generation-skipping transfer tax. Unless accumulated income, plus any growth in value of trust assets when added to the trust corpus, exceeds $1 million, the GSTT will not apply.

Qualifying Terminable Interest Property Trust (QTIP)

When structuring the credit-shelter bypass trust arrangement, one must consider whether a QTIP trust should be employed. In non-QTIP trust situations, the surviving spouse can leave the property that passed from the decedent to the surviving spouse to anyone. Sometimes the first spouse to die is reluctant to allow his or her estate property to pass in such a fashion. Often the reluctance is based on a fear that this estate property will ultimately pass to an individual or class of individuals who, in the view of the first spouse to die, is undeserving of such property (for example, new spouse, children from a different marriage, etc.). In these cases a QTIP trust should be used. With this device, the first spouse to die may direct where the estate property will ultimately end up at the death of the surviving spouse. Considering the facts and circumstances of the Kelley case, there is no logical reason to employ a QTIP arrangement. There is no fear on Curt's part that his estate assets will ultimately pass to undeserving recipients.

However, the wills do need to be rewritten. Focusing first on Curt's, his will should establish a credit-shelter bypass trust. Given the facts as shown on page 8.32, the estate settlement costs for Curt's estate will be somewhat more than $333,000. As will be shown later in an estate plan that takes into consideration all the changes, this figure can be reduced. However, $822,500 of life insurance proceeds, $125,000 of Treasury bonds, and $50,000 of Series EE bonds of Curt's property have yet to be considered. Indeed, the life insurance proceeds plus the Treasury bonds exceed the amount needed to fully fund the credit bypass trust and pay all estate settlement costs. This leaves the Series EE bonds available for charitable giving. Curt's will should specify the alternatives as developed below, as well as those that have been developed earlier in this case (such as the distribution of the automobile and the Aggressive Stock Growth Mutual Fund shares to Connie).

The Life Insurance and Life Insurance Trust

A life insurance trust could be established to own the policies, and if Curt were to live for 3 years, this would effectively remove them from his estate. However, the facts of the case indicate that he is not expected to survive that long. The costs associated with establishing the trust, the implications of the trust's beneficiaries' receiving gifts of a future interest, and bringing back the policies into the estate for estate tax purposes combine to preclude the use of the life insurance trust, at least according to how the Kelleys feel. They do not want to pursue this course of action and prefer to have the proceeds pass directly to Curt's estate by changing the beneficiary designation from Connie to his estate. The proceeds will be used to fund a credit bypass trust in an amount at least equal to $600,000. It is anticipated that the trust corpus will be invested in a portfolio comprised equally of corporate bonds and common stocks. This portfolio should have a total return of about 10 percent annually and a cash income of about 5 1/2 percent. Under the terms of the trust, described below, Connie will have additional income of about $16,500 in 1995 and that will increase 2 percent yearly. It is assumed that the stocks will increase in value at 8 or 9 percent annually.

Connie is to receive one-half of the trust income. The remainder can be either accumulated or distributed under a sprinkling power to either Connie or the grandchildren. The grandchildren will be the corpus beneficiaries of the trust, which will not be dissolved during Connie's lifetime. If she dies prematurely, the trust will be dissolved when the youngest grandchild-beneficiary attains age 21.

The Series EE Bonds

Curt has expressed a desire to make charitable contributions from his assets. He could use the $50,000 of Series EE bonds for this purpose. If the gift is made during his last few weeks and is made to a qualified charity, it will qualify for the charitable income tax deduction and will remove this amount from his estate. This gift will be made while he is still alive.

The Treasury Bonds

This asset is needed in Curt's estate to provide, along with some of the proceeds of the life insurance, the cash to pay the various estate administrative costs, debts, and taxes.

EFFECT OF THESE CHANGES ON CURT'S AND CONNIE'S ESTATES

At this point, the estates of Connie and Curt should be reviewed, with particular emphasis on Curt's estate. The effect of these changes is to reduce Curt's estate by the amount of the income tax paid (5-year averaging) and the gift to Connie as a result of taking the lump-sum distribution from the pension plan. In essence, Curt's gross estate will be reduced by $694,940, the total value of the retirement plan, but it will then be increased by one-half of the $496,565 ($248,283). An additional $248,282 will go into Connie's gross estate also.

It should also be noted that Curt's gross estate will be reduced in the amount of $50,000 due to the gift from Curt to the charity of the $50,000 in the EE bonds. There will be no requirement that any of this $50,000 be brought back into Curt's gross estate.

After the various changes, it appears that Curt will have $947,500 of assets in his estate (insurance—$822,500 and Treasury bonds—$125,000), after deducting those assets that will pass to Connie. The estate's administration costs and debts will be approximately $240,000, leaving a taxable estate of about $700,000.

The result is that the estate will have some federal estate tax liability in addition to the state inheritance tax. There are several possible ways for the Kelleys to reduce the estate taxes further and also meet Curt's desire to make charitable contributions. The first method is to sell some of the Treasury bonds and make a charitable gift of about $75,000 while he is still alive, which would enable the Kelleys to obtain the income tax deduction for the amount of the gift as well as removing that amount from his estate. The second method is to instruct the trustee to use any estate assets remaining after deducting all debts, administration costs, state inheritance taxes, marital deduction, and the $600,000 funding of the bypass trust for a qualifying charitable gift. A third method is to specify an amount, such as $75,000, to be given as a charitable gift from the estate. Use of any of the above methods would reduce the federal tax to a relatively inconsequential amount.

Alternatively, the $108,000 ($708,000 − $600,000) in his estate will have a lower marginal estate tax rate than if the money had flowed to Connie and were eventually taxed in her estate. Curt's will could specify that any excess assets be added to the bypass trust funded with $600,000 of estate assets.

The Kelleys' choice was to have the estate make the charitable contribution of $75,000, and any estate assets remaining in the estate are to be placed in the bypass trust.

At Curt's Death	Computations	Actual Expenses Incurred
Gross estate[1]	$2,120,163	
Less: Debts[2]	(76,327)	76,327
Less: Costs of administration[3]	(159,012)	159,012
Adjusted gross estate	$1,884,824	
Less: Charitable deduction	(75,000)	
Less: Marital deduction[4]	(1,173,282)	
Taxable estate	636,542	
Federal estate tax	206,321	
Less: Unified credit	(192,800)	
Federal estate tax owed	13,521	13,521
State inheritance tax		$ 2,380
Total costs at first death		$251,240
At Connie's Subsequent Death		
Gross estate[5]	$2,358,282	
Less: Costs of administration[3]	(176,872)	176,872
Adjusted gross estate	$2,181,410	
Federal estate tax marital deduction[6]	−0−	
Taxable estate	2,181,410	
Federal estate tax		
Less unified credit	192,800	
Federal estate tax owed	676,891	676,891
State inheritance tax		130,885
Total costs at second death		$ 984,648
Total combined costs at both death		$1,235,888

Notes

[1]Gross estate of $2,616,821 reduced by $50,000 (EE bonds), reduced by $694,940 (qualified plan), but increased by $248,282 (one-half of net proceeds of retirement plan).

[2] Curt's estate will pay off remaining mortgage on residence.

[3] Assumed to be 7.5 percent of gross estate

[4] The value of the property passing to Connie

[5] This figure represents $1,173,282 passing from Curt's estate to Constance plus $1,185,000, which is the sum of Connie's share of the jointly titled property and her separate property.

[6] There is no federal estate tax marital deduction available, as Constance is assumed to be unmarried at date of death.

Connie's Will

With the upcoming change in Connie's marital status, a new will becomes essential. Since Curt has provided some funds for the grandchildren by virtue of the terms of the bypass trust, it now behooves Connie to make her children equal beneficiaries, per stirpes, of her estate. The will could also direct that contributions be made to specified charities. These changes should enhance fulfillment of the goals the Kelleys have established.

Connie's Financial Status

Now that decisions concerning the use of the life insurance proceeds to further their objectives have been made a part of Curt's estate planning, an examination of Connie's estimated financial situation, including the trust income, is the last area of this case to review.

Revised Estate Costs

The effect of the changes that have been implemented is to reduce the total costs of Curt's and Connie's estates from $2,021,491, as shown on page 8.32, to $1,235,888, as shown on page 8.69. The combined estate cost reduction of almost $800,000 was achieved without sacrificing the Kelleys' goals. Most of the reduction came from using the credit-equivalent bypass trust and taking a lump-sum distribution from the pension plan. This saving is reduced, however, by approximately $195,000 of income tax paid on the lump-sum distribution from the pension plan.

[text continues on page 8.81]

CASE IV
Addition of Bypass Trust Earnings to Connie's Projected Income

CASE ASSUMPTIONS—CASE IV

New Assumptions

1. Connie will receive one-half of the income earned by the bypass trust. This is assumed to be $16,500 for 1994 and is expected to grow at 2 percent a year.

Continuing Assumptions

1. Curt arranges to take early retirement on December 31, 1994. All paperwork for a lump-sum distribution to be effective that day has been completed, and the Kelleys decide to pay the income tax using 5-year averaging. (Note that the assumption that Curt will die on this date still applies.)

2. The net proceeds of approximately $496,595 are placed into a jointly owned investment account on that date and used to acquire a bond portfolio earning 8.12 percent. Curt dies before he can make a gift of his half of the account balance.

3. The Aggressive Growth Mutual Fund will pass to Connie as part of her distribution from Curt's estate.

4. Social security benefits, in the amount of $10,000 annually, will begin in January 1995 and will have an annual inflation increase of 3.5 percent.

5. Connie will sell her car, receive Curt's from his estate, and reduce the automobile insurance by 50 percent.

6. Curt dies on December 31, 1994.

7. All jointly owned property passes to Connie.

8. Income from portfolio owned by Connie will grow at rates shown in table 8.3.

9. The checking account balance is maintained at $70,000; the account is non-interest-bearing.

10. The money market deposit account earns 3.1 percent annually.

11. Investable cash is invested and earns 5 percent annually.

12. Expenditures for food, clothing and cleaning, utilities, phone, vacations, and charitable contributions will increase annually at 3 percent.

13. Expenditures for transportation will increase 4 percent annually.

14. Expenditures for entertainment will increase 5 percent annually.

15. Expenditures for medical insurance and other medical expenses will increase 6 percent annually.

16. Decreases in the value of furniture have been ignored.

17. The automobile decreases in value at a rate of 15 percent annually.

18. The value of the home will increase at one percent annually.

Deleted Assumptions

1. Income from the portfolio equals $44,360 and will grow at rates shown in table 8.3.

2. Curt's salary is increased at 5 percent annually.

1995   **INCOME STATEMENT**

CONSTANCE KELLEY

CASE 4	1995	1996	1997	1998	1999
Interest/Dividends					
Money Market Fund	2,325	2,325	2,325	2,325	2,325
Corporate Bonds	7,300	7,300	7,300	7,300	7,300
Bond Portfolio	40,321	40,321	40,321	40,321	40,321
Galaxy Pharmceutcal	7,650	7,803	7,959	8,118	8,281
Acme Drug Company	1,298	1,337	1,377	1,418	1,461
Zenith Drug Company	812	824	837	849	862
Aggrssve Grwth Fund	1,969	2,067	2,171	2,279	2,393
International Fund	1,854	1,910	1,967	2,026	2,087
Utility Fund	7,725	7,957	8,195	8,441	8,695
Index Fund	5,150	5,305	5,464	5,628	5,796
CDs	1,050	1,103	1,158	1,216	1,276
Overall Investmnt	1,097	3,072	4,850	6,669	8,529
	78,551	81,323	83,923	86,591	89,325
Other					
Txbl Social Sec	8,500	8,798	9,105	9,424	9,754
By-PassTrust Income	16,500	16,830	17,167	17,510	17,860
	25,000	25,628	26,272	26,934	27,614
Adj Gross Income	103,551	106,951	110,195	113,525	116,939
Deductions					
Charitable 50%	2,060	2,122	2,185	2,251	2,319
State Tax Paid	2,661	2,748	2,831	2,915	3,001
Home - Property Tax	3,640	3,786	3,937	4,095	4,258
Gross Deductions	8,361	8,656	8,953	9,261	9,578
Standard Deduction	3,700	3,850	3,950	4,100	4,250
Allowed Deductions	8,361	8,656	8,953	9,261	9,578
Pers Exemptions	2,350	2,450	2,550	2,600	2,700
Taxable Income	92,840	95,845	98,692	101,664	104,661
Fed Income Tax	24,298	25,059	25,780	26,536	27,293
Fed Tax Bracket	31.0	31.0	31.0	31.0	31.0

1995   **BALANCE SHEET**

CONSTANCE KELLEY

CASE 4	1995	1996	1997	1998	1999
LIQUID ASSETS					
Cash Balance	70,042	70,046	70,069	70,075	70,090
Cash Deposits					
Overall Investmnt	44,971	80,999	117,855	155,562	194,110
CDs	22,050	23,153	24,311	25,527	26,803
Money Market Fund	75,000	75,000	75,000	75,000	75,000
	142,021	179,152	217,166	256,089	295,913
Stocks & Bonds					
Corporate Bonds	100,000	100,000	100,000	100,000	100,000
Bond Portfolio	496,565	496,565	496,565	496,565	496,565
Galaxy Pharmceutcal	583,200	629,856	680,245	734,664	793,437
Acme Drug Company	79,396	84,556	90,053	95,906	102,140
Zenith Drug Company	47,524	51,801	56,463	61,545	67,084
Aggrssve Grwth Fund	151,801	167,284	184,347	203,151	223,872
International Fund	171,735	183,756	196,619	210,383	225,110
Utility Fund	159,135	163,909	168,826	173,891	179,108
Index Fund	237,620	259,006	282,316	307,725	335,420
	2,026,975	2,136,734	2,255,435	2,383,829	2,522,736
Liquid Assets	2,239,039	2,385,933	2,542,670	2,709,993	2,888,738
NONLIQUID ASSETS					
Personal Property					
Home	408,040	412,120	416,242	420,404	424,608
Car - Curt	21,250	18,063	15,353	13,050	11,093
Car - Connie	8,500	7,225	6,141	5,220	4,437
Home Furnishings	125,000	125,000	125,000	125,000	125,000
Jewelry & Furs	50,000	50,000	50,000	50,000	50,000
	612,790	612,408	612,736	613,674	615,138
Nonliquid Assets	612,790	612,408	612,736	613,674	615,138
Total Assets	2,851,829	2,998,341	3,155,406	3,323,667	3,503,876
Net Worth	2,851,829	2,998,341	3,155,406	3,323,667	3,503,876

1995   **CASHFLOW STATEMENT**

CONSTANCE KELLEY

CASE 4	1995	1996	1997	1998	1999
BEGINNING OF YEAR					
Idle Cash On Hand	70,000	70,042	70,046	70,069	70,075
SOURCES OF CASH					
Cash Income					
Soc Security Inc	10,000	10,350	10,712	11,087	11,475
Interest+Dividends	76,404	77,148	77,915	78,706	79,520
By-PassTrust Income	16,500	16,830	17,167	17,510	17,860
	102,904	104,328	105,794	107,303	108,856
Sale/Withdrawals					
Car - Connie	10,000	0	0	0	0
	10,000	0	0	0	0
Total Cash Inflow	112,904	104,328	105,794	107,303	108,856
Tot Cash Available	182,904	174,371	175,840	177,372	178,931
USES OF CASH					
Partly Deductible					
Medical Ins Premium	530	562	596	631	669
Charity Contrb-50%	2,060	2,122	2,185	2,251	2,319
	2,590	2,684	2,781	2,882	2,988
Not Tax Deductible					
Food	5,000	5,150	5,305	5,464	5,628
Clothing	5,000	5,250	5,513	5,788	6,078
Entertainment	6,000	6,300	6,615	6,946	7,293
Vacations	5,000	5,150	5,305	5,464	5,628
Transportation	1,040	1,082	1,125	1,170	1,217
Home - Ins Premium	714	728	743	758	773
Auto - Ins Premium	624	649	675	702	730
Jewlry&Furs-InsPrem	1,020	1,040	1,061	1,082	1,104
UmbrellaPolicy Prem	191	197	203	209	215
Home - Repair/Maint	3,090	3,183	3,278	3,377	3,478
Utility/Phone	4,120	4,244	4,371	4,502	4,637
Other Persnl Expnse	4,000	4,120	4,244	4,371	4,502
	35,799	37,092	38,436	39,831	41,281
Taxes Paid					
Fed Tax Paid	24,298	25,059	25,780	26,536	27,293
State Tax Paid	2,661	2,748	2,831	2,915	3,001
Home - Property Tax	3,640	3,786	3,937	4,095	4,258
	30,599	31,593	32,548	33,546	34,553
Purchase/Deposits					
Overall Investmnt	43,874	32,956	32,006	31,038	30,019
	43,874	32,956	32,006	31,038	30,019
Tot Cash Outflow	112,862	104,325	105,771	107,297	108,841
END OF YEAR					
Cash Balance	70,042	70,046	70,069	70,075	70,090

8.77

1995   SUPPORTING SCHEDULE

CONSTANCE KELLEY

CASE 4	SINGLE 1995	SINGLE 1996	SINGLE 1997	SINGLE 1998	SINGLE 1999
Income					
Adj Gross Income	103,551	106,951	110,195	113,525	116,939
Allowed Deductions	8,361	8,656	8,953	9,261	9,578
Pers Exemptions	2,350	2,450	2,550	2,600	2,700
Taxable Income	92,840	95,845	98,692	101,664	104,661
Federal Tax Liab					
Regular Tax	24,298	25,059	25,780	26,536	27,293
Gross Fed Inc Tax	24,298	25,059	25,780	26,536	27,293
Fed Income Tax	24,298	25,059	25,780	26,536	27,293
Fed Tax Analysis					
Indexing Factor	46	51	56	62	68
Fed Tax Bracket	31.0	31.0	31.0	31.0	31.0
$ To Next Bracket	22,160	23,205	24,508	25,886	27,339
Next Bracket	36.0	36.0	36.0	36.0	36.0
Previous Bracket	28.0	28.0	28.0	28.0	28.0
$ To Prev Bracket	39,340	40,445	41,342	42,314	43,261
Alt Minimum Tax					
Adj Gross Income	103,551	106,951	110,195	113,525	116,939
Contributions	-2,060	-2,122	-2,185	-2,251	-2,319
Adjusted AMTI	101,491	104,829	108,010	111,274	114,620
AMT Exemptions	-33,750	-33,750	-33,750	-33,750	-33,220
AMT Taxable Inc	67,741	71,079	74,260	77,524	81,400
Gross Alt Min Tx	17,613	18,481	19,308	20,156	21,164
Fed Tax Less FTC	-24,298	-25,059	-25,780	-26,536	-27,293
Other Tax Liabs					
PA Taxable Inc	95,051	98,153	101,090	104,101	107,185
PA Regular Tax	2,661	2,748	2,831	2,915	3,001
PA Income Tax	2,661	2,748	2,831	2,915	3,001
Pennsylvania Tax	2,661	2,748	2,831	2,915	3,001
Tot State/Local Tx	2,661	2,748	2,831	2,915	3,001
Total Inc Tax	26,959	27,807	28,611	29,451	30,294

1995

FINANCIAL SUMMARY

CONSTANCE KELLEY

CASE 4	1995	1996	1997	1998	1999
Gross Real Income					
Interest Income	52,093	54,121	55,954	57,831	59,751
Dividends Rcvd	26,458	27,202	27,969	28,760	29,574
By-PassTrust Income	16,500	16,830	17,167	17,510	17,860
Soc Security Inc	10,000	10,350	10,712	11,087	11,475
	105,051	108,503	111,802	115,188	118,661
Income & Inflation					
Gross Real Inc	105,051	108,503	111,802	115,188	118,661
Total Inc Tax	-26,959	-27,807	-28,611	-29,451	-30,294
Net Real Income	78,092	80,696	83,191	85,736	88,366
Cur Real Inc =	78,092	80,825	83,654	86,582	89,613
Purch Power Drop	0	129	463	846	1,246
At Infltn Rate Of	4	4	4	4	4
Cash Flow					
Idle Cash On Hand	70,000	70,042	70,046	70,069	70,075
Norml Cash Inflow	112,904	104,328	105,794	107,303	108,856
Norml Cash Outflw	68,988	71,369	73,765	76,259	78,822
Cash Invested	43,874	32,956	32,006	31,038	30,019
Cash Balance	70,042	70,046	70,069	70,075	70,090
Net Worth					
Personal Assets	682,832	682,454	682,805	683,749	685,228
Investment Assets	2,168,996	2,315,886	2,472,601	2,639,918	2,818,649
Personal Net Worth	682,832	682,454	682,805	683,749	685,228
Investment Net Worth	2,168,996	2,315,886	2,472,601	2,639,918	2,818,649
Net Worth	2,851,829	2,998,341	3,155,406	3,323,667	3,503,876

COMBINED EFFECT OF ALL DECISIONS ON CONNIE'S FINANCIAL SITUATION

As shown on the income statement on page 8.75 in Case IV, Connie's income is within $1,500 of their target. This income statement follows the definitions of income as used for income tax purposes.. In 1995 Connie will receive social security benefits of $10,000. Given her level of income, 85 percent of these benefits will be taxable and will appear on the income statement. The remainder, $1,500, will be exempt from income taxation. This amount, when added to her taxable income, achieves the objective.

Examination of the cash-flow statement (page 8.77) indicates that in 1995 she will have an excess cash inflow of more than $43,000. If Connie desires to use more than that amount for charitable and family gifts, then some portfolio repositioning is desirable. Alternatively, if the situation is satisfactory, then little can be gained by such moves and it would be best to continue holding low-dividend-paying stocks.

Now that the income has reached the targeted level, one possible recommendation is for Connie to shift some of the portfolio from its dependence on the pharmaceutical industry. Curt suggests she consider disposing of most of the pharmaceutical stocks, as he will not be around to assess the future success of the corporations. For emotional reasons she could find it difficult to dispose of the full investment in Galaxy. However, at least half could be sold, using specific identification so that Curt's stock interest is sold. Unless Galaxy's stock rises in value from the date of the estate valuation, no capital gain would result. The full position in the Acme and Zenith stocks could be disposed of with a small amount of realized capital gains. The proceeds could be invested in several mutual funds, such as a growth and income fund, a balanced fund, and an additional investment in an index fund.

Connie's Expressed Interest for Life Insurance

The case situation shows there is no life insurance on Connie's life. After observing how the insurance increased Curt's estate, will provide income for her, and will benefit their grandchildren, she expressed an interest in acquiring some coverage on her life. Based on the estate analysis (pages 8.69–8.70) and her balance sheet shown in Case IV (page 8.76), Connie will have a large estate that will continue to grow over the years. Since she will not have the benefit of an unlimited marital deduction, the estate that she will be able to pass to her children will shrink as a result of the taxes due upon her death. If, for example, she were to die in 1999, the estate taxes would be in excess of $1 million.

Since Connie has made their four children the beneficiaries of her will, some provision to reduce some of the impact of the estate taxes now becomes paramount. One way to accomplish this is for Connie to establish a life insurance trust that will apply for and own the policies on her life.

> **NOTE TO STUDENTS**
>
> To avoid repetition of background material on life insurance trusts, that material has been omitted from this chapter. In an actual plan material such as that on pages 3.90–3.92, 5.85, 6.108–11 and pages 7.40–7.41 should be presented to the client. If the student is not totally familiar with the noted material from previous chapters, it should be reviewed prior to proceeding through this section of the suggested solution.

The recommendation is that the trust acquire a $1 million whole life policy, rather than a universal policy, on Connie's life since she prefers the guarantees of this type of policy. In today's market, for a nonsmoker in good health, such a policy can be obtained for about a $25,000 annual premium. This size premium is feasible for Connie, given the excess cash inflow she is expected to have during the next few years.

Little reason exists for any delay in acquiring the insurance policy. As a matter of fact, the policy could be acquired before Curt dies. Its acquisition will limit Connie's ability to make charitable and family gifts from her income, but if making such gifts is really important, she could further reposition her portfolio to provide increased income for these purposes.

Connie's Checking Account Balance

One last recommended change is to consider reducing the amount of the idle cash balance being maintained in the checking account. By shifting $40,000 into a money market account (2.9 percent current rate) or a short-term bond fund (4.5 percent current rate), Connie could increase her annual income by a minimum of $1,160 or $1,852. Connie has agreed that she would be comfortable with $30,000 in her checking account.

> **NOTE TO STUDENTS**
>
> The solution to the Kelleys' case is not meant to be the only way that this family's objectives could be achieved. Many other decisions concerning the use of the life insurance proceeds, accrued pension benefit, and the securities could have been made and be equally effective.
>
> What this case shows is that some last-minute, before-death planning can be effective, that sequential choices can be analyzed to show their effect in achieving objectives, and that using the personal financial statements can aid in the planning.

9

PLANNING FOR THE SUCCESSFUL CLOSELY HELD CORPORATION AND ITS OWNERS

The successful closely held business may be a corporation wholly owned by one or two families, or it may have a small number of shareholders who are unrelated to the majority shareholders but who are key employees in the business. In the first and second generation of management the general trend seems to be that all stockholders are active in the business. The problems of closely held businesses with both shareholders who are active in the business and shareholders who are inactive are entirely different from the problems of businesses whose shareholders are all employees, since the objectives of active shareholders and those of inactive shareholders are inherently different. Our concentration in this case will be on the typical second-generation closely held business with active shareholders.

Many of the problems of closely held businesses are the same regardless of the size of the business; that is, they differ in scope but not in type. On the other hand, the solutions to some of these problems may be relatively simpler for the larger, more successful businesses because they generally have more cash flow, more assets, and more types of assets, all of which can make more options available to them. This case attempts to highlight the difference in terms of options and choice of techniques that the size and type of a business can make.

In addition, this book has emphasized the importance of comprehensive financial planning in terms of serving the client's best interests in an organized and cohesive fashion. Many financial planners and financial planning firms are so committed to this concept that as a general rule they refrain from doing more limited planning. Sometimes, however, special clients—perhaps those who have already had a comprehensive plan done for themselves and their families—will need additional advice in a particular area, such as tax planning for business transition. In this case assume that comprehensive personal planning such as that for educating children and for dispositions at death was done for Jack Templeton 7 years ago when his father, John, was much more active in the business. Assume further that John Templeton was not interested in comprehensive financial planning at that time. Now that circumstances have changed, Jack seeks advice on a business tax plan addressing the particular issue of his father's withdrawal from the business.

CASE NARRATIVE

John Templeton, Sr., and Allen Lewis, an unrelated party, started a contracting partnership in 1956 as equal partners. When they incorporated the business in 1962, they became equal shareholders in Templeton and

Lewis Contractors, Inc. The corporation issued 3,500 shares of $10 par voting common stock to each partner in return for his partnership interest.

John Templeton, Jr., (Jack) entered the business in 1974 at the age of 25 and devoted himself to learning it from the bottom up with the idea of eventually taking over its management. Jack, an only child, is now 45.

When Allen Lewis retired 15 years ago at age 72, he sold his stock in the corporation to Jack since no member of his family was interested in becoming involved in the business. At the time of the sale the corporation was changed to Templeton Contractors. Jack purchased the stock for $490,000 under the following terms: $40,000 down and an installment note for 25 years at 7 percent. Although Allen Lewis died last year, Jack continues to make annual payments to his estate. Jack has been president of the corporation for 3 years and is now seeking advice on behalf of himself and the corporation.

John is now 65 and his stock in Templeton Contractors makes up approximately 80 percent of his total assets. He and his wife, Lottie, depend on his income from the corporation to support a fairly lavish life-style. John is currently earning approximately $150,000 annually in salary and bonuses. His stock had a book value of $2,345,050 at the end of 1993. (See page 9.4 for balance sheet.)

John has been decreasing his involvement in the daily operations of the corporation for about 7 years but remains the chairman of the board of directors. However, the time he spends in the business on a daily basis is now limited to no more than 2 days a week. During the period that Jack has been the president of the company, it has grown appreciably under his leadership. John, Lottie, Jack, and Jack's wife, Eve, make up the board of directors. The corporation presently has 40 permanent nonunion employees and a nonunion payroll of $1,600,000 annually.

John has become quite concerned that so much of his wealth is tied up in Templeton Contractors. He would like to remove himself even further from corporate operations but does not want to forgo his salary unless another way can be found to fund his life-style. Jack is concerned that he could not really justify as reasonable compensation the present salary and bonuses paid to his father if the corporation was audited by the IRS.

John has offered to sell his shares to Jack, but Jack still has 10 years during which he is obligated to pay for the shares he has already purchased from Allen Lewis. He does not feel that he can undertake another such obligation, at least until his three daughters and his son are educated and established in careers of their own. As a point of fact, Jack doesn't really want to incur this heavy obligation when it is likely that all or a majority of the shares will come to him at the death of his parents. At the same time he does not want to put his parents in a position that would require their giving up a life-style that they enjoy and for which they have worked very hard.

John has also suggested that he would be willing to have the corporation redeem all or a portion of his stock. Jack would be willing to consider a small partial redemption but feels that the corporation cannot afford a complete redemption of John's stock, even with an extended payout period.

Another concern that Jack has is his father's federal estate tax problems. Since John's estate is still appreciating through its investment in Templeton stock and is so illiquid, Jack is concerned that the corporation will be called on to redeem at least enough of his father's stock to pay estate taxes and funeral and administrative expenses at his father's death. He states that his father is uninsurable and says he would feel morally obligated to attempt this type of a redemption, despite the fact that there are no buy-sell agreements that would legally obligate him to do so.

Jack's children are still relatively young: Claudia is 20, LeAnne is 17, Lauren is 15, and Toby is 12. Only the oldest, Claudia, has expressed any interest in the business as a career. Although Jack wishes to preserve the opportunity for all his children to participate if they choose, he does recognize that he must prepare for the continuity of the business if his children discover other careers that they find more fulfilling. Jack is also determined that two unrelated key employees, Ron Harrell and Greg Manion, be allowed to begin to participate in the ownership of the company. He has discussed with John the possibility of selling Ron and Greg at least some portion of John's shares. However, since they are both in their late thirties with families, their financial capacity to undertake an obligation to purchase shares from John would be severely limited. Their salaries and bonuses from Templeton Contractors were approximately $62,000 each last year, and they have no other significant source of funds.

Jack's current compensation is $150,000 annually, which last year was comprised of a base salary of $75,000 and an end-of-the-year bonus of $75,000. John's base compensation is also set at $75,000 annually. Equal bonuses are usually paid to John and to Jack, and much smaller bonuses are paid to Ron, Greg, and no more than five other employees. Because there is no set bonus plan, bonuses are determined at the end of each year by the board of directors and are usually based on overall corporate profits.

Jack has accumulated approximately $400,000 in assets outside the corporation, the majority of which are growth oriented and consequently produce little current income. He feels that he is paying too much in federal income taxes and wonders if there are better ways to use the corporation and its assets to take advantage of tax benefits personally to accumulate assets other than value in his Templeton stock.

The primary business of Templeton Contractors in recent years has been doing heavy construction for the federal government, which serves to insulate them to some degree from the generally cyclical nature of the construction industry. Last year the corporation had taxable income of $480,000. The corporation offers all its full-time employees good medical insurance coverage and nominal amounts of group term life insurance. Disability income coverage is provided for only Jack, Ron, Greg, and five other management employees. The corporation operates on a percentage-of-completion method of accounting for tax accounting purposes.

Templeton Contractors has never provided its employees with qualified deferred-compensation plans, primarily because John thought they were too much trouble and that it didn't matter to the employees whether they were offered. Jack is interested in this employee benefit but does not want to involve the corporation in anything that would constitute an uncontrollable drain on its cash flow. The corporation's 1993 balance sheet follows.

TEMPLETON CONTRACTORS
12/31/93

Assets

Cash	$ 835,000
Accounts receivable	3,679,420
Building (net of depreciation)	380,000
Property and equipment (net of depreciation)	1,225,679
Total assets	$6,120,099

Liabilities and Capital

Current liabilities	$1,430,000
Common stock	70,000
Retained earnings	4,620,099
Total liabilities and capital	$6,120,099

INSTRUCTIONS TO STUDENTS

Based on these facts, prepare a working outline or a business tax plan for Templeton Contractors. When you have completed the outline, compare it with the suggested solution that follows. Then go to page 9.9 for further instructions.

WORKING OUTLINE

I. Client's objectives

    A. Explore methods that would allow John to withdraw enough of his investment in Templeton Contractors stock to continue funding his life-style after retirement

    B. Assure continuity of management when Jack retires regardless of whether his children participate in the business

    C. Explore some tax-advantaged ways to allow the corporation or its assets to provide Jack with some personal tax benefits

    D. Provide Ron Harrell and Greg Manion with some of the stock in the corporation

    E. Provide a mechanism that will provide John's estate with sufficient liquidity to assure that a corporate redemption for federal estate taxes will not be necessary

II. Business tax planning

    A. Present position

    B. Assuring business transition and continuity
       1. Redemptions
           a. Requirements for sale-or-exchange treatment
           b. Sec. 318 attribution problems
           c. Sec. 302(c)(2) election—the waiver approach
           d. Sec. 303 redemptions
       2. Qualified plans of deferred compensation
           a. Benefits of use
           b. Utilizing a special type of qualified plan (ESOP) for business transition and continuity
              • Definition of ESOP
              • Creating a market for all or part of the stock of a shareholder
              • Assuring continuity of management control
       3. Installment sales
           a. General requirements
           b. Avoiding the limitations on deductibility of investment interest
       4. Nonqualified stock bonus plans
       5. Buy-sell agreements

    C. Reasonable compensation considerations

INSTRUCTIONS TO STUDENTS

Now prepare a business tax plan for Templeton Contractors. When you have completed your solution, it should be compared with the suggested solution that follows.

Suggested Solution

BUSINESS TAX PLAN

for

TEMPLETON CONTRACTORS

CLIENT'S OBJECTIVES

A. Explore methods that would allow John to withdraw enough of his investment in Templeton Contractors stock to continue funding his life-style after retirement

B. Assure continuity of management when Jack retires regardless of whether his children participate in the business

C. Explore some tax-advantaged ways to allow the corporation or its assets to provide Jack with some personal tax benefits

D. Provide Ron Harrell and Greg Manion with some of the stock in the corporation

E. Provide a mechanism that will provide John's estate with sufficient liquidity to assure that a corporate redemption for federal estate taxes will not be necessary

BUSINESS TAX PLANNING

PRESENT POSITION

Although the Templetons have been very successful in their business, the bulk of the wealth of two generations is now tied up in Templeton Contractors. Both Jack and John are uneasy about having this situation continue and would like to explore some methods to alleviate it in John's case and to prevent it from recurring when Jack reaches retirement.

In addition, Jack wishes to assure that his two key management people will continue at Templeton Contractors and would like to do so by allowing them to own some stock in the corporation.

Jack would also like to explore using the corporation or its assets more efficiently for personal tax benefits.

ASSURING BUSINESS TRANSITION AND CONTINUITY

Redemptions

Many owners of closely held businesses fail to realize that after spending their working lives in a business, it may be very difficult to transform their investment in that corporation into another type of investment that may be more appropriate for their later years without paying a heavy price in taxes.

One problem with the corporate form of organization arises from the fact that dividends paid to corporate stockholders are not deductible by the corporation and are taxable to the shareholders as ordinary income. In many, if not most, wholly owned or family-owned corporations, dividends are either never paid or are paid rarely and in small, often insignificant, amounts. This is usually not troubling to the shareholders of these corporations, who are most often also employees of the corporation and who depend on salaries rather than dividends for their livelihood.

In the absence of the statutory restraints on a corporate redemption of its stock, any time a shareholder of a wholly owned and closely held corporation wished to take money out of the corporation without receiving dividend treatment, the shareholder could simply sell some shares back to the corporation for cash and pay tax on the gain.

There is now a maximum tax rate of 28 percent for long-term capital gains. But since capital gains are part of a taxpayer's adjusted gross income (AGI) the recognition of these gains can lead to a loss of some of the personal exemptions and deductions allowable against AGI. The net result is an effective tax rate in excess of 28 percent in some cases. However, capital-gain treatment still provides two significant advantages over ordinary income treatment in a redemption. First, it will allow the shareholder to recover his or her basis in the redeemed stock tax free. Second, capital gains can be fully offset by capital losses, while ordinary income can be offset by capital losses only to the extent of $3,000 per year.

An example of a dividend-type redemption follows:

Shareholder T owns 100 percent (500 shares) of ABC corporation, which has earnings and profits. Each share is worth $1,000. He causes ABC corporation to redeem 30 shares of his stock for $30,000. Result: T still owns 100 percent of ABC corporation although he now owns only 470 shares of stock.

T would like to treat the redemption as the sale of a capital asset and receive capital-gain treatment. The Internal Revenue Code provides that the redemption is essentially the same as if a cash dividend had been paid to T and that the entire $30,000 will be treated as ordinary income.

Requirements for Sale-or-Exchange Treatment

The Internal Revenue Code defines a redemption as the corporation's acquisition of its stock from a shareholder in exchange for property (excluding stock in the corporation) (IRC Sec. 317). For this purpose property is defined to include money.

As stated above, whether the redemption qualifies as a sale or exchange of a capital asset determines whether the taxpayer pays federal income tax on the entire amount of the money or other property distributed (if treated as a dividend) or only on the amount of the gain (amount distributed − basis = gain) the taxpayer realizes on the transaction. In terms of the above example this principle can be illustrated as follows: If T has a basis of $300 in each of his 500 shares of stock and he can effect a redemption of 30 shares that will qualify for treatment as a sale or exchange, he will only pay tax on the amount of his $21,000 gain ($300,000 − [30 x $300]). T's basis in his stock is returned tax free before gain subject to tax is determined. If, however, the redemption is treated as a dividend (as it inevitably would be in our example), the entire $30,000 distribution is taxable. T's basis in the 30 shares of redeemed stock is then preserved by allocating it to his remaining 470 shares.

Particularly as they get older, shareholders, like John, of closely held businesses may wish to take some or all of their investment out of the corporation so that their lifetime accumulation of wealth will no longer be subject to the frailties and errors of new management—even if the new management consists of their own children—or, as in John's case, will allow them to replace the salaries on which they have come to depend so that they can withdraw from the business.

If the shareholder is willing and able to sell his or her stock either to the children or to an outsider, the tax problem of dividend treatment triggered by a redemption is avoided.

Since the direct purchase of a substantial interest in a business may be difficult for younger family members or key employees to finance without altering their life-style, family businesses often consider redemptions in their business transition plans.

One might think that the fact that an older shareholder had refrained from taking dividend distributions from the corporation would not affect other shareholders. However, the Internal Revenue Code treats the shareholder's entire family as an economic unit for this purpose through the attribution rules of IRC Sec. 318. As a result in situations when one family owns all or a large majority of shares and when it is especially desirable to use a corporate redemption, it may be very difficult to qualify such redemptions for capital-gain treatment.

The type of redemption that has been discussed in the preceding example of shareholder T of the ABC corporation is clearly an attempt to take out the earnings and profits of the corporation without treating them as dividends. As such, this is a transaction that should be taxed as a dividend. Therefore in attempting to prevent such abuses the Internal Revenue Code has enacted provisions requiring that as a general rule a corporation's purchase of its own stock will be treated as a dividend (to the extent of the earnings and profits of the corporation) (IRC Secs. 302(d), 302(c)). This general rule will apply regardless of whether an attempt is being made to transform dividends into capital gains unless the taxpayer can meet one of the exceptions in Sec. 302(b) that will result in capital-gain treatment.

The exceptions include

- redemptions not essentially equivalent to a dividend (IRC Sec. 302(b)(1)). This is not a precise test, and the result under the test depends on whether there is a meaningful reduction of the shareholder's interest under all the facts and circumstances of the case. For this purpose the shareholder's constructive ownership under IRC Sec. 318 (discussed below) will be considered. Since the test is imprecise, this is a perilous exception upon which to advise a client to rely.
- substantially disproportionate redemptions. A redemption qualifies for capital-gain treatment under this exception to the general rule provided that *immediately after the redemption* (a) the redeemed shareholder's proportion of ownership of both the outstanding *voting* stock and the *common* stock of the corporation is less than 80 percent of his or her proportionate ownership before the redemption, and (b) the redeemed shareholder owns less than 50 percent of the total voting power of all classes of stock entitled to vote (IRC Sec. 302(b)(2)).

    An example of a redemption that would qualify as substantially disproportionate is the following:

    X Corporation has 100 shares of one class of voting common stock outstanding. A and B each own 50 of those shares. The corporation redeems 20 of A's 50 shares. It now has 80 shares of voting common stock outstanding, of which A owns 30 and B owns 50.

    A's proportion of ownership before the redemption was 50 percent (50 ÷ 100). Her proportion of ownership after the redemption is 37.5 percent (30 ÷ 80). Eighty percent of A's prior 50 percent ownership equals 40 percent. Since A now owns 37.5 percent, her proportion of ownership of voting and common stock

after the redemption (37.5 percent) is less than 80 percent of her proportion of ownership before the redemption (40 percent). Since A also now owns less than 50 percent of the total voting power in the corporation, both the 80 percent and 50 percent tests are met, and the redemption will qualify as substantially disproportionate.
- a redemption that is a complete termination of a shareholder's interest (IRC Sec. 302(b)(3))

For corporations whose stockholders are not subject to the attribution rules of IRC Sec. 318, these exceptions are relatively straightforward. However, when they are combined with the complexities of constructive ownership through the attribution rules, they can become quite difficult, so that redemptions that qualify for capital-gain treatment can become virtually impossible to achieve in family-owned corporations.

Sec. 318 Attribution Problems

For purposes of determining the ownership of a corporation before and after a redemption, the redeemed stockholder is considered to own

- all the stock he or she actually owns
- all the stock owned by the stockholder's spouse, children, grandchildren, or parents
- stock owned by an estate or partnership of which the stockholder is a partner or beneficiary (in proportion to his or her interest in the partnership or estate)
- stock owned by a trust of which the stockholder is a beneficiary (in proportion to his or her actuarial interest in the trust)
- stock owned by another corporation in which the redeemed stockholder also owns directly or indirectly 50 percent or more of the outstanding stock

A discussion of the complexities of the family and entity attribution rules is beyond the scope of this plan. However, a simple example of the application of the family attribution rules to John and Jack's situation can illustrate some of the difficulties.

When one applies the family attribution rules of IRC Sec. 318(a)(1) to the Templetons' situation, the results show that John owns

Directly	50 percent of stock
<u>Constructively (Jack's)</u>	<u>50 percent of stock</u>
Total ownership actually and constructively	100 percent of stock

The result is the same for Jack, who owns

Directly	50 percent of stock
<u>Constructively (John's)</u>	<u>50 percent of stock</u>
Total ownership actually and constructively	100 percent of stock

Because John will always be deemed to own the stock his son owns, he will not be able to effect a lifetime redemption that will qualify for capital-gain treatment and still remain active in the business.

Sec. 302(c)(2) Election—The Waiver Approach

Because the difficulties in redeeming shareholders in family-owned corporations could force some shareholders into very difficult tax situations even though they are making no improper attempt to withdraw the corporation's earnings and profits, the Internal Revenue Code provides a method that can be elected to waive the family attribution rules of IRC Sec. 318 and allow the redemption of a shareholder such as John to qualify as a complete termination of his interest (IRC Sec. 302(c)(2)).

In order to effect this result the shareholder must dispose of all stock. There is no requirement, however, that all the stock must be redeemed, and combinations of sales and redemptions are not unusual. In addition, immediately after the redemption the shareholder must have no continuing interest (including an interest as an officer, director, or employee) in the corporation except that of a creditor and must agree not to acquire an interest in the corporation (except by inheritance) within 10 years from the date of the redemption. Furthermore, the employee must file an agreement with the Internal Revenue Service agreeing to notify them if an interest is acquired within the prohibited period.

Even if these conditions are met, the redemption will not qualify for capital-gain treatment if either (1) any portion of the stock that is being redeemed was acquired within 10 years of the date of the redemption from a person whose ownership of the stock would be attributable to the person whose stock is being redeemed, or (2) any person whose stock would be attributable to the person whose stock is being redeemed has acquired that stock within a 10-year period directly or indirectly from the person whose stock is being redeemed, unless his or her stock is also redeemed. For example, a father cannot have given a portion of his stock to his son and have the corporation redeem the remainder of the stock he holds under a Sec. 302(c)(2) election and receive capital-gain treatment unless the gift took place more than 10 years prior to the redemption and Sec. 302(c)(2) election, or unless the son's stock is also redeemed.

Since John seems content to terminate his employment at Templeton Contractors, this election out would provide him a means to have all his stock redeemed and receive capital-gain treatment. It would require, however, that the corporation pay him in excess of 2.3 million nondeductible dollars. This is a tremendous cash drain on the corporation even if it is undertaken on an installment basis and could jeopardize the company's continued viability. This is especially true since contractors are required to maintain certain amounts of liquid and near-liquid assets to obtain bonding, without which they generally cannot operate.

If an installment payout is elected, the corporation would also have the additional cash drain of paying interest on the obligation, although the interest payment would be deductible.

Our conclusion is that a redemption would not be a suitable technique for effecting the transfer of John's stock into a more liquid investment.

Sec. 303 Redemptions

Many shareholders of family-owned businesses do continue to hold stock in their corporations until death, with the result that their estates are very illiquid. The rules for redemptions are not materially eased at death. However, to avoid hardship in these cases, IRC Sec. 303 provides a method for assuring that sufficient stock can be redeemed and treated as a sale or exchange of a capital asset to pay estate taxes and deductible funeral and administrative expenses if certain prerequisites are met. The test for utilizing a Sec. 303 redemption is that the value of the corporation's stock owned by the decedent exceeds 35 percent of the decedent's adjusted gross estate.

A second requirement is that the Sec. 303 redemption is available only if the shareholder receiving proceeds of the distribution is subject to an obligation to pay estate taxes and deductible funeral and administrative expenses. For example, in a typical will with a marital and a residuary trust, the marital trust will bear none of the expenses of administration or estate taxes. Therefore a Sec. 303 redemption could not be utilized to fund this marital trust. Instead the Sec. 303 redemption would be available to fund the residuary trust, which would be liable for administration expenses and estate taxes.

The assets in a decedent's estate receive a stepped-up basis generally equal to their fair market value at the date of the decedent's death (IRC Sec. 1014). Therefore there is usually little or no income tax liability resulting from a Sec. 303 redemption. The sales price is usually equal to the value of the stock at the time of the shareholder's death, allowing the estate to receive the proceeds as a tax-free return of its stepped-up basis in the stock. This makes capital-gain treatment particularly important when stock is redeemed from a decedent's estate.

If John were to die with his present stock holdings, his estate would qualify for a Sec. 303 redemption. However, since Jack has indicated a strong preference not to utilize this option unless he is forced to do so, other methods for providing liquidity to meet estate settlement costs must be explored.

Qualified Plans of Deferred Compensation

Benefits of Use

Rather surprisingly, the facts indicate that Templeton Contractors has never had a qualified deferred-compensation plan. Many entrepreneurs do have a great deal of trepidation about qualified plans because they perceive that these plans subject the corporation to more unwanted governmental interference. However, when a corporation has taxable income of almost $500,000, as Templeton Contractors did in 1992, and is not using a qualified plan, it is losing a valuable tax benefit.

> **NOTE TO STUDENTS**
>
> To avoid repetition of background material on qualified plans, that material has been omitted from this chapter. In an actual plan, material such as that on pages 3.38–3.48 and pages 5.46–5.50 should be presented to the client. If the student is not totally familiar with the noted material from prior chapters, it should be reviewed prior to proceeding through this section of the suggested solution.

Utilizing a Special Type of Qualified Plan (ESOP) for Business Transition and Continuity

ESOP Described. An employee stock ownership plan (ESOP) is either a qualified stock bonus plan or money-purchase pension plan that requires plan assets to be invested primarily in qualifying employer securities (IRC Sec. 4975(e)(7)). As a qualified plan it is subject to the requirements described in the materials referred to above. Most important, these rules require that the plan

- satisfy minimum coverage requirements
- meet minimum vesting requirements
- allocate contributions to participants using a method that does not discriminate in favor of the highly compensated employees
- meet special minimum contribution and vesting requirements when the plan is top-heavy
- does not exceed allocations to a participant of the lesser of 25 percent of compensation or $30,000 each year, counting all contributions and forfeitures allocated to a participant

The corporation can make annual tax-deductible contributions to an ESOP in cash or corporate stock. Under the stock bonus type of ESOP the maximum deductible contribution is 15 percent of covered compensation, while under the money-purchase type the maximum contribution is 25 percent of covered payroll. If an employer maintains more than one plan, the contributions in all plans are generally subject to the 25 percent limit. However, a special rule allows for greater deductions in leveraged ESOPs. The employer may find the stock bonus type more appealing, since the plan can be designed to provide for discretionary contributions, instead of fixed contributions as required in a money-purchase pension plan.

As with contributions to other types of qualified plans, ESOP contributions are not taxable to employees until they (or their beneficiaries) receive the benefits they have accumulated at retirement, disability, termination, or death. Earnings on amounts invested in a qualified plan are also not taxed until they are distributed.

In these ways an ESOP is subject to the same requirements as any other stock bonus plan or money-purchase plan. However, an ESOP is subject to some additional qualification requirements. These are summarized briefly below:

- The plan has to invest primarily in the employer's securities.
- The plan can invest only in "qualifying employer securities," which for the closely held company means stock containing both the greatest voting power of any class of stock and the greatest dividend rights of any class of stock.
- Voting rights have to be passed through to the participant in a publicly traded company. In a closely held company the voting rights pass-through applies only to major issues such as sales of the firm's assets, liquidations, or mergers and consolidation.
- Distributions generally must be available in the form of stock. However, employers whose charter or bylaws restrict ownership of substantially all outstanding employer securities to employees or a qualified plan may distribute cash only.
- Distributions do not have to be distributed in the form of cash. However, in a closely held company the participant must have the right to sell the stock back to the company within the 60-day period after stock is distributed, as well as during a 60-day period in the following year. This right is referred to as a "put option." If the put option is exercised, the company can repurchase the stock over a 5-year period when the participant has received a total distribution from the plan.
- Stock has to be valued at fair market value. A nonpublicly traded company must establish an acceptable procedure for appraising and determining the fair market value of stock. The determination must be made at least annually, and the appraiser has to be independent.
- An ESOP cannot be integrated with social security benefits.
- To protect the value of a participant's plan benefit, an ESOP must allow participants who are at least aged 55 and have completed 10 or more years of participation the right to direct the trustee to diversify the investment of a portion of their accounts. The plan must offer three (nonstock) investment options. In the first year that the right applies, the participant must have the right to diversify a minimum of 25 percent of his or her account. In each following year, the amount subject to the diversification requirement increases by 5 percent until the participant has the right to diversify 50 percent of the account after 5 years.
- Special rules apply to the timing of distributions from an ESOP. If an ESOP allows participants the option to receive a single-sum payment at the time of distribution, these special rules have no impact. However, if the plan wants to delay the timing of the distribution or limit the forms of the distribution by excluding a single-sum option, special rules applicable only to ESOPs will apply. The law requires that a distribution must begin within one year after the plan year in which an individual separates from service due to retirement, death, or disability and within 5 years if the individual terminates employment for any other reason. The plan must allow the participant to elect a payout period that does not exceed 5 years, unless the individual has an account that exceeds $500,000.

Although ESOPs are subject to additional qualification requirements, they are also eligible for special treatment. In the right situation an ESOP has significant advantages over other qualified plans. These advantages are summarized below:

- The corporation can make tax-deductible cash contributions that are used to purchase stock, either from the company or from another shareholder, creating a "market" for such stock.
- The corporation can also contribute its securities and receive a deduction for the fair market value of the contributions, resulting in an income tax benefit without a corresponding cash-flow drain.
- An ESOP can borrow money to purchase securities, allowing the plan to purchase large blocks of stock at one time. This type of ESOP, referred to as a "leveraged ESOP," has additional advantages. A company can raise capital by selling stock to the plan and retire the debt on a pretax basis by making tax-deductible contributions to the plan. A special rule allows an additional deduction for the amount of dividend payments paid on plan stock that are used to retire the loan. Also, a bank or other financial institution lending money to an ESOP may exclude from taxable income one-half of the interest received on the loan. This provision applies only when the ESOP owns more than 50 percent of the value of all stock and several other requirements are met.
- A leveraged ESOP can either borrow money from a "disqualified person" (a party related to the company or plan), or the company may guarantee the loan payments when the loan is made by the ESOP from an unrelated bank or other financial institution. Such loans or guarantees are allowed as long as the loan is set at a reasonable interest rate. The ESOP can use the stock purchased with the proceeds of a loan only as collateral. The stock held as collateral is placed in a separate suspense account. As the loan is repaid, shares are released from the suspense account and allocated to participants.
- In limited circumstances a shareholder may sell stock to the corporation and defer paying income tax on the gain due to the stock sale. To qualify, during the period 3 months before the sale until 12 months after the sale, the shareholder must use the entire proceeds from the sale to purchase "qualified replacement property." The stock sold must have been held by the seller for one year prior to the sale. Additionally, the ESOP has to own at least 30 percent of the total value of outstanding employer securities after the sale. Qualified replacement property that may be purchased includes debt securities or stock of another domestic corporation that does not have passive investment income in excess of 25 percent of its gross receipts and that uses at least 50 percent of its assets for the active conduct of a trade or business. Also, the selling shareholder (and family members) and any other person owning more than 25 percent of any class of the employer securities generally will not be able to participate in the ESOP if this option is exercised. An exception to this rule provides that lineal descendants (children, grandchildren) may participate in the plan if no more than 5 percent of the stock is

- allocated to the accounts of all such descendants during the 10-year period following the sale.
- In a closely held corporation where the owners are concerned about who holds corporate stock, the plan may contain a provision known as a "right of first refusal" in favor of the employer and/or the ESOP. Such provision would require that a participant who has received stock and wishes to sell it give the employer and/or the plan the first opportunity to buy the stock at the greater of the fair market price or the price offered by the buyer.
- The maximum annual allocation limit (the lesser of 25 percent of compensation or $30,000) applies to the amount of contribution made by the employer and not to the value of stock as it is allocated to a participant's stock or to dividends paid on such stock.
- Generally an employer is not allowed a tax deduction for dividends paid to shareholders. However, a deduction is allowed on dividends paid on stock held by the ESOP if the ESOP either pays the dividends currently to participants or if the dividends are used to repay a leveraged loan.
- In a leveraged ESOP the company can deduct contributions of up to 25 percent of covered compensation that is used to repay the principal of an ESOP loan. An additional deduction may be taken on contributions used to repay loan interest.
- Employer stock distributed as part of a lump-sum distribution is eligible for special tax deferral. The taxation of the appreciation in value from the time of purchase by the plan until the distribution may be deferred until the stock is actually sold by the participant.

Using an ESOP to Transfer John's Ownership Interest. John's stock in Templeton Contractors can be sold to the ESOP in one of several methods. The first and simplest is a series of periodic cash sales to the ESOP. On an annual basis the company can make a contribution to the plan, which can be used to purchase a portion of John's stock (see figure 9-1). This approach will give John a stream of income during retirement, and John will be taxed only on the purchase price of each sale, less his basis in the stock sold.

As an alternative, the ESOP can purchase all of John's stock at one time by financing the purchase (see figure 9-2). John can finance the transaction himself by agreeing to receive periodic installment payments. With this approach, John delivers all his stock to the plan. The company makes periodic contributions that are used to make promised installment payments to John. In order for John to have some protection, the stock can be held as collateral and kept in a separate suspense account. As the installment payments are made, a portion of the stock is released from the suspense account and allocated to plan participants.

Each installment payment that John receives contains three components: basis, capital gain, and interest. The capital gain (sale price less John's basis in the stock) will be prorated and recognized (taxed) over the years in which payments are received. The amount that represents interest payments will be recognized as ordinary income in the year received.

FIGURE 9-1
Periodic Cash Sales to ESOP

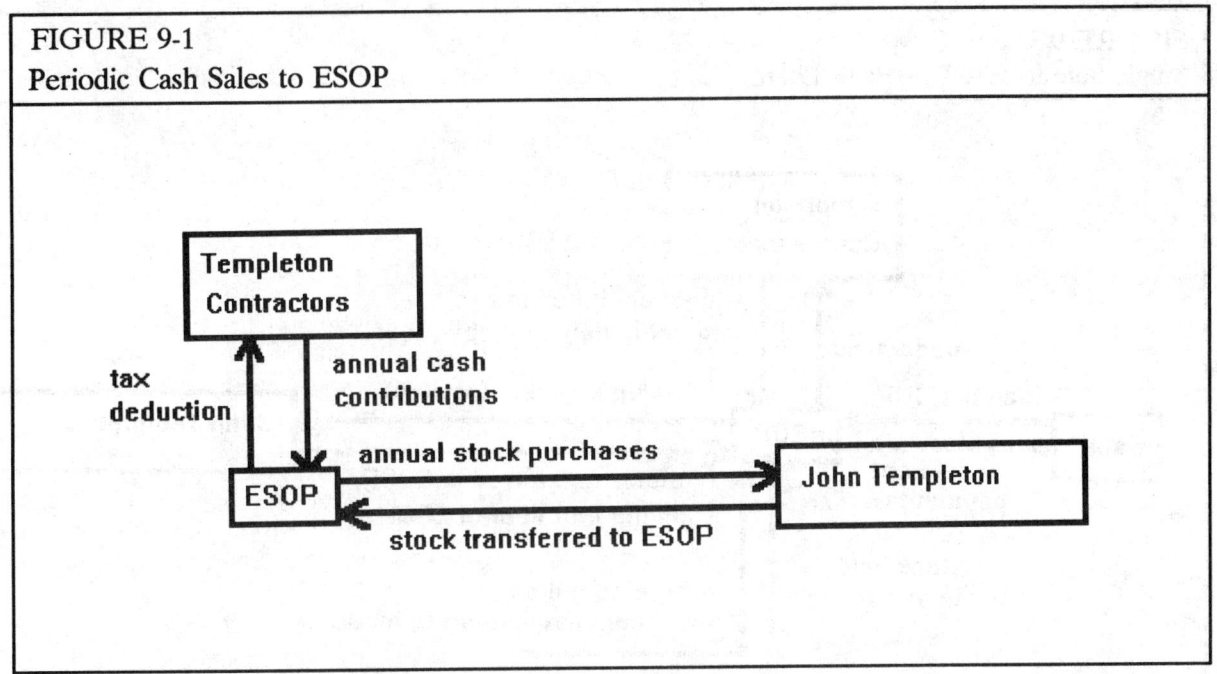

FIGURE 9-2
Single Sale to ESOP—Installment Payments

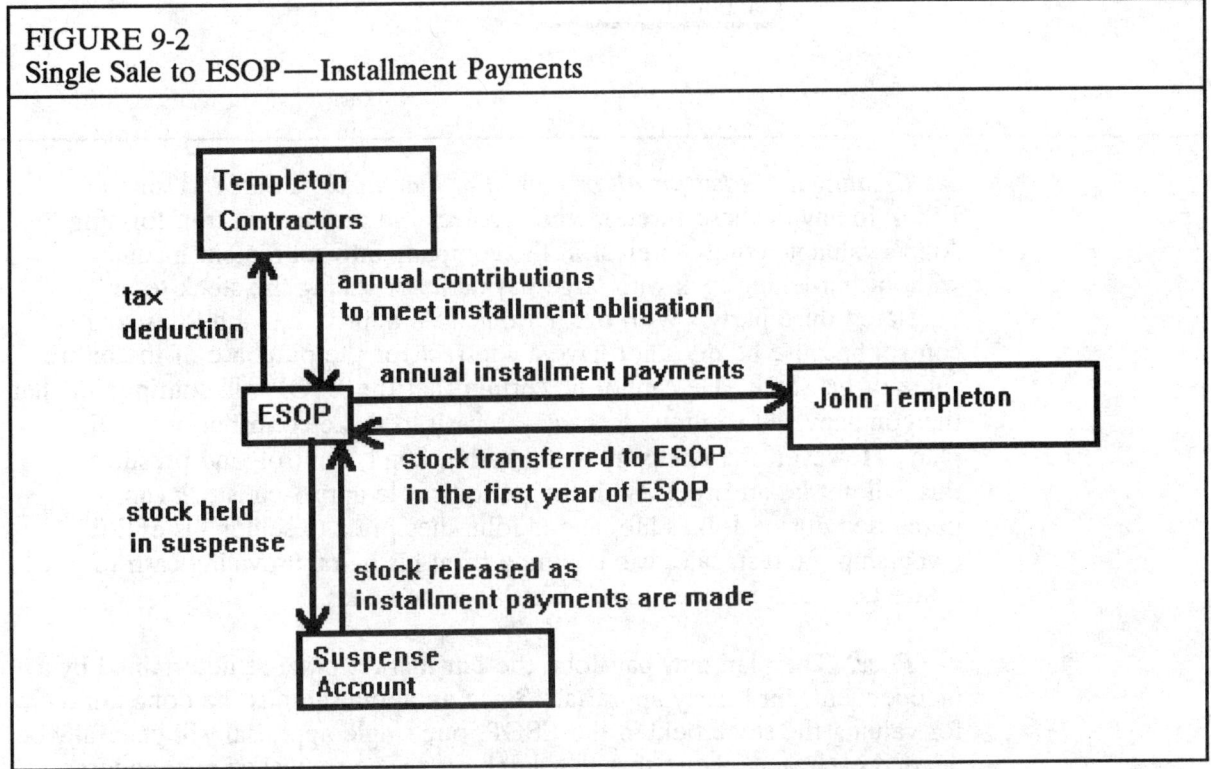

Another way in which the ESOP can purchase John's stock in one step is to borrow from a bank, repaying the loan with annual contributions to the plan (see figure 9-3). With a bank loan, the bank will generally require that the stock be held in suspense as described above. In addition, the bank will generally also require that the company guarantee the repayment of the note. With this approach, John receives the entire purchase price at one time. Such amount, less his basis in the stock, will be taxable at the time of receipt.

FIGURE 9-3
Single Sale to ESOP—Bank Loan

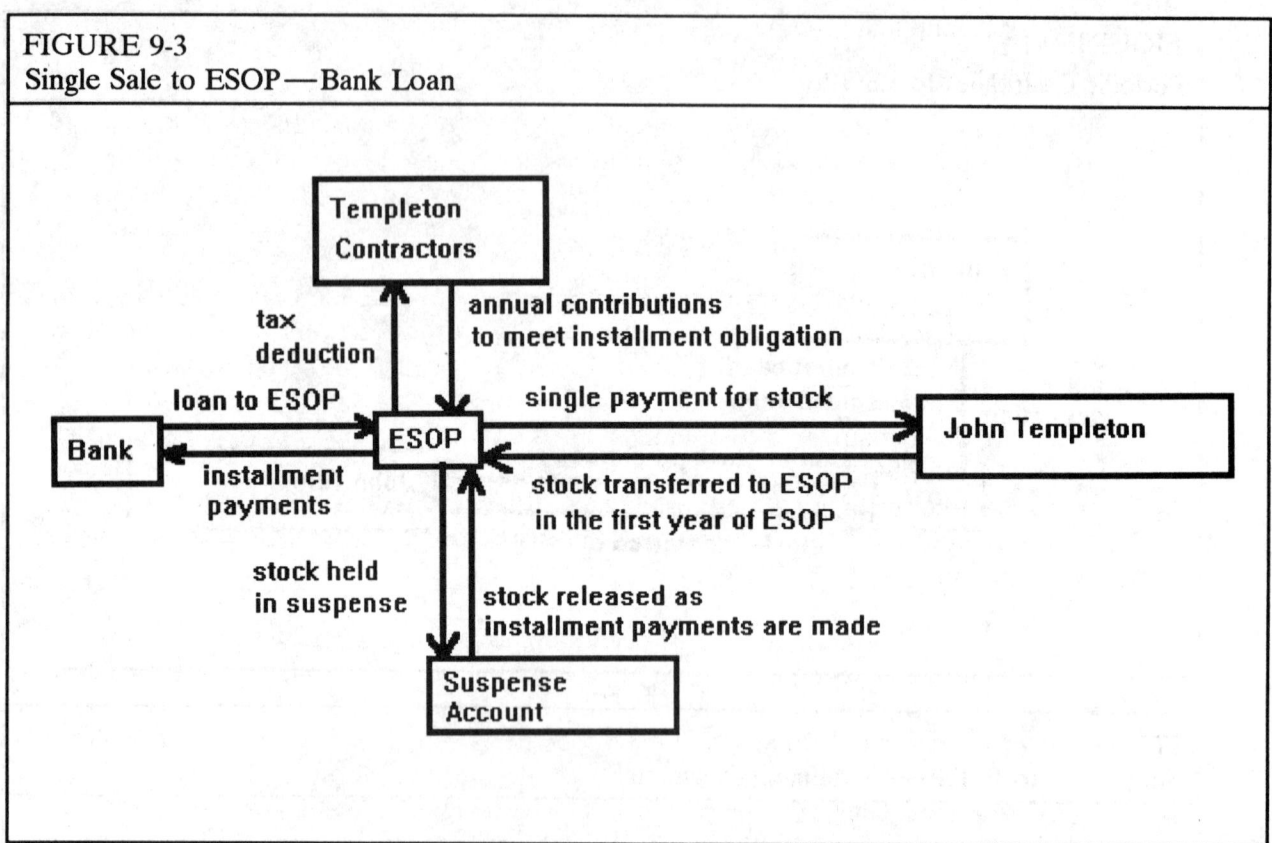

Creating a Market for All or Part of a Shareholder's Stock. Using an ESOP in any of these three methods solves the problem of transforming John's valuable equity interest in the company into retirement income without burdening Jack with large payments or selling the stock to an unrelated third party. With the periodic sale approach, John loses some control because he does not have a contract for the purchase of the entire value of his stock. He cannot be certain that the ESOP will continue or that the company will continue to have the cash to make contributions to the plan. However, the company is still within family control, and presumably this will not be an issue. With the periodic sale approach, stock can be purchased during John's life, and if John dies prior to selling his entire ownership interest, sales can continue from his heirs, providing cash to pay estate taxes and to meet John's heirs' income needs.

Price. The plan may pay John the fair market price as determined by a independent third-party appraisal. Since an appraisal must be done annually for valuing the stock held in the ESOP, one single appraisal will generally be needed each year. Note that the purchase price established may undergo scrutiny by the Department of Labor (DOL), since the stock is being purchased from a "prohibited party." The sale should occur as close to the date of valuation as possible, and if stock is purchased over a period of years, the value will have to be determined at the time of each sale. Therefore in a periodic sale, John will be subject to price uncertainty. The projected valuation of company stock is certainly a relevant consideration in determining whether a single purchase or periodic purchases are more advantageous. In contrast, in an installment sale or a sale financed with a bank loan, the purchase price for all of John's stock is based on the current fair market price.

Stock Redemption. A sale to the ESOP can generally avoid the previously discussed complicated redemption problems associated with a direct sale back to the corporation. Such a sale to the ESOP should be taxed as a sale or exchange of a capital asset.

However, under limited circumstances, the IRS has indicated that a sale of stock to an ESOP will be treated as a redemption for tax purposes (Rev. Proc. 87-22, 1987-20 I.R.B. 11). As specified in that ruling, dividend treatment will *not* result if the stockholder and his or her ancestors and descendants do not hold more than 20 percent of the beneficial interest in the ESOP after the stock is sold to the company and if none of the stock sold to the plan is subsequently sold to the company. The IRS will determine the tax implication of such sales in accordance with procedures set forth in the ruling.

In John's case the 20 percent beneficial interest rule is an issue that requires careful analysis. As discussed above, in normal circumstances Jack would be allowed to participate in the plan, and would probably like to participate to the fullest extent possible. Apparently, under the Rev. Proc. the 20 percent beneficial interest rule is tested after the completion of the sale. Therefore the plan needs to be designed accordingly to ensure compliance with the rule. In this case, it may be prudent for Jack to hire an attorney to request a ruling that the sale will not be deemed a redemption. The problem becomes somewhat more complex if John sells the stock over a period of time versus in a single sum to the plan. In the periodic sale situation, the issue will have to be considered each time a sale is made.

Deferring Taxes on Proceeds from the Sale of John's Stock. It may be possible for John to defer taxation on the sale of his stock to the ESOP as long as he sells at least 30 percent of his ownership interest to the ESOP at one time. However, if John wants to take advantage of the deferral, his son Jack (and any of Jack's children) will either have to forgo participation in the plan entirely or participate to a very limited extent. (All of John's descendants cannot have more than 5 percent of the stock purchased during the 10-year period following the sale allocated to their account.) If John does not try to take advantage of the tax deferral, under normal circumstances Jack would be allowed to participate fully in the plan (subject to the 20 percent limitations discussed above) and would ultimately be the beneficiary of a substantial portion of Jack's shares through the ESOP. Because of this conflict, the better solution may be for John to sell the stock over a period of time (using either the periodic sale or installment sale method), resulting in a deferral of taxation. Since John needs periodic retirement income, such periodic sales will defer taxation until the time of each payment.

Assuring Continuity of Management Control. It is impossible to ascertain at this time which, if any, of Jack's children will eventually enter the business and be able to succeed him in corporate leadership or whether that leadership will eventually go to unrelated key management personnel.

Naturally it is important to Jack that he continue to maintain control of the corporation until successors can be ascertained and he is ready to retire. With an ESOP Jack will still have almost the same control as if he owned all the stock directly. If the transaction is leveraged, some of the shares will be held in a suspense account, which can be voted by the trustee. The law allows Jack to be the trustee as long as the decisions that he makes as trustee are made "solely in the interests of the plan participants and beneficiaries." For the shares that are allocated to accounts of participants, the trustee can also vote on most issues. Only major issues, such as mergers or acquisitions or the sale of the company's assets, will require a voting pass-through to participants.

In an ESOP stock generally has to be distributed at the time of retirement or termination of employment. However, if Jack were willing to amend the company's bylaws to specify that only the plan or company employees can own stock, the plan could distribute cash instead. As an alternative, the plan could be designed to include a right of first refusal so that if participants wanted to sell their shares to outsiders, the company would have the right to purchase the stock instead. Assuming that there will continue to be no outside market for the stock, most participants are going to elect to cash in their shares at the time of distribution.

Estate Planning. The ESOP can also be helpful in transferring Jack's ownership interest to his children upon his death. At this point it is unclear which of his children will participate in the business. Typically, if all the children of a deceased businessowner are not active in the business, family friction can result. Those children who are active get direct benefits from the corporation in the form of salaries and fringe benefits, while children who are inactive can benefit from their stock ownership only if dividends are paid. Dividends, of course, are not tax deductible and deplete the company's net worth and working capital, a fact that frequently distresses the active children. This conflict of interest can lead to enormous dissension and can even result in litigation or an eventual sale of the business to outside interests.

Having an ESOP in place provides an excellent method of dealing with this problem. If some of Jack's children decide not to be involved in the business, there is now a market for stock they inherit. The ESOP can purchase their stock, and the proceeds can be invested to give them a return that does not depend on the corporation.

Preferred Method of Stock Purchase. Of the three proposed transactions, purchasing John's entire interest in the company with a bank loan to the ESOP is the least preferable. A bank loan may not be feasible because of the cyclical nature of the construction business. A bank might not be convinced that the company will be able to make annual contributions in amounts sufficient to meet the loan payments. Also, if John were to receive the entire purchase price for the stock at one time, he would have to pay income taxes on the payment. As discussed above, John would not be able to defer income tax by purchasing "qualified replacement property" without severely limiting Jack's ability to participate in the ESOP. Also, since John needs a source of annual income, he might not be able to purchase replacement securities (whether he takes advantage of the tax deferral or not) that generate enough dividend income to support his income needs.

Either the installment sale or the periodic payments method will work well. The key issues will be the current price of the stock and current "reasonable interest rate." As described above, the installment method will give John more security since his entire interest will be purchased at a fixed price. The price paid in an installment purchase will be the current fair market price plus interest payments (which must be based on a reasonable interest rate) on the unpaid balance. The real question will be whether the current fair market value and current interest rates will produce an income stream necessary to meet John's income needs. If the answer is yes, the installment method is probably the best approach. The installment method also fixes the value of John's ownership interest. If the value of the business rises, the increase will not be included in John's estate and will not be subject to estate taxes. Note, however, that the installment method is tantamount to a loan, and the ESOP will be treated as a leveraged ESOP and will be subject to "special scrutiny" by the DOL.

If the installment method does not generate sufficient income, then periodic sales to the ESOP is the preferable approach as long as the value of the company is expected to rise. The increasing value will support larger payments to John during his retirement. Also, the periodic sales approach is somewhat simpler since the ESOP will not be considered a leveraged ESOP.

Conclusion. An ESOP has many advantages for Templeton Contractors. For Templeton, as well as for other closely held businesses whose older shareholders have accumulated the bulk of their wealth in the business and cannot redeem less than their total interest and escape dividend treatment on the money received, an ESOP can be invaluable.

However, an ESOP does not come without its costs. The plan will have significant setup costs and ongoing administrative costs, including the annual appraisal. These costs should be fully understood before embarking on this course of action. Also, an ESOP cannot be easily unwound, and the transactions may result in scrutiny by the DOL and IRS. Before any corporation actually implements an ESOP, it should arrange for a thorough independent feasibility study that includes such things as a liquidity analysis for funding and projections for participants' account balances after 10 years. There should also be an appraisal to ascertain the fair market value of the company's stock since the value of the stock will allow the corporation to determine the number of shares it can contribute to the plan on a deductible basis. Like any other complex business plan, the success of an ESOP will depend on how carefully it is planned and implemented.

Installment Sales

General Requirements

A simple method of transferring some of John's stock to Ron and Greg is the use of an installment sale. An installment sale occurs when property is disposed of for payments, at least one of which is to be received after the close of the taxable year in which the disposition occurs (IRC Sec. 453(a)). The exceptions to the general rule—that is, the persons and types of property dispositions for which installment reporting is inapplicable—are not pertinent to this case (IRC Sec. 453(b)).

Interest payments made pursuant to an installment sale may be subject to the investment interest expense limitations of IRC Sec. 163, which will be discussed below as they apply to this case.

The seller receives capital-gain treatment to the extent of gain realized on the transaction (selling price less basis = gain realized). However, when the installment method of reporting is used, the capital-gain portion is recognized and reported as a percentage of each taxable year's payment. The interest portion of the installment payment is, of course, recognized as ordinary income in the year in which it is received. Use of the installment sale method can therefore spread a large gain over a number of years, with potentially significant income tax savings.

An installment sale also takes appreciating assets (Templeton stock) out of John's estate and replaces them with an asset that has a fixed value.

Avoiding the Limitations on Deductibility of Investment Interest

Generally an individual taxpayer can deduct investment interest only up to an amount of the taxpayer's net investment income (IRC Sec. 163(d)(1)).

INSTRUCTIONS TO STUDENTS

To avoid repetition of background material on the investment income and investment interest expense, that material has been omitted from this chapter. In an actual plan material such as that on pages 5.122 and 5.123 should be presented to the client. If the student is not familiar with the noted material from the previous chapter, it should be reviewed prior to proceeding through this section of the suggested solution.

Templeton Contractors is a C corporation. Interest payments on an installment obligation incurred by individuals in the acquisition of the stock of a C corporation are not treated as business-incurred interest and are therefore subject to the limitations on investment interest expenses. Therefore Ron and Greg will not be able to deduct interest payments in excess of their net investment income.

One additional potential problem of an installment sale such as has been proposed here should be noted, even though it is a purely personal one and not in any way tax related. The undertaking of such a purchase by a younger-generation successor of a closely held business means that for a very long period of time the purchaser's life-style may be curtailed, so that during the period when the family is being raised and educated, available cash flow may be limited. As long as the purchaser and spouse have thoughtfully considered this fact and are committed to the business, there may be no further problems. It is always advisable, however, to point out this potential problem to a client.

Nonqualified Stock Bonus Plan

An installment sale would not be a tax-favored method for Ron and Greg to acquire stock in Templeton Contractors. However, another alternative, a nonqualified stock bonus plan, would achieve this objective.

The stock bonus plan is a nonqualified plan of deferred compensation intended to benefit only "officers, shareholders, and other highly compensated individuals." Such a plan is specifically exempt from virtually all the rigorous regulations of ERISA. It is intended to be totally discriminatory in favor of a highly compensated group—generally shareholders and top management. The only type of governmental regulation that a nonqualified plan must comply with is that it must constitute "reasonable compensation" to the employee-participant.

Ron and Greg could participate in the plan as part of their compensation arrangement. A predetermined dollar amount of Templeton Contractors stock could be bonused to each of them annually. If it is desirable to keep the bonus amount level despite inflation, the amount of the stock bonus can be adjusted upward each year. This method assures that Ron and Greg will always receive the predetermined dollar amount of stock measured in today's dollars. This is a basic stock bonus plan and is not conditioned on performance.

If an incentive stock bonus plan is desired, the amount of stock awarded to Ron and Greg would depend on their performance based on established criteria. Either the basic stock bonus or the incentive-based plan can be used alone, or both can be used together.

For example, if both plans were implemented, Ron and Greg could each become eligible to receive an incentive stock bonus for achieving profitability in excess of a predetermined level in their areas of responsibility. The incentive plan could even require that to receive an incentive bonus, both the profit center for which the employee has responsibility and the corporation must achieve a certain level of profitability. This method balances the need to reward individual performance with the need to promote overall corporate cooperation among management personnel.

The bonused stock can vest in the employees at any time chosen by the corporation since nonqualified plans are not required to adhere to any specific vesting schedule. Care should be taken, however, that the vesting schedule chosen is not so lengthy that the employee is unable to view it as a substantial motivating influence. A reasonable vesting schedule for this purpose might be serial vesting over 5 to 7 years after the date on which the stock is bonused. If a 5-year-vesting plan is adopted, this type of vesting results in a recipient's being fully vested in stock received in the first year at the end of the fifth year.

In addition to the regular vesting schedule, the bonus plan could provide for complete vesting when an employee reaches retirement age, or if the employee becomes permanently disabled or dies prior to normal retirement.

Since the stock that is bonused to an employee under the plan is compensation, it is subject to federal income taxation the same as any other portion of salary. There is an option, however, regarding the time the fair market value of the stock is taken into the employee's income for income tax purposes.

IRC Sec. 83(a) allows the delay of reporting income until the earlier of the time that the property can be transferred by the recipient or the time that the property is no longer subject to a substantial risk of forfeiture. In a plan such as the one discussed, the fair market value of the stock would be included in the employee-recipient's income when the stock is vested, and the corporation would receive a tax deduction at that time. Since the value of the stock at the time it vests in the employee is impossible to ascertain in advance, this leaves the employee responsible for a tax liability that cannot be predetermined.

Another option for both the corporation and the employee is available under IRC Sec. 83(b). This option requires that the employee affirmatively elect to include the current fair market value of any stock bonus received during his or her taxable year in income for that year. This election must be filed with the Internal Revenue Service and is irrevocable as a general rule. The use of the Sec. 83(b) election allows the employee and the corporation to project the tax liability with much more precision and to plan for it effectively. The use of the Sec. 83(b) election has an additional advantage: it allows the corporation to take a tax deduction for the full value of the stock bonus in the year in which it is taken into income by the employee, regardless of whether it is fully vested.

Once an employee has affirmatively elected to take the value of a stock bonus plan into current income and has paid the associated tax liability, the stock will not give rise to taxation again until it is sold. At the time of a sale the increase in value since the stock was bonused is taxed as capital gains. The portion of the stock's value at time of sale that does not exceed the value when bonused will be received tax free as a return of basis.

If it appears that the tax liability associated with a stock bonus of this type may be difficult for an employee to pay without a change in life-style, the corporation can combine a stock bonus with a cash bonus sufficient to pay the employee's tax liability. Because both the stock and cash portions of the bonus are deductible despite the fact that the stock portion requires no cash expenditure, the corporation's aftertax cash-flow position is barely affected by this type of plan. Such a combination plan would seem to be a good one for Templeton Contractors.

If the combination plan is implemented, the bonus plan should require that the employee elect the IRC Sec. 83(b) option to take the amount of the combined stock and cash bonus into income in the year it is received.

If the employee does not remain with the corporation until all the stock vests, the unvested portion is forfeited. In that event the employee is entitled to a capital loss for the amount paid, if any, less any amount received upon forfeiture. The amount taken into income for income tax purposes is not considered to be an amount paid. If employees have been bonused cash in an amount to meet the additional tax liabilities attributable to the stock bonus, they are not harmed, in the event of forfeiture, when they are not allowed to take a tax deduction for the forfeited stock.

The corporation must include the deduction attributable to the forfeited stock in income in the year of the forfeiture.

Buy-Sell Agreements

Buy-sell agreements are usually of two basic types:

- redemption agreements in which the corporation and the shareholder enter into an agreement containing the provision that the corporation will redeem the shareholder's stock upon death or disability
- cross-purchase agreements that are agreements between and among the shareholders that in the event of death or disability, the remaining shareholders will purchase the deceased or disabled shareholder's interest

The effective use of redemption agreements may be difficult when family members are involved in a closely held corporation, because the family attribution rules of IRC Sec. 318 can produce adverse tax effects. Mandatory redemption agreements can also require enormous nondeductible corporate expenditures. Also if a C corporation receives proceeds of life insurance to fund a redemption agreement, it may be subject to income tax of up to 10 percent on those proceeds under the corporate alternative minimum tax.

Cross-purchase agreements are problematic when there are wide differences in shareholders' ages or if there is a shareholder whose health is impaired, because such agreements are usually funded wholly or partially with life insurance. The difference in ages or health conditions can result in the younger or healthier shareholders' being forced to pay high nondeductible insurance premiums for insurance on the life of the older or impaired shareholder. These problems would be particularly applicable in the case of Templeton Contractors as it appears that it may be impossible and will certainly be extremely expensive to insure John.

Since an ESOP has been recommended for Templeton Contractors, many of the objectives that are normally accomplished by buy-sell agreements can be accomplished more efficiently through the ESOP. It has already been noted that the employees who are ESOP participants should be required to give the ESOP (or the corporation) the right of first refusal to acquire their stock when they leave Templeton Contractors to prevent Templeton stock from remaining in the hands of outsiders.

In addition, either a contract or a stock restriction should require that other minority shareholders, such as Ron and Greg and other key management personnel who may own stock outside the ESOP, offer their stock to the ESOP or the corporation at the time they terminate their employment with Templeton Contractors.

A majority shareholder such as Jack can impose a stock-transfer restriction that requires that any of his children who inherit his stock and who are not directly involved in the business offer their stock to the ESOP (or the corporation) before offering it for sale to a third party.

REASONABLE COMPENSATION CONSIDERATIONS

Salaries are one method available to transfer funds from a corporation to shareholder-employees without subjecting them to double taxation—once at the corporate level and again at the individual level when it is received by the shareholder-employee. To avoid this double taxation the salary paid must be reasonable in amount and must be paid for personal services actually rendered (IRC Sec. 162 (a)(1)). If the salary meets this test, it is deductible by the corporation as an ordinary and necessary trade or business expense and is taxed only once—to the shareholder-employee.

As already indicated, the principal way in which salaries can lose their tax-favored status is a determination by the Internal Revenue Service that some amount of the salary is "unreasonable compensation." In making such a determination, the IRS is taking the position that the "unreasonable" portion is not salary at all, but a distribution of the corporation's earnings and profits—a dividend. If the IRS makes such a determination, the deduction to the corporation is disallowed because dividends are not deductible.

The issue of unreasonable compensation is generally raised only in closely held corporations where there is a strong identity of interest between the role of employee and that of stockholder or where a member of the employee's family is a stockholder. The Internal Revenue Service's position appears to be that an arm's-length transaction setting the value of personal services and effectively eliminating the unreasonable compensation issue cannot exist in most closely held corporations. Obviously the closer the identity of interest between the corporation and the employee, the more vulnerable to IRS scrutiny compensation becomes; for example, the most vulnerable situation occurs between an employee and the employee's wholly owned corporation. Because of the identity of interests the issue of unreasonable compensation is also frequently raised in family-owned corporations.

Effective planning in this area is very difficult, as there are no specific guidelines that have been uniformly applied. Even careful planning cannot assure that the IRS will not challenge a shareholder-employee's compensation. However, careful planning can diminish the chances of the IRS's being successful in a disallowance.

The appropriate test is to determine whether the compensation is reasonable under all the facts and circumstances of the particular case. That is, each case will be considered separately based on its particular facts, and this may account to some extent for the fact that the court cases in this area are decidedly less than definitive.

This somewhat confusing state of affairs does not mean, however, that no guidelines exist for setting shareholder-employee compensation arrangements that can withstand IRS scrutiny. The following points are critical and should always be kept in mind when negotiating compensation arrangements:

- All compensation, present or deferred, will be considered together to determine whether the total is reasonable.
- The compensation must be for services actually performed.
- Technically the appropriate time for measuring the reasonableness of a compensation arrangement is the time the arrangement was entered into, not at some later point when circumstances may have changed so dramatically that compensation payments exceed the expectations of all the parties. Although IRS audit agents often ignore this rule, it is a decided advantage to the taxpayer in litigation if the compensation plan was set long before the IRS challenge arose.

Corporations that are subject to severe fluctuations in business, such as contractors, may wish to utilize a bonus formula in addition to base salaries. Contingent compensation, such as bonuses, is not unreasonable in itself. Bonuses can actually provide incentives for both shareholder-employees and other employees to increase corporate profitability and can also build in flexibility to let total compensation adjust to any cyclical nature of the business. It would be appropriate in the case of Templeton Contractors to authorize a base salary and a bonus formula that would allow the board of directors to grant bonuses to the shareholder-employees and others based on established criteria, such as performance of various profit centers.

As a practical matter compensation arrangements should always be set in advance. It is unwise to wait until the close of the corporate year to determine bonuses or other contingent amounts. An advance determination of compensation should set out all compensation (base salaries, bonus formulas, deferred compensation, automatic cost-of-living adjustments, and any other payments). If a bonus is to be used, there are three principal guidelines that are very important: (1) the formula for computing the bonus should be predetermined, (2) the formula should never be based on the percentage of shares held or net profits, and (3) bonuses should not be restricted to shareholder-employees.

Corporate minutes and employment contracts can and should be used to document compensation arrangements and the reasons for establishing them at a particular level. Some helpful factors that should be included in employment contracts, corporate minutes, or both are the following:

- The employee's compensation is at or near the amount the employee earned in prior years, or if the compensation is adjusted materially, the reasons for the adjustment are fully documented.
- Compensation was set taking into consideration the employee's education, experience, skill, knowledge, standing in the industry, and other special qualifying attributes.
- Compensation was set taking into consideration responsibilities assigned to the employee.
- The employee's outside activities, if any, are not expected to interfere with the performance of the duties enumerated in the employment contract, and such outside activities, if any, are reflected in the compensation arrangements.
- The compensation arrangement reflects the standard compensation level in the trade or business.

Let's use John's situation to illustrate the effect of unreasonable compensation. John owns 50 percent of the stock of Templeton Contractors, a regular corporation. He is an employee of the corporation but devotes substantially less than his full time to its business. The corporation paid him salary and bonuses of $150,000 in 1990.

Assume that on audit the IRS seeks to disallow $100,000 of John's salary as unreasonable compensation. If the IRS is successful in the disallowance, the corporate deduction for the unreasonable amount is lost, and an additional $34,000 tax (assuming a 34 percent corporate tax rate) is due at the corporate level. It should be noted, however, that regardless of the outcome of the audit at the corporate level, the individual income tax result is the same—ordinary income taxable at the individual level.

Corporate Tax Results of IRS Disallowance of $100,000 of John's Compensation as Unreasonable

Corporation pays	$150,000
Corporation deducts	50,000
Additional corporate taxable income	$100,000
34 percent corporate rate	34%
Additional tax	$ 34,000

Based on the information given in regard to John's compensation, Jack's concern about a potential disallowance as unreasonable compensation appears warranted, particularly on the grounds that the compensation does not constitute payment for personal services actually rendered. John's withdrawal from the company will eliminate this problem after the period for auditing prior years' tax returns has expired.

There are, however, other problems with the way Templeton Contractors determines compensation, particularly bonuses. It is advisable for Templeton to keep paying bonuses, since they can provide incentives for shareholder-employees and other employees to increase corporate profitability, as well as to build in flexibility that allows total compensation to adjust to any cyclical nature of the business. However, the corporation should set base salaries and authorize bonuses that could be granted by either the president or the board of directors, based on a predetermined formula or on established criteria, such as the performance of various profit centers. A formula for bonuses should never be based on the percentage of shares held or net profits. Such an approach appears to be a disguised method of paying dividends to shareholders. This approach to bonuses appears to be a problem with Templeton Contractors' current method of determining bonuses.

If Templeton Contractors elected to be taxed as an S corporation, the problems of unreasonable compensation would be eliminated, since the corporation's income would be taxed directly to its shareholders. Templeton Contractors had approximately $480,000 in taxable income in 1991. If an S election were in effect, the corporation's taxable income would be taxed at the maximum individual rates (28 or 31 percent) rather than the maximum corporate rates (34 or 39 percent).

However, it is not recommended that Templeton Contractors elect to be taxed as an S corporation at this time. An S election would prevent the corporation from establishing the employee stock ownership plan (ESOP) previously recommended. An S corporation cannot have an ESOP because an ESOP is a qualified plan, and a qualified plan trust is not a type of trust that is permitted to own shares in an S corporation. Since the ESOP must invest primarily in employer securities, its ownership of employer stock would cause the termination of an S election. Also in this case the corporation could be subject to significant tax liability with respect to its "built-in gains" as a result of an S election. Therefore based on facts currently available, an election to be taxed as an S corporation is not appropriate at this time. (An additional relevant factor in the consideration of the S election is the recent release of the temporary regulations dealing with the effect of a deemed second class of stock.)

INDEX

Accelerated benefits, 8.35
Accumulated-earnings tax, 3.27

Borrowing from qualified plans, 3.61–63
Business insurance
    business overhead expense disability insurance, 5.56
    disability income insurance, 3.72, 5.54
    life insurance, 3.73, 3.90–96, 5.85–90
    professional liability insurance, 5.55–56
    property and liability insurance, 3.97, 6.112–13
Buy-sell agreements
    cross-purchase agreements, 3.67–69, 9.33
    funding methods, 3.68–70, 5.53
    provisions, 3.65–67, 5.50–53
    redemption agreements, 3.66–67, 9.27, 9.33
    special considerations for disability buyout, 3.82–83
    valuation of business interest, 3.68–69, 9.26
Bypass trust, 8.66–69

C corporation, 3.27–29, 5.44–45
Charitable giving, 8.30–31
Charitable remainder trusts, 8.30–31
Comprehensive financial planning
    distinguished from traditional problem solving, 1.1–3
    process, 1.3–12
    team approach, 1.4, 1.8-9
Constructive receipt, 6.84
Corporations. *See* C corporation; S corporation
Cross-purchase agreements. *See* Buy-sell agreements
Crummey provision, 3.92, 5.86, 6.108–9, 7.66

Data gathering, 1.4–6
Death-benefit-only plan, 6.86–87
Defined-benefit plan, 3.39–41, 7.31
Defined-contribution plan, 3.41–42, 8.36. *See also* Money-purchase pension
    plan; Profit-sharing plan
Determination letter, 3.45
Direct skip, 8.29

Economic benefit theory, 6.84
Education funding, 3.74–82, 3.109–23, 5.92–105, 5.119–22
EE bonds, 8.35–36, 8.68
Elimination period
    disability income, 3.72
    long-term care, 7.44–45
Emergency reserve, 3.98–99, 3.105, 3.109, 4.75–76, 5.92
Employee stock ownership plan (ESOP), 9.21–29
Employment contracts, 3.37–38

Employment of family members, 3.65, 3.80
Equalization of inheritance, 7.39–40, 7.55–56
Estate equalization, 6.94
Estate freezes, 6.77–78
Estate tax calculation, 5.72–83, 6.96–107
Excess accumulation tax, 5.69, 7.39

Family attribution rules, 6.74–75, 9.18–19
Family partnership, 5.64–65
Financial plan
    gathering data for. *See* Data gathering
    organizing data for, 1.6–7, 2.3
Financial planning. *See* Comprehensive financial planning
Financial planning process, 1.4–12, 2.1–4
Forward averaging, 8.53

Generation-skipping transfer tax (GSTT), 8.29, 8.34, 8.66–67
Gifts
    outright, 3.74, 5.58, 7.34
    Uniform Gifts to Minors Act (UGMA) and Uniform Transfers to Minors
        Act (UTMA), 3.75, 5.58–59, 7.37
Group insurance
    disability income insurance, 3.72, 3.82–83, 5.54, 5.68, 6.87–88, 7.57–58
    life insurance, 3.73, 6.88–89, 7.55–56
    medical expense insurance, 3.71–72, 4.73, 5.54, 7.58
Guardianship, 3.89

Hanging powers, 6.110–11
H bonds, 8.35–36
Home
    primary residence, 4.28–38, 4.49, 4.75
    vacation (second home), 3.84–85, 3.123–24
    refinancing, 7.60–62

Income-shifting techniques, 3.76–80, 5.59–66
Incorporation feasibility
    legal benefits, 3.34
    legal requirements, 3.30–32
    tax benefits, 3.34–37
Individual insurance
    disability income insurance, 3.72, 3.96–97, 4.72–73, 5.68, 7.57–58
    life insurance, 3.92–96, 4.73–74, 5.85–90, 7.31, 7.51, 7.55–56, 8.33–35,
        8.80–81
        annuity options, 8.34
    medical expense insurance, 3.71–72, 4.73
    personal property, 6.112–13
    trust, life insurance, 5.85, 6.108–11, 7.40–41
Individual retirement account (IRA), 5.67–68, 7.32
Inflation protection (long-term care policies), 7.48
Installment sale, 6.30–55, 6.71, 9.29–30
Insurance. *See* Business insurance; Group insurance; Individual insurance
Insurance planning, 1.15–17, 5.53–56

Integration with social security, 5.47–48
Intestate succession, 4.71–72
Investment planning, 1.17, 3.97–127, 4.75–78, 5.90–94, 5.98–99, 5.103–6, 5.119–40, 6.113–18, 7.60–67
Investment vehicles, 3.110–15, 3.124–26, 4.77–78, 5.105, 5.119–36, 6.113–16
Irrevocable insurance trust, 3.91–92, 5.86, 6.108–11, 7.40–41

Joint tenants with right of survivorship, 3.86–87, 4.49, 8.29, 8.31

Legal citations, 1.18–22
Long-term care protection, 7.44–51

Marital deduction, 3.87–90, 5.84, 6.93–95, 8.17
Money-purchase pension plan, 3.42–43, 5.49

Nonqualified deferred compensation, 6.83–87, 7.32–34
Nonqualified stock bonus plan, 9.31–33

Objectives, financial, 3.97–98, 3.106–8, 6.15, 7.17, 9.13
Outright gifts. *See* Gifts

Parental obligations, 5.65–66
Partnership, 3.22–23, 5.40–41
Personal use of company assets, 3.63–65
Planning for officer of a large organization, 9.1–37
Pooled-income fund, 8.31
Power of appointment, 5.84–85, 6.93
Preexisting conditions (long-term care policy), 7.45
Preretirement planning, 6.117–22
Private annuity, 6.79
Professional partnership, 5.40–41
Profit-sharing plan, 3.41–42, 5.47–48, 6.5–6, 6.82–83
Proprietorship, 5.39–40, 5.43

QPSA (Qualified Preretirement Survivor Annuity), 8.36
Qualified plans
    distributions from, 7.31
        forward averaging, 8.36, 8.66
        lump-sum, 8.36, 8.65
Qualified plans of deferred compensation, 3.38–48, 5.46–50, 6.81–83, 7.31, 9.20–29
QTIP (qualifying terminable interest property) trust, 6.93–94, 8.67

Rabbi trust, 6.85
Reasonable compensation, 3.34–37, 6.80, 9.34–37
Recapitalizations, 6.77–79
Redemption agreements. *See* Buy-sell agreements
Redemptions, 6.72–77, 9.15–20
Refinancing, 7.60–62
Renewability (long-term care policies), 7.48
Residuary trust, 3.87–90, 5.71, 6.95

Retirement income supplement, 7.41–44, 7.55
Risk
    investment, 3.100–1
    investor attitudes, 3.101
    trade-off, 3.101–3, 3.106

S corporation, 3.23–26, 5.41–44, 6.54–58
S corporation shares, 3.80–81, 5.42–43
Sec. 170(f)(2)(A), 8.30
Sec. 303 redemptions, 6.77, 9.20
Sec. 318 attribution rules, 6.74–75, 9.18
Sec. 1244 stock, 3.33–34
Sec. 2056, 8.17
Sec. 2503(b) trusts, 3.76–77, 5.59–60, 7.34–35
Sec. 2503(c) trusts, 3.77–80, 5.60–63, 5.89–102, 7.36, 7.63
Sec. 2612(a)(2), 8.29, 8.66
Sec. 2631, 8.66
Simple will, 8.31
Social security, 8.53, 8.65
Split-interest arrangements, 8.30–31
Sprinkle provision, 8.33–34

Taxable distribution, 8.29
Taxable termination, 8.29, 8.34
Tax authority, 1.18–23
Tax burden, reduction of, 3.83–84, 3.123–27
Tax-deferred annuities, 3.38–39
Tax planning, 1.12–15, 4.28–31, 5.57, 5.66–68
Top-heavy plans, 3.46–48
Trusts. *See* Sec. 2503(b); Sec. 2503(c); Individual insurance; Residual trust;
    Irrevocable insurance trust; Charitable trust

Unauthorized practice of law, 1.14–15
Unified credit, 3.86–88, 5.71, 5.84, 6.94–95, 7.38, 8.17, 8.29, 8.66
Uniform Gifts to Minors Act. *See* Gifts
Unlimited marital deduction, 8.17

Vesting, 3.44–48, 6.82–83
Viatical settlement, 8.35

Wills, 3.86–90, 4.71–72, 5.71–85, 6.92–95

Bibliography and Recommended In-depth Readings

Beam, Burton T., Jr., and McFadden, John J. *Employee Benefits.* 2d ed. Homewood, Illinois: Richard D. Irwin, Inc., 1988.

Bittker, Boris I., and Eustice, James S. *Federal Income Taxation of Corporations and Shareholders.* 6th ed. Boston: Warren Gorham Lamont, 1994 (with supplements).

Canan, Michael J. *Qualified Retirement and Other Employee Benefit Plans* (West's Handbook Series). St. Paul: West Publishing Co., 1992.

Grant, Irving M. *Subchapter S Taxation.* 3d ed. Tax and Estate Planning Series. Colorado Springs: Shepard's/McGraw-Hill, 1990 (with supplements).

Graves, Edward E., ed. *McGill's Life Insurance.* Bryn Mawr: The American College, 1994.

Lehmann, Michael B. *The Business One Irwin Guide to Using The Wall Street Journal.* 4th ed. Homewood, Illinois: Business One Irwin, 1993.

Leimberg, Stephan R., coordinator. *The Financial Services Professional's Guide to the State of the Art.* Bryn Mawr: The American College, 1989.

———, ed. *The Financial Services Professional's Guide to the State of the Art.* 2d ed. Bryn Mawr: The American College, 1991.

Littell, David A.; Cardamone, Donald C.; and Gruszecki, Wilhelm L. *Retirement Savings Plans: Design, Regulation, and Administration of Cash or Deferred Arrangements.* New York: John Wiley & Sons, 1993.

McFadden, John J., ed. *The Financial Services Professional's Guide to the State of the Art.* 3d ed. Bryn Mawr: The American College, 1994.

McKee, William S.; Nelson, William F.; and Whitmire, Robert L. *Federal Taxation of Partnerships and Partners.* 2d ed. Boston: Warren Gorham Lamont, 1990 (with supplements).

Stephens, Richard B.; Maxfield, Guy B.; Lind, Stephen A.; and Calfee, Dennis A. *Federal Estate and Gift Taxation.* 6th ed. Boston: Warren Gorham Lamont, 1991 (with supplements).

Tax Management United States Income Series. Tax Management, Inc., a division of The Bureau of National Affairs, Inc. Washington, D.C.

Tax Management Estate, Gifts and Trust Series. Tax Management, Inc., a division of The Bureau of National Affairs, Inc. Washington, D.C.

The statute and the regulations thereunder are available as the Complete Internal Revenue Code of 1986 (as amended), the Income Tax Regulations (as amended), and the Estate and Gift Tax Regulations (as amended) from various legal publishers, such as Prentice-Hall, Inc., Commerce Clearing House, Inc., and others.